WILLIAM GORDON WHEELER

Deirdre,

With love & good wishes.

James Hagey

5/11/16

WILLIAM GORDON WHEELER

A JOURNEY INTO THE FULLNESS OF FAITH

JAMES HAGERTY

GRACEWING

First published in England in 2016
by
Gracewing
2 Southern Avenue
Leominster
Herefordshire HR6 0QF
United Kingdom
www.gracewing.co.uk

ISBN 978 085244 851 9

Typeset by Gracewing

Cover design by Bernardita Peña Hurtado

CONTENTS

ACKNOWLEDGEMENTS

I AM ESPECIALLY GRATEFUL to Archbishop Arthur Roche, Archbishop-Bishop Emeritus of Leeds, and now Secretary of the Congregation of Divine Worship and Discipline of the Sacraments, for commissioning this biography and for his unstinting support and encouragement. I am greatly indebted to Bishop Marcus Stock who has kindly written the Foreword and the Trustees of the Diocese of Leeds who have generously provided financial support. I also thank Bishop John Wilson, formerly Administrator of the Diocese of Leeds and now Auxiliary Bishop of Westminster, for his interest and assistance.

I wish to thank His Eminence Cardinal Cormac Murphy-O'Connor, Archbishop Emeritus of Westminster, for generously sharing with me his memories and reminiscences of Bishop Wheeler.

I am indebted to Mgr Roderick Strange, former Rector of the Pontifical Beda College, Rome, for his permission to consult and quote the college archives and also to Fr John Breen, Vice-Rector, for providing the portrait of Bishop Wheeler which is reproduced by kind permission of the Trustees of the Beda. Canon Philip Gillespie, the current Rector, has also given generous assistance.

Robert Finnigan, Archivist of the Diocese of Leeds, has been particularly helpful in locating and facilitating access to Bishop Wheeler's papers, sharing his personal reminiscences of the Bishop, and reading the draft manuscript. I am deeply grateful for his advice and friendship.

Other archivists have been kind enough to answer my queries and allow me access to their collections. I thank the following: Dom Anselm Cramer, Ampleforth Abbey; Canon Anthony Dolan, Diocese of Nottingham; Dr Graham Foster, Diocese of Nottingham; Dr Simon Johnson, Downside Abbey; Rachel Kneale and Joanna Badrock, Manchester Grammar School; Rev Dr David Lannon, Diocese of Salford; Claire Mueller, Archdiocese of Westminster; Fr Nicholas Schofield, Archdiocese of Westminster; Rev Dr John Sharp, Archdiocese of Birmingham; David Smallwood, Diocese of Middlesbrough; and Dr Meg Whittle, Archdiocese of Liverpool.

Librarians at the Central Library, Manchester, The Minster Library, York, and the Curator of the Saddleworth Museum and Art Gallery have been most helpful.

From the Diocese of Leeds, Rev Dr John Berry, Mgr Anthony Boylan, Mgr John Dunne, Fr Bernard Funnell, Fr Gerard Hanlon, Mgr Peter McGuire (RIP), Mgr John Murphy and Mgr Bryan Sharp have all generously supplied information and shared their recollections of Bishop Wheeler. Vincent Canavan; Anne Forbes; Peter Fox; Francis Freeman; Dr Alana Harris, Lincoln College, Oxford; Ian Hurst; Dr Serenhedd James, St Stephen's House, Oxford; Liam Kelly, Ampleforth Abbey; Dr Kevin McNamara; Bernard Marriott, Association for Latin Liturgy; Colonel Victor Nicholls; Jan Niczyperowicz; Hugh Norwood; David Stockdale; Rev Geoffrey Turner, Louise Ward and Ian Wells have helped and supported me in a variety of ways. I express my thanks to them all.

Special thanks go to Archbishop Arthur Roche, Mgr Peter McGuire (RIP), Mgr Anthony Boylan, Rev Dr Paul Murray OP, Rev Dr Peter Phillips, Robert Finnigan and Chris Power who read drafts of the biography, corrected errors of style, accuracy and interpretation, and made many helpful suggestions.

I am grateful to Meredith MacArdle for compiling the Index. Tom Longford, Monica Manwaring and Rev Dr Paul Haffner of Gracewing Publishing have been most professional in their efforts to bring this book to publication. I thank them for their assistance and advice.

As ever, my greatest thanks go to Trina for her unfailing love, understanding and support.

ABBREVIATIONS

AAW, Griffin	Archives of the Archbishop of Westminster, Cardinal Griffin Papers
AAW, Godfrey	Archives of the Archbishop of Westminster, Cardinal Godfrey Papers
AAW, Heenan	Archives of the Archbishop of Westminster, Cardinal Heenan Papers
ABA, Couve de Murville	Archives of the Archbishop of Birmingham, Archbishop Couve de Murville Papers
ALA, GHC	Archives of the Archdiocese of Liverpool, Godfrey-Heenan Collection,
ALA BECK	Archives of the Archdiocese of Liverpool, Archbishop Beck Papers,
ALA WOR	Archives of the Archdiocese of Liverpool, Archbishop Worlock Papers
BDA	Brentwood Diocesan Archives
DAA	Downside Abbey Archives
LDA, WDC	Leeds Diocesan Archives, Wheeler Diocesan Collection
LDA, WPC	Leeds Diocesan Archives, Wheeler Personal Collection
LPL, Ramsey	Lambeth Palace Library, Archbishop Ramsey Papers

PBCA	Pontifical Beda College Archives
QR	Quinquennial Report to the Vatican on the Diocese of Leeds
SDA	Salford Diocesan Archives

ILLUSTRATIONS

Front cover: Bishop William Gordon Wheeler (Leeds Diocesan Archives)

Frontispiece: Bishop William Gordon Wheeler (Courtesy of Archbishop Arthur Roche)

1. Dobcross: Wheeler's birthplace. M. Fox and P. Fox, *Saddleworth Album* (Oldham: Taylor and Clifton, 1995)

2. The young Wheeler with his mother (Leeds Diocesan Archives)

3. Student at Manchester Grammar School. Wheeler is on the front row, sixth from the left. (Manchester Grammar School Archive)

4. The Anglican Priest: Wheeler in December 1934 (Leeds Diocesan Archives)

5. Student at the Beda with Cardinal Hinsley and other seminarians. Wheeler is on the second row, second from the left. (Leeds Diocesan Archives)

6. Student in wartime: Wheeler (standing extreme right) and other Beda students with Mgr Charles Duchemin at Upholland in 1940 (Leeds Diocesan Archives)

7. Administrator of Westminster Cathedral (Leeds Diocesan Archives)

8. Wheeler as Coadjutor Bishop of Middlesbrough 1964 (Leeds Diocesan Archives)

9. William Gordon Wheeler, Bishop, of Leeds, 1966 (Leeds Diocesan Archives)

10. Wheeler with his father following his consecration as Bishop of Leeds, 1966 (Leeds Diocesan Archives)

11. Wheeler visiting the Leeds Diocesan Mission in Peru (Leeds Diocesan Archives)

FOREWORD

ILLIAM GORDON WHEELER: *A Journey into the Fullness of Faith* is the biography of a remarkable twentieth-century British Catholic churchman.

Since the Restoration of the Catholic Hierarchy in 1850, there has been a long and distinguished line of Catholic prelates in our country who formerly were Anglican priests. Among them is William Gordon Wheeler, the seventh Bishop of Leeds. His early life was lovingly cradled in the care of a closely-knit northern Anglican family. There he was imbued with a strong sense and value of the Christian faith. This was further nourished by inspirational teachers at Manchester Grammar School who instilled in him a love of history and literature. At University College, Oxford, he became familiar with the writings of Cardinal John Henry Newman and at St Stephen's College with the traditions of High Anglicanism. Despite earlier, personal reservations about the Church of England's position he was ordained nevertheless as an Anglican priest in 1934. After curacies in Brighton and Chesterfield and a post at Lancing College, he made the momentous decision, greatly inspired by Newman, to convert to Catholicism. He was received into the Church at Downside Abbey in 1936.

It was with considerable relief and freedom that WG, as he was often referred to, embraced with conviction and enthusiasm the historical position and the teachings of the Church. In 1940, Cardinal Arthur Hinsley, a fellow Yorkshireman, ordained him a priest for the Archdiocese of Westminster where he served until his appointment as a bishop in 1964. The timing of his appointment by Blessed Pope Paul VI was to be of considerable influence on Bishop Wheeler for, as Coadjutor Bishop of Middlesbrough, he attended the last two sessions of the Second Vatican Council (1962-1965). As a convert, he had embraced with a deep love all that he had long sought and accepted from the Church of the 1930s. Not all of the Council's changes in style were entirely to his personal liking, but he embraced them with faithfulness and, as Bishop of Leeds, paved their implementation within the diocese with considerable creative pastoral energy. His years as bishop, however, were also buffeted by many contemporary social changes and defiant attitudes to religious authority which he found difficult to reconcile with his own steadfast faith in the Church and her teachings.

Looking back on his life, it is clear that Bishop Wheeler was a man of strong faith, self-deprecating humour, keen intellect, great personal charm, and impeccable style and taste. Many described him as 'the last of the prince bishops', but one thing is for certain he was a bishop for his time and a much loved one.

As a fellow convert to Catholicism, I warmly welcome Dr Hagerty's timely biography of Bishop Wheeler. His research has been extensive, having had access to Bishop Wheeler's personal and official papers from various sources as well as to living testimonies. He has left us with an admirable and important biography of a remarkable Bishop of Leeds which will be of considerable interest to many, and an important contribution to the history of the British Catholic Church in the twentieth century.

✠ Marcus Stock
Bishop of Leeds

INTRODUCTION

WILLIAM GORDON WHEELER was born in Yorkshire in 1910 but his parents were Lancastrians. He grew up in a stable and loving middle-class family and his early life was marked by a strict but willing adherence to the Anglican faith. His scholarly progress was a source of pride for his parents and grandparents and although his first academic love was History, he gravitated towards Theology as he sought to emulate one of his ancestors, Rev William Upjohn, and become an Anglican clergyman. After studies at Manchester Grammar School and University College, Oxford, he entered St Stephen's House, Oxford, and was ordained a priest of the Church of England in 1934.

Wheeler's Anglican priesthood brought him little satisfaction. This was no surprise for at Oxford and immediately before his ordination, he harboured serious doubts about the Anglican Church and particularly its relationship to the doctrines and liturgy of the Church of Rome. His study of John Henry Newman's writings and sermons, his discussions with many of his Oxford contemporaries and acquaintances, and contact with the Cowley Fathers had moved him almost inexorably from High Anglicanism towards Catholicism. In 1936, after much soul searching and prayer and to the utter devastation of his family, he left the Anglican Communion and was received into the Catholic Church at Downside Abbey. He wrote later that he had found no assurance in the Anglican faith and on his conversion, he felt 'enriched by the certainty which only the See of Peter can give'. He had 'Poped' and found his 'true home in this part of the Vineyard'. Among other things, he now fully accepted the teaching of Pope Leo XIII's *Apostolicae Curae* which proclaimed as part of the Supreme Magisterium that those who became Catholic priests were ordained absolutely and not, as in the case of Anglican priests, conditionally.

Wheeler never regretted his conversion to Catholicism. 'The joy of being a Catholic', he wrote later, 'has always far outweighed the sorrows, trials and even the changes that one has had to endure. After all, the gift of the fullness of Faith is the greatest gift—and I believe this with all my heart—that God can give to any man or woman in this life'. His Anglicanism, however, was not confined to oblivion for Wheeler forever held the Anglican Communion in great respect. He was profoundly grateful for the sound scriptural and prayerful foundations he had received as an Anglican and maintained correspondence and social contact with his many Anglican friends until the end of his life.

Wheeler's immediate ambition after conversion was to become a Catholic priest and, between 1936 and 1940, he undertook a course of training and formation at the Beda College in Rome. There he absorbed the history and traditions of the Roman Church and acquired *Romanità*—that unique sense of identification with the Eternal City and the primacy of the papacy over the Universal Church. It was for him a wonderful period when he quickly and with ease adapted to the life and liturgies of the one, true Church to which he now belonged.

His subsequent ministry in the Archdiocese of Westminster was marked by pastoral commitment, personal satisfaction and steady advancement. As a busy and successful curate in Edmonton during the Second World War, he endured the same life-threatening dangers, heartbreak and deprivations as his parishioners but found time to continue his reading, especially of Church history. His literary talents found expression in Catholic journals and he was in regular demand as a preacher. In 1944, he became a Chaplain of Westminster Cathedral and there participated in the hectic life of a large, very important and developing parish. He was also appointed editor of the *Westminster Cathedral Chronicle* and persuaded well-known Catholic and non-Catholic writers to submit articles on a range of historical, literary and theological topics thereby raising the magazine's profile and enhancing his own reputation. In 1950, at a time when few Catholic priests had the advantage of a university education, he was appointed by Cardinal Griffin as Catholic Chaplain to London University before being recalled in 1954 to be Administrator of Westminster Cathedral. This was a post which Wheeler loved and filled with devotion, dedication and panache. He took great pride in the unceasing spiritual support offered in the Cathedral, in its traditional and rich liturgies, in its music, art and architecture, and in its location at the centre of national Catholic life. It was a post which placed him in a position of ecclesiastical prominence and where he came to the notice of influential people.

There was a distinct possibility that Wheeler would be raised to the episcopate and, in 1964, he was appointed Coadjutor Bishop of Middlesbrough. He and some of his close friends regarded this appointment as an unwelcome and distant posting after the pivotal role he had played in

Westminster but this preferment provided him with one of the most exhilarating experiences of his life—attendance at the Second Vatican Council. Called by Pope John XXIII in 1959, this momentous event wrought enormous changes in the life of the twentieth-century Catholic Church. Among the faithful it led to joy, hope, frustration, bewilderment, anger, sadness and despair in varying degrees and Wheeler was not exempt from some of these reactions. He discovered that while some of the changes introduced by the Council were exciting and challenging, many of the certainties and characteristics of the Catholic Church which he had found so attractive, and the cause for his conversion, either disappeared or were transformed. As a bishop, he was entrusted with the critical role of implementing the changes he and his confrères had agreed at the Council but it was not an easy duty nor was it always palatable for someone as innately conservative as Wheeler. Nevertheless, he undertook his episcopal responsibility with fidelity to the Holy See and the decrees of the Council.

There can be no underestimating the impact of the Second Vatican Council on Wheeler as a convert, priest and bishop. At an intellectual level, he was especially influenced by what he and others considered the effect of Cardinal Newman's legacy on the Council. To Wheeler, Newman's nineteenth-century writings presaged much of the Council's deliberations and decisions and he continued to study Newman through-out his life, regarding him as the paradigm of the Anglican convert and educated Catholic priest. Just as Newman came to recognise the Truth in the Catholic Church, so too did Wheeler. As an aside, it may be mentioned that Wheeler paid no homage or made many overt references to Cardinal Manning, that other famous nineteenth-century Anglican convert and contemporary of Newman. Like Newman and Wheeler, Manning too had attended Oxford but was from a wealthier and more influential background and at the time of his conversion had already achieved high office in the Anglican Church. Wheeler considered Newman rather than Manning to have been more sympathetic to 'cradle Catholics' and to the Catholic historical and liturgical tradition than to converts and Anglican history. Where Newman's influence was doctrinal, historical and literary, Manning's was essentially political and practical and concerned with the leadership of the English and Welsh Catholic Church in times of radical economic and social change.

In 1966, Wheeler was translated from Middlesbrough to become Bishop of Leeds and was confronted with the daunting and practical task of being solely responsible for implementing the Second Vatican Council's decisions. Cardinal John Carmel Heenan wrote that after the Council, the bishop's task was more fruitful and attractive, when the episcopate, clergy and laity were subject to the enlightened Conciliar decrees which brought bishop, priest and people into a more simple and affectionate relationship. Wheeler welcomed this new relationship but other aspects of Vatican II troubled him throughout his episcopate and to the end of his life. He may have been prepared to accept *aggiornamento* or the renewal of the Church envisaged by Pope John's Council but he was distressed by some reforms which others considered integral and essential to the process of renewal. The Council changed the culture of the Church as he and millions of other Catholics knew it. The loss of the Latin Mass celebrated for centuries according to Pope Pius V's Roman Rite, the introduction of the vernacular into the liturgy, the reordering of churches and the unintended downgrading of devotions to Mary and the saints were less than appealing to him as they were to others.

Wheeler's two immediate predecessors in Leeds, Cardinal Heenan in Westminster and Archbishop George Patrick Dwyer in Birmingham, were still alive when he acceded to the diocese in 1966 and he wrote, 'it was almost an overwhelming challenge to succeed such vigorous and outstanding figures particularly in the post-Conciliar period'. It was, however, a challenge he rose to. He wrote later: 'I have tried...in my limited way, to do what the Pope asked of us: to make Vatican II present in a balanced way in the diocese entrusted to my care; handing on the unchanging eternal truths of the Gospel in a way understandable as far as possible in our time. It has not always been easy and often I have failed'. Despite this protestation of modesty, his achievements in Leeds were remarkable and the new relationship between bishop, priests and people referred to by Cardinal Heenan came to the fullness of expression. Relying heavily on others, Wheeler managed the diocese effectively and established structures for better administration and pastoral care, including the erection of the new Diocese of Hallam. He set up Commissions for Liturgy, Ecumenism, Justice and Peace, and Vocations and Adult Religious Education. He convened a Council of Priests, a Diocesan Pastoral Council, Area Pastoral Councils and Parish Councils. He opened centres for the development of catechesis and ecumenism and he became the first bishop to ordain married deacons. It was not a period of unbroken progress, however. The loss of priests and a sharp decline in Mass attendance, marriages and baptisms were sad aspects of Wheeler's time as Bishop of Leeds.

As a member of the Bishops' Conference of England and Wales, Wheeler played a full part in all its deliberations. As a new bishop, he was respectful to his seniors but was prepared to make his views known as, for example, on the education and training of priests. In this and other issues, he found a soul mate in the Benedictine Abbot Christopher Butler of Downside, another Anglican convert and a friend for over thirty years. Butler, however, was theologically to the left of Wheeler and though their friendship remained true, their views later differed, particularly on the reception in 1968 of Pope Paul's encyclical *Humanae Vitae* which restated the Church's ban on the use of artificial contraceptives.

Wheeler found being Chairman of the Bishops' National Liturgy Commission a difficult responsibility for he was never really a fervent advocate of the post-Conciliar forms of liturgical expression. Privately, he was saddened by the loss of the Mass celebrated according to the traditional Roman Rite, commonly called the Tridentine Mass, and the end of Latin as the universal language of the Church. He found some translations into the vernacular inelegant and meaningless and his less than enthusiastic commitment to his episcopal membership of the International Commission for English in the Liturgy (ICEL) was perhaps indicative of his approach to liturgical reform and renewal. In particular, he expressed concern over the Americanization of liturgical language and fought to have ICEL's headquarters transferred from Washington to London where the English bishops could exert direct influence. Never the one for the limelight, he was prepared to support others discreetly in the public struggle for the retention of the Latin Mass but he fought a long, losing battle as younger bishops, less attached to the old order, came to the Conference and as priests emerged from the seminaries with no knowledge of Latin or any nostalgia for the pre-Conciliar age.

In one significant respect, Wheeler could claim success. In 1975, he was instrumental in the selection of Abbot Basil Hume to succeed Cardinal Heenan as Archbishop of Westminster. Wheeler and Hume had been friends for many years and Wheeler felt that Hume's spirituality and his intimate knowledge of the European Christian tradition would stand the English and Welsh Church in good stead and be in contrast to the rather insular approach of Heenan and some of his colleagues. After an initial period of warmth, however, the relationship between Hume and Wheeler seems to have cooled.

Wheeler's arrival in Leeds coincided not only with the implementation of the reforms of the Second Vatican Council but also with changing generational attitudes towards established authority and institutionalised religion. The domestic Catholic Church, so long unchallenged, was subjected to internal criticism and external attacks and went through a very painful period. The questioning of episcopal authority by some priests and laity during the period before and after the Vatican Council was compounded by the wider negative Catholic response to *Humanae Vitae* and subsequent external developments such as the legalization of abortion and homosexuality and the general liberalisation of society's manners and morals. Permissiveness was the catch phrase of the time and religious observance and practice were deleteriously affected. It was not a comfortable time for bishops.

Wheeler was also a bishop in difficult political and economic times. The Vietnam War, the Cold War, the Arab-Israeli conflict, the Soviet invasion of Czechoslovakia and post-colonial conflicts in Africa dominated the international stage through the 1960s and 1970s and such huge issues demanded an episcopal response. Domestically, the British political landscape was often in turmoil with urban riots and economic unrest in 1970s and early 1980s, the Irish Republican Army's (IRA) bombing campaign in Ulster and on mainland Britain, the Falklands War of 1982, the national Miners' Strike of 1984, the continued influx of Commonwealth immigrants, and the reception of refugees from Uganda, Chile and Vietnam. Wheeler and his diocese were not exempt from these developments.

It is significant that Wheeler was never promoted to an archbishopric when vacancies occurred. His views and counsel were sought and respected; he was a man of discerning intellect and style and a bishop with practical experience of two dioceses. Yet perhaps his innate traditional approach, together with his delicate health, denied him promotion. By the end of his episcopate, he was regarded by some as reactionary and of a previous age but this was to overlook the many reforms he had introduced into the Diocese of Leeds. In retirement, he wrote to Archbishop Couve de Murville of Birmingham, another conservative, that he had ploughed 'a somewhat lonely furrow' in the Hierarchy, one which became lonelier as he became the oldest and most experienced bishop on the bench. He was certainly out of step with contemporary ecclesiastical fashion and taste yet his ecclesiastical and theological conservatism was always tempered by open-mindedness, humility, humour and experience.

Wheeler's style was legendary. He insisted on wearing his full episcopal regalia at religious and liturgical events and at his gentleman's residence at Eltofts, he generously dispensed hospitality to all social classes with aplomb. The journalist Patrick O'Donovan said 'there is no more civilized prelate in England than Bishop Gordon Wheeler'. Eltofts had a wonderful collection of antiques and paintings and when on parish visitations Wheeler was always on the lookout for interesting and tasteful pieces of furniture. The clerical limerick ran:

That episcopal gent named Wheeler
As he knelt on his Sheraton kneeler
Made this prayer to God:
As a bishop, I'm not much of a bod
But I'm a wonderful antiques dealer.

He later wrote to Archbishop Cardinale: 'I am thinking of starting a society for the preservation of old furniture on the lines of the Latin Mass Society.' Ever conscious of his status, he wrote to Professor H. P. R. Finberg in February 1972: 'My car will meet you at the station. The chauffeur will be at the barrier. He has a chauffeur's hat with the Papal Arms on it'.

Affable and unfailingly courteous, Wheeler chose his friends carefully and kept them for life. He acidly remarked that one bishop had been his acquaintance for over twenty years. Among the clergy and laity, he developed warm and lasting relationships and took great comfort in being able to share the ups-and-downs of their lives. Most of his lay friends, it was pointed out to him, had double-barrelled surnames and many inhabited the upper reaches of Catholic society. It did not worry Wheeler: to him friendship was a manifestation of truth and love irrespective of a person's origins and social status. His conversation was always made more captivating by his slight speech impediment and was, if the occasion demanded, full of wit and humour. Very often, his anecdotes were self-deprecating. He was, for example, fond of relating the story that after receiving a prestigious award from the Grand Master of the Sovereign Order Malta he descended into the Roman street in full episcopal attire with the medal around his neck. He hailed a taxi and got in only to find that an Italian lady had entered on the other side. They agreed to share the taxi and after a mile or so, the lady looked at Wheeler's new medal and said: "Oh, my husband's got a Benemerenti!" He would also tell the story of how he once became lost while travelling to a speaking engagement in Bradford. After driving around and unable to find the right street, he eventually saw a boy standing beside the road. Winding down the window, he said to the boy, "Listen, I'm hopelessly lost. Can you please tell me how to get to St. George's Hall?" "What do you want to go there for?" said the boy. "Because I'm due to give a talk," replied the Bishop, "and I'm already late." "What's the talk about?" the boy asked. "Well it's about how to get to heaven," said the Bishop, "would you like to come and hear it?" "Me come and listen to you?" the boy replied. "How will you be able to tell me how to get to heaven when you don't even know the way to St. George's Hall?" Of course, many humorous stories were also told about him. On one occasion, at a time when priests were leaving the ministry and clerical morale was low, Wheeler called to his secretary: "Oh, Father, Father, something tewwible has happened." The secretary thought another priest had defected but instead Wheeler said: "Lady—is coming and we've wun out of shewwy."

With his old friend Mgr Francis Bartlett in Westminster, Wheeler shared the view that priests had to be men of culture and learning—abreast of the arts, history, and literature as well as theology and spirituality. It was something of a forlorn hope but he never ceased to encourage his priests to broaden their minds. To some of the clergy in the Leeds Diocese, Wheeler was always a Westminster man. His friends were predominantly southerners and very English; not the sort normally associated with northern and Irish priests renowned for their practical approach and anti-intellectualism. However, with Fr Tommy Kilcoyne, also in Westminster, he displayed another interest and wrote in May 1972, after Leeds United had beaten Arsenal in the FA Cup Final:

> You will be amused to know that I watched the Leeds-Arsenal match on colour TV on Saturday afternoon. I found it more moving than anything I have seen since Champion the Wonder Horse and many lumps came into my throat, and when poor Jones managed to stagger up to the Queen after his injury, I was speechless with admiration. I at once sent a greetings telegram to the manager of the team! You will be interested to know that Fr Tim O'Shea went down to London with them because Bremner, Gray and Giles are Catholics.

Mgr Bruno Scott-James was a different kind of friend—one who for years taxed Wheeler's patience and generosity. Yet to the maverick and eccentric Scott-James, and to others like him, he demonstrated understanding, love and affection for someone whose personal circumstances were not as stable and as fortunate as his.

Wheeler had the wonderful gift of being at ease in any company. Whether with the King of Spain, President John F. Kennedy and his family, popes and cardinals in the Vatican, parishioners on a council estate, Knights of the Sovereign Order of Malta, peers of the realm, the Union of Catholic Mothers, or leading politicians, Wheeler was comfortable. If he delivered an after-dinner speech, played the piano at parish visitations, or sang a solo at a school prize giving, he was a natural performer. He could adapt his manner and style to suit any and every occasion.

In retirement, Wheeler wrote two books. The first, *In Truth and Love*, was a memoir of his life and ministry rather than an autobiography. It covered the people and factors which had influenced his religious development, the defining events of his long life and the issues which had confronted the Church in general and him as a priest and bishop. It gave nothing away and betrayed no confidences and was a rather bland and somewhat disappointing account of the life of a man who had witnessed and achieved so much. It revealed little that was new about Wheeler or about his relationships with the men who played such important roles in the life of the twentieth-century domestic Church. The second volume, *More Truth and Love*, was a collection of obituaries, sermons and articles which he had written over the years. Like the first volume, it was not a revealing book but it laid before its readers the love and respect he had for some of his contemporaries, the admiration he had for the saints and martyrs who had suffered for the faith, and the importance of some places in his life. The books, like his sermons, reflect Wheeler's discretion, wide reading and his acute and perceptive intellect.

This biography, based largely on his vast archive, is an attempt to rectify some of the deficiencies and shortcomings of Wheeler's published memoirs and obituaries. It is chronological in approach and sub-divided into sections designed to capture the essence of Wheeler's life, ministry and active retirement as they unfolded. It seeks to let Wheeler's own words, and those of others, speak for themselves. Wheeler was an inveterate correspondent and a hoarder. On the face of it, his archive is the historian's delight but the fact that he kept virtually everything has meant that being side tracked or immersed in detail was an ever-present threat and distraction.

This work is also an opportunity of recognising and sharing the notable achievements of a very human, talented and loyal northern bishop whose role in the development of the English and Welsh Catholic Church at a critical period in the twentieth century may be hastily judged, overlooked or forgotten.

1 NORTHERN ROOTS

An Anglican Family

WILLIAM GORDON WHEELER, son of Frederick and Marjorie Wheeler (née Upjohn), was born on 5 May 1910 in the Yorkshire Pennine village of Dobcross. Noted for the manufacture of fancy woollen cloth, shawls and flannel, Dobcross was an important crossing point of the River Tame and had been an ancient chapelry in the parish of Rochdale. Like many other Pennine hill villages in the early twentieth century, Dobcross was characterised by textile mills, small independent workshops, stone houses with stone slate roofs, and eighteenth-century handloom weavers' cottages redolent of the early Industrial Revolution. It was one of four villages in the Urban District of Saddleworth and according to the Census of 1911 had a population of 3,016.[1]

Wheeler's paternal grandparents were Lancastrians. His grandfather Samuel was born in Manchester while his grandmother Elizabeth was born in Walkden, six miles north-west of Salford. Samuel was a successful coal merchant and with his wife and their five children lived at Booth Bank Farm in the Urban District of Worsley. Frederick, their fifth child, was born in 1880 and on 6 October 1908 married Marjorie Upjohn at St Mark's, Worsley.[2] Frederick and Marjorie moved to Dobcross where Frederick established himself in the cloth bleaching trade. There he and Marjorie lived with William Gordon and Marjorie Elizabeth (born 1912) at 'Hillcrest' on Nicker Brow. A short time after the birth of the children, the family moved to nearby Greenfield.

The Wheelers and Upjohns were staunch Anglicans and William Gordon had Church of England clergymen among his antecedents. One of his mother's ancestors, Emma Upjohn, had married Rev John F Smith in the 1840s and his great-great-grandfather, William Upjohn (1774–1855), was Vicar of St Andrew's, Field Dalling, Norfolk, from 1811 to 1855.[3] William Gordon was duly baptised according to the rites of the Established Church at St Mark's Church, Worsley, on 3 July 1910.[4] He later recalled that he 'sprang from a deeply religious family and was brought up very much according to Catholic principles' in 'a High Church tradition in which the sacramental teaching of the Church was greatly valued'. 'All the household assembled daily at my home for prayers and we were most assiduous in our attendance at Church on Sundays and feastdays, usually two or three times per day'.[5] Both Wheeler's grandfathers were Freemasons but this, he said later in life, did not contradict with their 'sincere practice of religion'.[6]

At the outbreak of the Great War in August 1914, Frederick Wheeler joined the colours. William Gordon was deeply affected by the loss of his father to the army and recalled that even at the age of four he prayed for his safekeeping and return. The family home in Yorkshire was closed up and Marjorie took William Gordon (normally called Gordon) and Elizabeth to the Upjohn house in Worsley, Lancashire, where Wheeler experienced 'a memorable and extremely happy childhood in the midst of a patriarchal family'. The Upjohn family were numerous. Wheeler's maternal grandparents, William Barber Upjohn and Mary Mathieson Robertson, had fourteen children and Gordon and his sister had plenty of cousins. At weekends, they gathered at their grandparents' house in 'unspoilt country on what was then the estate of Lord Ellesmere'. William Barber Upjohn had worked for many years as head gardener at Worsley New Hall and occupied a substantial house. He was, recalled Wheeler, 'a landscape gardener in the mould of Carr and Capability Brown'. During the Great War, Worsley New Hall became a military hospital and, much to his grandfather's regret, the great house had fallen into disrepair by 1919 but Wheeler and his cousins were still able to play in the 'magical expanse' of its park and explored 'with insatiable delight every nook and cranny'. An additional diversion was being taken, with the dogs, by Grandfather Upjohn on ferreting expeditions on Saturday mornings.[7] In Worsley, Wheeler, his mother and sister and the whole family attended the Church of St Mark's where he had been baptised.[8]

Towards the end of the war, while on an Easter visit to York, Wheeler experienced what he later described as his first call to the priesthood. Waiting for a bus, he saw in a shop window a sepia picture of the Resurrection: 'An angel was within the tomb and there was awe and expectancy in the expression and posture of the first visitors'. He remembered the picture with intense joy as 'all the jubilation of Eastertide seemed to be crowded into it'. In the afternoon, he was taken to York Minister for a service and of that experience, he recalled:

> I think it was then that I received the first call to devote myself to the ministry of the Church. I can remember the singing, the procession, the vast beauty of the Minster, the Archbishop of the

Northern Province; but I can see too hundreds of people in sombre clothing. Many of them had no doubt been deprived by the War of all that they held dear. And my picture obtruded on all this and gave me what I believe was my first realisation of the necessity of God and Christ and Resurrection (indeed of Dogma) in a world that had gone astray.[9]

At the end of the war, the Wheeler family stayed on in Worsley rather than return to Yorkshire and in was during this period that Gordon, aged about nine, had his first taste of religious controversy. When Henry William Thorne, a priest of Anglo-Catholic sympathies, became Vicar of Worsley in November 1918, he abolished High Matins in favour of the Holy Eucharist. The Wheelers and Upjohns regarded this innovation as anathema and were unimpressed, but to the surprise of his family, the young Wheeler expressed the opinion that 'it was the most beautiful service I have ever seen' and he was supported in his view by his Aunt Ida.[10] His parents' overriding loyalty to the Church overcame their disapproval of Rev Thorne and Wheeler continued to attend sung Eucharist and Catechism classes on Sunday. From Thorne he learnt the first elements of the Catholic faith recalling later that 'I could never be sufficiently grateful to him for all his teaching and help'. He was confirmed by the Bishop of Blackburn at the age of twelve and thereafter became the Bishop's first altar boy at Sunday services. However, his parental distrust of Rev Thorne's religious leanings lingered and Wheeler was prevented from making his Confession before his Confirmation.[11] The Wheelers were not the only ones who objected to Thorne's ideas. The historian of the parish wrote that Thorne was a good and conscientious priest who 'served St Mark's well according to his beliefs' but 'it was unfortunate for all that those beliefs had not coincided with the majority of his parishioners'.[12]

Wheeler recalled that at about this time he 'became more and more obsessed by ecclesiasticism'—a phase manifested in the collection of religious objects and play-acting religious roles rather than any mature reflection on theology. In his room, he assembled a collection of artefacts, bought and given, which enabled him to construct an altar and conduct 'services' with his friend Vernon Knowlson. In later years, he regarded this phase as 'something excessively priggish' yet he was only doing what other boys of similar inclinations did at that time. There was a magnetic and imitative quality about contemporary church ceremonies and these often fired the youthful religious imagination. It was, he remembered, 'a very good game' but one tinged with a sense of reality. It was a period in his otherwise normal early life, he remembered, 'of real romanticism which is the accessory of early youth, manifested in other ways by the composition of ambitious and high falutin poems: each one with a moral'.[13]

Schooldays

Late in his fifth year, Wheeler commenced his formal education at Park View Preparatory School, Swinton. There he encountered the indomitable Miss Smith—'an Edwardian edition of the Victorian Dame'. Under her and in the company of others, he spent 'happy days' learning a range of basic skills while simultaneously developing a liking 'for art and civilisation'. His termly reports, while not exactly flattering, indicated that he was making good progress and his position in the class was never less than second. Perhaps conscious of his religious leaning, his art teacher Miss Peace warned him that under no circumstances should he give in, even under the threat of death, if Roman Catholic nuns ever tried to force him to join the Catholic Church. Wheeler conjured up images of nuns with revolvers secreted under their voluminous habits.[14]

His own faith, still decidedly Anglican at this point, was developing in its youthful way. In November 1921, aged eleven, he produced a poem entitled 'Hope':

Hope
Let us hope and not give in
Pray and believe
For Heavenly Father will receive.
Do not give in if you have done a sin
Confess and you will get Absolution!
Do not fret.
He hath hope and in the morn
Doth rise again at dawn
So let us be like he
for in front we cannot see.
In the city of Eternity
With all of the magnetic three
Faith—Hope—and Charity.[15]

Conscious of events elsewhere, he added:

O Almighty God we pray and beseech Thee to save all the dying and starving children in Russia. Give them food, clothing and a home. And grant that, when we die we may enter into Thy Heavenly Kingdom. Thro' Jesus Christ our Lord. Amen.[16]

Around the age of twelve, Wheeler left Park View and was enrolled at Eccles Grammar School where his father had been a pupil. An old-fashioned institution, Eccles Grammar School lived on the reputation of former glories established in the previous century. It was significantly different in Wheeler's day in that the regime was no longer excessively brutal. He wrote that he was happy there 'for the most part' but admitted to playing truant when faced with the wrath of the teachers. This disapproval centred mainly on the appalling quality of Wheeler's writing, a fault accentuated at a time when so much class time was given over to the practice and perfection of handwriting. Nevertheless, Wheeler progressed successfully and in 1923 was awarded the College of Preceptors Preliminary Certificate indicating proficiency in English Language and Literature, English History, Geography, Arithmetic, Algebra, Geometry and French. However, despite making good progress at Eccles, his mother took him to Manchester Grammar School and persuaded the Headmaster, John Lewis Paton, to admit her son. He left Eccles tearful and with profound regret and felt moved to present the school with a copy of *The Ingoldsby Legends*.[17]

Manchester Grammar School in Long Millgate, Manchester, was a huge school for the time. Over 1,200 boys attended the school and Wheeler admitted that his first term, in the autumn of 1924, was terrifying.[18] He quickly adjusted, however, and settled into an academic and scholarly routine aptly suited to his abilities. Spurred on by an ambition to do well and taught by men of high educational attainment, he made good if somewhat erratic progress. His teachers acknowledged his diligence, his 'distinct ability', his tenacity, and even his 'taste and feeling' but at various intervals they reported 'signs of staleness' and 'daydreaming'. Nevertheless, he was regarded as 'a fine lad' closely involved with the dramatic society and school magazine. His results were not particularly impressive and his class positions were: summer 1924, 4th out of 22; summer 1925, 21st out of 28; and summer 1926, 24th out of 24.[19]

His religious interests did not desert him. As he wrote later, his essays almost invariably seemed to take a religious or ecclesiastical turn: 'If the subject was Bathing, Books or Bicycles the Almighty turned up at the beginning or the end with a frequency which must have been exasperating to some of those who had to teach me'. A more physical and lasting experience came when he visited Paris on a school trip in 1926. He attended High Mass at Notre Dame Cathedral on Easter Sunday and was overcome by the ceremonial and processions. The scene, he recalled, 'was one of the most remarkable things I had ever witnessed'. His attempt to revisit the scene in Salford Catholic Cathedral on his return home, however, proved initially disappointing when his liturgical impressions and the harsh, cultural reality of Catholicism clashed. He found the cathedral 'packed with people: with men with rags around their necks and women with shawls and clogs and I had never seen people like that in a church before'. He looked at the Holy Water font and found it full of dirt—'it was all very unhygienic'. For the first time he had witnessed the Catholic working class and they were unlike the clean and well-dressed Anglicans of Worsley or stylish Parisians in Notre Dame. His experience at Salford, however, had a positive effect for he returned regularly to the cathedral to attend Mass and thought 'how wonderful this is because the people of God, so to speak, are here; it's not just the well-dressed'.[20]

At school, Wheeler admitted to his schoolboy failings but they did not prevent him developing his considerable talents for English and languages and his love of History. His facility with words and editorial experience on the school magazine seemed to draw him towards a career in journalism while a family friend offered to obtain for him a secretarial position in a commercial undertaking. Some of Wheeler's schoolboy poems, plays and translations survive but only one is dated—'The Legends of Aristaeus, Orpheus and Eurydice' of 16 December 1925. The other poems are 'The Spirit of Labour' and 'Music'; there is a translation of 'Orpheus' and a play entitled 'The Clerical Colouring Club'. All reflect Wheeler's adolescent literary aspirations.[21]

In the autumn of 1926, at the age of sixteen, and after sitting his School Certificate, Wheeler returned to the History Sixth at Manchester Grammar School and subsequently concentrated on the study of English Literature, English History, French and Economics supplemented by courses in Biblical History and Literature. Alongside entry into the higher academic and prestigious reaches of the school, there came the advantages of some of the best teachers and the privilege of wearing a special summer boater and being able to study at the famous and nearby John Rylands Library. Taught History by Richard Poskitt—a man to whom he 'owed so much'—Wheeler felt he was stepping into a great tradition of learning, one which resulted in 'a galaxy of University Open Scholarships and Exhibitions' to Oxford and Cambridge.[22]

Wheeler thrived in the academic atmosphere of the History Sixth. Surrounded by other able boys and taught by some inspirational teachers, he made notable progress. Richard Poskitt wrote that he was 'an interested student with sound literary tastes'. He added: 'He is inspired by spiritual idealism and I can confidently recommend him as most suitable for a university career'. In January 1928, the High Master, Douglas Miller, wrote that Wheeler was a boy 'of most gentlemanly leaning and excellent character'. A year later, when recommending him for university, Miller summed up Wheeler's general contribution to school life: 'He is a distinctly able boy, a school prefect and a leading member of the Dramatic Society. He has a strong personality and is a boy who I am sure, will make the very best of his opportunities'.[23] His results, however, had remained relatively unimpressive.[24]

A reference from his old mentor Rev (now Canon) Henry Thorne in support of Wheeler's application for a scholarship to Oxford portrays a picture of a teenager with a social conscience and one already determined to embark on formation for the priesthood. Thorne could not speak highly enough of his protégé's 'intellectual gifts and social talents and also the integrity of his character and general influence'. These qualities, the Canon remarked, 'peculiarly fit him for the work of the ministry, in which, I believe, from the highest motives, he feels that he can best serve his day and generation'. The reference divulges information about the younger Wheeler not included in the Bishop's later memoir. During the Great War, he and his sister had visited local hospitals entertaining wounded soldiers with songs and recitations. While at Manchester Grammar School, Wheeler had organized charity collections, concerts and amateur theatricals in aid of the National Society for the Prevention of Cruelty to Children and other local charities and hospitals. His many commitments to the parish church included playing the organ.[25]

In autumn of 1929, Wheeler left Manchester Grammar School and proceeded to University College Oxford, as an Exhibitioner to read History. He was in receipt of a bursary from the Kitchener Scholarship Fund which provided support for children of war veterans whose health had been undermined during the Great War.[26] Two of his companions in the History Sixth—Reginald Cadman and David Peck—were, like

Wheeler, to proceed to Holy Orders in the Anglican Church.[27] When Wheeler left Manchester for Oxford, Richard Poskitt wrote to him: 'You have strength of character, unbounded faith and many qualifications for leadership' and he advised him 'to be proud of MGS' and never forget 'its message and its ideals of service for all humanity'. He was confident that in later life Wheeler would 'be convinced of the supremacy of MGS in so many of the fundamentals of education'.[28]

Notes

1. Saddleworth Urban District Council was comprised of the villages of Uppermill, Dobcross, Delph and Greenfield. *Kelly's Directory of the West Riding (1912)* (London: Kelly's Directories Ltd., 1912), pp. 800–806; M. Fox and P. Fox, *Saddleworth Album* (Oldham: Taylor and Clifton, 1995). At Wheeler's birth, Dobcross was located within the Roman Catholic Diocese of Leeds. It remains so.

2. *Lancashire Online Parish Clerk Project*, Marriages at the Church of St Mark in the Parish of Worsley—Marriages recorded in the Register for the years 1903–1909.

3. I am indebted to David Stockdale for this information and for other details on Bishop Wheeler's family history.

4. LDA, WPC, WGW and Family; 1901 Census; 1911 Census; W.G. Wheeler, *In Truth And Love* (Southport: Gowland and Co., 1990), p. 9. St Mark's was opened in 1846 by its patron Lord Francis Egerton, 1st Earl of Ellesmere, and was in the Anglican High Church tradition.

5. Undated typescript; probably a paper given to the Converts Aid Society. LDA, WPC, Converts Aid Society.

6. Wheeler to Archbishop Bruno Heim on 'English Freemasonry', 25 March 1981. LDA, WDC, W14.

7. LDA, WPC, WGW and Family.

8. LDA, WPC, School/Oxford, Childhood; Wheeler, *In Truth And Love*, p. 9.

9. LDA, WPC, School/Oxford, Childhood.

10. Wheeler, *In Truth And Love*, p. 9.

11. LDA, WPC, School/Oxford, Childhood.

12. H. T. Milliken, *Changing Scene: Two Hundred Years of Church and Parish Life in Worsley* (Worsley: H. Duffy, 1985), pp. 31–32.

13. LDA, WPC, School/Oxford, Childhood. Vernon Knowlson was subsequently ordained into the Anglican ministry.

14. LDA, WPC, School/Oxford, Childhood.

15. LDA, WPC, School/Oxford, Childhood.

16. LDA, WPC, School/Oxford, Childhood.

17. LDA, WPC, School/Oxford, Childhood. Wheeler's handwriting did not improve with age.

18 *A Biographical Register of Old Mancunians 1888–1951* (Manchester: Manchester Grammar School, 1965), p. 370.

19 Manchester Grammar School Archive.

20 Wheeler, *In Truth And Love*, pp. 14–15.

21 LDA, WPC, School/Oxford, Childhood.

22 LDA, WPC, School/Oxford, Childhood.

23 LDA, WPC, School/Oxford, Childhood; Wheeler, *In Truth And Love*, p. 9.

24 Manchester Grammar School Archive.

25 H. W. Thorne to the Trustees of the Kitchener Scholarship Fund, 27 Jan 1928. LDA, WPC, School/Oxford, Childhood.

26 Marquis of Normanby to Wheeler, 23 Jan 1928. LDA, WPC, Letters Personal 1920s-1930s.

27 LDA, WPC, School/Oxford, Childhood.

28 J. R. Poskitt to Wheeler, 31 July 1929. LDA, WPC, School/Oxford, Childhood.

2 ANGLICAN DAYS

Oxford Undergraduate

WHEELER WENT UP to University College, Oxford, in the Michaelmas Term of 1929. The college's official name is 'The Master and Fellows of the College of the Great Hall of the University of Oxford', but is usually shortened to 'Univ'. It is claimed by some that the college was founded by King Alfred the Great in 872 but most agree that its likely foundation was in 1249 by Archbishop William of Durham. This later date still allows the claim that Univ is the oldest of the Oxford and Cambridge colleges, although this is contested by Balliol College (1263) and Merton College (1264). Until the sixteenth century Univ was only open to Fellows studying Theology. As the college grew in size and wealth, its medieval buildings were replaced with the current Main Quadrangle in the seventeenth Century. Although the foundation stone was placed on 17 April 1634, the disruption of the English Civil War meant it was not completed until sometime in 1676. Radcliffe Quad was built between 1716 and 1719, a new residential building was erected in 1842, and the Library was built in 1861. The college in which Wheeler took up residence would have changed little from the nineteenth century. Univ is known not only for its distinguished alumni but also for its especially long Grace before Meals which is recited by a scholar before every Formal Hall.[1]

Wheeler enjoyed himself enormously at Oxford and willingly and enthusiastically imbibed its history, traditions, and culture. He read History, which he regarded always as his first love, made many friends, and became deeply involved in the Oxford University Dramatic Society and the various Anglo-Catholic communities in and around the city. His undergraduate course was wide ranging and he spent time in the Radcliffe Camera consulting works on topics such as English Constitutional History, the Counter Reformation and Nineteenth Century Industrial Relations. As is the Oxford system, he went for tutorials to other colleges where the Professors, Fellows and Lecturers were in residence and he revelled in the company of the brilliant, the eccentric and the downright odd. Eccentrics and oddities appealed to Wheeler's sense of humour and his memoir is full of hilarious anecdotes about the characters of contemporary Oxford. He revelled in the ambience of the place and was impressed by the many men and women who combined their faith, scholarship and vocations with a high appreciation of European civilization. He felt completely enriched by his undergraduate experience.

The Master of Univ was the educationalist Sir Michael Sadler, formerly a senior government administrator and Vice-Chancellor of the University of Leeds from 1911 until 1923 when he returned to Oxford. Sadler was known as a connoisseur and an avid collector of modern art. When invited to the Master's Lodgings for breakfast, Wheeler the Fresher was in awe of the huge art collection arrayed before him. The Dean of Univ was Sir David Lindsay Keir, later to become Vice-Chancellor of Queen's University, Belfast, and then Master of Balliol. He was also Wheeler's Tutor in Constitutional History. As Dean, Lindsay Keir was responsible for discipline and it was Wheeler's misfortune to fall foul of him. After having inadvertently set a cushion on fire with ash from his pipe, Wheeler threw out the blazing cushion on to the lawn beneath his rooms in the Inner Quad. The lawn was consequently damaged and Wheeler was summoned to the Dean to be given 'a wigging' in 'unsurpassable prose' and fined £5.[2]

When he arrived in Oxford, Wheeler found Anglo-Catholicism 'in excelsis' but not at Univ. The source and location of this joy was Pusey House, opened in 1848 as a memorial to Edward Bouverie Pusey, former Regius Professor of Hebrew at Oxford and a Canon of Christ Church Cathedral. Pusey was a leading figure in the Oxford Movement and Pusey House was firmly in the Anglo-Catholic tradition of the Church of England. Wheeler attended and served at daily Eucharist at Pusey, went to Benediction there and was sacristan for a while. At Pusey, he met Anglican academics such as Darwell Stone, the famous Patristic scholar. Wheeler had great admiration for Stone and went to him for confession. Despite being much older than Wheeler, Stone and Canon Frederick Hood were also close and inspirational friends throughout his Oxford years. Among his younger acquaintances was Patrick McLaughlin of Worcester College, Francis Head, whom Wheeler met at Pusey and St Stephen's House, and Billy Clonmore, later Lord Wicklow. At Pusey, Clonmore was an Anglican deacon but he, Head and McLaughlin subsequently converted to Catholicism. Wheeler was to maintain contact with McLaughlin, Head and Clonmore and many other Oxford contemporaries throughout his life.

There was no shortage of Anglo-Catholic churches in and around Oxford and Wheeler attended services at St Barnabas, St Paul's, St Mary Magdalene, and the house of the Cowley Fathers. He recalled: '...one grew up in that sort of atmosphere. One got all the satisfaction of the full sacramental system and the beauty of worship and music and so forth in the High Anglican set up'. He added that he also attended lectures given at the Catholic Dominican house of Blackfriars.[3]

The socio-economic background to Wheeler's time at Oxford was dominated by the great economic depression of the late nineteen-twenties and early 'thirties and he acknowledged his good fortune that he and his family were not directly affected. He may have experienced financial shortages but his student life was not excessively restricted. Elsewhere, three million people were unemployed and successive National, or coalition, governments seemed unable to find solutions to the dire economic and social situation. Into this void in England came the Communists and a good number of prominent Oxford dons and students were among their ranks. In Europe, meanwhile, the extreme right provided another political alternative and the Italian Fascists and the German Nazis rose to power. These too, had their adherents in England and Oxford. Wheeler was certainly aware of political activity in Oxford but did not participate or become involved. Into this highly charged atmosphere there came, in 1928, the American Protestant Christian Evangelist Rev Dr Frank Buchman who proposed 'moral re-armament' as an antidote to extreme politics. Buchman's fundamentalist 'Oxford Group', 'a religious movement of great power', took the university by storm and persuaded many to surrender to God's will and change their lives. Frequent meetings gathered those who felt ready to publicly proclaim their unworthiness and follow the 'absolutes' of Truth, Purity, Selflessness and Love. It was not, as Wheeler recalled, everyone's solution to the world's problems or even their personal difficulties and it was certainly not his.[4]

Academically, Wheeler made good progress and remembered with affection most of his tutors. At the end of his undergraduate studies he was awarded 'a very good second' class degree.[5] He recalled that he loved Oxford and retained a deep affection for the university and city. He was always grateful 'for the good things' it did for him 'on the pilgrimage of life'.[6] As Wheeler went down, the Master of Univ wrote that 'he is a man of high character and his conduct has been exemplary'.[7]

St Stephen's House

In the autumn of 1932, Wheeler began his training for the Anglican ministry at St Stephen's House, Oxford. St Stephen's was founded in 1876 by members of the Tractarian movement and was in the Catholic tradition of the Church of England. The principal founder of the House is usually recognised as Edward King, Bishop of Lincoln, who was Regius professor of Pastoral Theology in the University of Oxford. King was acclaimed as an outstandingly holy man and had a considerable influence on the early history of the House. Associated with him were William Bright, Regius Professor of Ecclesiastical History; Edward Stuart Talbot, Warden of Keble College and subsequently Bishop of Winchester; Edwin James Palmer, Professor of Latin, Archdeacon of Oxford and later Bishop of Bombay; Edward Woolcoombe, a Fellow of Balliol who had a great interest in the missionary movement; John Wordsworth, Chaplain of Brasenose College; and finally Henry Scott Holland, senior fellow at Christ Church and one of the leading figures in the development of contemporary Christian social teaching. Holland recommended that the House be placed under the patronage of St Stephen.

The House's central purpose was to train candidates for ordination in the Church of England and other provinces of the Anglican Communion. Regarded as a seminary located in the Anglo-Catholic tradition of the Church of England, its courses were based on a very Catholic model of training priests in the use of the confessional and the practice of Ignatian meditation. Life was quasi-monastic with periods of greater and lesser silence, and prescribed times for prayer. Presiding over it was Fr Arthur Couratin, described by some as 'a Roman Catholic who uses the Prayer Book' and by others as a 'Noël Coward in a clerical collar'. His relaxed drawl and quick wit concealed a formidable intellect and with him as Principal, the House maintained high standards of liturgy, scholarship and morality. The House was located originally on the site which is now the New Bodleian Library in premises opposite the King's Arms public house. In 1919, it moved into buildings in Norham Gardens, North Oxford. These buildings were developed and a chapel was built to the side of one of the houses.

Wheeler entered St Stephen's at a time when the Church of England faced a manpower crisis. The shortage of priests began during the Great War with the loss of priests and ordinands. In 1918, the Church was short-staffed and by 1930, the situation was causing some anxiety. In

1924, *Crockford's Clerical Directory* suggested that curates were 'like rare migrant birds' and they 'promised to become scarce'. In 1927, it warned that if the ordination statistics of the previous decade were anything to go by, then 'the maintenance of the parochial system will become impossible in all but a few favoured localities'. In 1931, it reported that the situation was going 'from bad to worse and a crisis of the first magnitude draws nearer every year'. In 1932, it reckoned that there had been a loss of 550 priests and that 1,380 new clergy were required. The number of clergy had dropped from 19,053 in 1905 to 16,745 in 1930. New ordinands tended to be men who had served in other occupations but unlike many previous ordinands, few were of independent financial means and the cost to the Church to educate these men was high. Another complication for an ordinand was that although a bishop might accept him for study he had to find a vicar who would subsequently employ him otherwise he could not be ordained. Complicating the whole picture was the economic discrepancies between and within dioceses. Poor parishes could not always afford a curate.[8]

Wheeler's time at St Stephen's was not a happy experience. Unwisely, he had been persuaded to attempt an Honours course in Theology in one year as it would prepare him for the Anglican ministry but he had neither the time nor the inclination to undertake such a punishing schedule. He wrote of his mental state at this time:

> Academically this was a great mistake. Looking back, I think it is unwise to attempt in one year a second Honours School unless one is outstandingly brilliant. I was already disenchanted with the Anglican situation. And added to that I was passing through perhaps the lowest trough in my life and perhaps near to a nervous breakdown. I was certainly not in a mood to tackle the syllabus in the way I should have done and the result in the Schools was disastrous.[9]

Wheeler had been brought up to love the Scriptures but he wrote that studying Theology at Oxford, rather than deepening that love, had the opposite effect and the pre-occupation with German Higher Criticism seemed to him to be totally destructive. He recalled: 'It took me many years to rediscover the glories of the Old and New Testaments'.[10] His tutors and friends were surprised at his poor performance; Wheeler felt he had let them down very badly. Alongside this disappointment, there was a growing uncertainty over his Anglican faith and although he had immersed himself in Anglo-Catholicism during his time at Oxford, its features and trappings, despite their beauty, had begun to lose their appeal.[11]

Brighton and Chesterfield

Wheeler was so thoroughly disenchanted with the Anglican Church and the prospect of his ordination that he tried to fail the General Ordination Examination. However, he scraped through and was sent to be ordained deacon by Bishop George Bell of Chichester, the famous contemporary ecumenist. In spite of his doubts, his ordination to the diaconate took place on 21 December 1933 at Chichester Cathedral in the presence of all his family. As with all ordinands in the Anglican Church, Wheeler took the oath 'required by law'.[12]

Following his ordination, Wheeler took up a curacy with Talbot Dilworth Harrison, a priest he had met in Oxford. Dilworth Harrison was firmly in the Anglo-Catholic tradition and was the author of books on the Oxford Movement and the history of the Anglo-Catholic revival. Wheeler described Dilworth Harrison as 'a fine pastoral man' and was happy to accept his invitation to become his curate at St Bartholomew's Church in Brighton. Within a very short time of Wheeler's arrival in Brighton, however, Dilworth Harrison was appointed Archdeacon of Chesterfield and he invited Wheeler, still only a deacon, to accompany him as his assistant in the parish of St Mary and All Saints whose church was famous for its crooked spire. Before accepting the invitation, Wheeler sought the advice of the Bishop of Chichester. Bishop Bell said he 'knew of no finer instructor of young clergy' than Dilworth Harrison and so with Bell's permission, Wheeler went to Chesterfield.[13]

Under the careful attention of the dedicated and celibate Dilworth Harrison, Wheeler set about his ministry in Chesterfield. With his fellow curate, he had to submit to the parish priest a form on which was recorded details of previous week's house visits and other pastoral activities. This procedure was taken seriously by Dilworth Harrison who closely questioned his young assistants on their work. The occasional attempt to hoodwink the Archdeacon by furnishing false names and addresses of those visited failed miserably. On another occasion, Wheeler was asked to give a dictated lecture on the history of the Church of England in the place of Dilworth Harrison. He found it difficult as he was of the opinion that what Dilworth Harrison would have said was untrue. Nevertheless, he was required to say what his superior had written.[14]

As the time approached for Wheeler's priestly ordination, the pressure on him increased. He solicited the advice of an Anglican Benedictine, the Vicar of All Saints, Margaret Street, Chesterfield, but received only sympathy and encouragement to proceed with ordination.[15] Despite his unhappiness, he went ahead and was ordained at Derby Cathedral on Sunday 23 December 1934 by the Bishop of Derby. He assented to the Thirty-Nine Articles of the Church of England and became a stipendiary curate. He celebrated his first Mass on the following day at All Saints Church, Chesterfield.[16] Despite his misgivings, Wheeler engaged in the usual parish activities with enthusiasm and not content with visiting the homes of his own parishioners, he was known to pay calls on those of other denominations. He was actively involved in the parish's dramatic activities, in schoolwork and with the Scout troop, organizing a summer camp to the south coast in the summer of 1935.[17] His decision to proceed with ordination, however, had come at a physical cost and he was affected by a serious attack of jaundice which he ascribed to the strain 'of the question that had been going on for four years and to which I hadn't really faced up'. He was advised to return to 'a south climate' to recover his health. Providentially, in 1935 he was offered a way out of Chesterfield in the form of offers of a curacy at St Giles', Cambridge, or as Assistant Curate at Lancing College in West Sussex. The thought of Cambridge and further study appealed to him but he was advised and encouraged by Oxford friends to go to Lancing and restore its Anglo-Catholic traditions.[18]

Lancing College was a boarding school for boys aged between thirteen and eighteen and was located between Shoreham and Lancing in West Sussex. It was founded in 1848 by Reverend Nathaniel Woodard and was the jewel in the crown of the eleven schools eventually built across the country by the Woodard Corporation. They were not English public schools of the traditional type but catered for the middle classes which Woodard regarded as irreligious. They were graded according to Woodard's view of the Victorian class system with grade one schools for the boys of upper middle class families and inferior grade two schools for those of the lower middle classes. Fees varied accordingly. Lancing was a grade one school and the centre of its campus was the magnificent thirteenth century Gothic style chapel begun in 1868 and completed in 1911. The chapel was exceeded in height by only Westminster Abbey and York Minster. Nathaniel Woodard was a Tractarian and was accused of trying to impose the Catholic tradition of the Church of England on his students. Religious ceremonies centred on the sacramental and on the Eucharist.[19]

Wheeler was happy at Lancing and soon became a popular figure. He did not stay long but the school's history records that during his ministry 'he made a deep impression on masters and boys'.[20] He admitted that he would never make a good schoolmaster but he enjoyed the school community and his further involvement with the Boy Scouts. Lancing's atmosphere and its High Church services appealed to him but his doubts about the Anglican Church in relation to the truth and authority of the Catholic Church remained.[21]

Notes

1 See www.univ.ox.ac.uk

2 W. G. Wheeler, *In Truth And Love* (Southport: Gowland and Co., 1990), pp. 16–19.

3 The foregoing two paragraphs are based on Wheeler, *In Truth And Love*, pp. 16 and 19–24.

4 W. G. Wheeler, *More Truth And Love* (Southport: Gowland and Co., 1994), p. 136.

5 Wheeler, *In Truth And Love*, pp. 16–17.

6 Wheeler, *More Truth And Love*, p. 136.

7 M. Sadler, 16 Jan 1933. LDA, WPC, Anglican Documents.

8 R. Lloyd, *The Church of England 1900–1965* (London: S.C.M. Press, 1966), pp. 337–343.

9 Wheeler, *In Truth And Love*, pp. 16–17.

10 *Ibid.*, p. 150.

11 *Ibid.*, p. 17.

12 William Gordon Wheeler, Diaconate Certificate. LDA, WPC, Anglican Documents.

13 Wheeler, *In Truth And Love*, pp. 28–29.

14 *Ibid.*, p. 32.

15 *Ibid.*

16 William Gordon Wheeler, Ordination Card. LDA, WPC, Anglican Documents; *Crockford's Clerical Directory for 1935*, (London: Oxford University Press, 1935), p. 1049.

17 LDA, WPC, Anglican Documents.

18 Wheeler, *In Truth And Love*, p. 32.

19 LDA, WPC, Lancing College; *The Daily Telegraph*, 25 April 1991.

20 B. Handford, *Lancing College: History and Memoir* (Chichester: Phillimore, 1986), pp. 208–209. Many years later, after he became Bishop of Leeds, Wheeler was invited to preach at Lancing and expressed his joy that the ecumenical movement had enabled

him to be in a pulpit which he had never expected to mount again.

[21] Wheeler, *In Truth And Love*, pp. 32–33.

3 CONVERSION AND ORDINATION

Conversion

THERE CAN BE no doubt that his decision to become a Catholic was the greatest in Wheeler's life. It was not made hastily but after years of discernment and discussion, prayer and thought, and a series of providential experiences. It was a journey in faith, which began in Oxford and before his ordination to the Anglican ministry. There was 'no dark night of the soul' but there were times of physical torpor, deep emotion, anxiety and close spiritual examination. His movement towards Catholicism appeared almost inexorable.

Wheeler's contacts with Catholics in Oxford were rare. He had come across the Jesuit Fr Martin D'Arcy and Fr Ronald Knox when he was an undergraduate. Both contacts were somewhat superficial but Wheeler chose to remember them later in life. D'Arcy was a notable Catholic theologian in 1930s Oxford and, from Campion Hall, he exerted an immense influence. He had been invited to dinner by Wheeler when the latter was involved with the Oxford University Dramatic Society but of that meeting, there is little to add.[1] Wheeler's encounter with Knox, however, through Knox's reputation and through social contact is perhaps more important. Knox's conversion reflected Wheeler's own journey from Anglicanism to Catholicism—a strong attraction to the rituals of Anglican Catholicity, an affinity with the history of English Catholicism, attendance at Pusey House and Cowley, and contact with the monastic life (in Knox's case, the Anglican Benedictines of Caldey Island).[2] Wheeler's imagination was stirred by seeing the old-Etonian Knox, then Catholic Chaplain to the University, walking across Christ Church Meadows in the afternoon reading his breviary. It was an impression further strengthened when Wheeler, with some Catholic friends, attended a soirée at the chaplaincy and heard Knox deliver a humourous paper on 'The Man Who tried to Convert The Pope'—an account of the visit to Rome in 1850 by the Bishop of Durham and his wife, the highpoint of which was an audience with Pope Pius IX. Wheeler wrote later that: 'Ronnie loved priests, and he was admired and loved by them in return. One can think of no other priest, cradle-Catholic or convert, who made so deep and affectionate an impression on his generation. He became a legend but never just a period piece. He was, in a sense, an incarnation of all that priests most value'.[3] As such, Knox was a role model to the impressionable Wheeler.

Wheeler's change of confessional direction seemed to emerge mainly after discussions and experiences with his Anglican friends and mentors. Of these, he identified Canon Herman Leonard Pass as having a particular influence on him. Principal of Chichester Theological College and a friend of the Wheeler family, Pass invited Wheeler to accompany him as his secretary to a Conference of Theologians of Eastern and Western Churches at Berne in Switzerland. There the young Wheeler, still an undergraduate, absorbed the academic papers and discussions of some of Europe's greatest ecumenical figures but was especially fascinated by Pass's recollection of his meeting with Pope Pius XI when, as Fr Achille Ratti, he was Librarian of the Ambrosian Library in Milan. Pass and Wheeler attended the Old Catholic Church in Berne but Pass dismissed the Old Catholics as an intellectual movement with little following and asked Wheeler to search out a Catholic Church.[4] There they subsequently attended Mass but did not receive Holy Communion. Pass told Wheeler: 'I am, as you know, anxious that you should, as soon as possible, devote yourself to the problems of reunion'.[5]

Another influence on Wheeler during this time was Francis Head who had befriended him at meetings at Pusey House and St Stephen's House. The two corresponded frequently and Wheeler recalled that Francis 'helped to clear the path of my thinking and drew me on my pilgrim way'.[6] In 1933, Head told Wheeler that he had 'been received into the Roman Church' and explained his reasons. After two years at St Stephen's, he had spent three months in an Anglican parish but could not continue either with his ministry or his membership of the Anglican Church. He told Wheeler of his difficulties: 'To believe in one religion and act as though one believes in another is really no good when it comes down to parish work and trying to convert others'. His painful decision was to leave the Anglican Church.[7]

Head eventually became a Catholic priest in the Diocese of Portsmouth after trying his novitiate with the Jesuits. It was during his time with the Jesuits, throughout 1934 and 1935, and in the immediate months before Wheeler's own conversion that Head wrote regularly to him urging him to convert. He was of the view that the Church of England was 'illogical' and could not be explained. He derided the religious atmosphere and posturing at Pusey House, where they had spent time together, and regarded it as an unhealthy influence on Wheeler. It was, he wrote, 'Modernism clothed in chasubles'. Wheeler's poor performance in the Theology exams had been a sign from the Holy Ghost 'that he should not shine in Theology of that kind' and added that the Jesuits at Stonyhurst were cleverer than all those in Pusey House put together.[8] Having made the step to Catholicism himself, Head was in a position to offer advice: 'You must not let any human influences affect you one way or the other, nor follow any advice save your own conscience'.[9] He acknowledged that 'coming over' was a step in the dark' and was 'a terrific act of faith' but almost in a sense of exasperation he wrote, 'I do really believe it is time for you to act, as you may go on for ages groping about in the dark, and it is only <u>one jump</u> with Our Lady and all the company of Heaven pulling you, is what you need. If I were you I should do it at once'.[10]

The other strong influence on Wheeler was Patrick McLaughlin, a scholar of Worcester College and, like Wheeler, a member of the OUDS. McLaughlin introduced Wheeler to the Dominicans at Blackfriars where they attended lectures on St Thomas Aquinas and discussed the relevance of papal encyclicals to social problems. However, by the time he took his degree in 1932, Wheeler did not intend to become a Catholic for despite his conviction of 'the Catholic position', he felt that he did not have 'the fullness of faith' and felt no particular urge to abandon his Anglicanism.

In 1933, during his year at St Stephen's, there occurred a providential event in Wheeler's life. Due to a cancellation, he was asked to accompany two friends to the Catholic Benedictine Buckfast Abbey where they stayed for a few days. Wheeler knew of the monastic tradition and rule from his historical studies but the fact that the monastic life survived so strongly in the modern world took him by surprise. He was even more impressed by Abbot Anscar Vonier who sat up late into the night with the three young visitors in the Abbey Guest House discussing religious topics. He recalled that they sat 'with this Austrian Catholic wondering whether we ought to become Roman Catholics' and then they wrote in the Visitors' Book 'For mine eyes have seen thy salvation'.

They returned to Oxford and Blackfriars and asked to be instructed in the Catholic faith but the Dominican priest recognised the immediacy of their emotional and spiritual experience at Buckfast and advised that they went away to think about their decision and seek instructions in their own Catholic parishes. Accordingly, Wheeler went to see Canon James Walters at Our Lady of Ransom in Eastbourne, near to where his parents were living, and explained his difficulty — that he wanted to be received into the Church but he was currently training for the Anglican ministry. Wheeler asked if he might be able to enter a Catholic seminary but it was not a decision that Walters could make. Instead, he arranged for Wheeler to see Bishop Peter Amigo of Southwark who was shortly to visit Hastings. The venerable bishop was sympathetic but advised Wheeler to inform his parents of his intentions. A difficult task confronted Wheeler.

His father, normally a taciturn man, was tearful as Wheeler told him what was in his mind and how he had lately been in the company of priests and other members of the Catholic faith. The situation, Wheeler told his father, had reached a climax and he felt that he could not return to St Stephen's. His father's firm advice was that he should not tell his mother and that he should return to Stephen's and prepare for ordination. A devastated but dutiful Wheeler informed Canon Walters that he could not proceed with instruction and that he would give himself more time to consider his future. Wheeler returned to Oxford disconsolate and progressed towards Anglican ordination, despite trying to fail his exams.

As we have seen in the previous chapter, Wheeler was ordained to the diaconate and priesthood in the Anglican Church and it was as an assistant in Brighton that his advice was sought by a young woman considering conversion to Catholicism. After a number of meetings, she suggested to Wheeler that as he could put forward more reasons for becoming a Catholic than he could in defence of the Anglican faith then he too ought to become a Catholic. She had been convinced by his arguments in favour of the Catholic faith and on his advice took a train to Bath and subsequently to the Benedictine Abbey at Downside to meet a convert Anglican called Dom Christopher Butler. Wheeler's advice and the young woman's consequent defection were not welcomed by the Vicar.

Despite some satisfaction with his ministry as a deacon in Brighton and as priest in Chesterfield, Wheeler was never completely free of doubt about his membership of the Anglican faith and for this reason was less than convinced about his ordination. It was while he was employed at Lancing College, however, that Wheeler took the decision to leave the Anglican Church and Anglican orders.

Wheeler was very happy at Lancing although he doubted his abilities and future prospects as a schoolmaster. He was active in the general life of the school and was a popular figure. While teaching religion at the college, however, his religious doubts re-surfaced and began to fill his thoughts. In the summer vacation of 1936, he went with a Lancing housemaster Patrick Halsey on a tour of Italy. A high point of the journey was an audience with Pope Pius XI at Castelgandolfo and following this unique and influential experience Wheeler felt that he must speak with a Catholic priest and wrote to Mgr William Godfrey, Rector of the English College in Rome, who had arranged the papal audience. Godfrey had been at the College's summer residence at Palazzola in the Alban Hills but went to meet Wheeler at his hotel in Rome. The conversation was fruitful. Wheeler outlined his difficulties to Godfrey who listened sympathetically and 'provided the final clarification'. 'If one has the fullness of faith,' said Godfrey, 'one must grasp it'. Aware of Wheeler's domestic situation, he reminded him that Jesus had said that if a man loves his parents and family 'more than me, he is not worthy of me'. On hearing and dwelling on that remark, Wheeler finally resolved to join the Catholic Church.[11] The meeting with Mgr Godfrey was remarkably coincidental and Wheeler will no doubt have recognised this but failed to mention it in his memoir. While in Italy in 1832, John Henry Newman had visited the English College and met with Nicholas Wiseman, then Rector of the College and future Archbishop of Westminster.[12] Like Wiseman, Godfrey held both offices.

When he returned to England, he immediately told his mother of his decision to become a Catholic. She was naturally upset but told him to leave for Downside and instruction while she broke the news to his father and the rest of the family. Shortly after he arrived at Downside, Wheeler received a telegram asking him to go home. Faced with this difficulty, he sought the advice of Abbot Bruno Hicks who told him to go home and be strong in his convictions. In the midst of his family, Wheeler was under constant pressure to explain his reasons and motives. His mother seemed resigned to the situation and in spite of her sadness, said, 'You will I hope, go on to be a priest'. It was brave of her to express such a sentiment for she knew that as a Catholic priest he would have to take the vow of celibacy. At this point, however, Wheeler claimed he had not decided on his future course of action. The weekend was a draining and emotional experience but Wheeler held his position and eventually returned to

Downside where, on 18 September 1936, he was received into the Catholic Church by Dom Richard Davey. The two witnesses were Dom Christopher Butler and Dom Oswald Sumner. Mrs Bell, the young lady he had advised at Brighton was also present. After years of spiritual struggle and emotional torment, the uncertainty was now over. Wheeler recalled: 'the outcome was a great joy and a great relief'.[13]

Reactions

Wheeler was acutely aware that his conversion would provoke a range of strong and probably bitter reactions among his family and friends and he took pains to alert some of them of his decision before his reception at Downside.

The Catholic Francis Head was 'speechless' with joy at the news of his forthcoming conversion. He wrote: 'You are becoming a Catholic—it is the will of God'. He advised kindness but firmness in dealing with those who questioned his decision.[14] The Anglican reaction, however, was not universally joyful or understanding and there was a mixture of sadness at his decision and anger at the Church of Rome's poaching of such a talented priest. His sister Betty wrote that their father was deeply upset and very quiet.[15] His Aunt Ida was shocked by the news and 'it gave way to uncontrollable grief'. She admitted that it must have taken a lot of courage and now she somehow had to find the courage to tell his ninety-three-year-old Grandfather who was so proud of Wheeler's work at Lancing.[16]

His friend Nora Wallis, meanwhile, was conscious of Wheeler's deep concern over wounding his family and in particular the effect that his conversion would have on his mother. She wrote to Mrs Wheeler that her heart went out to her in her 'great distress.' She had suspected that Gordon had been 'rather playing with Rome' while at Oxford, and their meetings in London, when they had visited Westminster Cathedral, had pushed them both towards Catholicism. She, however, had taken the step before him. Wallis could only imagine a mother's anguish but tried to reassure Mrs Wheeler that 'days will dawn when she will be a proud mother'.[17] Wheeler said later that his father was a man of strong Anglican principles who had sacrificed so much for his education; there was little wonder that he opposed his conversion. They were to be estranged for many years.[18]

Among his friends there was sadness but understanding. In some responses to his letters, there was an admission that his defection was expected but most hoped that the decision had been his own. Humphry

Beevor had heard that he had 'poped' and wondered if Francis Head had exerted influence. He acknowledged Wheeler's courage but could not understand why he had given up such a comfortable job and good ecclesiastical prospects.[19] From Lancing, Frank Doherty urged him to discuss the matter with him before leaving not only the Church but the priesthood and the College.[20] Other staff and boys were desperately upset at his departure although the level of understanding naturally varied enormously. Once he had made the decision to leave the Anglican Communion, he had to resign from Lancing but the Headmaster and staff were anxious to keep the news from the boys. Shortly after he had left the College, a boy approached him and said: "Oh, hello Sir, what's happened to you? Why haven't you been back this term?" Wheeler replied, "Well don't you know?" The boy said, somewhat naively, "The boys do say, Sir, that you've run off with a barmaid". "Well", said Wheeler, "I don't think she's generally called a barmaid, but I've heard her referred to as a scarlet woman".[21]

Hugh Frazer, now a vicar in Scarborough, wished he had been told sooner so that they could have discussed Wheeler's position. The Church of England's loss, he wrote, would be far greater than Rome's gain. He remained convinced that 'the dear old Church of England is inherently Catholic and part of the Body of Christ' but, recognising the gulf between the two Communions, he hoped that Wheeler would not regard the Anglican Masses he had said 'as being no Masses at all'.[22] Another friend agreed that Wheeler's loss would be deeply felt by the Church of England and that he should be prepared for unpleasant things to be said to him and about him.[23] Bishop George Bell of Chichester was completely taken by surprise at Wheeler's forthcoming conversion: 'I had no idea when we last met, you were contemplating so serious a step'. He had thought that Wheeler was happy as a priest and at Lancing and wondered why he had not been informed of his 'difficulties'. He asked if Wheeler had taken any advice from Anglicans or had been more influenced by Roman Catholics.[24]

A minority of Anglicans tempered their answers to Wheeler's letters, or responses to the news of his conversion, with very strong anti-Catholic views. They were, it seemed, angry at his defection and at the same time warned him about the Church he was joining. From Sheffield, Ethel Reynolds thought he had been enticed by the Church of Rome whose priests 'were cunning, deceitful and unpleasant'. Wheeler could not possibly live in that environment and his happiness would be short lived.[25]

From Lancing, Rev J. R. Missen felt that Wheeler's great gifts could have been used without the 'natural grief that anyone must feel who separates himself from the Church of his upbringing: and you with your generous and appreciative nature must of necessity feel that grief very acutely'. He warned Wheeler of the dangers of the Roman Church: 'Truth is not her strong suit', he wrote, and the morality of the Catholic Church was defective and suspect.[26] From Chesterfield, Archdeacon Dilworth Harrison, Wheeler's former vicar, was even more vitriolic in his anti-Catholic views. It was no coincidence, he wrote, that that the Catholic Church allied itself to the contemporary dictatorial regimes in Italy, Spain and Mexico, for that was its normal *modus operandi*. The Catholic Church, he concluded, would not acknowledge its responsibilities for all the faults of the world's ills.[27] As if to reassure him, the Catholic William Home welcomed Wheeler and wrote that Church of England was not a Church but 'a compromise' and 'an establishment'.[28]

Francis Head wrote that he was 'desperately pleased' at Wheeler's reception: 'You don't know what you are in for'.[29] He warned him, however, that the first few months would be strange and difficult but that the future was indeed something to savour. 'It gives me terrific joy to think of you so new in the faith and the happiness that will grow in you as you get used to it'.[30] Mgr Charles Duchemin, Rector of the Pontifical Beda College, Rome, where Wheeler would later go to be trained for the Catholic priesthood, wrote to him that he had taken a difficult step but that it would lead to great things, 'at least if you take advantage of what the Church offers'; 'reception was only the beginning'.[31] From Downside, the former Anglican Dom Christopher Butler also offered Wheeler cautionary advice: 'Don't worry too much about your temper. You've been through a rather stressful experience in becoming a Catholic, and you may have been feeling a certain amount of nervous "groundswell" now that the whole thing is done'.[32] His school and university friend, Rev David Peck, sent Wheeler his good wishes and the promise of prayers and continued friendship. He concluded: 'Preserve your humour and your individuality. For Heaven's sake, don't become a stereotyped convert'.[33]

Wheeler recalled that the whole experience of conversion 'was a very traumatic one' but he had no regrets: '…the joy of being a Catholic has always far outweighed the sorrows, trials and even the changes that one has had to endure. After all, the gift of the fullness of the Faith is the greatest gift—and I believe this with all my heart—that God can give to any man or woman in this life'.[34] In old age, he reflected on his Anglican background and especially its influence on his prayer life. In his upbringing, he had the joy of family prayers and Bible stories. As a youth, he worshipped at church, attended confirmation classes and went on retreats. He loved the Authorised Version of the Bible and read it daily: 'Indeed I had been brought up not only on the Gospels but all the lovely stories of the Old Testament'. At Oxford, he discovered the spiritual classics—'I tried to follow some of their inspirations. But one didn't always find it very easy'. It was at Lancing, however, that he resorted more to prayer than at other times in his pre-Catholic days:

> This was because I felt very strongly that I needed God's help in teaching religion throughout the school to these young men and boys. I found myself giving more time to it and trying to understand more fully what it meant to make progress at prayer. One of the things that happened was that it became very clear to me that I must become a Catholic.[35]

Essentially, he had come to a point where he could no longer accept the doctrine and authority of the Anglican Church. As he later recalled:

> I must admit that I was repelled from the Anglican Church by the idiosyncrasies that I found and the uncertainties regarding fundamental things. Fundamentally, the call to me was to be one with one with the Universal Church. I had never really thought of the Anglican Church as a Universal Church in the sense that the Catholic Church is. Nor have I ever regarded any authority in the Church of England as measuring up to that authority which Our Lord gave St Peter and consequently to his successors.[36]

The Beda

Once he had been received into the Church, Wheeler sought admission to the monastic Order of St Benedict. To become a postulant or a novice, however, the Benedictines required that men had to first experience the Catholic Church in the lay state but it was not a prospect that immediately appealed to Wheeler. Abbot Bruno Hicks of Downside wrote to him: 'If God wishes you to join a religious order he will let you know in his time. You will lose nothing by going into the priesthood now and throwing yourself into all the duties and obligations of that sacred calling with all your strength and fervour'.[37] Providentially, while discussing his situation with the monks of Downside he encountered Mgr Charles Duchemin,

Rector of the Beda and an old Gregorian. The Beda specialised in preparing mature men and ex-Anglican priests for the Catholic ministry and Duchemin agreed to take Wheeler to the Beda immediately. At about the same time, Wheeler's friend Nora Wallis, also an Anglican convert, had agreed to pay for his studies on the understanding that he would be ordained for the Diocese of Westminster. Wheeler therefore sought the advice of Archbishop Hinsley of Westminster who agreed to sponsor him and generously told him that he would not force him to return to the diocese if he wished to exercise his ministry with the Benedictines. On 4 October 1936, Wheeler was confirmed by Bishop Brown in Southwark Cathedral and later in the month set out for the Beda and preparation for the Catholic priesthood.[38] His friend Francis Head had warned him against the Beda for the 'atmosphere will be rather convert' and advised that he waited a while to consider his options.[39]

Despite its high profile and solid reputation, the Beda had a relatively recent history. In 1851, Mgr George Talbot, Cardinal Nicholas Wiseman's representative in Rome, alerted the Cardinal to the problems experienced by convert Anglican clergymen who had gone to Rome to study for the Catholic priesthood. They were, Talbot reported, attending lectures at the Gregorian University but were living separately in rented accommodation. He suggested that a special college ought to be established for them where they could live in community and prepare for ordination in a fitting and appropriate way. Cardinal Wiseman approached Pope Pius IX with the idea and immediately received the Pontiff's support. A suite of rooms was found in the Piazza Scossacavalli near St Peter's and in 1852, the college was opened as the Collegio Ecclesiastico. From 1854, because of the Pope's intimate connection with the college, it became known as the Collegio Pio. Coincidentally, the rooms in the Piazza Scossacavalli had formed the nucleus of a hospice called Domus Conversorum where English converts had stayed in the seventeenth century.

In 1854, the college was relocated to the Venerable English College on Via di Monserrato and the two very distinct institutions were accommodated under one roof. The Rector of the English College was in overall charge of the house while the Moderator of the Collegio Pio had responsibilities for the education, training and behaviour of the convert clergymen. There were inevitable problems of finance, administration and control but above all, there were huge differences in ethos. The *Venerabile* took younger men while the Collegio Pio was dealing with mature men who had already received an education, usually at either Oxford or Cambridge Universities, and had already served as priests. When Cardinal Merry del Val, the *Venerabile's* Cardinal Protector, visited the college in 1898, he determined that the two institutions should be separated and a new home found for the Collegio Pio. As a result, in 1898, Pope Leo XIII issued a new constitution for the Collegio Pio and placed it under the patronage of the Venerable Bede, the great English scholar of the eighth century. In the following year, the Pope raised Bede to the dignity of Doctor of the Church and the Collegio Pio became the Pontifical Beda College. The Beda remained on Via di Monserrato but in 1916, following an Apostolic Visitation of the *Venerabile*, it was formally recommended that the two colleges be separated and new accommodation found for the Beda. The separation finally occurred in 1917 and, under the rectorship of Mgr Horace Mann, the Beda at first occupied temporary premises in the Prati di Castello but in 1921 moved to the Via San Niccolo da Tolentino. By this time, the Beda was not only accepting convert Anglican clergymen but also mature Catholic men who wished to study for the priesthood.[40]

In 1928, Mgr Mann was replaced as Rector by Fr Charles Duchemin, a man who was to have a great influence on Wheeler. Duchemin was born in Birmingham in 1886. His family were of French extraction and his father was a friend of John Henry Newman. Duchemin was educated at Downside and Trinity College, Cambridge. After training as a solicitor, Duchemin began his studies for the priesthood at the Beda when it was housed in the *Venerabile* and was ordained in 1918 for the Diocese of Northampton.[41] Duchemin's appointment to the Beda signalled the start of an extraordinary period in its development. Wheeler recalled that Duchemin was attentive to the needs of the students and assiduous in the care and advice he gave them. His administration was efficient, effective and understanding but college life under his rule was characterised by enthusiasm, virility and vigour. As a priest, the rector impressed Wheeler and others and he recorded that Duchemin 'set a high example in this matter'. When asked to define the Beda tradition under Duchemin, Wheeler said: 'I pointed out that it was Roman and yet English; that it was "cradle Catholic" and yet "convert"; that it was both ordinary and extraordinary'. For Wheeler, the Beda was the manifestation of St Bede's ideals—devotion to study, a love of the scriptures, and an undying participation in the Church's liturgies — and these were all bound together with a deep spirituality and a love of community.[42]

Although students at the Beda followed a different course of study from that undertaken by younger seminarians, the route was not a short cut to the priesthood. The daily routine was that stipulated by the Council of Trent and the four-year condensed course consisted of one year of philosophy and three years of theology. It was 'quick going', wrote Duchemin. It was expected that a man knew Latin but because the courses were delivered in English it 'preserved the essentials of the scholastic system' without men being placed under 'the strain of listening to the explanations in an unfamiliar tongue'. To those who thought that four years might be too long given their previous experience, the Rector wrote that 'men become so interested in their training that they do not find four years at all too long...for once they have caught a glimpse of the educational system evolved through the centuries by the Church for her ecclesiastical students, they do not want to lose any of the benefits it offers them'.[43] However, the house rules and discipline for mature men were different from those imposed on 'youths whose character has yet to be formed'. In Duchemin's view, the Beda was designed to strengthen and mould men sufficiently to carry out the duties of a priest. It was into this milieu that Wheeler arrived in the autumn of 1936.[44]

For Wheeler, the Beda was 'the greatest welcome that the Church could give to the convert clergyman'. It was difficult, he recalled, for a mature man, already well educated, theologically trained and with sound pastoral experience, to have to begin his studies all over again but the college regimen with its emphasis on study, prayer and meditation appealed to him. The 'testing' had already been done in a former life but he recognised that although the years of study might seem 'like an epoch', they were necessary and studying in Rome was a great experience for him: 'It is a wonderful privilege to be plunged into the heart of Christendom and have the opportunity of acquiring that special 'genius' which is known as Romanità'.[45] To Wheeler, the Beda was the best of both worlds, being English and Roman. It had the characteristics of an Oxbridge college, an officers' mess and a Roman seminary. The translation to Rome was made easier for Wheeler by the presence at the Beda of men he knew either from Oxford or from his Anglican training and ministry. Some who had been former acquaintances now became firm friends, among them George

Arthur Tomlinson, Roscoe Beddoes, Vernon Johnson, Ken Oliver Carter, Bryan Houghton and Tim McCarthy.

After his comfortable lodgings at Lancing, the accommodation at the Beda was a complete physical contrast. The college had taken over a run-down property and his room, at the top of a flight of stairs and overlooking a *cortile* of noisy flats, was sparsely and primitively furnished. His bed, he recalled, collapsed when he sat on it. These disadvantages though were more than offset by the wonderful spirit among the staff and the fifty mature students from a variety of backgrounds and from across the English-speaking world.[46] Spiritually, academically and socially, Wheeler was radiantly happy. He even played, rather unspectacularly, in the college cricket eleven at the Villa Doria Pamphili against a team from the *Venerabile*.[47]

His course, as already mentioned, lasted for four rather than the customary seven years and he and other Beda students attended lectures in the college. Students attending other Roman universities were taught in Latin but at the Beda, lectures and tutorials were delivered in the vernacular. He felt enriched especially by the Dogmatic Theology course delivered by Dr Schutt which, he wrote, was superior to anything he had experienced in Oxford. He described his course as 'magnificent' and claimed that it never gave him any reason to feel academically inferior. The course was enlightening and challenging, the college was near the centre of Rome, and high table was always full of visiting bishops and important Catholic lay people. He regarded Rome as 'the perfect completion of Oxford' and described his time at the Beda as 'one of the greatest things in my life'. He looked back on it 'with great thanksgiving'.

At this time Rome had become the centre of Italian fascism and in 1937 as Wheeler strolled through the Borghese Gardens, he saw Hitler, Goering and Goebbels in their cars with great escorts of outriders. The city was decorated with swastikas but Wheeler sensed a deep unease among Italian people at the Axis between Fascist Italy and Nazi Germany. On another interesting but less ominous occasion, Wheeler met Alphonso XIII, the exiled Bourbon-Hapsburg King of Spain. Fr Walter Meyjes, a friend of Wheeler's and a student of the Menevia Diocese, had asked him to serve his first Mass. Wheeler agreed and turned up at the Church of Santa Andrea delle Fratte in Rome where the exiled monarch was sitting in a gold chair on the sanctuary. As was the custom in those days, Wheeler took the Book of the Gospels for the king to kiss after the Gospel had been read. The king was a friend of the Meyjes family and had given the newly ordained priest a gold chalice. Wheeler and Meyjes were later invited to lunch with the king and his family in the Royal Suite at the Grand Hotel. There, Wheeler and other guests were welcomed by the haemophiliac king wearing grey suede gloves and were shown his study where he kept up to date with the events of the Spanish Civil War.

While at the Beda, Wheeler had his second papal audience. It was, he recalled, 'an extraordinary experience'. In October 1936, Archbishop Hinsley took his Westminster students from the *Venerabile* and the Beda to be received by Pope Pius XI in his private study. After he had genuflected three times before the Pontiff, Wheeler and two other ex-Anglican clergymen were introduced in Italian by Hinsley as former Anglican clergymen but the words he used translated as 'antique Anglican clergymen'. It caused the Pope to laugh.[48] The Pope, Wheeler wrote, 'looked me full in the face and patted me on my cheek'.[49] Later in 1937, with other Westminster students, Wheeler was present at the *Venerabile* when Hinsley took delivery of the *biglietto* or official notification that he had been admitted to the College of Cardinals. He subsequently attended the service when Hinsley received the red biretta and then the great public consistory when Hinsley and the other new cardinals paid homage to the pontiff and received the huge *galero* or scarlet hat. The religious and social aspects of these events greatly impressed him and increased his familiarity with the Roman and universal Church.[50]

The saddest occurrence for Wheeler during his time in Rome was the death of his mother in January 1938. In 1937, Cardinal Hinsley had given him permission to return home to Sussex to be with his mother 'until all danger has abated'.[51] He was able to attend to her needs, continue his studies and attend Mass at the nearby Catholic church. In the autumn of 1937, however, Wheeler had to return to Rome to begin his course in Theology and while there, his mother died. On the day of her death, he was to perform in a college play. His friends advised that he should withdraw but he insisted that he should continue and worked 'through the strain'.[52] His mother's death was a great blow to him and he was devastated that he was unable to attend the funeral; but that was his choice. He felt that she understood why he had become a Catholic and a priest. It was, he wrote, an extraordinary acceptance by her; some of his relatives were less than sympathetic over his conversion and ordination, especially as it was expected that as an only son he would carry on the family name.[53]

The final Church events of Wheeler's time in Rome came with the death of Pope Pius XI on 10 February 1939 and the election of Pope Pius XII on 2 March 1939. Once again, he was privileged to see at first-hand the majesty of papal ceremonies and the centrality of Rome in the life of the Universal Church. The Beda students were invited to kneel around the body of Pope Pius XI as it lay in state in St Peter's Basilica. There for one hour, between ten and eleven o'clock at night, the students prayed in darkness except for the light shining from twenty-four candles around the bier. Wheeler again absorbed the atmosphere of a great Roman occasion and with others engaged in the gossip surrounding the election of the new Pope.[54] Despite reporting to Nora Wallis that 'Pacelli is not talked about a great deal', Wheeler later told her that Cardinal Pacelli had been elected as the new Pope and had taken the name Pius XII.[55] In 1958, on the death of Pope Pius XII, Wheeler recalled in more detail the day when news of the Pope's election was given to thousands, like him, who were standing in St Peter's Square on 2 March 1939:

> On that day I was standing in the Piazza of St Peter's when the white smoke went up announcing the election of a new Pope. From all quarters of the city a vast concourse poured down the narrow defiles which have since become the Via della Conciliazione and as the news spread like wildfire the Piazza filled with a tightly packed and highly excited throng. I remember that I could not even raise my hands to remove my hat. And I shall never forget the thrill of that moment when the doors were opened on the balcony in the middle of the façade of St Peter's and Cardinal Caccia-Dominioni, then the first of the Cardinal Deacons, came out and told us through the microphones that Cardinal Pacelli had been elected. The Romans went mad with joy that one who was in every sense a Roman had been elected and we were overjoyed also that one so well-known to us as Secretary of State and in other ways had been chosen. We had often seen him on our afternoon walks in the Borghese or Pincio Gardens and we had always found that if we raised our hats to him we received a friendly salute in return.[56]

His final Roman event was attending the Papal Coronation with the other students but for him it was a personal anti-climax. They had a good vantage point of the 'marvellously moving ceremony' but he saw little due to the extreme physical discomfort of his seating and consequently having to go to a first aid post because he felt unwell.[57]

In the summer of 1939, Wheeler returned to England for the summer vacation. When war with Germany was declared in September, it became impossible for the students to return to Rome and the Beda was evacuated to St Joseph's College, Upholland, the Liverpool diocesan seminary.[58] It was a very different setting and as Wheeler remarked, 'There was a sort of bathos in changing your address from Rome to Wigan!'[59] Cardinal Hinsley told Wheeler that he was happy the Beda had been given such a warm welcome but agreed that its students would miss Rome 'and all its religious associations'.[60] As in earlier years, the Beda once again shared premises with another and very different institution. Nevertheless, despite the dislocation Wheeler found the experience to his advantage.[61] The college routine continued in much the same way and he progressed towards ordination.[62]

There were many differences between the Roman Beda and the Lancashire Beda yet Wheeler felt privileged at being in 'such a magnificent place' with its own English history and traditions. He could see at first-hand how other, younger seminarians were being formed. Wartime restrictions affected diet and recreational opportunities and some of the mature Beda men chafed at the presence and antics of young people but Wheeler took it all in his stride and had nothing but praise for Upholland. 'The Uphollanders are certainly a splendid crowd', he wrote.[63]

While at the Beda and after ordination Wheeler continued to write for *The Beda Review* in most cases contributing review articles. Upholland's location in the seat of Lancashire recusancy was not lost on him and in an article celebrating the third and fourth centenaries of some of the English martyrs he placed their 'diabolical murder' in the context of the lives of the many recusant families who had lived around the college. It was perhaps the beginning of his life-long devotion to the martyrs and to his support of the cause for their beatification and canonization. In another edition, he celebrated the life and martyrdom of Blessed Philip Howard[64] while in a later review, published seven years after his ordination, we can see the church historian in Wheeler. Reviewing Fr Philip Hughes's *History of the Church*, he wrote:

> Nothing is more indicative of the Divine institution and maintenance of the Catholic Church than her history. Had she been merely human, she would have perished like other empires long ago. The reading of history, even when it is unpleasant, should therefore always be a tonic to a Catholic: for he can have it both ways in the

edification of the lives of the saints and in admiration of the Divine steering of a barque that has frail humanity in its crew.[65]

It was at Upholland that Wheeler completed his training for the Catholic priesthood. When in Rome he had told Nora Wallis that he expected to receive the Tonsure and Minor Orders when he returned home but he had not then imagined he would be resident at Upholland.[66] Under the direction of Mgr Moss, Vice Rector of the Beda, Wheeler and the other ordinands started 'practising the Mass' and went on retreat to the Redemptorist house at Bishop Eaton in Liverpool to prepare themselves for ordination. On 7 December 1939, he was ordained to the diaconate by Archbishop Richard Downey of Liverpool in the chapel at Upholland.[67] In late 1939, he returned to Westminster for the final preparations for his ordination. Cardinal Hinsley had earlier congratulated him on his forthcoming ordination to the diaconate and wished him well.[68] Where he was to be ordained remained unsettled with Upholland, Ushaw College, Wonersh, the Brompton Oratory or even a local church being under consideration.[69] Aware of the very great financial and spiritual support given to Wheeler by Nora Wallis, Mgr Duchemin wrote to her a week before Wheeler was to be ordained: 'You will be blessed I am sure for doing so much to bring this about and I look forward to him doing splendid work. He has a charming nature combined with great and varied talent'.[70]

Ordination

Cardinal Hinsley ordained Wheeler on 31 March 1940 in Westminster Cathedral. The long service was not conducted on the sandbagged cathedral's magnificent sanctuary but in the crypt because of the threat of German air raids. With Wheeler, four other Beda students were ordained to the priesthood and one to the diaconate and their backgrounds illustrated the particular nature of the Beda. Only Wheeler had experience of the religious life; the other five had worked in banking, farming, business, insurance and the electrical industry.[71] Some of Wheeler's contemporaries at the Beda were present at the ceremony as was his sister, her husband and his aunt but not his father. After his ordination, they left for Norfolk, in a blacked out train because of wartime restrictions, so that Wheeler could say his first Mass on 1 April in the fourteenth-century Slipper Chapel at Walsingham, since 1934 the Roman Catholic National Shrine of Our Lady. Walsingham was both a shrine for Catholics and Anglicans and this fact would not have been ignored by Wheeler.

Wheeler had written on Marian devotion before his ordination and in 1936 had written five verses under the title '*Monstra Te Esse Matrem*', in which he linked the loss of the old Faith and the fate of the martyrs during the Reformation to the place of Mary in English worship and religious fealty. The first verse ran:

Lady of Walsingham, once Queen of England,
What now is left thee of all that was thine?
One lonely arch overlooking sad ruins,
Gone are the cloisters and empty thy shrine.

From this desolation, however, there comes the hope of restoration through the intercession of Mary and the blood of the martyrs. In the last verse, he writes:

Lady of Walsingham, England is waking,
Thousands acclaim thee as Lady and Queen;
Queen of our martyrs, we ask through their dying,
Bring back the loyalties England has seen.[72]

In 'The Madonna at Oxford', which he wrote for *The Beda Review*, he placed the Church of St Mary's at the centre of the university and the city. Oxford, he wrote, was one of the most Catholic cities in England and its buildings, carvings, art and seats of learning manifested its historical devotion to the Madonna. The recent reintroduction of the contemplative life in the colleges was 'a signal mark of the special favour of the Mother of God'.[73]

Wheeler's choice of Walsingham was also partly due to his close friendship with Fr Bruno Scott-James, an eccentric scholarly priest of the Northampton diocese who had met Wheeler in Rome. Born in 1906, Scott-James was an Anglican convert and had studied at the Beda. He was ordained in 1935 and in the same year was appointed by Bishop Youens of Northampton to re-establish the Shrine of Our Lady at Walsingham thus becoming its first Roman Catholic custodian since the Reformation.[74] Scott-James had ample but very primitive accommodation near Walsingham and Wheeler spent summer holidays there from 1937 possibly because he felt uneasy at returning to his parental home given the distress his conversion had caused.[75] In his obituary of Scott-James, Wheeler later recalled:

The small house in those days had no washing facilities, and he and his friends literally got under the pump each morning. This rather eccentric priest, enveloped in a black cloak, his head shorn, and with a Siamese cat perched on his shoulder, squatting on the steps of the Slipper Chapel as he poured out pearls of patristic wisdom, was an inspiration to many.[76]

By coincidence, Archbishop Godfrey, the Apostolic Delegate, was also in Walsingham and attended Wheeler's first Mass.[77] To Wheeler it was a remarkable twist of fate: he had spoken with Godfrey about becoming a Catholic when they had met in Rome in 1936 and again in 1940, before his ordination, Wheeler had asked Godfrey to consecrate the chalice he would use at Mass on and after his ordination. Godfrey had willingly agreed.[78]

Wheeler was now a priest of the Catholic Church. He was also a priest of the Westminster Diocese but was uncertain where he might be sent as a curate. Bishop David Mathew, Hinsley's Auxiliary Bishop, told him that the demand for military chaplains would almost certainly lead to unexpected vacancies.[79] In July 1940, he was informed by Mgr Francis Bickford, the Vicar General, that 'the Cardinal wishes you to go to Lower Edmondton as 2nd assistant to Fr J. G. McGrath'.[80] In September 1940, *The Beda Review* noted that 'Father Wheeler was assisting at the large parish of Edmonton'.[81]

Notes

[1]   A. Hastings, 'Some reflexions on the English Catholicism of the late 1930s' in A. Hastings (ed.), *Bishops and Writers* (Wheathampstead: Anthony Clarke, 1977), p. 109.

[2]   Hastings, 'Some reflexions on the English Catholicism of the late 1930s', p. 110. Hastings refers to Knox as a 'man of letters' not a theologian. For Knox's life at Oxford and his conversion see T. Tastard, *Ronald Knox and English Catholicism* (Leominster: Gracewing, 2009) and C. Williams, *Harold Macmillan* (London: Phoenix Books, 2010). Martin D'Arcy preached at Knox's funeral in 1957.

[3]   See Wheeler's review of Fr T. Corbishley's *Ronald Knox the Priest* in *Catholic Herald*, 20 Nov 1964.

[4]   The term *Old Catholic Church* refers to European Christian groups separated from the Roman Catholic Church over certain doctrines but especially that concerned with the apostolic succession and papal authority. The term 'Old Catholic' was first used in 1853 to describe the members of the See of Utrecht who did not recognize infallible papal authority. Later Catholics who disagreed with the doctrine of Papal Infallibility as made official by the First Vatican Council (1870), had no bishop and so joined with Utrecht to form the Union of Utrecht. The formation of the Old Catholic

communion of Germans, Austrians and Swiss began in 1870 at Nuremberg. Episcopal succession was established in 1874 with the consecration of an Old Catholic German bishop by a prelate of the Church of Utrecht. The 1889 Declaration of Utrecht accepts the first seven ecumenical councils and doctrine formulated before 1054 but rejects communion with the pope and certain other Roman Catholic doctrines and practices. The Utrecht Union of Old Catholic Churches is in full communion with the Anglican Communion but not the Holy See. Since 1925, Old Catholics have recognized Anglican ordinations and they have had full communion with the Church of England.

5   Pass to Wheeler, 18 Aug 1930. LDA, WPC, Anglican Documents; W. G. Wheeler, *In Truth And Love* (Southport: Gowland and Co., 1990), pp. 21–35. Wheeler had attended the Fourth Anglo-Catholic Congress at Westminster in July 1930.

6   Wheeler, *In Truth And Love*, p. 24.

7   Head to Wheeler, 26 Oct 1933. LDA, WPC, Anglican Documents.

8   Head to Wheeler, 4 Feb 1934. LDA, WPC, Letters 1936; Wheeler, *In Truth And Love*, p. 24.

9   Head to Wheeler, 25 March 1934. LDA, WPC, Letters 1936.

10 Head to Wheeler, 19 April 1934. LDA, WPC, Letters 1936.

11 Wheeler, *In Truth And Love*, pp. 21–35. After many years as an Anglican priest, McLaughlin was received into the Catholic Church in 1962. He and Wheeler remained in contact throughout their lives.

12 R. Strange, *John Henry Newman: A Mind Alive* (London: Darton, Longman & Todd, 2008), p. 17.

13 Wheeler, *In Truth And Love*, pp. 21–35; L. E. Whatmore, *The Story of Our Lady of Ransom, Eastbourne* (Sussex: privately printed, 1977), pp. 111, 195.

14 Head to Wheeler, 8 Sept 1936. LDA. WPC, Letters 1936.

15 Betty to Wheeler, n.d. (1936?). LDA. WPC, Letters 1936.

16 Ida to Wheeler, 11 Sept 1936. LDA, WPC, Letters 1936.

17 Wallis to E. Wheeler, 10 Sept 1936. LDA, WPC, Letters 1936.

18 Wheeler, *In Truth And Love*, p. 37.

19 Beevor to Wheeler, 10 Oct 1936. LDA, WPC, Letters 1936.

20 Doherty to Wheeler, 28 Aug and 6 Sept 1936. LDA, WPC, Letters 1936.

21 W. G. Wheeler, 'The Converts Aid Society: It's Validity Today', 1976. LDA, WPC, Biography and Obituaries.

22 Hugh Frazer to Wheeler, 14 Sept 1936. LDA, WPC, Letters 1936.

23 Stewart (?) to Wheeler, 22 Sept 1936. LDA, WPC, Letters 1936.

24 Bell to Wheeler, 14 Sept 1936. LDA, WPC, Letters 1936.

25 Reynolds to Wheeler, 23 Sept 1936. LDA, WPC, Letters 1936.

26 Missen to Wheeler, 5 Sept 1936. LDA, WPC, Letters 1936.

27 Dilworth Harrison to Wheeler, 5 Sept 1936. LDA, WPC, Letters 1936.

28 Home to Wheeler, 10 Oct 1936. LDA, WPC, Letters 1936.

29 Head to Wheeler 16 Sept 1936. LDA, WPC, Letters 1936.

30   Head to Wheeler, 6 Oct 1936. LDA, WPC, Letters 1930s-1950s.

31   Duchemin to Wheeler, 21 Sept 1936. LDA, WPC, Letters 1936.

32   Butler to Wheeler, 11 Oct 1936. LDA, WPC, Letters 1936.

33   Peck to Wheeler, n.d. (1936?). LDA, WPC, Letters 1936.

34   Wheeler, *In Truth And Love*, pp. 37–38. For a discussion of the responses to conversion, see S. Gilley, 'Loss and gain: Conversions to Catholicism in Britain, 1800–1994 (Annual Lecture to the Friends of Cardinal Newman, 1994), typescript.

35   Quotation and preceding sentences based on Wheeler, *In Truth And Love*, pp. 133–134.

36   *Ibid*, p. 41.

37   Hicks to Wheeler, 29 Sept 1936. LDA, WPC, Letters 1930s-1950s.

38   Fr J. Collings to Wheeler, 22 Sept 1936. LDA, WPC, Letters 1930s-1950s; Wheeler, *In Truth And Love*, pp. 36–37, 52;

39   Head to Wheeler, 16 Sept 1936. LDA, WPC, Letters 1936.

40   C. L. H. Duchemin, 'The Evolution of the Beda' in *The Beda Review*, Sept 1942, vol. 4, no. 8, pp. 14–17; M. J. McConnon, 'The Pontifical Beda College: A History' in *The Beda Review*, June 1985, vol. 12, no. 1, pp. 2–10.

41   *The Catholic Who's Who* (London: Burns, Oates and Washbourne: 1940), p. 142.

42   W. G. Wheeler, 'Tribute to Mgr Duchemin on His Retirement' (Typescript, 1961). LDA, WPC, Beda.

43   C. L. H. Duchemin, 'What is the Beda?' in *The Beda Review*, vol. 3, no. 8, Sept 1937. pp. 6–9.

44   C. L. H. Duchemin, 'The Beda', *Catholic Herald*, 19 Sept 1941.

45   W. G. Wheeler, 'The New Beda', Typescript, Oct 1960 LDA, WPC, Beda; Wheeler, *In Truth And Love*, p. 134.

46   *Log Book 1936–38*. PBCA.

47   *Ibid.*.

48   Fr Meyjes was of Dutch-Jewish origin. A former Anglican, he served in London, Spain and Gibraltar after ordination. Wheeler maintained contact with him throughout his life. LDA, WDC, W64; Wheeler, *In Truth And Love*, pp. 41–49.

49   Wheeler to Wallis, 7 Oct 1936. LDA, WPC, Nora Wallis.

50   Wheeler to Wallis, Advent 1937. LDA, WPC, Nora Wallis.

51   Hinsley to Wheeler, 22 March 1937. LDA, WPC, Letters 1930–1950s.

52   Wheeler to Wallis, 15 Jan 1938. LDA, WPC, Nora Wallis.

53   Wheeler, *In Truth And Love*, pp. 41–49.

54   Wheeler to Wallis, 19 Feb 1939. LDA, WPC, Nora Wallis.

55   Wheeler to Wallis, 2 and 3 March 1939. LDA, WPC, Nora Wallis.

56   'The Pontificate of Pope Pius XII'. LDA, WPC, The Popes.

57   Wheeler to Wallis, 2 and 3 March 1939. LDA, WPC, Nora Wallis.

58   *Log Book 1939–40*. PBCA.

59   Wheeler, *In Truth And Love*, p. 45.

60 Hinsley to Wheeler, 7 Dec 1939. LDA, WPC, Ordination.

61 Wheeler, *In Truth And Love*, p. 45.

62 *Log Book 1939–40.* PBCA.

63 Wheeler to Wallis, 5 and 19 Oct 1939. LDA, WPC, Nora Wallis.

64 *The Beda Review*, March 1941, vol. 4, no 5; Sept 1942, vol. 4, no 8.

65 *The Beda Review*, Sept 1947, vol. 5, no 10.

66 Wheeler to Wallis, 22 May 1938. LDA, WPC, Nora Wallis.

67 Wheeler to Wallis, 23 Oct and 26 Nov 1939. LDA, WPC, Nora Wallis.

68 Hinsley to Wheeler, 7 Dec 1939. LDA, WPC, Ordination.

69 Wheeler to Wallis, 16 Feb 1940. LDA, WPC, Nora Wallis.

70 Duchemin to Wallis, 24 March 1940. LDA, WPC, Nora Wallis.

71 *The Tablet*, 5 April 1940.

72 W. G. Wheeler, 'Monstra Te Esse Matrem' (1936 typescript). LDA, WPC, Beda.

73 W. G. Wheeler, *The Beda Review*, Sept 1942, vol. 4, no 8.

74 P. Rollings, *Walsingham: England's Nazareth* (Walsingham: Roman Catholic National Shrine, 1998), pp. 54–55. Scott-James was the Custodian until 1944. Scott-James was but one of many eccentric characters befriended by Wheeler down the years.

75 'Tribute to Mgr Bruno Scott-James'. LDA, WPC, Bruno Scott-James. Wheeler met Scott-James (1906–1984) at the Beda. His priestly life was full of controversy. He was, wrote Wheeler, 'a man who delighted or divided communities' and his autobiography was aptly entitled *Asking for Trouble*. Wheeler maintained a life-long, strong and caring friendship with him. Such were Scott-James's peculiar habits that when Wheeler stayed with him at Walsingham, they would not have a proper meal for days and then, led by Scott-James, they would embark on an eating spree. See also Wheeler, *In Truth And Love*, pp. 49–51.

76 *The Tablet*, 7 April 1984.

77 Wheeler to Wallis, 1 July 1940. LDA, WPC, Nora Wallis; *The Universe*, 5 April 1940. Wheeler sang his first High Mass in July 1940 at Preston Park, Brighton.

78 Godfrey to Wheeler, 14 April 1940. LDA, WPC, Ordination.

79 Mathew to Wheeler, 24 April 1940. LDA, WPC, Ordination.

80 Bickford to Wheeler, 12 July 1940. LDA, WPC, Ordination.

81 *The Beda Review*, vol. 3, no. 4, Sept 1940, p. 4.

4 CURATE, EDITOR AND CHAPLAIN

Curate in Edmonton

I N JULY 1940, shortly after the Fall of France and the evacuation of the British Expeditionary Force from the beaches of Dunkirk, Wheeler took up his appointment as the second curate at St Edmund's, Hertford Road, Edmonton.

From the 1790s onwards, Catholics in the Edmonton area had attended Mass at a house in Tottenham where French émigré priests had settled following the French Revolution. In 1805, a chapel and presbytery were built in Queen Street and this and its successor in White Hart Lane continued as the centre of worship for the Catholics of Tottenham and Edmonton. By the end of the nineteenth century, the population of Edmonton had almost doubled due to new rail connections with London and residential development, and the many working-class Catholics in the area, still without priest or church, attended Mass either at St Francis de Sales in High Road, Tottenham, or at Ponders End. Through the direct intervention of Miss Teresa Weld-Blundell, Cardinal Herbert Vaughan of Westminster invited the Redemptorists to assume the pastoral care of the Catholics in Edmonton and in early 1903 land was acquired on which to build a church and a neighbouring house was taken for use a temporary presbytery. Two Redemptorists arrived in June, and in July, a small temporary chapel was opened. This was replaced by a new and more permanent church in May 1907. It was dedicated to the Most Precious Blood (after Westminster Cathedral and at Cardinal Vaughan's wish) and to St Edmund, King and Martyr. In 1926, the Redemptorists, whose charism was essentially giving missions rather than running parishes, handed over the church and parish to the Archdiocese of Westminster. In twenty-three years, the parish had grown and features normally associated with a thriving faith community—a convent, a school, a parish hall, hostels, sodalities, and a scout troop—had all been established.[1]

The transition from the even tranquillity of seminary life to the untempered blast of the ordinary parish is a difficult one',[2] wrote Wheeler, and his first appointment as a Catholic priest was a memorable experience. The parish priest of St Edmund's was Fr John George McGrath, a sober and on the surface a rather humourless man. He had a reputation among young curates for being a strict disciplinarian and the presence of an Oxford-educated and well-spoken priest inexperienced in Catholic ways appeared to be a trial for him.[3] To Wheeler, however, McGrath was 'a dear'. The presbytery was 'splendidly run'; it was spotlessly clean, there was constant boiling water, and the meals were adequate 'without being flashy'. He became immediately immersed in parish life—celebrating Mass and Benediction, leading the Rosary, hearing confessions, visiting the sick, teaching in the primary school and supporting the St Vincent de Paul Society. The parishioners, he wrote, were 'nice and unpretentious'.[4]

Wheeler took up his duties in the midst of aerial bombing by the German Luftwaffe, blackouts, rationing and the evacuation of children to safer areas. Mass was celebrated in the church's side altars as this was considered safer than being exposed on the church's sanctuary. With Fr McGrath and the other curates, he visited parishioners during the day and at night acted a firewatcher in the parish school. Sleep, therefore, was in short supply and for consecutive nights, the priests were unable to take to their beds.[5] The raids were frequent and death and destruction commonplace. Parish work was restricted as the raids, lasting for hours, began to occur during the day as well as at night. During one night raid, Wheeler slept under a table in the presbytery; others slept in the public shelter.[6] In early October 1940 a high explosive bomb landed in the street near the church, blew open the church doors and smashed the church windows. Nearby churches in Enfield and North London were damaged and there was much improvisation as attempts were made to maintain religious services. The 'normally silent Fr McGrath' told Wheeler that he was very pleased with the way he was getting to know the people in such difficult circumstances.[7]

Wheeler, however, succumbed to the physical strain and became quite ill. Fr McGrath posted daily bulletins on the presbytery door. One read: 'Fr Wheeler's life is drawing peacefully to a close'. Visitors were implored not to ring the doorbell or knock on the door for fear of disturbing the ailing curate. In the absence of antibiotics, the local doctor, Dr Atkins, poured Cognac down Wheeler's throat. The remedy had the desired effect. During his convalescence, Wheeler was visited by his father. Fr McGrath's response was: 'Your father is a fine man. Pity you took after your mother!' Wheeler recalled his time at Edmonton with fondness and while recognising that Fr McGrath ruled with a rod of iron, he nevertheless acknowledged the parish priest's spirituality and genuineness. He recognised too the warmth of the parishioners: 'They were lovely people in that parish and I became extremely devoted to them'. His normal parish duties together with his work with the Knights of St Columba and the Young Christian Workers, and his productions of school nativity plays enabled him to meet and advise and befriend parishioners of all ages.[8]

In 1944, Wheeler was unsettled by an approach from Mgr Duchemin that he might return to the Beda as a lecturer, a move that would be 'well received by everyone'.[9] Wheeler's response was lukewarm. He felt that his academic attainments were 'meagre' and that he would feel uncomfortable while some of his contemporaries were still in training at Upholland. He wrote to Duchemin that he was devoted to Edmonton, Fr McGrath and the other curate Dr Cuming, 'not to mention the people'. He continued: 'Parish life in the C of E was so trying that I shuddered at the thought of ever doing it again. I have found it so different, however, in the Catholic Church that I should be quite happy if God saw fit for me to remain in it...' It was not the time to return to the Beda: he had experienced so much change in his 'short life' that he wanted 'a period of stability'.[10] To seek affirmation, Wheeler sought Bishop David Mathew's advice. The Bishop agreed with Wheeler and Duchemin let the matter rest.[11]

Despite the pressures of wartime duties and pastoral work, Wheeler managed to write articles and book reviews for *The Tablet*, the *Westminster Cathedral Chronicle*, *The Clergy Review* and the *Beda Review*. Soon after his arrival in Edmonton, he published an historical account of St Edmund, the ninth-century East Anglian Martyr and patron of his new parish. While it was important to recognise the Church universal, he wrote, English Catholics had to remember that 'the blood of the English martyrs flows in our veins'. It was necessary to recognize 'the saints of our own land' and acknowledge their heroic part in the history of the English Church. For the conversion of England, he proposed that Catholics could best worship at the shrines of Saints Edward at Westminster, Thomas at Canterbury, Edmund at Bury, and Our Lady at Walsingham, the source of cures, miracles and protection.[12]

He was a more frequent contributor to the *Westminster Cathedral Chronicle* and in October 1941 published an article on 'The Maids of France'—a review of the lives and influence of St Joan and St Thérèse of Lisieux.[13] This was followed by articles on Montague House, a recusant refuge in sixteenth- and seventeenth-century London, the life and death of Blessed Philip Howard, and the 'Spirit of Walsingham'.[14] In these, he emphasised the example of the martyrs and recusants, their spirit and fortitude in the face of intolerance and violence, and their supreme legacy to the English Church. His article on Blessed Philip Howard was followed up by the publication of a sermon he delivered at Solemn High Mass in Arundel Chapel on the Feast of Blessed Philip Howard in October 1943.[15] It seemed that Wheeler had not only crossed the doctrinal threshold into the Catholic Church, he had immediately and wholeheartedly absorbed its history and traditions.

Like others, Wheeler was affected personally by the war. He was especially fearful for his former Lancing students who were on military service, many of whom maintained contact with him. In the college's *Roll of Service*, he identified thirty-two of his students who had died and twenty-eight who had been wounded. Many had been decorated for bravery and outstanding conduct.[16] There were two deaths, however, both unconnected with the war, which caused him particular grief. Less than one month after his ordination as a Catholic priest in Winchester, Francis Head died of injuries sustained in a motorcycle accident at the end of January 1944. His ministry, wrote Wheeler, was brief, conscientious and enthusiastic but it could not be measured by the human notion of time, 'for it is what we are, not what we do, that counts in the long run, and the soul's activity is an eternal one'. Looking back to Oxford and St Stephen's House, Wheeler recalled that Head's views were 'extreme' and many thought him intolerant. While there, he attended Mass and Benediction at Catholic churches and visited Walsingham and Assisi 'but like many good Anglicans he saw no clear reason why this should not be combined with membership of the Church of England'. Shortly after his ordination into the Anglican Church at St Paul's in London, 'all his doubts came to a head' and after a few months he was received into the Catholic Church by the Jesuits. This event, wrote Wheeler, 'was the logical fulfilment of all his ideas and beliefs' and thereafter he never experienced the smallest reaction or nostalgia for the past. Acknowledging the value of Head's frequent letters to him—'a perpetual joy'–Wheeler concluded: 'It is to the clarity of these that at least one of his friends owes, under God, his possession of the Faith'. Wheeler's journey of faith was reflected in Head's.[17]

Perhaps Wheeler's biggest personal loss came with the death during the war of Nora Wallis his close friend and benefactress. There can be no doubt that he owed Wallis a great deal and cared deeply for her. He addressed her as 'Dearest Madre' and his letters to her were frequent, personal and informative. There is, however, scant reference to her in his published memoir. Wallis was born in 1881 into the Anglican faith and was later a daily worshipper at the Church of All Saints, Margaret Street, London. The source of her wealth is unknown but when Wheeler came to know her at Oxford, she was already a wealthy businesswoman, an artist, and an intrepid traveller. She was a socialite, a person of great charm and had a wide circle of friends. She undertook much charitable work and was a governor of Middlesex Hospital. Like Wheeler, Wallis entered the Catholic Church in 1936 and from then on, he wrote, 'she saturated herself in the life of the Church and in the shortest possible time breathed and radiated the ethos of Catholicism'. She was a daily communicant and a woman of daily prayer and meditation. Her contribution to Wheeler's journey towards the Catholic priesthood cannot be underestimated.[18]

In 'The Sublime Identity', written in 1942, Wheeler reflected on his early ministry in the Catholic Church. It is a youthful paper manifesting Wheeler's obvious delight in his priesthood yet revealing his difficulties in balancing prayer and contemplation with the practical demands of a parish. The young priest, he wrote, enters parish life with 'a barrage of attendant graces' accumulated during his years of training and preparation. However, the many calls made on him in a parish soon begin to erode these graces for in his uncontrolled zeal to fulfil his immediate sacred duties the curate neglects his prayer life and especially contemplation. Recalling the words of the late Pope Pius XI's Universal Constitution *Umbratilem* and those of St Thomas Aquinas, Wheeler argued that 'no other type of life is more perfect than the contemplative life' and that mixing teaching and preaching with contemplation 'causes a decline' as it had done within some contemplative orders. Using the Pope's words, he wrote that those who devote themselves to prayer and penance contribute much more 'to the propagation of the Faith and the salvation of mankind, than those who till the Master's vineyard with active apostolic labour'. Having argued that prayer comes before work, he then asked himself, how could this fundamental and apparently uncompromising philosophy apply to a busy priest operating in a parish? His answer is derived from the inherent sanctity of the priestly state—that is 'the identification of each priest with the Word Incarnate'. This sublime identification pre-destines the faithful priest to a degree of sanctity and 'everything that is magnificent in the order of Grace is included in the Priestly vocation'. To maintain this state the priest has to seek continually conditions most favourable to contemplation—solitude and silence and an avoidance of all secular distractions—but each ordinary act, taken in conjunction with apostolic work, study and spiritual reading, may be identified as having the capacity to glorify God. Just as Christ's 'smallest actions' gave glory to God, so too the priest 'on account of his quasi-hypostatic union with Christ, can give quasi-infinite, that is inconceivably enormous glory to God, by his most ordinary actions, walking, writing, breathing'. The priesthood, he concludes, brings with it the obligation of being a saint; to fulfil this obligation, priests must lead lives of 'heroic sanctity'.[19] According to Fr Bruno Scott-James, it was a 'pompous' paper, lacking in style and replete with exaggerated language.[20]

The Carthusian Fr Andrew Gray at St Hugh's, Horsham, was more sympathetic to Wheeler's difficulties, particularly regarding the balance between parish work and private prayer and in a way became Wheeler's spiritual counsellor. The monk acknowledged that the young priest had 'to live in the terrible rush and complications of modern life' whereas at least he had a cell where he could contemplate without interruption and pray regularly. He advised that Wheeler should place his 'mental prayer' alongside the Divine Office and that there was no dichotomy between the two or anything wrong with this approach. The secular priest, wrote Fr Gray, needed time for 'mental prayer' or contemplation although it was hard to find in wartime. He also added that Wheeler should not use spiritual reading merely in preparation for sermons but should use it 'for one's own spiritual perfection'.[21]

Editor and Cathedral Chaplain

In April 1944, Wheeler was asked by Archbishop Griffin to become editor of the *Westminster Cathedral Chronicle* and a chaplain at Westminster Cathedral.[22] Despite the opportunities which the move offered, Wheeler recalled that he was sad to leave Edmonton, his first parish, and was unsure of Fr McGrath's reaction to his departure. He need not have been concerned. The parish priest generously praised his contribution to the parish and said that during the sleepless nights of fire watching he found great consolation in reading the books recommended by Wheeler.[23] In a more private letter, the parish priest enclosed a cheque to cover Wheeler's outstanding salary and expressed his true feelings for his erstwhile curate: 'I need not say that I am sorry to lose you. Your help to me has been more than I can say, especially in the Blitz days. I only hope you will go gently until you get acclimatised to the new surroundings'. He concluded: 'remember me sometimes in your prayers'.[24] McGrath had watched the new priest fit smoothly into the ranks of the Catholic clergy and adjust conscientiously and enthusiastically to Catholic parish life.

As a Cathedral Chaplain, Wheeler joined the ranks of the other priests who conducted daily services in the Cathedral and served its parish in and around the bomb-damaged central London districts of Victoria and Pimlico which he described as 'a very run down and very poor part of the city'. Worshippers at the Cathedral, however, included wealthy and influential Catholics from a wide range of national and international backgrounds.[25] The Cathedral Administrator was Mgr Martin Howlett who had occupied the post since 1906. A Kilkenny man, Howlett was born in 1863 and ordained in 1886. He was educated at Downside, studied in Rome, and had been secretary to Cardinal Vaughan. As Cathedral Administrator, he served Cardinals Bourne, Hinsley and Griffin and had been responsible for arranging many important ceremonies in the Cathedral. It was said that he always 'did things in a big way'. From 1907 until 1918, he was also the editor of the *Westminster Cathedral Chronicle.*[26]

The *Westminster Cathedral Chronicle* had begun life in 1896 as *Westminster Cathedral Record.* Its purpose was not to be a chronicle of Cathedral services or a record of parish activities; its prime objective was to raise money for Cardinal Herbert Vaughan's new cathedral at Westminster. In this, it was successful and its eleven editions from 1896 until 1902 were effective in raising subscriptions from prominent and wealthy Catholics. In January 1907, under Archbishop Francis Bourne, the magazine was re-launched and renamed the *Cathedral Chronicle* although it later became known as the *Westminster Cathedral Chronicle.* It lasted under these titles for another sixty years and in Cardinal Bourne's and Cardinal Hinsley's times, reflected more of the Archbishop's activities, Cathedral ceremonies, and diocesan and parish news.

Under Wheeler's editorship, from 1944 until 1950, the magazine assumed a different and unique character. It remained a monthly magazine dedicated to publicising and recording cathedral and diocesan life but it developed into a lively wide-ranging journal whose contents went well beyond the Cathedral's boundaries. Church history, liturgy, scripture, literature, art and music all came under Wheeler's purview and articles were submitted by high-profile Catholic scholars—an indication of Wheeler's growing circle of contacts and his persuasiveness. There were thoughtful obituaries, reflective and prayerful pieces, and columns on Roman documents and Vatican affairs. The *Westminster Cathedral Chronicle* did not match the quality and stature of journals such as the *Ampleforth Journal*, the *Downside Review*, *The Month*, or *The Dublin Review*, but its purpose and readership was quite different. The *Catholic Herald* described it as being 'in the van of the smaller Catholic productions'.[27]

Wheeler's own literary output continued and his most memorable contributions to Catholic history were *Homage to Newman 1845–1945* published in 1945, and *Richard Challoner 1691–1781*, published in 1946. *Homage to Newman* and *Richard Challoner* were collections of essays, edited by Wheeler and published under the imprint of the *Westminster Cathedral Chronicle*. *Homage to Newman* marked the centenary of Newman's conversion and was produced to make the Cardinal 'more widely known and more greatly loved'. Catholic contributors included Fr Herbert Keldany of Westminster, the Catholic historian Denis Gwynn, and the Oratorians Frs Vincent Baker, Henry Tristram and Vincent Reade. Wheeler ensured that an Anglican appraisal of Newman's influence on the Church of England was included and this was provided by Rev R. D. Middleton.

From an early age Wheeler had been fascinated by Newman's life and time at Oxford, and his own contribution to the *Homage*—'A Newman Pilgrimage in England'—was a synopsis of the Cardinal's life related to the places he had lived and which had influenced him. Wheeler identified and visited Newman's three most important Oxford connections—Trinity College, Oriel College and St Mary's University Church—which contained 'a wealth of associations'. Trinity was Newman's first contact with the university and his first love. Oriel, where he was a tutor and fellow, gave him the academic seal and recognition of his alma mater, while the University Church of St Mary's 'gave him the platform and the apostolate amid the intellectuals which made him the Morning Star of that great dogmatic revival, the return to the Ancient Faith, itself the soul of Oxford, the Second Spring'. It was in Oxford, where Newman fulfilled his pastoral ministry among Anglicans of the city, that seeds of religious doubt were sown in his mind and it was from Oxford that he went on to Littlemore, the tearful sermon on 'the parting of friends', and conversion by Blessed Dominic Barberi. The similarities between Wheeler's own journey of faith and that of Newman's were obvious but left unwritten.[28]

In 1946, a unique event occasioned a publication edited by Wheeler of a series of articles on the life of Bishop Richard Challoner, a former Vicar Apostolic of the London District. A convert to Catholicism, Challoner had laboured on the English mission for fifty years. He died in 1781 aged ninety but the general civil and particularly anti-Catholic unrest of the time meant that he did not receive a Catholic burial. On 1 May 1946, the remains of Bishop Challoner were transferred from the tomb of the Barrett family at Milton in Berkshire to the Chapel of Saints Gregory and Augustine and the English Confessors in Westminster Cathedral. It was, recalled Wheeler, 'a fascinating but somewhat macabre assignment'. He had driven to Milton with Bishop Edward Myers, Mgr James Scanlan and Fr Francis Bartlett followed by a hearse. The Bishop and priests met with Home Office officials, Anglican representatives and local undertakers, and identified Challoner's remains by the plate on the coffin and the Anglican burial register. On the return journey to Westminster, but unknown to Bishop Myers and the priests, the hearse broke down and the 'precious burden' arrived much later than expected by the assembled prelates. While the undertakers were preparing to open the coffin, the prelates were involved in animated but subdued conversation. The object of their curiosity was Mgr Scanlan, now attired in bishop's robes. There was episcopal confusion: no See was vacant and no bishop had requested a coadjutor. It transpired that earlier in the day Scanlan, because of his Scottish ancestry, had been created Bishop of Dunkeld. When the coffin was eventually opened, Challoner's remains appeared to be intact but their lordships were soon disappointed as before their eyes the body rapidly disintegrated to bones and dust when exposed to the air. Doctors then identified each bone which was transferred to a new inner coffin.[29]

Richard Challoner included articles by Bishop David Mathew, Mgr Ronald Knox, Fr Gordon Albion, Fr Nicholas Kelly, Michael Trappes-Lomax, Stanley Morrison and Wheeler, indicating his ability to call upon an increasing and widening circle of literary and religious luminaries. Wheeler's contribution was a synopsis of Challoner's life and influence through his steadfastness, his example, his instructional *Penny Catechism* and his meditative writings such as *The Garden of the Soul*. Wheeler was impressed by Challoner's struggle to keep the faith alive in England and his optimism in a period of violent intolerance and persecution. "There will be a new people", said Challoner, and soon after his death there were migrations of Catholics from the French Revolution to England. These were followed by Irish immigrants in the 1840s and converts from the Church of England in 'the Second Spring'. Challoner was regarded by many as a saint in his lifetime and to Wheeler his 'supreme relevance' was personal and spiritual. Like Newman, he was an example to his contemporaries and to those who were to follow him. The cause for his beatification was opened by Cardinal Griffin on the day of Challoner's re-interment.[30]

The sociable Wheeler soon developed friendships among the Cathedral clergy. Fr Francis Bartlett and the Liverpudlian Fr Thomas Kilcoyne were particularly close to him and he maintained life-long links with them both. Wheeler and Bartlett, who was appointed to the Cathedral a few months after Wheeler, had shared interests: both were avid followers of Newman and both understood the sense of the Church's enduring history. Both also enjoyed Mgr Howlett's malapropisms which made their lives 'quite joyful even in wartime London'. Bartlett happily worked with Wheeler on the production of the *Westminster Cathedral Chronicle*.[31] Wheeler also developed a strong attachment to Archbishop David Mathew who lived close by the Cathedral. Like Wheeler, Mathew had been a student at Oxford and the Beda. He was ordained in 1929, became Catholic chaplain to Cardiff University and then, in 1934, Catholic chaplain to London University. In 1938, he had been made Auxiliary Bishop to Cardinal Hinsley in Westminster before being appointed Apostolic Delegate to British East and West Africa in 1946. Mathew was a Balliol man and an academic with an impressive list of major historical titles to his name. Wheeler revelled in Mathew's company and in his wide and interesting circle of friends and acquaintances. Mathew encouraged Wheeler to continue with his researches and writing, was responsible for him becoming a chaplain to the Knights of Malta in 1958, and introduced him to membership of the Athenaeum.[32]

In addition to his parish work and editorship of the *Westminster Cathedral Chronicle*, Wheeler was involved, with the other nineteen Cathedral clergy, in the daily singing of the Divine Office which went on at different hours during the day. The priests were divided into two teams and were responsible for singing the Office on alternate weeks.[33] This huge commitment—placing a monastic regimen on secular priests—was introduced by Cardinal Vaughan and it consequently ate into the time available for other activities and interviews and school visits, for example, could only be undertaken between the Divine Office. Despite the much harder work at the Cathedral and the restrictions imposed by the singing of the Divine Office, Wheeler found it very pleasant for anyone who liked the liturgy: 'It suited me because the daily High Mass and the offices of Matins, Lauds, Prime, Terce, Sext, None, Vespers and Compline gave a wonderful framework to the day'.[34]

Throughout these busy days, Wheeler maintained contact with Mgr Duchemin, now responsible for transferring the Beda from Upholland back to Rome and refurbishing its post-war premises. In November 1946, intimating that he still harboured the hope that Wheeler might return, now possibly as Rector, Duchemin wrote: 'So you see we are getting the college ready for you. I wonder when the Lord will think it wise to send someone else to guide its destinies'.[35] Wheeler, however, continued at the Cathedral where he established a good reputation as a devoted pastoral priest. His reputation as a writer and a speaker had also begun to spread. When Cardinal Mindszenty of Hungary was in London for a brief visit in the summer of 1948, he marvelled at the large number of people who came into Westminster Cathedral to pray. Similar numbers assembled to pray for his release after he was later arrested for treason by Hungary's Communist government. On 7 February 1949, over 5,000 flocked to the Cathedral. For an hour they prayed, together and in silence, before the brightly lit high altar where the Blessed Sacrament was exposed. They listened to Wheeler as he reminded them of previous persecutions and other martyrs who had gone before. After his sermon the vast congregation went down on its knees and for five minutes prayed silently. The *Catholic Herald* reported that these five minutes 'were among the most impressive of that sad and solemn hour'. Benediction followed and then *Faith of our Fathers*, and the five thousand who had come to watch and pray went silently out into the streets of Westminster. Similar scenes were reported at Farm Street, Walworth, Somers Town, and Brompton Oratory.[36] Later, a huge assembly gathered in the Albert Hall to hear the Hierarchy and prominent Catholics speak out against the treatment meted out to the beleaguered Cardinal.[37]

One of Wheeler's final duties as editor of the *Westminster Cathedral Chronicle* was his contribution to a commemorative volume marking the centenary of the Restoration of the English and Welsh Hierarchy in 1950. Edited by Bishop George Andrew Beck, Coadjutor Bishop of Brentwood, the book included a range of articles by prominent Catholic historians and educationalists. Wheeler's contribution, concerned with the history of the Archdiocese of Westminster since 1850, displays a perspicacious understanding of recent Catholic history by one so lately received into the Church. His narrative of events is succinct and accurate while the issues he enlarges upon indicate his background and particular interests. Thus, he writes of Cardinal Nicholas Wiseman, Archbishop of Westminster and the leader of the restored Hierarchy, having contact with European scholars and 'converts of the Romantic period'. He emphasises the importance of Wiseman welcoming converts from the Church of England and synthesising them, and the immigrant Irish, with 'the new elements of English Catholic life'. He acknowledged that Manning, Wiseman's successor at Westminster, was a difficult man but his social conscience, asceticism, sympathy for Ireland and devotion to the papacy won him friends at home and abroad. Conversions continued and under Manning the Church 'clearly emerged from its penal shades'

Of the animosity between Manning and Newman, Wheeler blamed the intervention and machinations of Wilfrid Ward and the allegations of Lytton Strachey, but significant differences remained between the two eminent converts, especially over papal infallibility. There was room for two 'dynamic influences' in the universal Church, wrote Wheeler, 'but England was too small for them to flourish side by side'. Under Cardinal Herbert Vaughan, the Archdiocese developed significantly but for Wheeler, Vaughan's greatest achievement was the erection of Westminster Cathedral. It was to be 'a live Cathedral', the heart and head of the Church in England 'and the vivifying centre of its spirit and worship'. As Wheeler knew personally from his own position as a chaplain, Vaughan's 'high conception of Liturgical worship' had a lasting influence 'through the adhesion in the main to his plans for the Cathedral'. On the Papal Bull of 1896 (*Apostolicae Curae*) that declared Anglican Orders null and void, Wheeler felt that Vaughan had little room for manoeuvre and that the papacy did not consult the Hierarchy in sufficient time to prevent a subsequent affair of spectacular proportions. This was something of a misinterpretation of events by Wheeler, however, for Vaughan was positively against the recognition of Anglican Orders and demanded absolute re-ordination for convert clergymen.

Cardinal Francis Bourne's long episcopate was eventful and not without controversy and Wheeler dealt competently with the more significant issues—ecclesiastical training, deficiencies in diocesan education, the Great War, the erection of the Provinces of Birmingham, Liverpool and Cardiff, Irish Home Rule and the partition of Ireland, and above all Bourne's determination to be recognised as the undisputed leader of the Hierarchy and Primate of the British Empire. Wheeler claimed that Bourne, a determined and single-minded but reserved and reticent prelate, had received no favours from a poor biographer. Of Hinsley, the man who ordained him, Wheeler was as accurate and objective as he had been with his treatment of Hinsley's predecessors. Hinsley too had many gifts and achieved great things but also had faults and weaknesses. In summary, wrote Wheeler: 'Each Cardinal Archbishop of Westminster has been in his own time the providential leader of his people. The very variety of their characters and gifts has borne witness to the unity of their principles'. All spoke and acted with authority and left no one in doubt as to their Christian responsibilities. They were at one with the historical tradition of Augustine of Canterbury, Thomas Becket and the English martyrs.[38] *The Tablet* reviewer was of the opinion that Wheeler wrote with 'the independence of phrase which distinguishes the true historian'.[39]

Throughout this period, Wheeler continued to be involved with The Converts' Aid Society which had cared for him after 1936. Under the protection of Our Lady and the English Martyrs, the Society had been established in 1896 to provide for Anglican convert clergymen who by leaving the established Church had lost their livelihood. Wheeler was eternally grateful to the Society for the support it provided him and particularly for the personal friendship of the Catenian Freddie Chambers and Mgr Vernon Johnson. Chambers was a former Anglican clergyman who had been received into the Church in 1919. In 1922, he became secretary of the Converts Aid Society and held that position when Wheeler sought its assistance. Chambers had extensive contacts in the publishing world. Like Chambers and Wheeler, Vernon Johnson was a former Anglican priest and was received into the Church by Fr Vincent McNabb in 1929. He preceded Wheeler at the Beda and was ordained for the Archdiocese of Westminster in 1933.[40] Wheeler recalled that the Society, Chambers and Johnson gave him a 'marvellous welcome' and that 'all the difficulties that I encountered were dissipated by the splendid influence of those two people'. From 1950, Wheeler was a member of the Executive Committee and felt especially valuable in an organization in which he encountered some notable Catholic converts. In October 1950, at the Church of The Assumption, Warwick Street, London, he spoke on 'The Great Return' in which he traced the recent development of the English and Welsh Catholic Church and emphasised the role of the two most famous convert Cardinals, Manning and Newman.[41] He was to recount his own journey of faith many times in the future.

University Chaplain

In May 1950, Cardinal Griffin appointed Wheeler to be Joint Chaplain with Mgr Frederick Kerr McClement at London University. McClement had been chaplain since 1945 and had consolidated on the work done by Fr Vernon Johnson and Fr David Mathew. His responsibility was the spiritual care of Catholic students at London University, the Inns of Court, and the increasing number of Catholics students from the United Kingdom and the Commonwealth. It was envisaged by Cardinal Griffin that Wheeler would at first assist and then eventually take over from McClement. Given his views on university education and on an educated Catholic laity, it was an ideal appointment for Wheeler and one which he welcomed. As one of the few secular priests with an English rather than a continental university education, he seemed to be an obvious choice.[42] Mgr Duchemin was delighted: 'With the change in status of the older universities a central body like that of London may come to be of hitherto unknown importance in the Catholic life of the country. You will give it a prestige it needs and has not yet had'.[43]

Henry Outram Evennett, a Catholic Fellow of Trinity College, Cambridge, wrote that the chaplaincy at London differed markedly from those at Oxford and Cambridge and at provincial universities. It was *sui generis* because of its size, its intrinsic importance and its location in the heart of Empire. It was also unique in that many of its students were non-resident, living in halls, residences and lodgings away from the university's urban and disparate campuses. The chaplain at London University was not a chaplain to a college but ministered to a large and diverse Catholic Society, federations of student unions and other Catholic groups. It was, wrote Evennett, this wide-range of scholarship, students and groups which gave the London Catholic chaplaincy its special character.[44]

During the Second World War, the chaplaincy had occupied a number of different and unsuitable properties but Griffin gave Wheeler the task of finding a more permanent home. A new centre was acquired by Wheeler in Devonshire Place, near Regent's Park, and the Cardinal invited Wheeler's friend, Viscount (Tony) Furness, to become chairman of an appeal committee entrusted to collect part of the sum required for the maintenance of the new chaplaincy. The chaplaincy, named Bourne House, was formally opened on 30 January 1951 by Bishop Myers, deputizing for Cardinal Griffin, and it was blessed by Bishop Craven, 'parish priest' of the centre. Present too were Bishop Cowderoy of Southwark and Bishop Beck of Brentwood. The main function of the chaplaincy was to provide a spiritual and cultural focal point for Catholics in the university, particularly for those from overseas, and co-ordinate the activities of the various Catholic societies in the colleges of the university. The chaplains gave lectures and conducted courses but as in most universities it was expected that social activities would be organized by the students themselves. Membership was free, the only qualification being that members should be Catholics studying or teaching at one of the colleges or at the Inns of Court. One of the major problems facing the chaplains was that the students were dispersed over a twenty-five mile area and it was the chaplains' objective to minimize this disadvantage. The situation, as Wheeler recalled, was most unlike Oxford. Furnishing and redecorating the very stylish Adams house cost over £8,000 and annual running costs were £12,000. The chapel had great dignity; behind the altar was a painting of the Baptism of Christ from the Tintoretto School and donated by Fr Martin D'Arcy SJ.[45]

At its Low Week meeting in 1951, the Hierarchy confirmed Wheeler as successor to Mgr McClement who left to take overall charge of visiting Commonwealth students in England and Wales.[46] Over 300 students attended the Freshers' Mass at the beginning of the Michaelmas Term, 1951 and the new life of the chaplaincy began.[47] Under Wheeler, Bourne House became 'the stateliest and grandest chaplaincy in the country', and the army of Catholic students in London University could claim that their common home was 'fit to be an embassy or a nunciature'. It was, recalled Wheeler with pride, 'a dream of a house'. The centre, it was noted, was as delightful to the eye as it was useful to the soul. Wheeler arranged with the Rosminian Fathers at St Etheldreda's, Ely Place, that on each Sunday of term High Mass *pro populo Universitatis Londoniensis* was sung. This was a liturgical act of corporate worship by Catholics for the University as a whole. Wheeler felt that such a ceremony was exactly the way to break down any sense of isolation or separation on the part of the Catholic minority. He argued that if Catholics could not bring back the days when Christianity was the core of Western universities, there was nothing to prevent them asserting and living the spiritual bond between them and their separated and doubting brethren. In St Etheldreda's they had a church whose beauty and history so intimately linked the present with the past but whatever the nature of the conditions, Wheeler felt that the Catholics of all universities should live and assert their full Catholic spiritual role. Mgr Ronald Knox was the preacher at the first of these High Masses.[48]

So successful was Wheeler's chaplaincy that Bourne House was soon overcrowded. On Sunday evenings, an ever-increasing number of students attended Benediction and then crowded into the canteen and danced and socialized in the common rooms. On Tuesdays the chapel and adjoining rooms were filled to capacity for Compline and Benediction and even the stairs were crammed with students joining in the hymns and prayers. The chaplaincy provided a focal point for all Catholic students, including those from overseas, in the numerous colleges, medical schools and institutes which made up the university. It was in constant use for meetings of college study groups, for lectures and discussions as well as spiritual and social functions.[49] By 1953 there were over 2,400 Catholic students and staff at the university.

Wheeler's wholehearted commitment to his duties was rewarded. In March 1952, he was informed by Cardinal Griffin that he had been created a Privy Chamberlain to Pope Pius XII and had been awarded the title of Monsignor. It was a mark of Wheeler's meteoric rise within the Catholic priesthood. The Cardinal wrote: 'I know that my pleasure in this honour will be shared by your many friends'.[50]

In January 1953, Wheeler published a leaflet on 'The University Apostolate' in which he set out his views on the importance of the medieval and religious roots of university life, the debt owed to Cardinal Newman, and the higher education of the modern laity. The papacy, he wrote, had founded thirty-three of eighty-one pre-Reformation universities. It was Pope Honorius III who, in 1219, first used the universal term 'faculty' with regard to university departments of study and nearly all university terminology had its origins in the medieval and largely ecclesiastical frame-work of higher education.

Newman, however, was Wheeler's inspiration. In his preface to *The Idea of a University*, Newman wrote:

> The view taken of a university in these discourses is the following: That it is a place of teaching universal knowledge. This implies that its object is, on the one hand, intellectual, not moral; and, on the other, that it is the diffusion and extension of knowledge rather than the advancement. If its object were scientific and philosophical discovery, I do not see why a university should have students; if religious training, I do not see how it can be the seat of literature and science. Such is a university in its essence, and independently of its relation to the Church. But practically speaking, it cannot fulfil its object duly, such as I have described it, without the Church's assistance; or, to use the theological term. The Church is necessary for its integrity. Not that its main characters are changed by this incorporation: it still has the office of intellectual education; but the Church steadies it in the performance of that office.

In other words, commented Wheeler, the university cannot be divorced in its true sense from the common life of the Christendom that nurtured it. Where there is such a break, the university will become less a university. Contrariwise, when the university has the traditional Christian life as its basis it has something by which it is incomparably enhanced.

The Church, Wheeler continued, had an important contribution to make to modern university life. It can infuse something strengthening like concrete into the defective foundations, and especially in philosophical and theological spheres. At the same time, it would be arrogant to imagine that Catholics go to the universities merely to 'give' something. The late Fr Bede Jarrett, OP, realized that the Dominicans would 'get' from Oxford as well as 'give'. All truth comes from God. There can never be any real conflict between sound theology and sound science or sound philosophy. It was the Catholic mission after the fiascos of the nineteenth century and the dichotomy between these subjects to show that the truth is one.

It followed that the Church's first apostolate in the universities is that of intellectual integrity. The best Catholic action in this sphere, other things being equal, is a good degree, and a full participation in the intellectual life of the milieu. Here Catholics are in a strong position, for they have the solid sanction of sources of revelation. The more Catholics can hold the day in their faculties, the more 'they would command that respectful attention which is the Church's due'. That was why Pax Romana, the international university organization under the aegis of the Holy See, was anxious to promote specific faculty studies to relate Catholic traditional teaching to every discipline. This was already being done in London, by the United Hospitals Catholic Society in its systematic study of medical ethics, and also in the London School of Economics with its study groups on social, population and other relevant subjects.

In the university milieu, the individual was strengthened by the community and corporate life—spiritually, intellectually and socially. This, he stated 'is why a university chaplaincy is desideratum everywhere' for it has profound effects on the whole life of the university. The chaplaincy enables individuals to realize that they do not stand alone but have 'the power of Christendom' behind them and in addition it presents a corporate and unified life to those outside and security to those within. A chaplaincy had an impact beyond its doors. There were chaplains in schools, he continued, but there had to be recognition of the value and importance of the 'university apostolate' as the university is 'the crown of the educational system'. University education in England had been granted grudgingly to Catholics, he concluded, but now that it had been given the Hierarchy recognized that the possibilities for the Church's involvement and contribution were enormous.[51]

The success of Wheeler's chaplaincy was acknowledged outside the university. Michael de la Bedoyere wrote that Cardinal Griffin understood the importance of intellectual and cultural leadership in the life of the Catholic community and had invested heavily in 'the establishment in London of a most attractive new university chaplaincy under the direction of so outstanding a priest as Mgr Gordon Wheeler...'[52] In 1953 Wheeler was appointed Ecclesiastical Adviser to the Union of Catholic Students and became involved in the running of their Summer Schools. A Conference of University Chaplains was established and meetings were held at Bourne House under the chairmanship of the legendary Mgr Alfred Gilbey, Catholic chaplain to the University of Cambridge.[53]

Wheeler was of the strong opinion that Catholic lecturers in universities had the responsibility of not simply making an important academic contribution; they had the duty to influence the spiritual development of their students. Students also had the responsibility to increase the knowledge of their faith in proportion to the acquisition of secular knowledge; not to do so was likely to create a dichotomy from which they would suffer. Where chaplaincies had been established, the vitality of

Catholic life in universities had 'increased a hundredfold'. The future impact of such an investment was enormous for educated Catholics could take their place in all spheres of national life.

Running alongside his views on Catholics in higher education was Wheeler's opinion that seminary training should be more closely related to the universities. It was a sensitive issue but he tackled it directly. While Newman and others recognized that secular education was incomplete without a spiritual dimension, so too, Wheeler argued, was seminary education incomplete if religious students were educated in isolation from the secular world. The influence of Oxbridge and an increasing number of other universities could not be denied and Catholics should not ignore this. Some bishops had begun to allow church students to take degrees at varying stages in their training and this was commendable but the five major seminaries 'constituted entirely isolated units; isolated from each other, and almost entirely isolated from the ordinary university life of the country'. The situation, he wrote, was largely an accident of history but could be rectified, and the many erudite and learned professors in seminaries could make a greater contribution to general academic life. Like students in the religious orders, diocesan students could attend secular universities and derive great benefit from their faculties while adding to university life and learning. St Edmund's House, Cambridge, had already given a lead in this respect and was making an important contribution to Catholic higher education and the life of the university. The Holy See had allowed Catholic students to attend universities and young Catholics had begun to maximize the opportunities. There were great benefits to accrue from allowing seminaries and seminarians to develop closer links with other institutes of higher education. He concluded: 'Nothing revolutionary has been stated or envisaged, but only a line of further development of a theme which has already been initiated, and an attempt to foresee the advantages which the Church can expect in co-operation with modern secular development in universities'.[54]

In the summer vacations Wheeler usually went on supply to Our Lady of Ransom in Eastbourne, but in 1951 he was asked by Fr Alfred Blount, a Senior Catholic Chaplain to the British Forces, to give Passiontide and Easter retreats to Catholic officers and men of the British Army of Occupation on the Rhine. It was an opportunity he readily grasped and there followed a tour of military bases in West Germany from Dortmund to Monchengladbach and Cologne, and finally to Berlin where he was able to walk through the Brandenburg Gate and into the eastern Communist sector of the city. There, he wrote, 'as one encounters the atmosphere of distrust and despair amongst the ruins, a glimpse may be caught of Europe without the Faith'. While complimenting the military chaplains on their ministry and allaying the fears of parents who thought the army might ignore the religious duties of their sons, he became conscious of the fact that many Catholic youths had lost the practice of their faith between leaving school and beginning National Service.[55] A short time later he was invited to give a lecture on Newman in New York and this too proved to be a memorable experience. There he met the Franciscan Fr Angelus Delahunt who was subsequently instrumental, with Wheeler, in saving the ailing Catholic Central Library and locating it near Westminster Cathedral.[56]

While at the chaplaincy, Wheeler was given the opportunity to develop his communication skills on radio. A popular daily morning slot on the BBC Home Service was 'Lift Up Your Hearts', when a prominent religious personality was given a few minutes to deliver a message based on scripture or philosophy. In spring and summer 1951, Wheeler gave a number of short talks on 'Christ The Way'. These were subsequently included in the *Westminster Cathedral Chronicle*.[57]

Notes

[1]   G. P. Joyce, *St Edmund's Edmonton: A Short History* (London: Fr G. P. Joyce, 1991), pp. 9–11, 13–14, 38–40.

[2]   Sacerdos Juvenis, 'The Sublime Identity'. LDA, WPC, Letters 1930s-1950s.

[3]   W. G. Wheeler, *In Truth And Love* (Southport: Gowland and Co., 1990), pp. 52–54.

[4]   Wheeler to Wallis, 30 July 1940. LDA, WPC, Nora Wallis Letters.

[5]   Wheeler to Wallis, 31 Aug 1940. LDA, WPC, Nora Wallis Letters.

[6]   Wheeler to Wallis, 12 and 15 Sept 1940. LDA, WPC, Nora Wallis Letters.

[7]   Wheeler to Wallis, 11 Oct 1940. LDA, WPC, Nora Wallis Letters.

[8]   Wheeler, *In Truth And Love*, pp. 52–54; Joyce, *St Edmund's Edmonton: A Short History*, p.42.

[9]   Duchemin to Wheeler, 9 Sept 1944. LDA, WPC, Duchemin Letters. Presumably by 'everyone' Duchemin meant those within the Beda.

[10]   Wheeler to Duchemin, 17 Sept 1944. LDA, WPC, Duchemin Letters.

[11]   Wheeler to Mathew, 15 Sept 1944; Duchemin to Mathew, 20 Sept 1944. LDA, WPC, Duchemin Letters.

[12]   *The Tablet*, 16 Nov 1940.

13 *Westminster Cathedral Chronicle*, vol. xxxv, no. 10, Oct 1941.

14 *Westminster Cathedral Chronicle*, vol. xxxvi, no.1 Jan 1942; vol. xxxvi, no 5, May 1942; and vol. xxxviii, no 3, March 1944.

15 LDA, WPC, Miscellaneous Publications.

16 Lancing College, *Roll of Service*. LDA, WPC, Lancing College.

17 W. G. Wheeler, 'The Reverend Francis Head RIP', Typescript, Oct 1944. LDA, WPC, Beda.

18 W. G. Wheeler, 'The Late Nora Wallis' (undated). LDA, WPC, Nora Wallis Letters.

19 Sacerdos Juvenis, 'The Sublime Identity'. LDA, WPC, Letters 1930s-1950s.

20 Scott-James to Wheeler, 12 Dec 1942. LDA, WPC, Bruno Scott-James.

21 Gray to Wheeler, 13 and 17 Oct 1943. LDA, WPC, Charterhouse Letters.

22 E. Morrogh Bernard to Wheeler, 5 April 1944. LDA, WPC, Letters 1930s-1950s.

23 Wheeler, *In Truth And Love*, pp. 53–54.

24 McGrath to Wheeler, 14 April 1944. LDA, WPC, Letters 1930s-1950s.

25 Wheeler, *In Truth And Love*, pp. 54–55.

26 *The Catholic Who's Who 1947* (London: Burns Oates and Washbourne, 1947), p. 242. In 1947, Howlett was replaced as Administrator by Mgr Cuthbert Collingwood.

27 *Catholic Herald*, 6 June 1959.

28 W. G. Wheeler, 'A Newman Pilgrimage in England' in *Homage to Newman 1845–1945* (London: *Westminster Cathedral Chronicle*, 1945), pp. 7–16; Wheeler, *In Truth And Love*, p. 56.

29 *The Friends of Westminster Cathedral, Newsletter*, Autumn 1989; *The Tablet*, 4 May 1946.

30 *Richard Challoner 1691–1781* (London: Westminster Cathedral Chronicle, 1946), pp. 12–24; Wheeler, *In Truth And Love*, pp. 141–142. A portrait of Bishop Challoner hung in the Dining Room at Clergy House, Westminster. Nothing came of the cause for Challoner's beatification. Wheeler tried to revive it in 1990 although he felt that Challoner would have disapproved.

31 W. G. Wheeler, *More Truth And Love* (Southport: Gowland and Co., 1994), pp. 36–38.

32 Wheeler, *In Truth And Love*, pp. 57–59; *The Catholic Who's Who* ((London: Burns Oates and Washbourne, 1952), p. 302.

33 *Catholic Directory* (1945), p. 83.

34 Wheeler, *In Truth And Love*, p. 55.

35 Duchemin to Wheeler, 21 Nov 1946. LDA, WPC, Letters 1946–1950.

36 *Catholic Herald*, 11 Feb 1949.

37 *The Tablet*, 12 Feb 1949.

38 Gordon Wheeler, 'The Archdiocese of Westminster' in G. A. Beck (ed.), *The English Catholics 1850–1950* (London: Burns Oates, 1950), pp. 151–186. Wheeler relied heavily on David Mathew, *Catholicism in England*; Wilfrid Ward, *The Life and Times of Cardinal Wiseman*; Shane Leslie, *Edward Henry Manning: His Life and Labours*; John George Snead-Cox, *The Life of Cardinal Vaughan*; Ernest Oldmeadow, *Francis*

Cardinal Bourne; and John Carmel Heenan, *Cardinal Hinsley*. Wheeler also refers to Lytton Strachey's, *Eminent Victorians*.

39   *The Tablet*, 23 Sept 1950.

40   *The Catholic Who's Who* (1940), pp. 75 and 252.

41   The Converts' Aid Society, *Annual Report* (1950). LDA. WPC, Converts' Aid Society.

42   Wheeler, *In Truth And Love*, p. 60; *Catholic Herald*, 19 May 1950.

43   Duchemin to Wheeler, 13 May 1950. LDA, WPC, Duchemin Letters.

44   H. O. Evennett, 'Catholics and the Universities, 1850–1950' in Beck (ed.), *The English Catholics 1850–1950*, pp. 291–321.

45   *Catholic Herald*, 2 Feb 1951; Wheeler, *In Truth And Love*, p. 60. The Chaplaincy was subsequently moved in Cardinal Godfrey's time to St Patrick's, Soho. Furness was to remain a very close friend of Wheeler throughout his life.

46   *The Tablet*, 12 Jan 1952.

47   *Catholic Herald*, 19 Oct 1951.

48   *Catholic Herald*, 14 Dec 1952; Wheeler, *In Truth And Love*, pp.60–61.

49   *Catholic Herald*, 19 Dec 1952.

50   Griffin to Wheeler, 20 March 1952. LDA, WPC, Letters Early 1950s; Griffin to Godfrey, 12 Feb 1952. AAW, G.1–5; *Catholic Herald*, 28 March 1952.

51   W. G. Wheeler, 'The University Apostolate', 23 Jan 1953. LDA, WPC, Miscellaneous Publications.

52   M. de la Bedoyere, *Cardinal Bernard Griffin* (London: Rockliff, 1955), pp. 110–111.

53   Wheeler, *In Truth And Love*, pp. 62–63.

54   W. G. Wheeler, 'The Universities And The Seminaries' in *The Dublin Review*, no. 472, Winter 1956–57, pp. 114–119.

55   W. G. Wheeler, 'Reflections on the Rhine' (undated typescript). LDA, WPC, Miscellaneous. Wheeler wrote of his experiences in Germany in *The Tablet*, 5 May 1951.

56   Wheeler, *In Truth And Love*, pp. 61–62.

57   *Westminster Cathedral Chronicle*, Feb–July, 1951.

5 CATHEDRAL ADMINISTRATOR

A Wider World

ON 20 JANUARY 1954, Cardinal Griffin appointed Wheeler as Administrator of Westminster Cathedral in succession to Mgr Cuthbert Collingwood who had occupied the post since 1947. 'Lovers of the cathedral and its great liturgical traditions', wrote Michael de la Bedoyere, 'owe to the Cardinal... the happy appointment of Monsignor Gordon Wheeler as its Administrator, to carry out his own plans to make Westminster Cathedral the liturgical centre of the country and an inspiration to non-Catholics as well as Catholics'.[1] It was the beginning of an interesting, fruitful and important period in Wheeler's ministry. For ten years, he was to play a central role in Cathedral affairs, furthering his diocesan and national reputation as a priest of ability, intellect, style and taste.

His standing at the Cathedral was already well established. In its February 1954 edition, the *Westminster Cathedral Chronicle* introduced its readers to 'Our New Administrator'. 'Mgr Wheeler', it began, was already well known and 'he returns to the Cathedral having securely established the Chaplaincy of the University of London in its beautiful headquarters in Devonshire Place'. Alongside his significant contribution to the pastoral life of the parish, 'he is best remembered', the editorial continued, 'for his vigorous preaching, his brilliant editing of the *Cathedral Chronicle*, his authorship of several brochures, notably his *Homage to Newman* and *Richard Challoner*, and his enthusiasm for the Guild of Our Lady of Walsingham'. Wheeler, the editorial concluded:

> ... was a man who has absorbed to an unusual degree the spirit of the two cities, Oxford and Rome, which have formed him. Mgr. Wheeler brings to the great task which lies ahead a wide vision and magnanimity imbued with *Romanitàs* and deep Marian piety.[2]

Mgr Duchemin was delighted to hear the news of Wheeler's appointment and pointed out the opportunities associated with the post. The move, he wrote, 'releases you from the burdens of the chaplaincy while it is at the height of its success, and it introduces you to a wider world'. He continued: 'You will inherit a grand tradition of liturgy, you will be the meeting point for national and international movements; you will have a position that will not depend on your own initiative'.[3] Wheeler's major responsibility, undertaken on behalf of the Archbishop, was care of the Cathedral, the supervision of its staff, and the maintenance of its liturgical life and fabric. It was a great challenge—rather like being abbot of a small monastery, he recalled—but he received the strongest support from Cardinal Griffin and his previous experience of the Cathedral stood him in good stead.[4] His relations with Griffin's successor, Cardinal Godfrey, were more distant and formal yet Godfrey too supported the Cathedral's liturgical life and was a generous personal benefactor of the Cathedral.[5] Cardinal Vaughan's vision of daily Cathedral life had been well established for nearly half a century and Wheeler was anxious 'to maintain this liturgical tradition and to be present myself as often as all my other obligations allowed'. This often proved difficult for the Administrator, like the other Cathedral clergy, had parish responsibilities. Nevertheless, with the agreement of the other chaplains, Wheeler introduced daily Confessions and the Cathedral acquired a new life and bustle. In addition, the Cathedral continued to be the scene of many national and state events.

The post-war period witnessed an astonishing increase in the Catholic population of England and Wales and Westminster's diocesan population had reached 470,000 by 1960. The Cathedral parish had also grown in terms of population and had undergone many social, cultural and ethnic changes. According to Peter Doyle, Wheeler responded imaginatively and enthusiastically to the new circumstances: '... [he] was no cloistered Dean; he understood the demands of the Cathedral's pastoral mission not just to its own parishioners but to the many hundreds of people who used it regularly as their place of worship, and to the large numbers who 'dropped in' from time to time for Mass, the Sacraments, the music or just for anonymous advice and comfort'. Such needs called for a creative and varied response by the Cathedral authorities. One such response was the provision of daily Confessions which drew even more people to the Cathedral. It was a way of providing pastoral support and 'breaking down the barrier which a highly formalised liturgy created between the congregation and the clergy'.[6] The parish included Royal Parks, famous London landmarks, huge hospitals and popular and busy locations. Its housing stock ranged from royal residences to council houses; and from mansions to bed-sits. It was incredibly varied in social composition with extremes of poverty and wealth. The chaplains had pastoral responsibility for all the divisions of the parish including the outlying districts of Pimlico and Horseferry. This placed heavy burdens on them for these responsibilities and the care of numerous sodalities and societies had to be undertaken alongside their confessional and liturgical duties. In 1957, Wheeler told Cardinal Griffin that he was desperately searching for sites on which to build new churches. Chapels of Ease were used before both Pimlico and Horseferry were established as separate parishes in the early 1960s.[7]

The Cathedral was the scene of many important events and Wheeler had complete responsibility for their arrangement. The first big occasion over which he presided was the funeral of Cardinal Griffin in August 1956. As ever, the rumour mills focussed on Griffin's successor. Wheeler wrote to Patrick McLaughlin: '… England is very out of touch really with what is the real mind of the Holy See and it will make the appointment all the more interesting and acceptable'. The choice, thought Wheeler, was between Archbishop Godfrey of Liverpool and Bishop Beck of Salford.[8] *The Daily Telegraph*—under the heading 'Room for a Convert?'—considered that both Abbot Christopher Butler of Downside and Wheeler himself ('the very able Administrator of Westminster Cathedral') were candidates to succeed Griffin.[9] Eventually, Godfrey was appointed to Westminster in December 1956 and Wheeler supervised the televised enthronement on 11 February 1957.[10]

A later ceremony at which Wheeler officiated was the baptism of Anna Christina, daughter of Princess Lee Radziwill, in June 1961. This was to be no ordinary baptism for the Princess was the sister-in-law of John F. Kennedy, President of the United States of America, and he and his wife Jackie would be attending the service. After many discussions with security men, Wheeler eventually welcomed the President, Mrs Kennedy and members of the Radziwill family to the Cathedral and duly conducted the baptism in the Crypt where the President stood as godfather. Wheeler and Cardinal Godfrey were then invited to a reception at the Radziwill home in Buckingham Gate where Kennedy, his family, and Prime Minister Harold Macmillan were among many distinguished guests.[11]

Enriching the Cathedral

In Wheeler's time, the huge Byzantine-style Cathedral was hidden away at the back of commercial and residential properties on Victoria Street.

One of his first responsibilities was to complete the decoration of the Cathedral's overwhelmingly dark but dignified interior. His predecessor, Mgr Collingwood, had made the mistake of interfering with Bentley's original design by removing a pillar in order to facilitate processions. Collingwood's decision caused an artistic outcry and he was subsequently divested of his responsibilities. Griffin had earlier assembled an Advisory Art Committee of eminent artists and architects to advise him and Wheeler reconvened the Committee and launched 'the Million Crown Fund' to raise the required sum to beautify the church. In line with Bentley's original designs, Wheeler and the Committee started at the West End of the Cathedral and began to complete the permanent furnishings and affix mosaics to bare brick walls.

Almost every project was the subject of intense debate among the Committee but Wheeler maintained that work must proceed strictly in line with Bentley's vision. The balustrade on both sides of the nave was completed as were the Blessed Sacrament Chapel, the Shrine of St Thérèse of Lisieux, the Chapel of St Paul, and the installing of the alabaster shrine of Our Lady of Westminster under Eric Gill's thirteenth Station of the Cross. The fifteenth-century alabaster carving of Our Lady and the Holy Child had appeared on the market and after prompting by Fr Francis Bartlett, the Sub-Administrator, Cardinal Griffin became so determined to acquire it that he had given Wheeler a blank cheque to buy it. The Dean and Chapter of York Minster, however, had first choice on the alabaster but were unable to meet the cost. Wheeler therefore stepped in and acquired the precious statue for the Cathedral. The Shrine was blessed and inaugurated by Archbishop Edward Myers on 8 December 1955 in the presence of the Dean of York's representative.[12] Another of Wheeler's innovations was Roy de Maistre's Stations of the Cross hung in the long corridor linking the Cathedral Sacristy with Clergy House, Archbishop's House, and the Choir School. Like Wheeler, the Australian de Maistre was a convert and had been confirmed by Bishop Craven in the chapel of London University Chaplaincy in 1951.[13] His cubist work was not to everyone's taste and some have compared his work in paint with Eric Gill's in stone. Encouraged by Mgr Duchemin, in 1954 Wheeler commissioned de Maistre to paint the Stations and they were unveiled and blessed by Cardinal Griffin in 1956. Wheeler arranged for them to be paid for by private subscription but they were not intended for public viewing.[14] De Maistre also painted portraits of Wheeler and

Duchemin but Wheeler was somewhat embarrassed by his, fearing that other priests might think him presumptuous. Nor did he like de Maistre's emphasis on the red of the monsignorial robes; he thought this was to the detriment of the subject.[15] In later life, Wheeler used to relate the story that Fr Bartlett had seen the portrait on display and while not mentioning that he knew it was Wheeler said at lunch that he had seen at an exhibition '... a portrait of a Monsignor who looked like the Gamekeeper at Ushaw'.[16]

The historian of the Cathedral wrote that during Wheeler's time as Administrator the decoration of the Cathedral was substantially enhanced:

> Much of the credit for this achievement must go to Wheeler himself, for it is always the Administrator who sets the tone...for what is done in the Cathedral and it is abundantly clear that Wheeler had taken a close and knowledgeable interest in the various artistic projects during his term of office.[17]

Wheeler did not shoulder the burden alone and he later paid generous tribute to the contribution made by Fr Francis Bartlett whom he had chosen as his Sub-Administrator in 1954. He and Bartlett worked closely on projects designed to complete and enrich the Cathedral and both shared a love for the Cathedral and its liturgical round. Wheeler wrote that they both wished to maintain the Cathedral's reputation as a great house of prayer 'and to develop its growth pastorally and materially'. Bartlett and his brother Aelred devised ways to complete the Cathedral's marble revetment; they visited Greek marble quarries and went to Italy for mosaics; and they persuaded the Art and Architecture Commission to sanction the great Balustrade. Bartlett persuaded Cardinal Griffin to have a representation of St Thérèse of Lisieux in the Cathedral and moved the Cathedral authorities to commission new mosaics by Boris Anrep in the Blessed Sacrament Chapel.[18]

The Cathedral's important musical tradition continued alongside artistic and architectural developments. During his long tenure as Master of Music, George Malcolm, in Wheeler's words, had 'built up the notable post-war tradition of the choir, liturgically, and traditionally in the line of the chant but also in that of polyphony and the classics together with the best of modern developments'. The Malcolm tradition 'was carried on magnificently by others and especially Colin Mawby'.[19] The choir was faced with heavy routine demands and the Cathedral authorities had imposed severe restrictions on its external performances and the use of the consecrated Cathedral as a venue for recitals and concerts. About this, Wheeler, like his predecessors, 'had an absolute phobia'. While there were recordings of scared music in Wheeler's time and the attendance of composers such as Benjamin Britten, he was as anxious as his predecessors to maintain the sanctity of the Cathedral and the choir's liturgical focus.[20]

Ecumenism and the Heythrop Conference

Wheeler continued to be an avid observer of relations between the Established Church of England and the Church of Rome and an advocate of their improvement. He had taken an initiative in January 1955 when the Church Unity Octave was observed for the first time in the Cathedral. The week was marked by special services and sermons but it was essentially a Catholic affair. The Unity Octave became an annual event and Wheeler continued to be an active supporter of the advancement of unity but the lack of support from the Hierarchy, whose policy was to discourage religious contacts between Catholics and other Christians, meant that Wheeler and others like him were ploughing a lone furrow.[21] The early shoots of ecumenism encouraged by Cardinal Hinsley through the Sword of the Spirit had not been nurtured by either Griffin or Godfrey. Nor was the Anglican approach enthusiastic. He wrote to Dilworth Harrison that he found Archbishop Geoffrey Fisher less sympathetic than some of his predecessors.[22] At a personal level, however, contacts were more sociable: 'I am on very friendly terms with the Dean of Westminster and (Bishop) George Bell of Chichester is always very nice when I bump into him', he wrote to Dilworth Harrison in 1956.[23]

Wheeler's Anglican background proved useful for Griffin. In May 1955, he was summoned by the Cardinal to advise him on a letter from Anglo-Catholics in Southern India. Dissatisfied with the workings of the local Anglican Church and its possible merger with the previously united Congregationalist, Presbyterian and Methodist Churches, the Anglo-Catholics sought Griffin's views on a possible approach to the Pope regarding their relationship with the both the Catholic Church and the Lambeth Conference. In particular, they sought to stay free of the Conference and become 'Papalists'. It was not a controversy which Griffin sought to enter or a question he could easily address without upsetting someone and so he convened a temporary advisory group consisting of his secretary Mgr Derek Worlock, Abbot Christopher Butler, Fr George Patrick Dwyer of the Catholic Missionary Society and Wheeler. It was thought that through his informal contacts Wheeler might be able to sound out senior Anglican opinion in England. Such a case, however, went beyond the realms of informal contacts and Wheeler could provide little of substance. While some of the Anglo-Catholics in Southern India converted to Catholicism, others distanced themselves from the petition to Westminster and submission to Rome.[24]

Wheeler's sermons and lectures on ecumenism and specifically on the relationship between the Roman and Anglican communions were always charitable but firm and based on his personal experience. Addressing the Newman Association in the mid-1950s, he made the distinction between a corporate or institutional approach to unity and personal conversion, an approach he frequently repeated. In the former, the Catholic Church trod warily 'for she has the dire responsibility of scandalising no-one' but for individuals seeking a spiritual home in Catholicism, conversions had to continue. In this, Catholics had to be sympathetic: 'We are indeed privileged to have the grace of the Faith whether by birth or conversion; but we should always be mindful of the fact that far from it being our right, we have done nothing to deserve it and that we should show a great reverence for the working of God in others who like the Roman tribune obtained their citizenship "with a great sum."' To Anglicans, and others considering conversion, he advised prayer, strength of purpose and use of free will.[25] At the corporate level, unity had to be achieved by understanding and prayer but not by forsaking principles in order to co-operate with other Christians: '... it is only by bearing witness to the absolute sacredness of our own principles that we can dissipate their blindness.' By joining in the prayers and services of other denominations 'we should be bearing a false witness and doing them a great disservice by implying a compromise such as Our Lord Himself would never tolerate.'[26] In 1960, in the context of developing Anglican-Catholic relations, he welcomed the meeting in Rome between Pope John and Archbishop Fisher of Canterbury but warned his congregation not to expect 'immediate or fantastic results' despite the meeting being of 'immense significance.' He called for more ecumenical discussions and prayer.[27]

The Second Vatican Council was to have a profound influence on the Church's relations with other faiths and Wheeler, always sympathetic to Christian unity, became much more closely involved in ecumenical issues. The Council, he felt, was to be welcomed by friend and critic because 'it is inspired in considerable measure by the general desire among Christians for renewal and unity.'[28] Through the efforts of Pope John XXIII, he wrote, 'there is a new and happier relationship between Christians...a spirit of friendship and closer understanding...'[29] Wheeler's previous attempts to build bridges between Catholics and Anglicans in particular were based largely on personal friendships but during and after Vatican II, these were replaced with semi-official contacts. The Council's ecumenical deliberations bore heavily upon Anglican-Catholic relations in England and Wales where religious history remained haunted by the lasting and bloody memories of the sixteenth-century Reformation.

Ecumenism assumed a very different guise and level of importance in consequence of Pope John XXIII's initiative. Under the influence of the German Jesuit, Cardinal Augustin Bea, a confidant of Pope John on ecumenical matters, the Pope established a Council body to deal with separated Christian churches but fearing curial opposition he declared that, rather than it being called a Commission or Congregation, it was to be named the Secretariat for Promoting Christian Unity. This, Pope John felt, would deflect critics and offer more unrestricted movement in 'a new and unique field'. The Secretariat had two specific functions: first, to inform non-Catholic Christians of the Council's work and to receive their views relating to the Council; and, secondly, to aid non-Catholic Christians by establishing common ground and identifying means by which the Catholic Church could help them to true unity. The Secretariat was not meant to replace existing local or national initiatives for the study of ecumenical matters. It was to become an indispensable link between the Catholic Church and the wider Christian ecumenical movement.[30]

In June 1960, Bea was appointed to chair the Secretariat and he recruited men he knew and could trust. The Secretariat's permanent staff included Bea, Mgr Jan Willebrands, the Dutch bishops' representative for ecumenical matters, the American Paulist Fr Thomas Stransky, and the Italian Mgr Jean-Francois Arrighi. The dynamic Willebrands was a well-known ecumenist and in 1952 had set up the Catholic Conference for Ecumenical Questions as a conduit between Catholic ecumenists and the non-Catholic World Council of Churches. In September 1960, Archbishop Heenan of Liverpool was also appointed to the Secretariat along with the American Frs Gerald Corr and James Cunningham, the Belgian Bishop Emile de Smedt and Archbishop Lorenz Jäger of Paderborn. Heenan felt that the appointment of an English prelate went against a Vatican custom which seemed to assume that English and Welsh bishops were uninterested in ecumenical matters and therefore relied on European continental bishops as authorities on English and Welsh affairs.[31] Heenan was of the view that there were 'few countries in which ecumenism presented more problems than in England'[32] but found that few in the Secretariat, and even Pope John, understood the reasons for this situation. Consequently, he spent some time relating the religious position in England to the Secretariat, informing them of the history of the English Catholic Church and its relationship to the State and the established Church of England.

The England and Welsh Hierarchy made its preparations for the Vatican Council. A reluctant Cardinal Godfrey was appointed to the Central Preparatory Committee and the bishops drew up the topics they wished to be discussed and a list of the committees on which they wished to have representation. Among the many issues discussed by the bishops was that of ecumenism and Archbishop Heenan was appointed to chair the Hierarchy's Committee for Christian Unity—a high-profile and an extremely sensitive role for there was no one episcopal interpretation of the word 'ecumenical'. Godfrey interpreted it to relate to the calling of a General Council of the worldwide Catholic Church whereas a few others, including Heenan, saw it in part as a movement towards the unity of Christian denominations. Godfrey remained 'suspicious' of the ecumenical movement and, wrote Heenan, was not sufficiently enthusiastic enough to open an ecumenical secretariat in Westminster. Nevertheless, he allowed Heenan to do so in Liverpool. The Committee for Christian Unity was empowered to give directives on ecumenical matters and had powers to control all official approaches to non-Catholics. On the Committee were Heenan and Bishops Rudderham of Clifton, Murphy of Shrewsbury, Holland (Auxiliary in Portsmouth) and Cashman (Auxiliary in Westminster). Heenan made it clear that henceforth ecumenism would be under the direction of the bishops who alone would guide, advise, and take the initiative.[33] Cardinal Bea expressed his satisfaction with this initiative.[34]

Archbishop Heenan's strategic aim was to bring ecumenical developments under episcopal control and make ecumenism acceptable to the bishops, priests and laity of England and Wales at a time when to most Catholics both the concept and the word were novel and threatening. To some bishops and priests who were overseeing significant numerical and material Catholic expansion, ecumenism was neither needed nor welcome.

The majority of Catholics were unaware of previous contacts between Catholic leaders and those of other Christian denominations; religious differences had been drummed into them at school and from the pulpit. Consequently, ordinary Catholics were ignorant and suspicious of other Christians and, according to Heenan, even the ecumenical ideas and language of the Church and Council were rudimentary. Protestant Churches were referred to as 'ecclesial communities' and Council decrees stated unequivocally that salvation was only possible through the Catholic Church. Pope John stated what all Catholics believed and wished to hear: that the faith and the Church were not going to change. He was simply welcoming back those who were 'separated'.[35]

One of the episcopal committee's first actions was to convene a national conference on ecumenism in July 1962 at Heythrop College, the Jesuit House of Studies in Oxfordshire, and to invite Cardinal Bea to attend. Six bishops and seventy secular and regular priests were present. Heenan's objective was that the conference should set in motion a programme that would enable the Hierarchy 'to instruct priests in the nature of the Ecumenical Movement and not leave the initiative on this field to non-Catholics' or Catholics who were likely to give the wrong message and cede too much ground.[36] Heenan invited Wheeler to 'give a talk on relations with the Church of England'. The main speaker was to be Cardinal Bea and he would be accompanied by Mgr Willebrands, Secretary of the Secretariat for Promoting Christian Unity.[37]

Before the conference, Wheeler sought the views of others. Cardinal Godfrey, who had instructed the young Wheeler in Rome, stressed the difference between institutional reunion and individual conversion. He advised that 'it would be as well for you to emphasise that nothing is to be gained from disguising the fact that the issue of Anglican Orders has been judged definitively and absolutely'. They remained 'utterly null and void'. If an Anglican minister feels in conscience unable to conduct Anglican services, 'then he is ready for instruction with a view to reception in the Church. There can be no question of remaining in error in order to bring in others later...To remain in error is only to encourage others in the belief that their position is tenable'.[38] The Jesuit Fr Bernard Leeming offered advice on assistance to converts and the faults of the contemporary seminary system training but essentially agreed with Wheeler that although individual conversions were to be welcomed, they did not really amount to ecumenism and that a different approach was required. He concluded: 'I think it a great mistake to tie ourselves up with Anglicans alone'.[39]

Wheeler read his paper on 'English Catholicism and the Anglican Tradition' to the conference on 7 August, and made the distinction between individual conversion and ecumenical dialogue. Addressing the issue of unity from an Anglican perspective and the views of Anglican clergymen, he said there were some Anglican clergymen who were ready for conversion but faced difficulties doing so, and there were those opposed to both conversion and unity. While individual conversions must continue, he urged that as a Church 'we must enter into dialogue with non-Catholic Christians without the motive of conversion'. He called for a new Catholic approach through a serious adjustment of thought, collaboration on scriptural and dogmatic issues, use of the vernacular, revised seminary training, education of the laity, and a deeper understanding of the inherent national nature of Anglicanism and the influence of the Free Churches, a dimension either often overlooked or misunderstood by continental European Catholics. Both sides had faults, he admitted, and there was a sad historical legacy of mistrust and even hatred, but the present divisions between the Roman and the Anglican Churches were scandalous. Pope John had called for *veritas et caritas* and that had to be the basis of any new approach.[40] Fr Leeming wrote to Wheeler: 'Your paper was smashing!'[41] The historian Fr Gordon Albion wrote that 'your paper had me purring with delight'.[42] *The Tablet* reported that 'a penetrating and enlightening analysis of the Anglican position' was presented by 'that distinguished convert Mgr. Gordon Wheeler'.[43]

Heenan summarised twenty-eight suggestions arising from group discussions. From the group chaired by Wheeler came the 'essential recommendation' that the bishops 'give the priests of England and Wales a lead in the ecumenical spirit by giving to their flocks a strong an unambiguous directive'. The Catholic faithful in England, conscious of the harsh treatment meted out to them in penal times and with the blood of the martyrs in their veins, needed a reason to change their attitudes and without this lead 'the ecumenical movement will make no more than minimal progress and this conference will prove a waste of time'.[44] Heenan did not consider the conference particularly successful yet its outcomes reached to the heart-of-the-matter as far as many priests were concerned. He felt that much had to be done in the wider English Church to offset 'the war psychology which still determines some of our attitudes towards our separated brethren'. To Heenan, ecumenical progress in the British Isles had been slow for obvious historical reasons. There were also, he continued, sound doctrinal reasons for caution. As for Cardinal Bea, Heenan thought that he did not fully understand the English religious tradition and was insensitive to the subtleties of the English Anglican Church. He was later to say that he doubted if Bea 'really appreciated the delicacy of the religious situation in England'. Bea's concluding reflections at Heythrop simply expressed the view 'that conditions... in the British Isles are different from conditions elsewhere, and full account must be taken of this'. The British Isles, he continued, could learn from continental experiences and said that 'some few matters need adaptation to conditions in these islands'.[45] The crux of the differences in interpretation was that Heenan saw the position solely from the lingering and damaging effect of history upon contemporary English Catholocism while Bea saw the English situation from the standpoint of the Universal Church. Heenan did not wish to cede ground to other denominations in England and wrote to Wheeler: 'Nothing, it seems, could be more foolish in our ecumenical unity than to assume that it is we who have to do all the changing'.[46]

One of the biggest obstacles to the development of Anglo-Roman relations, and one which Bea did not appear to understand, was the cause for the canonization of the English martyrs and Heenan felt that Wheeler's intervention on behalf of Cardinal Bea was unhelpful. Wheeler seemed to be operating as an interlocutor between Cardinal Bea and Archbishop Ramsey and it was not to Heenan's liking. He wrote to Wheeler:

> Personally, I would regard it as a mistake for you to see Dr. Ramsey or anybody else officially as a sort of intermediary—unless, of course, Cardinal Bea tells you to do so. I am very much afraid that eventually it would become known and this would almost certainly do great harm to the cause of unity which we both value so highly.[47]

Wheeler was not to be deflected and continued his discussions with leading Anglicans. In September 1962, he informed Bea that he had discussed the issue of the martyrs with the Anglican Dean of Westminster and was of the opinion that 'if carefully worded' the Bull of Canonization would cause little trouble and 'might even be made into an eirenic document especially if the new notions of toleration were embodied therein'. There was no doubt, he told the Cardinal that the old Catholic body would be irritated and even more embittered if the canonisation were held up for unity reasons but 'they would be placated if the Bull urged the faithful to emulate the sacrifices made by the martyrs for their faith in the light of modern materialistic dangers rather than that of anti-Protestant feeling'.[48]

In January 1963, he informed Bea that much had happened since Heythrop and that he had been given permission by Bishop Craven, Vicar Capitular following Cardinal Godfrey's death, to attend a dinner at Lambeth Palace as Archbishop Ramsey's guest. Included in the Catholic party were the Jesuits Archbishop Thomas Roberts and Fr Thomas Corbishley, and Fr Ronald Pilkington who accompanied Wheeler. The meeting, reported Wheeler, was very friendly and many matters of common interest were discussed. Ramsey asked his guests to pray especially 'for his own conflicts with the more Protestant representatives of his Communion' and 'looked forward to the day when he would have the opportunity of visiting the Holy Father'. Wheeler concluded: 'I thought you would like to know all these interesting and historic developments of our friendly relations'.[49]

In the interregnum between Cardinal Godfrey's death in January 1963 and Archbishop Heenan's appointment to Westminster in September of the same year, Wheeler continued to develop links with Lambeth Palace. Aware of Archbishop Ramsey's serious concerns that the cause for the canonization of the English martyrs 'might be a hindrance to our new ecumenical friendships,' he sent a list of points which set out the Catholic view and the anticipated Anglican response. Ramsey replied that he was very impressed particularly by Wheeler's plea that Anglican interference and objection to the cause would damage the ecumenical spirit among Catholics and he would take further soundings among his brethren.[50] Inspired by Ramsey's tact and grace, Wheeler wrote to Bea: 'It seems to me a wonderful answer to prayer that the Archbishop has so changed his attitude, and I sincerely hope that that these may help you in furthering the Cause of our Martyrs'.[51] Abbot Butler, meanwhile, was of the opinion that the process of canonization ought to be quietly slowed down for the sake of improving ecumenical relations.[52]

The bonds between Ramsey and Wheeler were further strengthened when the Archbishop asked the Administrator if he might make a private visit to the Cathedral. So secret was the occasion that the Archbishop arrived under the cover of darkness when the Cathedral was closed.[53] Unable to conceal his excitement, Wheeler wrote to Dilworth Harrison: 'Did I tell you that the Archbishop of Canterbury is coming privately here for a dinner on Ascension Night. I think he is a really sound person and we are in close contact'.[54] He informed Cardinal Bea that 'Last night was a very historic occasion here: the Archbishop of Canterbury came to dinner with the clergy, and afterwards visited the Cathedral and prayed for some time before the Blessed Sacrament'.[55] So close had contacts with the Anglicans become under Wheeler, that Canon John Satterthwaite of the Church of England's Council on Foreign Relations wrote to him that 'your Cathedral is becoming a kind of second home.'[56] Mgr Duchemin thought that Wheeler 'had made history' and was now 'pivotal' in ecumenical relations.[57]

The Second Vatican Council

The most important developments at the Cathedral during Wheeler's time emanated from the Second Vatican Council (1962–1965), often referred to as Vatican II. The Council, convened by Pope John XXIII, became the most significant event in the history of twentieth-century Catholicism and ushered in a momentous and challenging period in the history of the modern Church. Its impact and reverberations were enormous. For some Catholics it was the sad end of a golden era; for others it was a time of new hope. The Council's sessions in Rome directly involved the 2,500 bishops and their clerical and lay experts (*periti*) but the consequences affected the Universal Church. As Edward Norman commented, 'although the bishops were unaware of it, a distinct phase of Catholic history was drawing to an end'.[58] For the majority of the English and Welsh Hierarchy attendance at the Council was the first time they were compelled to address anything of significance beyond the domestic needs of their own dioceses. They were henceforth confronted with liturgical changes, new attitudes to relations with non-Catholic Christians, and the transformation of the centuries-old model of a centralized, disciplined Catholic Church. These developments were met with episcopal responses ranging from mildly enthusiastic to extreme hostility. The Cathedral, like other churches, was affected and Wheeler, responsible for its liturgy was confronted by the innate conservatism of Cardinal Godfrey and the slightly more modernising tendencies of Archbishop Heenan.

The calling of the Second Vatican Council was unheralded and unexpected. On 25 January 1959, at the Basilica of St Paul Outside the Walls, and a little under ninety days after his election, Pope

John XXIII suddenly announced that he had decided to hold a diocesan synod for the city of Rome and a Council of the Universal Church. A Council had hitherto been the climax to an apparently insoluble problem or controversy in the Church. The Pope's decision was therefore astonishing as nobody knew of any current problem or controversy that could not be solved by the normal means at the disposal of the Holy See; but as the Pope said later, the Council was not the fruit of lengthy reflection but the spontaneous flower of an unexpected springtime.[59]

Many assumed that the Council would simply be a ceremonial demonstration of unity within the Church and of support for one or two papal projects, but the objective of Pope John's Council was rather different and surprising. It was to address nothing less than

> the development of the Catholic faith and the renewal along the right lines of the habits of the Christian people, and the adapting of the Church's discipline to the needs and conditions of the present time. The event will surely be a wonderful manifestation of truth, unity and charity; a manifestation, indeed, which we hope will be received by those who behold it but who are separated from this Apostolic See, as a gentle invitation to seek and find that unity for which Jesus Christ prayed so ardently to His Heavenly Father.[60]

The Council was to be a modernizing exercise with pastoral and ecumenical dimensions. Its essential driving force was to be *aggiornamento*—bringing the Church up to date—but it was also to be an opportunity for the Church to encourage and develop fruitful dialogue with both its separated brethren. The 'Ecumenical Council' was to be a catalyst for Christian unity. Of necessity, the Council would impinge on other Christian denominations, both East and West.

On 5 June 1960, Pope John XXIII signed the Motu Proprio *Superno Dei nutu*—a document prepared on his own initiative—which set up a central commission and ten other commissions for thematic areas to be considered at the Council. The direction which the Council would take depended very much upon the Commissions. Abbot Christopher Butler was able to attend the Council as President of the English Benedictine Congregation and his radical view of the Council influenced Wheeler. In September 1962, before the opening of the Council, he had written to Wheeler to say that he intended to use his vote 'regularly on the minority side'. He feared that 'the Council has come too soon; the new life of the Church hasn't yet bitten deep enough into the ranks of the Old Guard. May the Holy Ghost see to it that, however little actual progress is made, fresh obstacles are not set up'.[61] Later, in December 1963 towards the end of the Second Session, Wheeler expressed his delight on learning of Butler's appointment to the Theological Commission: 'This is a feather in our cap and more than compensates for the election of that ridiculous old gentleman from Brentwood (Bishop Wall) on to the Seminaries Commission'.[62]

The leadership, personnel, and remits of the Commissions were vital for the outcome of Vatican II. The agenda of the Council was formulated after cardinals, bishops and religious superiors had submitted their views to Rome. Preparatory commissions drew up the schemata or proposals arising from the responses and these were then to be dealt with by commissions of nominated and elected bishops. Pope John summoned the Council with the Apostolic Constitution *Humanae Salutis* on 25 December 1961 and formally opened it with the declaration *Gaudet Mater Ecclesia* on 11 October 1962. The first session commenced under the presidency of the French Cardinal Eugene Tisserant on 13 October. Three more sessions followed in 1963, 1964 and 1965.[63]

Wheeler had tremendous respect and admiration for Pope John XXIII. John, a gentle and courteous man, died in June 1963 after a whirlwind papacy of four-and-a-half years and was succeeded by Cardinal Montini who took the name Pope Paul VI. To Wheeler, Pope John had been 'fully attuned to God's plan for our time' and 'fully committed to the whole *aggiornamento*', or modernization of the Church. Petrine and Johannine in tradition, Pope John 'completed the fullness of the divergent apostolic charisma by his Pauline approach' and his Christo-centric emphasis 'so redolent of the Scriptures and early tradition' had been the paramount effect of the *aggiornamento*. Vatican II had been the crowning achievement of his papacy; the Church was now truly universal and John had ushered in 'a reorientation of the whole of the Catholic outlook in ecumenical matters'. Wheeler confidently asserted that Pope John XXIII had 'set the compass for his successor'.[64]

The Vernacular Question

The introduction of the vernacular into the sacred liturgies during and after Vatican II marked a huge change in Catholic tradition and in the nature of ceremonies at the Cathedral and other churches. There had been some liturgical and other innovations prior to the Council, however. Pope Pius XII's 1947 encyclical *Mediator Dei* had permitted liturgical changes which were the result of a genuine theological renewal. In the 1950s, the hours of fasting before receiving Holy Communion were reduced, evening Masses were introduced, the Dialogue Mass in Latin encouraged congregational participation, and the vernacular was introduced into the Easter liturgies in 1955. With Cardinal Godfrey's permission, Wheeler introduced Sunday evening Masses at the Cathedral in 1956 and daily evening Masses in the following year, thus enabling workers to attend Mass on their way home. Wheeler was a cautious supporter of all these developments but argued that the Cathedral, like other large European cathedrals, should be taking the lead. In 1961, changes were introduced to the Divine Office and these allowed the chaplains more time for the confessional and their parochial duties.[65]

The use of the vernacular, however, was a more complex and divisive issue and the prospect of this reform greatly troubled the liturgically conservative Wheeler. In 1960, he was invited by the editor of *The Lamp* to respond to an article which had in appeared in the magazine *America* on 'The Language of the Liturgy'. Wheeler took the opportunity to state his views clearly and firmly. He began by referring to the recent Eucharistic Congress in Munich where, he wrote, an 'occasion which ought of its very essence to have stressed universality' was marred 'by the intrusion of loudspeakers which drowned the sacred liturgy in a non-stop German commentary'. 'The uncontrolled use of the vernacular', he continued, 'can only result in stressing the national at the expense of the supra-national'. There was more to the issue than loudspeakers broadcasting a German commentary, however.

Wheeler considered the idea of dualism in the Mass—that is combining the Mass of the Catechumens in English with the Mass of the Faithful in Latin. It would, he argued, be destructive of the unity of the Mass which had evolved over centuries, a unity which reflected the unity of the supreme sacrificial act which in itself promises unity and completeness. The Mass simultaneously gave adoration and thanksgiving, he wrote, and 'the edification and inspiration which can be derived from the actual words of this offering are in a sense secondary and the literal understanding of them is by no means essential to the worshipper. Otherwise, we should be stigmatising the devoted worship of countless millions in many ages as worthless'. By providing liturgical manuals and visual aids, and involvement through the *Dialogue* and *Commentary*, the Church had encouraged a fuller participation 'while preserving the great Latin tradition'. Meanwhile, the 1958 Decree *Musica Sacra* had achieved 'a norm of intelligent participation'. He asked: 'Is anything further either necessary or desirable?'

To those who argued that apathy enveloped the vast majority of Sunday congregations and was a cause of lapsation, he replied that the reasons for apathy and defections could not be proved and participation of mind and heart were of far greater importance than being vocal. To those who claimed that Latin was a 'formidable roadblock to conversion', he responded by saying that it had not stopped him. He continued: 'if a man is put off from becoming a Catholic by anything so trivial as a question of language certainly he has not got the gift of faith. I have yet to meet a convert who was deterred from joining the Church by its Latin tongue. On the contrary, it has an impelling dignity and action'. To those who asserted that the Catholic vernacular movement was a threat to English Protestantism, he commented that compared with the 'bathos' of many Catholic English translations, the dignified English of the Book of Common Prayer and the Authorised Version of the Bible 'would establish the Protestant ascendancy for years to come'.

To Wheeler, the Mass was not primarily didactic; rather, 'It is the supreme act of worship'. Its true meaning could be taught in sermons and catechetical instructions. The importance of true instruction was over-looked and here was the real need. 'This is surely of far greater importance and having incomparably more far-reaching results than this minor issue can ever have. Believe me—and I know from my own experience in the Church of England—that the vernacular is no universal panacea'.[66]

In late 1964, following the promulgation of the Constitution on the Sacred Liturgy, Wheeler again addressed the issue in 'The Council: the Mass and the Vernacular'. By this time, definite principles had been laid down regarding the use of the vernacular and could be implemented at the discretion of local hierarchies. All Catholics, wrote Wheeler, should welcome this 'important and magnificent decree' which 'is destined under God's guidance and with our co-operation' to achieve something of the *aggiorna-mento* promised by Pope John XXIII. More than anything else, he wrote, liturgical reform was designed to reinvigorate Christian life, adapt to modern times those institutions subject to change, and encourage ecumenism.

The Hierarchy had to decide how much of the vernacular was really needed and as if by way of a warning to the bishops, Wheeler asked: 'What is the real feeling of the laity about all this?' He scorned the idea 'so commonly fomented by the liturgical enthusiasts' that laity 'are avidly awaiting the vernacular in the Mass'. This did not ring true in England and Wales where many cradle Catholics were aghast at the very thought of the overthrow of tradition while many converts who 'found stability and security in the lingual unity of the Mass are distressed beyond measure at the thought of a change which could spell loss.' Many know, he wrote, that 'familiarity with words does not always deepen the realisation of acts'. The Latin Mass was a symbol of the Faith and the history of Catholics in the British Isles had made them 'afraid of losing one jot or tittle of that for which we have lived and often died'. He added: 'It will take time for us to adapt to those distinctions between doctrine and discipline which are more clearly evident to other people'.

He then asked: 'How much of the vernacular do the laity in this country really need in the Mass?' and answered by citing the contemporary use of bi-lingual missals and the reading of the Epistle and Gospel and the restored Prayer of the Faithful in English. Beyond this, he asked, what more was necessary? He referred to the kind of vernacular to be employed and was especially anxious that it held its own with the 'incomparable non-Catholic versions'. 'Our separated brethren', he continued, 'have had four hundred years in which to experiment in these matters and it would certainly be in accord with the Decree for the whole of this matter to be treated ecumenically. The form of any vernacular responses or canticles should surely be in accord with the country's highest traditions' which were linked closely 'to the translations used by our Catholic forefathers'. Anglican translations had a universal currency in the English-speaking world and the introduction of the vernacular in the Catholic Church 'could be a chance to further a common tongue amongst all English-speaking Christians'. One item of liturgical reform which particularly worried Wheeler was the merits and continued use of the terms 'Thee' and 'Thou'. Would these 'hieratic' and 'sacral' forms relating to an unchanging God, he asked, 'be sacrificed for a modern basic English which itself is constantly changing?'

He concluded on a note of cautious optimism. Recognising the innate conservatism of the English and Welsh hierarchy, he was confident that no hasty or irrevocable decisions would be made. The feeling in some quarters that 'the more vernacular the better' would be far remote from those who had the responsibility for making so important a decision. He thought that the bishops would confine themselves to Low Mass and not to Sung or Solemn Masses where so much specialist guidance was necessary. The Church, he concluded, had not imposed a radical interpretation on the use of the vernacular but 'wisely orders that they should be adopted locally and in many different contexts and without undue haste. He concluded: 'Those who are apprehensive—and they are not a few—can take heart from this and know that it will be done for God's glory and man's betterment in the fullness of time'.[67]

A year earlier, Abbot Christopher Butler had written to Wheeler regarding the use of English in the Mass—an especially sensitive issue at the Cathedral, the centre of Catholic liturgical practice in the country. 'I am thankful that you are keeping an eye on the quality of English for the Mass', he wrote, 'It's a horribly tricky matter, especially in these days of stylistic decadence'. With his Anglican background to the fore, he concluded: 'Personally, I should like to see us plundering Cranmer's magnificent liturgical English'.[68] Wheeler too looked to his Anglican roots and the dignity of Cranmer's English but saw another positive dimension to its adoption. In January 1964, he wrote to Cardinal Bea on the implementation of the vernacular informing him that he was trying very hard 'to persuade our Hierarchy how ecumenical a thing this could be if they were to appropriate the wonderful wealth of literary culture which Anglicans have developed in the Book of Common Prayer'. He called upon the Cardinal to speak to any members of the Hierarchy he might encounter, 'in favour of the adoption of a vernacular which would be so according to the mind and word of Pope John and Pope Paul'. It could become, he concluded, 'a common language between us and all our separated brethren'.[69]

A Successor to Cardinal Godfrey

Cardinal William Godfrey died on 22 January 1963 and Wheeler became immediately involved in the preparation of the Cathedral and its staff for the Cardinal's obsequies and solemn requiem. While this activity was expected, the inclusion of Wheeler's name in the list of possible successors to Godfrey was quite unexpected.

In his capacity as Administrator of the Cathedral, Wheeler delivered his own panegyric on the late Cardinal. His comments were realistic yet kind and accurately reflected Godfrey's mild manner and his old-fashioned brand of Catholicism. The Cardinal's death, he said, 'marks the end of a very simple and pious man who was noted for his imperturbable and measured wisdom'. He was 'venerated in all circles' and exerted a tremendous influence over English Catholic life for a quarter of a century but his traditional approach and demeanour was not to everyone's liking and taste. Cardinal Godfrey's faith, Wheeler noted, was 'rock-like' but to some this was 'the epitome of a kind of dye-hard intransigence'. He was utterly obedient to the papacy even when asked or directed to implement something he did not understand. Godfrey, he concluded, 'somehow was of another age'.[70]

It was assumed and hoped by some that Godfrey's successor would be a modern bishop more suited to the contemporary world rather than past times. So traditional was he, that the Second Vatican Council alarmed him. Douglas Woodruff wrote that 'Cardinal Godfrey would have been far more at home at the First Vatican Council'.[71] There were a few outstanding contenders and because of his position at the Cathedral, Wheeler was perhaps more anxious than most to get the right man. Archbishop Heenan of Liverpool and Bishop Beck of Salford were the front-runners. Wheeler kept his ear to the ground: '... there seems to be no sign of a new Archbishop', he told Dom Iltud Evans; 'I get the impression from talking to other bishops of the English Hierarchy, that they do not want Heenan. I think their choice would be Beck...'[72] Newspapers canvassed names, analysed credentials and added other possibilities. Archbishop Heenan, Bishop Beck and Abbot Christopher Butler were among those whose names were most frequently mentioned but so too was Wheeler's. In *The Observer*, 'Pendennis' wrote that 'it was most likely that a man with a national reputation will become Archbishop of Westminster' and the most obvious candidate was Archbishop Heenan, 'the celebrated fifty-seven year old Archbishop of Liverpool'. However, Pendennis continued: 'Another well-favoured candidate is MONSIGNOR GORDON WHEELER of Westminster Cathedral. He may not have a national reputation, but, he too, would be the first man of exceptional talent to be chosen Archbishop (and hence in due course a Cardinal) since HINSLEY'. Both Heenan and Wheeler had established themselves as 'Christian Unity men' and each had singular strengths and characteristics. Heenan had developed a masterly manner on television; he was a good dialectician and an outstanding orator; and, importantly, had a sound record of episcopal success. However, his Irish name and background was considered a problem as, rather perversely, was the fact that he had been 'almost too successful at Liverpool'. Wheeler, on the other hand, was in the great tradition of the convert Churchmen of the nineteenth century and as Heenan had been inspired by Cardinal Hinsley, Wheeler had been inspired by Cardinal Newman. 'Pendennis' continued: 'Though very much the Catholic intellectual without as yet any popular following, Gordon Wheeler has shown he has exceptional administrative ability since he took over the administration of the Cathedral'. To support this, it was stated that Wheeler ran the Cathedral like clockwork and that over 20,000 people passed through its doors every week to attend scores of Masses. In addition, Wheeler was a notable preacher and an inspired pastor. There were, however, three serious handicaps to his candidacy: first, he was a convert; second, he was an intellectual and as such 'would make other bishops feel insecure'; and finally the odds on him being chosen were too long as he had not yet worn a mitre.[73] Abbot Butler wrote that while he was 'not unduly worried by the risk of being sent to Westminster' he was aware that Wheeler 'was also in the running…'[74] He later wrote: 'Like you, I prefer Heenan to any of the other bishops. He will have to contend with his temperament and his upbringing and past. But at least he can see things with his intellect, even if he can't translate the truth into feeling'.[75] In line with most predictions, Heenan was appointed Archbishop of Westminster by Pope Paul VI on 2 September 1963 while Wheeler remained in his post at the Cathedral.

No sooner had Archbishop Heenan arrived at Westminster, where he received 'a great welcome on all sides', than he was on his way to Rome to attend the Second Session of the Vatican Council which opened on 29 September. Bishop Craven, wrote Wheeler to Dom Rudesind Brookes, 'was to rule the diocese' until the Archbishop returned. Reflecting on the fact that Abbot Butler had been overlooked for Westminster, Wheeler hoped that he would be given a post to match his abilities: 'I will be sorry to see him sent to a lesser See than Westminster. I think he is far more important as Abbot of Downside'. He hoped that 'Heenan will bring him even more into things'.[76]

One of the major Council debates during this session was on the ecclesial position of non-Catholic Christians and the Catholic Church's relations with other Churches. During the debate, Heenan said that Catholics must work for the conversion of 'our separated brethren' and that 'Rome could never be satisfied until they have become one with us'. In England, the Anglican newspaper, *The Church Times*, seized upon Heenan's remarks as a betrayal of his earlier and more sensitive understanding of the Anglican position. Wheeler was quick to defend the Archbishop. *The Church Times*, he wrote, appeared to 'impugn the good faith' of the Archbishop and had misunderstood the true nature of the debate which was not about ecumenism but about the nature of the Church itself (*De Ecclesia*) and its mission to proclaim the faith to all mankind. At the centre of the misunderstanding, he argued, was the use of the word 'conversion' which, he said, Heenan had not used. He concluded: 'It is sad to read expressions which cannot but be hurtful to the ecumenical cause and the more so since Dr Heenan himself is well known for studiously avoiding wounding phrases'. The editor was unconvinced: more than one source, some of whom were present at the debate, affirmed that Heenan spoke of the obligation to work for the conversion of separated brethren.[77] Wheeler saw no reason to change his opinion. He had re-read the Latin text of the debate and said that Heenan had used the word '*reconciliatio*'; he spoke therefore, not of conversion but of reconciliation. The Archbishop, he averred, remained committed to dialogue.[78]

Notes

1   M. de la Bedoyere, *Cardinal Bernard Griffin* (London: Rockliff, 1955), p. 117; *Catholic Herald*, 29 Jan 1954.

2   *Westminster Cathedral Chronicle*, vol. XLV, no. 2, Feb. 1954.

3   Duchemin to Wheeler, 20 Jan 1954. LDA, WPC, Letters Early 1950s.

4   W. G. Wheeler, *In Truth and Love* (Southport: Gowland and Co., 1990), p. 64.

5   LDA, WPC, Other Bishops; Wheeler, *In Truth and Love*, p.64.

6   P. Doyle, *Westminster Cathedral 1895–1995* (London: Geoffrey Chapman, 1995), p. 100.

7   Doyle, *Westminster Cathedral 1895–1995*, pp. 98–99.

8   Wheeler to McLaughlin, 16 Oct 1956. LDA, WDC, Westminster Personal.

9   *Daily Telegraph*, 21 Aug 1956.

10   B. Plumb, *Arundel to Zabi* (Warrington, 1987).

11   Wheeler, *In Truth And Love*, pp. 70–71. See also *The Tablet* 16 Nov 2014.

12   Doyle, *Westminster Cathedral 1895–1995*, pp. 86–91; Wheeler, *In Truth and Love*, pp. 67–69.

13   Wheeler, *In Truth And Love*, p. 68.

14   H. Johnson, *Roy de Maistre: The English Years 1930–1968* (New South Wales: Craftsman House, 1995), pp. 141–143.

15   Johnson, *Roy de Maistre: The English Years*, pp. 145–147.

16   I am grateful to Archbishop Arthur Roche for this reference.

17   Doyle, *Westminster Cathedral 1895–1995*, p. 90.

18   W. G. Wheeler, *More Truth And Love* (Southport: Gowland and Co., 1994), pp. 39–40. Giacomo Manzù sculpted the relief of St Thérèse. I am grateful to Archbishop Arthur Roche for this reference.

19   Wheeler, *In Truth And Love*, p. 69.

20   Doyle, *Westminster Cathedral 1895–1995*, pp. 66–67.

21   Doyle, *Westminster Cathedral 1895–1995*, pp. 106–107. An offshoot of the Unity Octave was that Wheeler was invited by the American Friars of the Atonement to preach at their Unity Octave at Providence Cathedral, Rhode Island, in January 1959. Wheeler took the opportunity to visit New York, Washington and Boston. In New York, he went to see the musical *My Fair Lady*. 'Priests are allowed to go to the theatre in New York', he recorded. He flew to the United States but came back on the liner *Queen Elizabeth*. LDA, WPC, Oddments.

22   Wheeler to Dilworth Harrison, 5 Sept 1956. LDA, WDC, Westminster Personal.

23   Wheeler to Dilworth Harrison, 28 Oct 1956. LDA, WDC, Westminster Personal.

24   Griffin to Archbishop O'Hara, 18 June 1955. AAW, G.1–5, Apostolic Delegate. See M. Yelton, *The South India Controversy and the Converts of 1955–1956: An Episode in Recent Anglo-Catholic History* (London: Anglo-Catholic History Society, 2010).

25   W. G. Wheeler, 'The Catholic Attitude to the Anglican Approach'. LDA, WPC, Ecumenism.

26   W. G. Wheeler, 'Chair of Union Octave', 18 Jan 1958. LDA, WPC, Ecumenism.

27   W. G. Wheeler, 'Chair of Union Octave', Jan 1960. LDA, WPC, Ecumenism.

28   W. G. Wheeler, 'Token For Good: Some Reflections on the Council and Unity' in *The Tablet* , 13 Oct 1962.

29   LDA, WPC, Ecumenism. W.G. Wheeler, 'The Council and Unity' (no date). LDA, WPC, Ecumenism.

30   'The Background to the Secretariat for Promoting Christian Unity'. SDA, Holland Papers, F.141; A. Hastings, *A History of English Christianity 1920–1985* (London: Collins, 1986), p. 522.

31   T. F. Stransky, *'The Foundation of the Secretariat for Christian Unity'* in A. Stacpoole, *Vatican II by those who were there*, (London: Continuum, 1986), pp. 62–67.

32   J. C. Heenan, *A Crown of Thorns* (London: Hodder and Stoughton, 1974), p. 320.

33   Heenan, *A Crown of Thorns*, p. 324.

34   Bea to Holland, 7 July 1961. SDA, Holland Papers, F141.

35   Heenan, *A Crown of Thorns*, pp. 322–323.

36   Heenan to Hierarchy, 15 Aug 1962. LDA, WDC, Westminster Administration.

37   Heenan to Wheeler, 21 April 1962; Heenan to Hierarchy, 15 Aug 1962. LDA, WDC, Westminster Administration.

38   Godfrey to Wheeler, 30 June 1962. LDA, WDC, W55.

39   Leeming to Wheeler, 27 July 1962. LDA, WDC, W55.

40   W. G. Wheeler, 'English Catholicism and the Anglican Tradition' (typescript), 7 Aug 1962. LDA, WDC, Westminster Administration.

41   Leeming to Wheeler, 15 Aug 1962. LDA, WDC, Westminster Administration.

42   Albion to Wheeler, 28 Nov 1962. LDA, WDC, W55.

43   *The Tablet*, 18 Aug 1962.

44   Heenan to Hierarchy, 15 Aug 1962. LDA, WDC, Westminster Administration.

45   Report on the Heythrop Conference, 15 Aug 1962. ALA, GHC, SI/II/A/44.

46   Heenan to Wheeler, 10 Jan 1963. LDA, WDC, Westminster Administration.

47   Heenan to Wheeler, 23 Aug 1962. LDA, WDC, Westminster Administration.

48   Wheeler to Bea, 5 Sept 1962. LDA, WDC, W55.

49   Wheeler to Bea, 15 Feb 1963. LDA, WDC, Westminster Administration.

50   Ramsey to Wheeler, Low Sunday, 1963. LDA, WDC, Westminster Administration.

51   Wheeler to Bea, 3 May 1963. LDA, WDC, Westminster Administration.

52   Butler to Wheeler, 5 March 1963. LDA, WDC, Westminster Personal.

53   Doyle, *Westminster Cathedral 1895 -1995*, p. 107.

54   Wheeler to Dilworth Harrison, 17 May 1963. LDA, WDC, Westminster Personal.

55   Wheeler to Bea, 24 May 1963. LDA, WDC, Westminster Administration.

56   Satterthwaite to Wheeler, 24 Sept 1963. LDA, WDC, Westminster Administration.

57   Duchemin to Wheeler, 24 May 1963. LDA, WDC, Westminster Personal.

58   E. Norman, *Roman Catholicism in England* (Oxford: Oxford University Press, 1986). p. 129.

59   G. Alberigo, *A Brief History of Vatican II* (Maryknoll, New York: Orbis Books, 2008), p. 1; Y. Congar, 'A Last look at the Council' in A. Stacpoole, *Vatican II by those who were there*, p. 338; *The Tablet*, 31 Jan. 1959.

60   Statement by Cardinal Tardini, 29 June 1959. ALA, GHC, SI/II/A/7.

61   Butler to Wheeler, 14 Sept 1962. LDA, WPC, Vatican II.

62   Wheeler to Butler, 2 Dec 1963. DAA, Butler Papers.

63   Alberigo, *A Brief History of Vatican II*, pp. 13–16, 21.

64   W. G. Wheeler, BBC *Christian Outlook*, 7 June 1963. LDA. WPC. The Popes.

65   Doyle, *Westminster Cathedral 1895 -1995*, pp. 98–99.

66   W. G. Wheeler, 'The Vernacular Question', Aug 1960. LDA, WPC, Articles.

67   W. G. Wheeler, 'The Council: the Mass and the Vernacular'. 1964. LDA, WPC, Articles.

68   Butler to Wheeler, 28 Feb 1963. DAA, Butler Papers.

69   Wheeler to Bea, 31 Jan 1964. LDA, WDC, Westminster Administration.

70   LDA, WPC, Articles; LDA, WPC, Other Bishops.

71   Quoted in Plumb, *Arundel to Zabi*.

72   Wheeler to Evans, 17 May 1963. LDA, WDC, Westminster Personal.

73   *The Observer*, 27 Jan 1963.

74   Butler to Wheeler, 5 March 1963. LDA, WDC, Westminster Personal.

75   Butler to Wheeler, 10 Sept 1963. LDA, WDC, Westminster Personal.

76   Wheeler to Brookes, 20 Sept 1963. LDA, WDC, Westminster Personal.

77   *The Church Times*, 18 Oct 1963.

78   *The Church Times*, 1 Nov 1963.

6 COADJUTOR BISHOP OF MIDDLESBROUGH

The Pope's Choice

O N 25 JANUARY 1964, Wheeler was invited to lunch with Archbishop Igino Cardinale, the newly appointed Apostolic Delegate, at his residence in Wimbledon. Before lunch, the Archbishop took him to one side and said: 'The Holy Father would like you to become the Coadjutor Bishop of Middlesbrough in Yorkshire. Would you be ready to say *Volo* or *Nolo*—Yes or No to that?' Seeing that Wheeler was taken by surprise, Cardinale asked him if he would like time to think about it. Probably to Cardinale's relief, Wheeler quickly replied: 'No, I wouldn't want any time to think about anything the Holy Father had asked me to do.' Therefore, after twenty-four years in the Diocese of Westminster, Wheeler found himself destined to return to the north of England as Coadjutor to Bishop George Brunner with right of succession.[1]

Wheeler returned to the Cathedral in a state of shock. The appointment, he recorded, 'had come out of the blue' and he immediately looked for a map of Yorkshire to locate Middlesbrough. As a native of the West Riding of Yorkshire, he was familiar with some parts of the county but not Teesside and certainly not the steel producing town of Middlesbrough.[2] He later wrote to Fr Michael Hollings at the Catholic Chaplaincy in Oxford that 'The whole thing was a great shock and could only have been thought up by the Good Lord himself, and so, as you can imagine I unhesitatingly said "Yes"'.[3]

Many of Wheeler's colleagues, friends and acquaintances felt it highly likely that he would eventually be raised to the episcopate. His appointment to Middlesbrough, however, came at a time of change for the Diocese of Westminster and may have had as much to do with the newly appointed Archbishop Heenan clearing the diocesan decks as with Wheeler's personal qualities, pastoral experience and successful stewardship of Westminster Cathedral. Whether Heenan manoeuvred Wheeler out of Westminster or not is open to debate. Certainly, the Archbishop knew Wheeler from Westminster Cathedral; he knew of his contacts among influential Catholic clerical and lay figures; and he knew of his ecumenical leanings and his close friendship with senior Anglicans. He would also have been aware that Wheeler had been considered as a possible but unlikely successor to Cardinal Godfrey. Wheeler was indeed a powerful, well-connected and popular behind-the-scenes figure but there is no reason to suggest he would be disloyal to his new Archbishop for, as we have seen, he had only recently defended him in the *Church Times*. It was Heenan's style, however, to sweep into a diocese and impose his authority and the quickest and easiest way to do this was by moving priests. The *Catholic Herald* described Heenan as a 'Dynamo in Bishop's Robes'.[4]

Changes were therefore expected following Heenan's appointment to Westminster in September 1963 and one of the most high profile translations came in 1964 when Mgr Derek Worlock, who had been secretary to both Cardinal Griffin and Cardinal Godfrey, was moved to a parish in Stepney. It was seen by many as the marginalisation of a talented, knowledgeable and highly influential priest who had been at the centre of Westminster affairs for twenty years but who was a possible threat to Heenan's authority.[5] Longley, however, writes that Heenan had raised various possibilities for Worlock's future but that Worlock himself chose to become a parish priest realising that such experience was necessary if he were to become a bishop.[6] The Cathedral too was affected by Heenan's arrival. Wheeler told his father that: 'Things are moving very fast here under the magic wand of the new Archbishop'.[7] Using a different metaphor, he wrote to Mgr Curtin at the Beda: 'The hatchet is out here, and to our great sorrow we are losing Francis Bartlett our Sub-Administrator. He has been appointed to (Our Lady of The Assumption) Warwick Street'. He concluded: 'Pray for us all'. To Abbot Butler he wrote: 'Axes are falling in all directions'. Bartlett and Wheeler had enjoyed a 'perfect partnership' for a decade but the Sub-Administrator had been ordained for thirty years and, according to Wheeler, Heenan correctly felt it was time for him to assume 'his own responsibilities'.[8]

As is customary with episcopal appointments, no public announcement is made until Vatican ratification is received and so Wheeler had to wait for nearly three weeks and continue as Administrator of the Cathedral until his preferment to Middlesbrough was announced. On 11 February, the Feast of Our Lady of Lourdes, he informed Archbishop Heenan that his appointment was to be announced during the day. Heenan would have known that Wheeler's appointment was in the offing for he said: "Oh, it's come through has it?" At noon, Heenan and Wheeler met with colleagues in the priests' Common Room at Clergy House where Heenan, according to custom, placed a zucchetto, or skullcap, on the new bishop's head.[9]

Reactions

Once news of his appointment became public, Wheeler was overwhelmed with congratulations and messages of goodwill from prelates, priests, parishioners, students, schoolboys, friends and converts. His replies were gracious but he only revealed his true feelings to his closest friends.

On behalf of the Middlesbrough Diocesan Chapter, Provost William Brunner, Bishop Brunner's brother, assured Wheeler 'of a very sincere welcome to Middlesbrough'[10] while Fr Mark Crowley of Sacred Heart parish, Middlesbrough, wrote: 'You will find the people of Middlesbrough a friendly, lovable people and you need not have the slightest fear but that you will experience tremendous joy in working for them and with them'.[11]

Cardinal Bea sent his congratulations and good wishes[12] while from his Roman *alma mater* the telegram was short and succinct: 'The Beda is honoured in the dignity which is yours'.[13] Archbishop Grimshaw of Birmingham telegrammed: 'Praise to God for these Godly and Comfortable tidings'.[14] From Leeds, Bishop George Patrick Dwyer wrote that he was delighted at the news and 'still more at the prospect of you being in the Northern Province'.[15] The Jesuit Archbishop Thomas Roberts, formerly Archbishop of Bombay and now Titular Bishop of Sugdaea, wrote, 'we who are titular bishops do not usually know very much about our spiritual brides' but, he added, 'I know well enough about the Catholics of the north east to congratulate you on that connection and to pray that it may bring you every happiness'.[16] Archbishop David Mathew told Wheeler than he could not be Coadjutor to 'a pleasanter and nicer man' than Bishop Brunner but warned 'don't expect too much of your cathedral if by any chance you have not seen it'.[17] Archbishop Joseph Walsh of Tuam penned a fulsome tribute:

> Not for a long time have I heard any news that gives me greater pleasure than the news of your Lordship's appointment as Coadjutor Bishop of Middlesbrough. To my mind, nobody could be more suited or more competent, and I feel sure that your Lordship will do very good work indeed.[18]

Like Archbishop Walsh, Abbot Christopher Butler could not conceal his joy but for a different reason:

> I suppose your birth in Yorkshire had something to do with their
> choosing you for this diocese; I should have liked you to have gone
> to Salford. The main thing is that you have broken the 'closed
> shop' and have become our fifth column in the episcopal citadel.
> This delights me.

He rejoiced 'that Ampleforth will have you for their Father in God'.[19]
Dom James Forbes of Ampleforth, like Wheeler a chaplain of the
Sovereign Order of Malta, confirmed this sentiment when he told the
new Bishop that 'a wave of rejoicing' swept through the monastery at the
news of his appointment[20] while Abbot Basil Hume offered him a
pre-consecration retreat.[21]

The Tablet reported that those connected with Wheeler in the
Westminster diocese, at the Cathedral and the University Chaplaincy,
were generous in their appreciation of his various contributions. His
appointment as Cathedral Administrator had been one of Cardinal
Griffin's inspired appointments and his ten years' administration had been
'remarkable'. Those privileged to live in the parish were blessed with the
excellence of all his arrangements and 'the lightly touched combination
of humanity and efficiency'. The report concluded: 'Lucky the North'.[22]

Archbishop Heenan wrote that as Cathedral Administrator, Wheeler
was responsible for 'the smooth precision of all Cathedral functions' which
'were never late, never hurried and never slipshod'. He had never been
satisfied simply to maintain the best traditions of the Cathedral's liturgy but
had placed them within the context of and at the disposal of the ever-
increasing numbers of Londoners and tourists who attended the Cathedral
services. The Cathedral had won 'world-wide recognition as a centre of
liturgical worship' and this was due to Wheeler's inspiration and application:

> Everything in the Cathedral is geared to the needs of the faithful.
> Westminster is renowned for its ability to provide a splendid setting
> for great national events. But this has not prevented the Adminis-
> trator from catering for the spiritual needs of the humblest visitor.
> Perhaps future generations will thank him most for making sure that
> at any hour of the day a priest is available in the Cathedral to hear
> confessions and give counsel and consolation to those in distress.

'London will bid him farewell with the utmost reluctance', concluded
Heenan[23] but this may not have been an entirely honest sentiment. The
new Archbishop was anxious to proceed with the liturgical changes
ushered in by Vatican II and these conflicted with Vaughan's vision of

Westminster Cathedral so strongly championed by the Administrator. Wheeler's tenure at the Cathedral had been successful from many points of view and Doyle argues that he probably left at the right time for it was difficult to see how Wheeler could have worked comfortably with Heenan. In particular, he did not agree with the rapidity with which the Archbishop pushed ahead with experimental liturgical changes and called for a longer period of preparation of the people. Wheeler complained to Heenan that the new liturgical arrangements were out of sympathy with Vaughan's vision and the Cathedral was now regarded as a 'glorified parish church'. The Second Vatican Council, he argued, had not required the abandonment of the Cathedral's monastic liturgical tradition but Heenan retaliated by saying that the secular clergy now refused to accept it and he left further decisions about the Cathedral to the new Administrator.[24]

Roy de Maistre congratulated Wheeler and hoped that 'the translation' had made him happy but he added: '… I cannot help feeling a personal sense of loss… there will be a lamentable gap at the Cathedral when you are no longer there'.[25] The Catholic historian E. E. Reynolds wrote:

> You will no doubt have many regrets at leaving the Cathedral where you have done so much, and you will doubtless have doubts of your capacity to fill your new high office. Your friends, however, will have no such doubts and will rejoice that larger fields have been opened for you.[26]

In an obviously personal expression, Fr John Milne of Hatfield thanked Wheeler for his contribution to Cathedral affairs: 'May I say that my experience of your Administratorship was very happy and tension-free. The grey skies broke to reveal the blue skies and warm sunshine'.[27] Mgr (now Saint) Josemaria Escrivá, founder of Opus Dei, sent Wheeler a very personal letter of congratulation[28] while the Opus Dei priest Fr Cormac Burke wrote that he would miss Wheeler's 'constant aid and presence' and that 'his friendship meant a great deal'.[29] Eileen Noel spoke for many Catholic graduates when she recalled his days at the University Chaplaincy of which she retained 'very happy memories'. There was, she recalled, 'a very special privilege and intimacy about being involved in the re-establishment of a university chaplaincy in London'.[30] Beyond the Cathedral and chaplaincy, many others sent congratulatory messages. The Sovereign Order of Malta sent good wishes to one of its chaplains.[31]

There were those who alerted Wheeler to the mixed blessings of his northern appointment. Some of his correspondents spoke of it as an exile and warned him of the fog, soot and grime of the north, the lack of aesthetic pleasures, and the simple but delightful people. The *Northern Echo* reported Wheeler as saying: 'I am thrilled. I am returning to my own people',[32] but his correspondence reveals his apprehension about the move. To Freda Molyneux-Seel he wrote: 'I have been going through a very strong reaction at the thought of leaving all my friends behind, so I shall badly need your prayers'.[33] To the Franciscan Fr Ralph he wrote: 'I am going to very wild and isolated parts, but I believe the people are warm hearted'.[34] In a similar vein, he wrote to Fr Bruno Scott-James that he felt 'like Abraham setting off from Ur' and added: 'I have no house to go to at the moment in those wild parts'.[35] From Ipswich, Fr Alfred Bull, Wheeler's contemporary at the Beda, wrote: 'In all honesty I am glad it is you and not me! I hope you will be more successful than I should in finding coincidences between north-country religion and Catholicism'.[36] Wheeler replied that the whole situation 'seems improbable'; 'I rather feel as if I were setting out for the foreign missions'.[37] Twenty years later, he wrote: 'Although I was returning to my native Yorkshire, there had been an absence of something like 50 years. And in fact I felt as though I had died'.[38] He told Dom Oswald Eaves that his appointment to Middlesbrough had come as 'a great shock' and his Yorkshire birth 'seems to have been one of the things which influenced the Holy See when sending me there'.[39]

The Scottish-born Cardinal William Theodore Heard, resident in Rome and himself a convert, wrote: 'You will find the hard headed Yorkshiremen rather a change from Westminster; but I believe you yourself are from the north, and whether or no, I am quite sure you will know how to tackle them.'[40] Fr Patrick McEnroe, a Middlesbrough priest based with the BBC in Manchester, admitted to Wheeler that it was 'impossible to think that a Londoner can have unmixed feelings about this move—the North and East Ridings of Yorkshire must have some-thing of the appeal of Siberia'. However, he added that Wheeler's qualities were sorely needed in Middlesbrough: '... I am inclined to think of our great need of you and I hope you will be compensated by the thought that you will be able to contribute to the diocese'. Incorrectly reflecting that Wheeler was the first Bishop of Middlesbrough to come from outside the Diocese, he ended: 'We have been rather inbred, backwater sort of people—Yorkshire Irish ...But I have always believed we were capable of growth, given the leadership. And I am quite sure we will respond to your Lordship's rule'.[41] Wheeler may have expressed uncertainty about the move but must have realised that Heenan would probably have moved him from the Cathedral and sent him to other pastures in Westminster. He admitted that a change would be beneficial: 'It's a great adventure really, and should have the effect of preventing me sinking into a rut—which one can so easily do if one is too long in one place'.[42]

Some Catholics took the opportunity to both congratulate Wheeler on his appointment and plead with him to bring his influence to bear at the Second Vatican Council. Some wished him to be progressive; others wished him to speak in favour of retaining traditional rites and customs. Abbot Butler, present at the Council as the Abbot President of the English Benedictine Congregation, wrote: 'You can be sure that you have behind you the urgent good will of those who are most alive to the real challenge and opportunity presented to the Church in this country in the second half of this century'.[43] From St Hugh's Charterhouse, Horsham, Sussex, Fr Andrew Gray reminded Wheeler of his Lancing days but brought him right up-to-date when he spoke of the Second Vatican Council which Wheeler would be attending in the autumn: 'Don't be too progressive, will you, and leave us poor converts lagging behind. Sometimes, like the late Cardinal (Godfrey), I find the pace a bit too much for me'.[44] H. P. R. Finberg, Professor of Local History at Leicester University, pleaded with Wheeler 'from his new position' to 'shield us' from the loss of the Latin Mass. 'It will be a tragedy', he wrote, using the words of Archbishop Grimshaw, 'if we throw away Latin and get in exchange something no better than the extempore prayers at a back-street meeting house'.[45] Others expressed similar concerns about the emerging liturgy. From Neuchatel, Leonard Wilde, whom Wheeler had met at Oxford, wrote that he had followed Wheeler's career with interest 'and it has certainly been a spectacular one'. However, he added in a state of frustration:

> ... if you have any influence with the Vatican do tell them to stop all these gymnastics which are taking place in the churches here. We are made to stand, and sit, and listen to long diatribes in French. The 'bad old days' when one could sit quietly and listen to the soft murmur of the Latin, and really concentrate on what was going on at the altar seem to have gone.[46]

The messages Wheeler received from his non-Catholic friends and acquaintances were equally generous and indicated the strength and warmth of Wheeler's connections and long-standing friendships outside the Catholic Church. The Lord Mayor of London sent congratulations[47] as did the United States Embassy, adding that: 'London's loss will be Middlesbrough's gain'.[48] Canon John Satterthwaite, on behalf of the Church of England's Council on Foreign Relations, wrote that the Council was delighted at his promotion 'but would be sad to see him go'.[49] No doubt echoing the sentiments of his senior Anglican colleagues, Satterthwaite lamented in a more personal letter, that 'we shan't see our beloved GW so frequently'. He added: 'We know who are our friends are and give thanks to God for these... And soon you are to be a Bishop of the Church of God. I knew it would come to you and have often said so. Dear Pope Paul must have especial love for his Anglican friends'.[50] Peter Mason, High Master of Manchester Grammar School, sent his congratulations and those of the staff and students of Wheeler's schoolboy *alma mater* and at the same time sought Wheeler's views on the place of Direct Grant Schools under a future Labour government.[51] Wheeler was unable to enlighten Mason but asked instead for an introduction to Lord Eric James of Rusholme, the former High Master of Manchester Grammar School who had recently been appointed Vice-Chancellor of the new University of York. 'I am very anxious to help in the light of the development of the University of York', he wrote.[52]

From St Deiniol's Library, Hawarden, the Warden, Dr Stewart Lawton, wrote of the responsibilities of the contemporary episcopate:

> My Dear Gordon,
>
> ... If anybody deserved recognition for wholehearted loyalty and perseverance, it is certainly you. I am well aware too that there is no worldly satisfaction in a call of this kind—all of us share the fate of being looked upon as a rather queer minority in the XXth century; and I am sure that no-one must feel this more keenly than a bishop.[53]

On 8 March, Wheeler attended a reception in his honour and four days later, less than two months after learning of his appointment, left Westminster for Teesside in a car which had been presented to him by the Diocese. He had expected that Heenan would arrange a farewell lunch but this did not materialise. His passenger on the drive north was Abbot Hume of Ampleforth where Wheeler had arranged to spend his pre-consecration retreat. Hume had called to Clergy House the day before Wheeler's departure and asked Wheeler if he would like company on the journey. Wheeler regarded this sensitive act of kindness typical of Hume and it marked the beginning of a long and fruitful friendship between the two men.[54]

The five-day silent retreat proved difficult for Wheeler so accustomed was he to the bustle of the Cathedral and being variously surrounded by bishops, priests, choristers, cathedral staff and hundreds of daily visitors. His retreat, he recalled was 'a strange experience', a preparation for a ministry completely unknown to him. He felt, he wrote, 'very isolated', 'as though I had died'. His depression almost took over until, praying in the side chapel housing the famous Ampleforth statue of Our Lady with a grin on her face, he looked at the statue and started laughing. He felt that Our Lady was laughing at him 'for being so ridiculous'. 'This', he wrote, 'broke the ice for me and I never looked back after that. I laughed all alone in the church'.[55] He was given further encouragement by the famous American evangelist Bishop Fulton Sheen, Auxiliary Bishop of New York and Director of the Society for the Propagation of the Faith, who sent his congratulations to Wheeler prior to his consecration:

> With the coming of the Holy Spirit and your consecration there will be an influx of power and spiritual dynamism which will often make you wonder at its marvels. Not in the brilliance of its ornaments, but in the soul decorated with virtue is the honour of the episcopacy—or better still its burden, for that is what it is called in the liturgy. It is a burden, however, that is sweet for it is the yoke of the Divine One by which we pull the ploughs that tear up the hard soil of rebellious hearts to make them ready for the planting of the seed that is the Word.[56]

Consecration

Wheeler's consecration as Coadjutor Bishop of Middlesbrough and Titular Bishop of Theudalis took place in 'the not unpleasing Gothic' Cathedral of St Mary's, Middlesbrough, on 19 March 1964.[57] St Mary's was begun in 1876, before the erection of the Middlesbrough Diocese, to a design by George Goldie, but was later equipped with painted altarpieces and the other accoutrements of Victorian churches to add to its dignity as a cathedral.[58] Wheeler wrote to Fr Aelred that 'some day when I have succeeded to the See, you must tell me what can be done to Middlesbrough Cathedral. You may feel that demolition is the only answer'.[59] To Mgr John Mostyn in Rome he wrote that the cathedral was 'ghastly'.[60] He had earlier written to Freda Molyneux-Seel that 'Middlesbrough is very primitive' and I don't think the Mass (of consecration) will be a sung one'.[61] He recalled, however, that:

... it was a very memorable occasion for me. St. Mary's Cathedral was filled to capacity for the event. In the nave were about 120 priests from the Middlesbrough Diocese, together with former colleagues from Westminster, representatives of other denominations and civic dignitaries from Teesside and the North and East Ridings. In the sanctuary...were Abbot Hume, Mgr Casey VG, as well as old friends from Westminster: Monsignor Canon Bartlett, Mgr Row and Fr Kilcoyne. The Bishops of Leeds, and Hexham and Newcastle, and the Auxiliary Bishop of Lancaster were also present in the sanctuary. My co-consecrators were Archbishop Cardinale, Bishop Brunner, and Bishop Craven, the Auxiliary in Westminster.[62]

'Amid scenes of colourful pageantry and ceremony' Fr Liam Carter read the Papal Bull of Appointment and the new bishop was examined as to his beliefs and intentions. Wheeler then lay prostrate before his consecration and anointing. Holy water was sprinkled over the mitre on his head. His pectoral cross had belonged to Bishop Lacey[63]; his episcopal ring had belonged to Cardinal Griffin.[64] For Archdale King, 'the most moving incident was the singing of the *Te Deum*, when his Lordship the Coadjutor Bishop... led by the assistant bishops and now for the first time vested in the full *pontificalia*, went round the church giving his blessing to the faithful of his new diocese and to his loyal friends from Westminster who had been privileged to witness the honour conferred on him by the Holy See'. After the ceremony, Wheeler and his guests drove to the Coatham Hotel, Redcar, for a celebratory lunch.[65]

There remained the matter of Wheeler's coat of arms. The Bishop had no shortage of inspiration and by mid-March 1964, a clever and meaningful design had been agreed with J. P. Brooke-Little, the Bluemantle Pursuivant of Arms. The new bishop took as his motto *Veritas et Caritas* ('In Truth and Love') from St Paul's Epistle to the Ephesians and inspired by a phrase used by Pope John XXIII—'Follow the Truth in Charity'—in connection with the ecumenical movement. The Catherine Wheels were a play on the bishop's name but also a symbol of martyrdom and a reminder that a bishop must be ready to give his life to God. The White Rose represented the county of his birth and the location of his new see while the Maltese Cross was a reminder of his link with the Sovereign Order of Malta. The martlets were the symbols of University College, Oxford, and Westminster Cathedral while the dominant colours were those of his mother's family, the Upjohns.[66]

Wheeler became a member of a comparatively young Hierarchy. Of twenty-three bishops, twelve were in their fifties, seven in their sixties, two in their seventies and two in their eighties. The oldest, Bishop John Henry King of Portsmouth, was born in 1880, ordained in 1904 and consecrated in 1938. Bishop George Craven, Auxiliary in Westminster, was born in 1884, ordained in 1912 and consecrated in 1947. Ten had been consecrated in the 1950s and 1960s and some were relatively inexperienced bishops. Most were from Irish or Anglo-Irish families and from lower middle class or working class backgrounds. Twelve had been trained abroad—nine at the English College, Rome, one at St. Sulpice, Paris, one at Louvain, and one at Valladolid. Others had been trained at English seminaries.[67] Two—Dwyer and Rudderham—had been educated at Cambridge while Cowderoy was the only convert. Wheeler, therefore, a convert with an Oxford education, was in a definite minority.[68] Abbot Christopher Butler wrote: 'I thank God that at last we have someone on the bench who shares the mind of Oxbridge—which is far more important still than might seem to be the case in these proletarian days'.[69] The dominant personality on the bench was Archbishop Heenan but all were men of independent mind, secure in attitudes and actions which were derived from their education, training and autonomous episcopal jurisdiction. Decisions taken at the Bishops' Conference were reached with no more binding force as a common policy than that of a gentleman's agreement.[70]

Coadjutor

The Diocese of Middlesbrough, in the Province of Liverpool, was erected in 1878 when the Diocese of Beverley, co-terminus with the county of Yorkshire, was divided into two dioceses centred on Middlesbrough and Leeds. Middlesbrough Diocese consisted of the North and East Ridings and the City of York north of the River Ouse.[71] The serving Bishop in 1964 was George Brunner who was born in Hull in 1889. Brunner was educated at Ushaw College and read Classics at Durham University. Ordained in 1917, he had spent all his priestly life in the Middlesbrough Diocese, initially as a curate in Hull and subsequently as parish priest in Hessle. From 1931 until 1937, he was parish priest of St Patrick's, Hull, and in 1935 became a Canon of the Diocese. From 1937 until 1951, he served as parish priest of St Charles's, Hull, and while there was consecrated, in 1946, as Titular Bishop of Elide and Auxiliary Bishop to Bishop Thomas Shine, who had been the Ordinary since 1929. In 1951, he was appointed Vicar

General and because of Bishop Shine's advanced age and infirmity, went to reside in Bishop's House. On Archbishop-Bishop Shine's death in 1955, Brunner was elected Vicar Capitular and was appointed third Bishop of Middlesbrough by Pope Pius XII in 1956. Reserved by nature but with a sense of humour, Bishop Brunner was essentially a pastoral priest, a man of prayer who quietly went about his ministry. Nonetheless, he was an active bishop and ensured the development of schools and churches in a diocese whose ports and industrial areas had been ravaged in the Second World War. For fifteen years, he was the Hierarchy's representative to Catholic women's organizations and became known as 'the Women's Bishop'.[72] At the time of Wheeler's appointment, Brunner was seventy-six years of age.[73] In his panegyric at Brunner's requiem in 1969, Wheeler remarked that the late Bishop was a prayerful, diligent, self-effacing, kind and gentle man, "Well loved by God: well loved by men".[74]

In 1964, Middlesbrough was the third smallest diocese in England and Wales with a population of 86,000—the two smaller ones being Plymouth with 46,000 and Menevia with 33,000 Catholics. By comparison, the Diocese of Liverpool had 500,000 Catholics while the Diocese of Westminster had 454,000.[75] The Diocese was served by 149 diocesan priests. Twenty-four men were in senior seminary while twenty boys were in junior seminary. The majority of seculars ministered in the urban areas of Middlesbrough, Stockton-On-Tees, Hull, York and Redcar but there were also a Catholic presence in market towns such as Malton, Richmond and Leyburn, and in seaside resorts such as Scarborough, Whitby and Bridlington. There were 129 churches and chapels for public worship but the diocese had an unusually large (thirty-eight) number of private chapels, reflecting the historical tradition of recusancy and wealthy Catholic families in the region. The Benedictines of Ampleforth Abbey provided the largest number (fifty-six) of regulars but there was also a significant Marist presence (nineteen) in Hull. There were also twenty-four convents for female religious. Marriages, baptisms, and conversions were in significant annual numbers while there were approximately 20,000 students in Catholic diocesan and independent primary and secondary schools.[76]

Bishop Brunner was often dubbed 'the quiet man'—he said little and wrote little—but his episcopacy witnessed a substantial growth of the Catholic community, an increase in churches and schools, and the introduction of more efficient methods of diocesan administration.[77] Brunner, however, was getting old and was unwell and the historian of the Middlesbrough Diocese wrote that 'The ageing bishop needed help; Rome provided it by giving a priest of great experience to be his co-helper, his Coadjutor'. On 11 February 1964, Brunner 'announced with much relief and satisfaction that Mgr. W. G. Wheeler was to be his Coadjutor, and that the Bishop-elect would have the right to succeed him'.[78] Brunner and Wheeler were very different characters and their upbringing, education and outlook contrasted sharply. Once the announcement of his prelacy had been made, Wheeler arranged to visit Brunner. His reception, he recorded, was warm and welcoming but the old bishop's vague answers to his questions about practical things such as jobs to be done and places to live were 'rather frustrating for somebody who had been used to a very business-like sort of life'. The only useful piece of advice Brunner offered was that as Wheeler was to succeed him then it might be useful to live near Middlesbrough where 80% of Catholics in the diocese lived.[79] To his friend 'Flo' Roscoe, Wheeler wrote: 'The Bishop of Middlesbrough is a dear old man who is getting rather old for the job, so I imagine I shall do most of his work for him'.[80] Brunner was so impressed by Wheeler that he is reported to have said: 'I expected a Mini, but they've sent me a Rolls'.[81] To the end Brunner was formal in his relations with his Coadjutor.

Brunner had suggested that Wheeler take up temporary residence in York[82] but accommodation was found for him at the presbytery of St Alphonsus, North Ormesby. There he lived happily with Mgr Alban Nolan and his curates for some months before a house was bought for him. He eventually settled at the lovely 1930s-style White Lodge, Newby, set in two acres of North Yorkshire farmland and overlooking the Cleveland Hills.[83] He may have missed his friends but he derived consolation from some beautiful items of furniture which they had presented to him and which now adorned his episcopal residence. He may also have been detached from his busy ministry at Westminster but there was some compensation in the wonderful scenery to be enjoyed on the drive from Newby into Middlesbrough and around his new diocese. It was, he wrote, 'small enough to be a very family affair; wide enough to present an apostolic field of great variety and beauty, and spacious enough to enable local initiative'. He came to appreciate the deep-rooted Catholic history of the diocese in which were located the ruins of great monastic abbeys such as Whitby, Byland and Rievaulx and the Charterhouse of Mount Grace. The diocese had also inherited 'much of the ethos of the

Vicars Apostolic of the North with their strong tradition of the martyrs and the great Catholic houses'. There were many areas in the diocese where the Faith had never died out and it had 'a wealth of local centres where the Faithful, in addition to the great Catholic Families, aided by apostolic priests like Blessed Nicholas Postgate, preserved the ancient truths and worship…'[84]

From Newby, Wheeler assumed his episcopal duties. Bishop Brunner did not overburden him with administrative duties for he realised it was important that his Coadjutor should get to know the diocese before succeeding him. White Lodge, therefore, became the springboard for his many subsequent visitations of the diocese. In 1964, he administered the Sacrament of Confirmation at seventeen locations and in the following year made parish visitations to Driffield, Hull, Middlesbrough, Staithes, Pocklington and Malton.[85] Carson wrote that; 'in an amazingly short time Bishop Wheeler knew every priest, every parish, and every religious house in the Diocese. And perhaps what is equally more important, his priests and religious and people all got to know him'. He became 'a familiar figure' and was able to give 'freely to all of himself, his time and his talents in his genial, courteous and most hospitable way'.[86] He became Chairman of the Diocesan Finance Committee and dealt with the prosaic but necessary practicalities of church property, accounts, insurance, and the Diocesan Housekeepers' Fund.[87] At a different level, Wheeler was appointed as the Hierarchy's representative on the central committee of the National Catholic Youth Association and, with the Bishops of Dunkeld and Portsmouth, sat on the Central Religious Advisory Committee of the Independent Television Authority.[88] They were roles that enabled Wheeler to come to terms with his wider episcopal duties and become familiar with the workings of the Hierarchy. Bishop Brunner, meanwhile, was delighted with Wheeler's assistance in the diocese. 'I appreciate you relieving me of so many burdens—I shall come to lean on you more as the days go by'. He advised him to get a holiday before leaving for the Third Session of the Second Vatican Council in the autumn of 1964.[89]

One of Wheeler's final undertakings in Middlesbrough was to acquire for the diocese the Anglican Church of St Leonard's, Malton. It was the kind of project that he loved—an ecumenical venture restoring the area's pre-Reformation past. St Leonard's had been a chapel-of-ease to the parish church of St Michael's and the Anglican authorities, faced with the rising cost of maintaining a church badly in need of restoration and repair, reluctantly decided to discontinue services at St Leonard's. The church dated from the twelfth century when it was established by the Gilbertines, the only religious order of purely English origin, and was a chapel-of-ease to the Gilbertine priory of St Mary at Malton. The priory survived until 1539 when, during the dissolution of monasteries, it finally surrendered to the Royal Commissioners but St Leonard's continued to serve the Church of England for more than another four centuries. Early in1966, Wheeler, had a meeting with the Archdeacons of York and Cleveland to see if a way could be found to allow the Catholic community of Malton to worship at St Leonard's. The result was a magnificent and unprecedented gesture whereby after the necessary Order in Council had been obtained St Leonard's was transferred into Catholic hands as a completely free gift. When the 'new' Catholic church came into use, in 1972, it bore the combined names of St Leonard and St Mary.[90]

Notes

[1]   W. G. Wheeler, *In Truth And Love* (Southport: Gowland and Co., 1990), p. 77. A Coadjutor had right of succession to his See. At this time there was only one other Coadjutor Bishop—Bishop Thomas Holland who was Coadjutor to the ageing Bishop John Henry King of Portsmouth. There were five Auxiliary bishops—two in the Archdiocese of Westminster, and one each in the Archdiocese of Birmingham and the Dioceses of Lancaster and Northampton. See *Catholic Directory* (1964), (London: Burns and Oates, 1964). Auxiliaries do not have right of succession and are usually appointed in large dioceses or where the Ordinary specifically requested assistance. Unlike Coadjutors, they have no jurisdictional authority. Coadjutors and Auxiliaries are styled 'titular bishops' in that they are consecrated to extinct sees. See *A Catholic Dictionary* (London: Burns and Oates, 1954), pp. 83–84 and 192.

[2]   Wheeler, *In Truth And Love*, p. 77.

[3]   Wheeler to Hollings, 12 Feb 1964. LDA, WDC, 28. Like Wheeler, Hollings was a former student of the Beda.

[4]   *Catholic Herald*, 13 Sept 1963.

[5]   C. Longley, *The Worlock Archive* (London: Geoffrey Chapman, 2000), p. 192.

[6]   *Ibid.*, pp. 187–188.

[7]   Wheeler to Frederick Wheeler, 31 Dec 1963. LDA, WDC, Westminster Personal.

[8]   Wheeler to Curtin, 30 Dec. 1953 and 2 Feb 1964; Wheeler to Butler, 30 Dec 1963. LDA, WDC, 54 (a).

[9]   LDA, WPC, *In Truth And Love* Transcript, Tape 3; Wheeler, *In Truth And Love*, p. 77. Wheeler's appointment was announced in the *Catholic Herald* and other Catholic papers on 14 February 1964.

10   Brunner to Wheeler, 12 Feb 1964. LDA, WDC, 28.
11   Crowley to Wheeler, 17 Feb 1964. LDA, WDC, 28; *Catholic Directory* (1964), p. 295.
12   Bea to Wheeler, 12 Feb 1964. LDA, WDC, 28.
13   Beda to Wheeler, 12 Feb 1964. LDA, WDC, 28.
14   Grimshaw to Wheeler, 12 Feb 1964. LDA, WDC, 28.
15   Dwyer to Wheeler, 12 Feb 1964. LDA, WDC, 28.
16   Roberts to Wheeler, 12 Feb 1964. LDA, WDC, 28.
17   Mathew to Wheeler, 12 Feb 1964. LDA, WDC, 28.
18   Walsh to Wheeler, 13 Feb 1964. LDA, WDC, 28.
19   Butler to Wheeler, 13 Feb 1964. LDA, WDC, 54. Dom Christopher Butler had been Abbot of Downside since 1946 and Abbot President of the English Benedictine Congregation since 1961. The Diocese of Salford became vacant when Bishop Beck replaced Heenan as Archbishop of Liverpool. See B. Plumb, *Arundel to Zabi* (Warrington, 1987).
20   Forbes to Wheeler, 12 Feb 1964. LDA, WDC, 28.
21   Hume to Wheeler, 13 Feb 1964. LDA, WDC, 28.
22   *The Tablet*, 15 Feb 1964.
23   J. C. Heenan, 'The New Bishop' in *Westminster Cathedral Chronicle*, vol. LVIII, no. 3, March 1964, p. 41.
24   Heenan to Wheeler, 14 March 1973 and Wheeler to Heenan, 19 March 1973. LDA, WDC, Westminster Personal. Long after Wheeler had left Westminster, Heenan continued to seek his advice on Cathedral matters, especially on rising costs associated with the choir. Wheeler was insistent that economies 'should not jeopardise or even reduce the liturgical traditions of the Cathedral which are the entire cause of its unique standing both nationally and internationally. In particular, it could be catastrophic from the viewpoint of the whole tradition of Catholic Church music.' See also P. Doyle, *Westminster Cathedral 1895–1995* (London: Geoffrey Chapman, 1995), pp. 109–111.
25   de Maistre to Wheeler,12 Feb 1964. LDA, WDC, 53.
26   Reynolds to Wheeler, 13 Feb 1964. LDA, WDC, 28.
27   Milne to Wheeler, 13 Feb 1964. LDA, WDC, 28.
28   Escrivá to Wheeler, 13 Feb 1964. LDA, WDC, 28.
29   Burke to Wheeler, 13 Feb 1964. LDA, WDC, 28.
30   Noel to Wheeler, 16 Feb 1964. LDA, WDC, 28.
31   Sovereign Order of Malta to Wheeler, 21 Feb 1964. LDA, WDC, 28.
32   *Northern Echo*, 12 Feb 1964.
33   Wheeler to Molyneux-Seel, 17 Feb 1964. LDA, WDC, 28.
34   Wheeler to Ralph, 17 Feb 1964. LDA, WDC, 28.
35   Wheeler to Scott-James, 17 Feb 1964. LDA, WDC, 28.
36   Bull to Wheeler, 24 Feb 1964. LDA, WDC, 28.

37 Wheeler to Bull, 26 Feb 1964. LDA, WDC, 28.

38 W. G. Wheeler, 'Twenty Years A Bishop'. LDA, WPC, Biography and Obituaries.

39 Wheeler to Eaves, 9 March 1964. LDA, WDC, Westminster Personal.

40 Heard to Wheeler, 12 Feb 1964. LDA, WDC, 28.

41 McEnroe to Wheeler, 14 Feb 1964. LDA, WDC, 28. Bishop Richard Lacy, first Bishop of Middlesbrough had gone to Middlesbrough from St Patrick's, Bradford, in 1872. Both towns were then in the Diocese of Beverley. Thomas Shine, second Bishop of Middlesbrough had gone as Coadjutor to Bishop Lacy in 1921 from St Anne's Cathedral, Leeds. He was given the personal dignity and title of Archbishop by Pope Pius XII in 1955. See Plumb, *Arundel to Zabi*.

42 Wheeler to Greensmith, 27 Feb 1964. LDA, WDC, 28.

43 Butler to Wheeler, 13 Feb. 1964. LDA, WDC, 54.

44 Gray to Wheeler, 18 Feb 1964. LDA, WDC, 28.

45 Finberg to Wheeler, 12 Feb 1964. LDA, WDC, 28.

46 Wilde to Wheeler, 18 Feb 1964. LDA, WDC, 28.

47 Farmiloe to Wheeler, 13 Feb 1964. LDA, WDC, 28.

48 US Embassy to Wheeler, 12 Feb 1964. LDA, WDC, 28.

49 Satterthwaite to Wheeler, 12 Feb 1964. LDA, WDC, 28.

50 Satterthwaite to Wheeler, 13 Feb 1964. LDA, WDC, 28.

51 Mason to Wheeler, 15 Feb 1964. LDA, WDC, 28.

52 Wheeler to Mason, 17 Feb 1964. LDA, WDC, 28.

53 Lawton to Wheeler, 17 Feb 1964. LDA, WDC, 28.

54 LDA, WDC, 28.

55 LDA, WPC, *In Truth And Love* Transcript, Tape 3; Wheeler, *In Truth And Love*, pp. 78–79; *Catholic Herald*, 28 March 1984.

56 Fulton Sheen to Wheeler, 11 March 1964. LDA, WDC, 52.

57 LDA, WDC, W5; A. A. King, 'The Consecration of Bishop Wheeler' in *Westminster Cathedral Chronicle*, April 1964, p. 70. Theudalis was a see in Carthage during the days of Imperial Rome. Archdale Arthur King was a graduate of Keble College, Oxford, who trained for the Anglican ministry at St Stephen's House, Oxford. He converted to Catholicism in 1914. It is likely that Wheeler came across him in through the Converts Aid Society. When King died in 1972, Wheeler said his requiem in St Anne's Cathedral, Leeds. The Mass was in the Tridentine Rite and Wheeler wore black vestments. Wheeler was instrumental in the winding up of King's estate.

58 B. Little, *Catholic Churches Since 1623* (London: Robert Hale, 1966), p. 97.

59 Wheeler to Fr Aelred, 26 Feb 1964. LDA, WDC, 28.

60 Wheeler to Mostyn, 18 Feb 1964. LDA, WDC, Westminster Personal.

61 Wheeler, *In Truth And Love*, p. 77.

62 *Ibid.*, pp. 80–81.

63 *Northern Echo*, 20 March 1964.

64   Confident that they would both become bishops, Cardinal Griffin bequeathed his
      ring and pectoral cross to Mgr Wheeler and Mgr Worlock. Whoever was consecrated
      first had choice of the items. Wheeler took the ring. On his death, it was returned
      to the Cardinal Archbishop of Westminster. When Mgr Arthur Roche, Bishop
      Wheeler's secretary in Leeds, was created Auxiliary Bishop in Westminster in 2001,
      Cardinal Cormac Murphy-O'Connor gave him the ring. I am grateful to Archbishop
      Roche for this information. Paul Kennedy claims that Griffin 'gave his ring to Gordon
      Wheeler and his pectoral cross to Derek Worlock' who was 'a close friend' of Wheeler.
      This is a different slant on the story. It is also debatable that Wheeler and Worlock
      were close friends. See P. Kennedy, *The Catholic Church in England and Wales,
      1500–2000* (Keighley: PBK Publishing, 2001), p. 269.

65   King, 'The Consecration of Bishop Wheeler' in *Westminster Cathedral Chronicle*,
      April 1964, p.70.

66   Brooke-Little to Wheeler, 18 and 20 March 1964. LDA, WDC, 28. Brooke-Little
      was a Knight of Malta. *The Universe*, 13 March 1964.

67   *Catholic Directory* (1964); Plumb, *Arundel to Zabi*. In 1964, bishops were not
      compelled by the Holy See to retire at the age of 75.

68   *Catholic Directory* (1964); Plumb, *Arundel to Zabi*.

69   Butler to Wheeler, 13 Feb 1964. LDA, WDC, 54.

70   D. Worlock, *English Bishops at the Council: Third Session* (London: Burns and Oates,
      1965), p. 43.

71   R. E. Finnigan and J. Hagerty, *The Bishops of Leeds—Essays in Honour of Bishop David
      Konstant* (Leeds: PBK Publications on behalf of the Diocese of Leeds, 2005), p. 9.

72   Anthony Bickerstaffe to Wheeler, 23 March 1969. LDA, WDC, 38.

73   Plumb, *Arundel to Zabi*

74   *Middlesbrough Diocesan Yearbook (1970)* (Middlesbrough: 1970).

75   *Catholic Directory* (1964), p. 768.

76   *Catholic Directory* (1964), p. 306.

77   R. Carson, *The First Hundred Years: A History of the Diocese of Middlesbrough
      1878–1978* (Middlesbrough: Middlesbrough Diocesan Trustees, 1978), pp. 268,
      270–271.

78   Carson, *The First Hundred Years*, p. 281.

79   Wheeler, *In Truth And Love*, p. 78.

80   Wheeler to 'Flo' Roscoe, 12 Feb 1964. LDA, WDC, 28.

81   *The Tablet*, 28 Feb 1998.

82   Wheeler to Mostyn, 18 Feb 1964. LDA, WDC, Westminster Personal.

83   LDA, WDC, 10. White Lodge Sale Catalogue. White Lodge was sold by the
      Diocese in 1969. AAW, He4/M.4/2.

84   LDA, WPC, Other Bishops. W. G. Wheeler, 'Panegyric for the late Bishop
      McClean of Middlesbrough' (1978). The diocese claimed connection with twenty-
      nine martyrs of the sixteenth and seventeenth centuries. See R. Connelly, *No Greater
      Love* (Great Wakering, Essex: McCrimmon, 1987) and Wheeler, *In Truth And Love*,
      pp. 126–127. Wheeler received numerous letters from Martin Gillett on the history

of Our Lady's Chapel at Mount Grace. See LDA, WDC, Gillett, for the correspond-ence. Gillett, a former Anglican deacon, was received into the Catholic Church in 1932. He was heavily involved in ecumenical ventures and in the Shrine at Walsingham. He founded the Ecumenical Society of the Blessed Virgin Mary in 1966. *The Tablet*, 3 May 1980.

85 LDA, WDC, 52. Confirmations in Middlesbrough.

86 Carson, *The First Hundred Years*, pp. 281–282.

87 LDA, WDC, 10. Middlesbrough Diocesan Matters.

88 LDA, WDC, 52. N.C.Y.A. and I.T.A. Files.

89 Brunner to Wheeler, 20 April 1964. LDA, WDC, 41.

90 *Catholic Herald*, 13 Jan 1984. The Gilbertines were an order of nuns and canons founded by St Gilbert of Sempringham in 1130. Malton Priory was founded about 1150.

7 COUNCIL FATHER

The Second Vatican Council

ISHOP BRUNNER HAD attended the First and Second Sessions of Vatican II (autumn 1962 and autumn 1963) but thereafter, because of ill health, remained in Middlesbrough. Wheeler was present at the Third and Fourth Sessions (autumn 1964 and autumn 1965) and attended his first Hierarchy meeting in October 1964 at the English College in Rome.[1] Some of the fiercest battles among the bishops, he recalled, had been fought in the Vatican Council's first two sessions but only one Constitution and one Decree had been promulgated. When he arrived in Rome in autumn 1964 there remained another fourteen to be debated, voted upon and ratified. The battles continued, he noted, until the last session.[2]

Abbot Christopher Butler wrote to Wheeler: 'It will be glorious having you on the Council, where England needs a clear voice speaking for real *aggiornamento*. One thing about the Council: as the reactionaries tend to be the older men, time and Death are on the side of the angels'. He warned Wheeler that he would have 'a hard task' to teach some of his episcopal brethren the elements of ecumenical theology but hoped he would be able to stimulate and lead some of the younger bishops and encourage them to 'speak up more boldly for the right ideas and policies'.[3] Butler himself continued his own radical path. In May 1963, before the Second Session of the Council, he had written to Wheeler: 'I feel that the Council is of almost over-riding importance and if the Pope is really out for 'results' at the next gathering, our deliberations will be critical—and rather frightening'.[4] Two months later, after the election of Pope Paul VI, he wrote: 'Montini was the man I wanted as Pope, but I thought the reactionaries would keep him out'. 'Montini', he continued, 'had committed himself to the late Pope's line before the Conclave'. There would therefore be no going back.[5]

Wheeler found the Council an enriching and spiritually uplifting experience offering him the opportunity to be present at a unique occasion in the history of the Church, attend Mass and services in different rites, and meet and socialise with the world's bishops.[6] The overriding impression on him, he later recalled, was deeply spiritual—'a very precious and almost tangible presence of the Holy Spirit'. On arrival, he had much catching up to do 'not only with developments but also with the mechanics of the whole event' and it quickly became, he recalled, 'the most fascinating gathering in which I had ever participated'. While most of the Hierarchy stayed at the English College, Wheeler was resident at the new *Beda* near the Basilica of St Paul Outside the Walls, with the Bishops of Southwark, Northampton, Hexham and Newcastle, and Brentwood. In the Council, the bishops sat in order of the date of their consecration; this meant that when Wheeler attended Council Sessions he was so far removed from the centre of action that he frequently went to the Observers' Box where John Moorman, the Anglican Bishop of Ripon enlightened him on proceedings.[7] The English College became the venue for the Bishops' Conferences normally held in Westminster and for discussions on Council matters. In Council, Archbishop Heenan frequently spoke on behalf of the Hierarchy but other bishops contributed. On some issues, the Hierarchy was not of one mind; for instance on nuclear disarmament and contraception.[8] Wheeler's own contributions related to seminary training and the priestly life, the problems of the Third World, and the issue of nuclear weapons.

Seminary Studies and the Priestly Life

In October 1964, within a month of his arrival in Rome for the Council, Wheeler gave a press conference on 'Priestly Life and Service'. His conference 'had little of the *éclat* attached to the great issues of the Council' but for those concerned with *aggiornamento*, the theology of the priesthood was a critical dimension of the contemporary Church. By implication, said Wheeler, the place of the priest in modern societies predicated upon his training and world-view and as the concept of the Church as 'The People of God' developed, so must importance be attached to the *new dialogue* between clergy and laity, especially if the latter was to play a more significant part in the life of the Church. He continued:

> This new conception of the "People of God", together with the high intellectual development of our laity, demands a priesthood of a kind which speaks and understands their language. This, to my mind, can only be achieved in the long run by a radical adaptation of seminary training to the ordinary cultural institutions. If the dangerous dichotomy at present in existence continues,

we shall have only ourselves to blame for the growth of anticleri-
calism from which we have blessedly been free.

He added: 'I think our separated brethren have something to offer us in
this matter' and that this new approach to education and training need
not conflict with the spiritual, scriptural, patristic and pastoral formation
of seminarians. More importantly, it did not imply an end to celibacy; the
new Schema before the Fathers, he continued, 'commends an ever-
increasing regard for the celibacy of the Priestly life'. The Fathers may
also have approved of a married diaconate but they did not abandon
celibacy—'a high spiritual vocation which leaves a man unencumbered to
exercise that pastoral freedom which makes him a member of every family
and yet belonging to none'.[9]

The debate on seminary studies had begun in England before the
Third Session. In September 1960, following an increase in defections
among junior clergy, the Vatican ordered that episcopates look closely at
both the selection of candidates for the priesthood and the nature of
seminary studies.[10] Wheeler was particularly critical of the poor quality
of seminary courses and training and the weak relationship between
seminaries and universities. This view was shared by some Catholic
university lecturers and the Conference of Catholic University Professors
established an *ad hoc* committee consisting of four Catholic university
lecturers and Fr Edward Sillem to consider the situation. Their Memorandum, presented to Archbishop Beck of Liverpool, the Bishops'
Conference spokesman on Education, was highly critical of many aspects
of seminary training, noting that seminarians often found themselves
intellectual strangers to both non-Catholic and Catholic graduates.
Seminarians were unaware of and not trained to meet current theological
and philosophical challenges advanced against Catholic teaching. The
reasons, it was suggested, lay in the remote geographical location of most
English seminaries, the monastic regimen of seminary life, the retention
of outdated curricula and teaching methods, and inadequate libraries. The
result, the Memorandum claimed, was self-imposed educational and social
isolation. Traditional links with the Gregorian University in Rome, with
its emphasis on lectures rather than tutorials, also led to an unhelpful
'un-English' strain running through clerical higher education. On the
European continent, meanwhile, Catholic universities and seminaries
were undergoing a revival of theological and philosophical studies and
reacting to a traditional situation which imposed attachment to one

particular school of theology rather than allowing the possibility of nourishment by a diversity of schools. The present English situation could not be ignored, the Memorandum noted, and unless changes were introduced to seminary education, the Catholic laity receiving high quality secular university education would in future have an academic and theological influence on the Church and Catholic schools greater than that of the bishops and priests.

The recommendations of the academics were hard-hitting. The Bishops' Conference was advised that the system should not be allowed to continue and that it should express its concerns to the Congregation of the Universities and Seminaries as well as the Commission for the Education of the Clergy of the Second Vatican Council. It was recognised, however, that the seminaries were the responsibility of the bishops and that their independence could not be compromised. While bishops had to retain control of the spiritual and theological formation of seminarians, there was a great need, the committee recommended, for the whole structure and content of seminary training to be reorganised, re-orientated and modernised in order to equip the Church and its priests for the challenges of the twenty-first century.[11]

Wheeler, of course, had received an Oxford education, attended an Anglican theological college, trained in Rome for the Catholic priesthood, and had been a university chaplain. Therefore, he had some experience in these matters and his opinion, especially on the dichotomy between the seminaries and the universities and its deleterious effect on Catholic life, was well formed.[12] He informed Archbishop Beck that he was 'thrilled' with the Memorandum and that it dealt with a matter close to his heart. The Memorandum's critique of the present situation, he wrote, presented a first rate diagnosis but some of its content, he felt, would prejudice the bishops' acceptance of the principles and recommendations being advanced. He wrote that a blanket criticism of current seminary teaching could alienate modern scholars such as Fr Charles Davis and others who did not fit the traditional mould of seminary professors and he advised caution in accepting the suggested changes to the nature and content of seminary courses in theology and philosophy. Radical changes here, he warned, would meet episcopal opposition unless handled carefully. Praising British universities was also a double-edged sword; they too had their old-fashioned dons, trained in the methods of yesteryear and still peddling outdated research. Above all, he was concerned that in order to make progress the seminaries should be related to the modern world and the universities, especially the newer ones. Reform of the seminaries, he concluded, was for him 'a number one priority for the conversion of England and the continued growth of the Church in our country'.[13]

The Hierarchy discussed the Memorandum on 8 November 1964 at the *Venerabile*. Naturally, it did not receive much approbation as it criticised the very system under which most of the bishops had been trained and over which they now ruled. Some were critical of the Memorandum and said that its recommendations were of little value as they were based on a misconception of the current state of seminary training. Others agreed but a minority suggested that as new Catholic Teacher Training Colleges were now being located near universities might not this principle be applied to seminaries. Wheeler spoke of the mutual advantage of a close association between seminary teachers and university professors. He referred 'with praise to the practice of Anglican Theological Colleges, situated close enough to Universities for all their students to benefit from the stream of university thought, even though only those with the greater intellectual capacity only attended University lectures. He also referred to the recent example of religious in establishing houses of residence in Oxford and Cambridge'. His intervention was to no avail: the bishops continued to discuss various other ways of improving seminary training but with the emphasis on general pastoral rather than specific intellectual training. A committee of bishops was set up to give further consideration to the matter.[14]

In the same month, Wheeler published an article on 'Catholics and the Universities' in *New Blackfriars*, the magazine edited by the Dominican Fr Herbert McCabe.[15] Ostensibly, a discourse on the place of theology in university studies, Wheeler took the opportunity to carry the debate on seminary studies much further. Taking his inspiration from Newman's *The Idea of a University*, he identified theology not as a separate discipline but 'as an interpreter of the whole academic process'. Modern Catholic scholars, he noted, emphasised the need for theology and philosophy to be studied in an academic milieu, by laity as well as priests and religious and, importantly, in dialogue with those of other faiths. He was against creating a Catholic University 'with a ghetto mentality' but instead wanted 'full participation on the highest levels of objective scholarship, by scholars in all disciplines, who are committed to the Christian way of life'. Having argued the need for a highly educated

Catholic laity, Wheeler then claimed that there had to be a new relationship between the seminaries and universities which could only be 'achieved by a complete and drastic rethinking, topographically and from the point of view of syllabus and curriculum of the system in which secular clergy are trained. For this remains an anachronistic legacy of penal times and creates an alarming dichotomy between the clergy and the laity'. As more Catholics entered universities, there was an increasing probability that the laity would be better educated than their priests and with this the concomitant possibility of the emergence of an anti-clerical laity. The 'cleric-dominated' Church would eventually give way to a community of the people of God.[16] A closer relationship between seminaries and universities was, therefore, to their mutual advantages and the good of the Catholic community. The success of Pope John's *aggiornamento*, he wrote, was dependent upon an intelligent and educated laity playing their full part in the life of the Church. Christians had a significant contribution to make to academia and perceptions of secular universities should be unhampered by 'any imaginary fear of conflict between verities...' The Church, he concluded, had to be humble and accept that secular universities had a contribution to make to the life of the living Church by their impact upon the process of theology.[17] Wheeler and others may have felt they had good evidence to support a change in seminary studies but their efforts achieved little immediate success. There was, as Wheeler pointed out, little point in producing anything definitive or prescriptive until the Council's decrees on priestly formation and the priestly ministry had been issued.[18]

Conciliar Contribution

Wheeler's modest contributions to Council business came in his interventions in the debate on the Church in the Modern World when the Fathers sought to define the Church within the contemporary world—the setting for its existence and self-understanding.

The long-awaited Schema on the Church in the Modern World, eventually to lead in 1965 to the Pastoral Constitution *Gaudium et Spes*, was concerned more with contemporary and urgent human problems rather than speculative theology, and debates gave rise to diverse and opposing views, even among the English and Welsh bishops. So wide was the range of problems before the Fathers that the Schema was summarised as 'from the Pill to the Bomb'. During the Third Session,

Wheeler made a brief written intervention on the obligation of the Church to ensure social justice and the fair distribution of material wealth.[19] In the Fourth Session, again in the debate on the Church in the Modern World, he made two verbal interventions—one on the problems of the Third World and one on nuclear weapons.

The emphasis of his comments on relationships between rich and poor countries was on increased collaboration between rich and poor nations. While the Christian had the right to defend the right of private property, such a defence was only valid in the context of justice augmented by love and compassion:

> The distribution of the fruits of the earth and the control of productive factors must accord with justice so that each is given his due and none may usurp for his private enjoyment products and property which should be shared by many.

He argued against the prevalent view that charity begins and ends with financial support from richer nations; this resulted in aid being ineffective. Instead, he called for meaningful dialogue between nations and international aid organizations to ascertain the real and urgent needs of poorer countries and in this exchange the Church had to play a major role not only in the provision of aid but also to ensure justice and morality. Aid and support, he said, had to be given 'in a spirit of brotherly partnership without any bias or imperialistic or economic exploitation on the part of the aiding nations'.[20]

Regarding nuclear weapons, Wheeler emphasised the need for a strong Christian witness in the universal search for peace and reconciliation. Like others, he considered an earlier text on the condemnation of nuclear weapons to be weak and implicitly condone their use in certain situations. The Church had traditionally defended human life: not unilaterally condemning the use or retention of a nuclear deterrent appeared to contradict that view. In addition, it was his opinion and that of others that there had not been enough moral support for the conscientious objection to nuclear weapons. His views on these issues and on the authority of governments in war followed the lead of Abbot Christopher Butler. On the Council's previous statement on conscientious objection, for example, Butler said that 'Some conscientious objectors may in fact be prophets of a truly Christian morality'. Wheeler said:

> The words describing the conscientious objector are so weak and
> patronizing as to suggest that he is a milksop. The witness of a
> conscientious objector is something to be valued and welcomed as
> a special factor in modern life even by those of us who would not
> be classed as conscientious objectors. I would like to see these weak
> descriptions changed to 'as a witness of the Christian vocation to
> bring about peace'.

He was supported by Bishop Grant and Archbishop Beck and by some
bishops from Canada, Europe and South America who had pragmatic views
of the retention of nuclear weapons but many North America bishops were
against this stance.[21] The hope of some—that the Council would unequivocally condemn the use of nuclear weapons—was not fulfilled.[22]

In the Fourth Session, Wheeler prepared a *relatio* for the Hierarchy
on the Ministry and Life of Priests and an Intervention in the Council
which was not called. His intervention was designed to advise the Council
Fathers on the relationship between bishops and priests and the lesser
groupings of the faithful outside the confines and extent of cathedrals
where the local pastor liturgically takes the place of the bishop. Wheeler
argued that the Council Fathers would be missing a great opportunity if
they 'did not stress here and now the canonised liturgical bond between
Bishops and Priests and do all in our power to promote a closer
relationship in worship'. The laity, he continued, should be given the
opportunity of experiencing 'pontifical occasions' outside the cathedrals
and not only during episcopal visitations: 'It is a great loss for priests and
people if they only see their high priest (the bishop) on the infrequent
occasion of Visitation'. Liturgical possibilities, such as concelebration,
could enable priests to take the place of their bishop 'and on these
occasions they should, wherever possible, underline the unity of the whole
people of God...' This need not conflict with the parochial idea and
priests will be 'hallowing their *fraterna conjunctio* in a highly spiritual
manner which can bear fruit in their own priestly lives and ultimately in
the lives of all their people'. Liturgical practice was not the only way of
manifesting unity: there was 'a common life or common table' but here
Wheeler emphasised the increasingly practical experiences of priests living
alone. Many large presbyteries and fortunate individual priests had
religious working as housekeepers but the pastoral efforts of a priest living
alone were often vitiated by personal domestic concerns. He urged a more
professional approach to the provision of housekeepers.[23]

Wheeler was of the firm opinion that the Council's thinking especially on the Church, Revelation, Conscience and the Dignity of the Laity had been influenced by Cardinal Newman and that the whole mind of the Council was imbued with his thought. He was not alone in this view and he was deeply influenced by Abbot Butler who in 'Newman and the Second Vatican Council' had claimed that Newman's was indeed a 'prophetic voice' and that Vatican II 'proved the fact'.[24] It was difficult to see, wrote Wheeler, how the Council's deliberations and decisions on these issues could have been formulated without the intellectual groundwork done by Newman in the nineteenth century. The ecclesiology of the Council's Dogmatic Constitution on the Church (*Lumen Gentium*) could not have emerged without reference to Newman's *The Development of Doctrine* and the Constitution on Divine Revelation drew upon Newman's study of Patristic sources and his insight on scripture and tradition. Similarly, the Decrees on the Laity, on Ecumenism, Christian Education, and the Declaration on Religious Liberty together with some aspects of *Gaudiam et Spes* all bear the hallmark of Newman's thought and influence, his growth and development. He wrote:

> Newman and the Council had a similar purpose, a missionary intention, to reform the Church so as to be able to carry the Gospel of Christ more effectively to the Modern World—and in that task everyone and especially the laity were and are expected to play their part.

For Wheeler, however, there was more to Newman than just his writings and intellectual endowments. His personal sanctity, spirituality, humility, prayer, honesty, pastoral care and dedication 'showed people of our times how to live a deeply Christian life in the midst of indifference and all the hostile influences of today'.[25] Some Council Fathers had remarked on Newman's 'hidden presence' while others doubted that it was discernible. Wheeler wrote:

> My own feeling is as follows: Whilst it seems clear that the name of Newman does not often appear in the Council's interventions, the entire ethos bespeaks of a kind of approach to a whole range of matters that was his. Now one might say this was a case of great minds thinking alike. But one also has to remember that in the immediate pre-Conciliar period there had been a considerable revival of Newman studies, and especially in France and Germany, from which areas a good part of the new approaches had come.

To prove that Newman's lucidity of thought, perfection of expression and literary clarity really did actually influence the Council, Wheeler later called for more research on the *periti* and Council Fathers 'concerning their philosophical and theological foundations'.[26]

Wheeler forever saw humour in events and people and Vatican II was no exception. To him, the human touches were in watching the vast gatherings of posturing prelates and their *periti* and especially in reading the Latin limericks composed by the Anglo-Saxon bishops to relieve the personal, theological and spiritual tensions of the Council. Bishop Wall of Brentwood and Bishop O'Loughlin of Darwin, Australia were notorious for their acid Latin verse.[27]

A Modern Bishop

As Wheeler had related the higher education of Catholics to Pope John XXIII's modernising approach, his elevation to the episcopate was seen by some in the same context: '... it augurs well for the *aggiornamento* so dear to the heart of the late Holy Father', wrote A. A. King.[28]

In 'The Bishop and the Liturgy', published in January 1966, Wheeler set out his view of the nature and purpose of the episcopacy. It was a modern approach deriving inspiration from the recent Vatican Council document *Lumen Gentium* and emphasising the centrality of the liturgy in the inter-dependent relationship between bishop, priests and people. It was also closely related to the press conference he had given in October 1964 on 'Priestly Life and Service'. He first identified the bishop's pastoral function—'the bishop is to be considered as the high priest of his flock, from whom the life in Christ of his faithful is in some way derived and dependent'. The ultimate sign of unity was the local bishop in communion with the pope and one with his fellow bishops throughout the world. It was an ideal stressed and manifested above all in the liturgy when the bishop celebrated with his priests and people. The liturgical life of the diocese centred around the bishop and all had to be convinced that 'the pre-eminent manifestation of the Church consists in the full active participation of all God's holy people in the same liturgical celebrations, especially in the same Eucharist, in a single prayer at one altar, at which there presides the bishop surrounded by his college of priests and ministers'. It was of course impossible for a bishop to conduct such services on a frequent basis and so parish liturgies, not 'private functions', were signs of unity and the bishop had to safeguard this unity. In fulfilling this responsibility, the bishop was dependent on his priests with whom he should seek 'more and more understanding'. In the past, he wrote, 'the Church has too often been considered merely as a juridical society. Vatican II now emphasises, as the early Fathers did, that the Church is truly and pre-eminently a spiritual thing, but also and essentially a human and sensible one in as much as it is incarnate'. In such a situation, the bishop was not to be seen simply as an efficient administrator or a papal legate, but one at the very heart of the Church's life with God-given powers for the fulfilment of his mission among his people. He concluded:

> ... there is no doubt that it is the mind of the Church, expressed in the Liturgical Constitution, that the bishop is no longer to be thought of juridically or as an administrator. This is only one aspect of his office which is or should be gathered up liturgically in his High Priesthood. We can no longer afford to think of the bishop, if in the past we have sometimes done so, as an obscure figure of a distant nature who appears every few years to give the Sacrament of Confirmation. This is, of course, an important duty but again only one aspect of his being the High Priest of his flock.[29]

Middlesbrough, he recalled later in life, was one of the less organised dioceses from an administrative perspective but there was 'the very loving relationship of the priests with one another, the priests with their bishop and the Bishop with his priests'. There was, he admitted, something much more important than ecclesiastical authority and intellectual and theological analysis.[30]

'The Council Fathers had been together for four years and had been enriched by a greater vision of the unity, holiness and apostolicity of the Church', wrote Wheeler, and they had promulgated Constitutions and Decrees of the utmost significance for the Church of the future, but their experiences and achievements could not be quickly or easily be passed on. On his return to Middlesbrough, he informed the clergy of Council developments but realised that imparting the true nature and meaning of Vatican II would take years rather than months, weeks or days.[31] He was especially concerned that the meaning of the Council was faithfully and adequately conveyed to the faithful and that they were protected from 'garbled and sometimes alarming reports from the press which is so often preoccupied with sensationalism'. The consequence, he continued, 'is distress and uncertainty'. If it had been a privilege to attend the Council, bishops were left with the huge responsibility of communicating its innovations and recommendations.[32]

One of the most momentous changes wrought by the Council was the introduction of the vernacular into the liturgy and especially into the celebration of the Mass. Some priests and laity welcomed the changes but for others they caused anguish, complaint and heartache — no one was left unmoved or unaffected. For Wheeler, who had entered the Church because of its possession and guardianship of the truth and its scriptural, liturgical and cultural traditions, it cannot have been an easy decision to support but he did: 'It doesn't really matter whether the Mass is in English or Latin. It is the Mass itself that matters'. His subsequent explanation, however, concentrated on the nature, purpose and structure of the Mass rather than on the reasons why Latin had been discarded. He did not reveal his personal feelings about the changes.[33] Nearly thirty years later, he said that much as Latin was the language of the universal Church in the early 1960s and had been for centuries, there was a deep feeling within the Council that many in the Church, particularly those outside Europe, had different linguistic roots from Latin and that these had to be recognised.[34] The Church could no longer afford to be Eurocentric but had to be multicultural.

In the *Northern Echo*, Wheeler wrote 'End and Beginning' in which he summarised the Council's achievements and outlined future developments within the Church. Pope John XXIII, he recalled, had convened the Council so that the Church would engage in a process of renewal and in attempts to restore Christian unity. In both developments there had to be a return to 'the original sources, and especially the Scriptures' now covered with twenty centuries of 'encrustation' which 'confused the seekers of truth and sometimes blinded them'. Following the truth in the spirit of charity, he wrote, was the basis of Pope John's programme now enthusiastically assumed by Pope Paul VI. The bishops' debates, he wrote,

> Had given a new look to the whole of theology and brought it up to date in the terms of contemporary thought. As these documents, now promulgated, are studied and implemented, they can have a revolutionary effect within and without the Church. For Catholics it is the same, unchanging Church, in a new garb. For non-Catholics it will have an entirely new look. Many will soon realise that considerable stumbling blocks have been removed. And this can especially assist the unity of Christians.[35]

The 'new garb' was not welcomed by all Catholics, however.

In September 1965, *The Guardian* included an article on the social make-up of the English and Welsh Hierarchy. It opined that the bishops had no intellectual aspirations and there were no alumni of the great English public schools among them. The Hierarchy was of 'uncompromisingly middle-class origins, and not by any means always from the upper middle class'. Catholics, it continued, were once described by an Anglican vicar as 'a rather rough and tricky lot, notoriously deficient in taste and manners'. If this applied to rank-and-file Catholics, the article concluded, it could well apply to the Bishops.[36] Bishop Wheeler replied with a limerick 'On the lowly origins of the English Bishops':

Hierarchical stratification
Is a hazard of human creation;
But we middle class thugs
(e'en though less than bugs)
Are the heart of the new dispensation.[37]

If Wheeler differed from his fellow bishops in his approach to ecumenism, nuclear disarmament and the nature of seminary studies, he was also very different from them culturally, socially and above all in style. The writer George Scott visited Wheeler at White Lodge. He recalled that Wheeler displayed the true hallmarks of an English gentleman: 'His style of living is English: the green-tiled house in the country just outside Middlesbrough; the dogs that come to the door to greet me; the tea served by his housekeeper; the manner of his speech'.[38] According to Scott, 'It was in his familiarity and sympathy with the cultural and educational background shared by the majority of fellow countrymen that Wheeler differed from most of his fellow bishops'. Scott was anxious to portray Wheeler as 'a new kind of bishop'—'a figure of significance and hope to those who wished to reform the Church'. His background and attitude of mind, according to one admirer, made him 'one of the most hopeful appointments for a long time'. Wheeler, however, was not disposed to be singled out and refused to criticise his fellow bishops now grappling with the changes wrought by the Second Vatican Council. 'The more I've seen of the other bishops', he said, 'the more I've been impressed by their open-mindedness and their anxiety to carry out to the full the renewal of the Church's life as expressed by the Pope and the Council'.[39]

Aggiornamento, however, was to be more complicated and tortuous than expected. There were iconoclasts who took every opportunity to use the Council as a means not simply to modernize but to discard and destroy and there were traditionalists who set their faces against any scintilla of change. In the midst of the feverish excitement surrounding Vatican II and the impending changes in Church life, Wheeler felt obliged to remind others of the need to recognize both the authority of the Church and the need for prayer and spirituality in such turbulent times. He deliberately pointed to those who were exploiting changes according to their own personal agenda. In *The Tablet*, he wrote:

> There is a great deal of talk nowadays about the crisis of authority. There are good aspects of this in so far as it is the consequence of maturity. Whereas the child obeys blindly, the mature person obeys in accordance with reason, or at any rate not entirely without good reason, even if he cannot always comprehend it in its entirety. The abuse enters in when the subject of authority is so preoccupied with his own ego, and with his flowering and development as he sees it, that he loses all objective standards and becomes self-centred instead of God-centred.
>
> Now I am convinced that the real crisis of our day is not so much this crisis of authority as the crisis of spirituality. The two are not unconnected. Preoccupation with self instead of with God, or our neighbour, can be at the heart of both. In recent years there has been a stress on personal edification in the spiritual life rather than the objective worship of God. The Church in her wisdom is always redressing balances. She has passed through an age when it was perhaps important to stress pure worship at the expense sometimes of understanding. The new legislation on the vernacular has remedied this by familiarizing the People of God daily with a wealth of scriptural understanding. By enabling articulate participation as well as understanding it has brought the liturgy to life. The edification derived should assist our growing up in Christ which is the means of our spiritual renewal.[40]

His article brought many letters of approval and support, including from those in monastic orders.

For traditional Catholics the Second Vatican Council was an unwanted break in the Church's history and its liturgical practices; moderate reformers saw it as another stage in the Church's long development and opportunity for renewal at all levels; a vocal minority welcomed it as moment for radical change. From all angles of opinion, Vatican II had an enormous impact. As Bernard Bergonzi wrote in January 1965, English Catholics—still a defensive minority with an acute sense of religious identity—were being shaken not only by cultural developments in English society but also by 'the wave of new thinking in the Church which is associated by the genius of Pope John and the work of the Second Vatican Council'.[41] For the Church as a whole and for the Church in England and Wales, things would never be quite the same again. Wheeler, by nature orthodox and traditional, would now become a change agent.

Notes

1   W. G. Wheeler, *In Truth And Love* (Southport: Gowland and Co., 1990), p. 81. The principle of 'one diocese, one vote' operated and Wheeler was allowed to vote only on 'consultative issues' unless Brunner was absent.

2   Wheeler, *In Truth And Love*, pp. 82–83.

3   Butler to Wheeler, 13 Feb 1964. LDA, WDC, WDC, 54 (a).

4   Butler to Wheeler, 7 May 1963. LDA, WPC, Vatican II.

5   Butler to Wheeler, 6 July 1963. LDA, WPC, Vatican II.

6   Wheeler, *In Truth And Love*, pp. 82–83.

7   *The Clergy Review*, Aug. 1986, vol. lxxi, no. 8.

8   'Life Among the Purple People', *Sunday Times*, 5 Dec 1965.

9   W. G. Wheeler, 'Priestly Life and Service', 15 Oct 1964. LDA, WPC, Vatican Council; D. Worlock, *English Bishops at the Council: Third Session* ((London: Burns and Oates, 1965), pp. 59–60, 155–159.

10   'Notes on the Training of Students prepared by the Archbishop and Bishops of the Northern Province for Seminary Professors and Seminary Confessors', Feb 1962. LDA, WDC, Northern Bishops.

11   Memorandum prepared at the request of His Grace the Archbishop of Liverpool, the Most Reverend George Andrew Beck A.A., on Seminaries and Universities by Professor Hilary Armstrong, Professor A. C. F. Beales, Timothy Potts, Justin Gosling and Reverend Edward Sillem. LDA, WDC, 52.

12   G. Scott, *The RCs: a report on Roman Catholics in Britain today* (London: Hutchinson, 1967), p. 183.

13   Wheeler to Beck, 17 Aug 1964. LDA, WDC, 52.

14   Bishops' Conference on Seminaries, Venerable English College, Rome, 8 Nov 1964. LDA, WDC, 52.

15   W. G. Wheeler, 'Catholics and the Universities' in *New Blackfriars*, vol. 46, no. 533, Nov 1964, pp. 78–81.

16   The Council Fathers had noted this prospect. Alberigo writes that the two Council Decrees on Priestly Formation and on the Ministry and Life of Priests (*Apostolicam*

Actuositatem, 1965, and *Presbyterorum Ordinis*, 1965) suffered from a lack of adequate reflection on the state of the priesthood and the absence of alternative models of priesthood. See A. Alberigo, *A Brief History of Vatican II* (Maryknoll, New York: Orbis Books, 2008), pp. 112–113.

17 W. G. Wheeler, 'Catholics and the Universities' in *New Blackfriars*, vol. 46, no. 533, Nov 1964, pp. 78–81.

18 Fr John McHugh of Ushaw College, to the Northern Bishops, 17 Jan 1965. LDA, WDC, Northern Bishops.

19 'Intervention by Bishop Gordon Wheeler on Chapter IV of the Schema *De Ecclesia In Mundo Huis Temporis*'. LDA, WDC, Vatican II; Wheeler, *In Truth And Love*, p. 83; X. Rynne, *The Third Session* (London: Faber and Faber, 1965), pp. 143–145.

20 'Intervention by Bishop Gordon Wheeler on Chapter IV of the Schema *De Ecclesia In Mundo Huis Temporis*'. LDA, WDC, Vatican II; *Catholic Herald*, 15 Oct 1965.

21 *Council Digest Prepared for the Council Fathers of the United States, 143rd Congregation, 6 Oct 1965*. LDA, WDC, 25; X. Rynne, *The Fourth Session* (London: Faber and Faber, 1965), pp. 112–113, 117–118, 132; *Daily American*, 7 Oct 1965.

22 *The Catholic Worker*, July-August 1965.

23 W. G. Wheeler, 'Schema on the Ministry and Priestly Life' and 'Intervention on the Schema on the Ministry and Priestly Life', (no date; 1965?). LDA, WPC, Vatican Council.

24 B. C. Butler, 'Newman and the Second Vatican Council' in J. Coulson and A. M. Allchin, *The Rediscovery of Newman* (London: Sheed and Ward, 1967), pp. 235–246.

25 Wheeler, *In Truth And Love*, pp. 84–85; W. G. Wheeler, 'Newman and Holiness' in *Mount Carmel*, vol. 38, no. 1, Spring 1990, pp. 34–39.

26 Wheeler, 'The Hidden Presence: Newman and Vatican II' in W. G. Wheeler, *More Truth And Love* (Southport: Gowland and Co.,1994) , pp. 86–94. Wheeler acknowledged his debt to the influential writings of Abbot Butler.

27 Vatican II, Limericks composed by English Bishops. LDA, WDC, Vatican Council. For example, Bishop O'Loughlin of Darwin, Australia, wrote:

The fault of the Doctrinal Commission
is by no means a sin of omission
for Progressives are saddened
and Conservatives gladdened
that everything needs its permission.

Bishop Rudderham of Clifton wrote:

There was an old priest of Dunleary
who stood on his head at the Kyrie;
when some asked why,
he made this reply:
'It's the latest liturgical theory'.

28 A. A. King, 'The Consecration of Bishop Wheeler' in *Westminster Cathedral Chronicle*, April 1964, p. 70.

29 W. G .Wheeler, 'The Bishop and the Liturgy' in *Liturgy*, vol. xxxv, no. 1, Jan 1966, pp. 6–11. See also B. Harbert, 'Flaminian Gate to Eccleston Square' in *Priests & People*, Oct 2000, vol. 14, no. 10, pp. 389–391. Mgr Harbert writes that following Vatican II many accretions of a fundamentally secular character were removed in order 'to allow rich and ancient signs of episcopal dignity to shine forth more clearly'.

30 Wheeler, *In Truth And Love*, Transcript, Tape 3. LDA, WPC; W G Wheeler, 'Your Bishop and You' in *Catholic Herald*, 11 March 1966.

31 Wheeler, *In Truth And Love*, p. 83.

32 W. G. Wheeler, *The Council at a Glance* (London: Burns and Oates, 1966), p.3. By the time this had been published, Wheeler had become Bishop of Leeds.

33 W. G. Wheeler, *Let's Get This Straight: The Church after Vatican II* (London: Catholic Truth Society, 1969), pp. 5–6.

34 W. G. Wheeler, Address to the Association for Latin Liturgy (13 Oct 1990). LDA, WPC, Liturgy.

35 *Northern Echo*, 11 Dec 1965.

36 *The Guardian*, 13 Sept 1965.

37 Limericks composed by English Bishops. LDA, WPC, Vatican Council. Vatican II.

38 Scott, *The RCs: a report on Roman Catholics in Britain today*, p. 183. Unknown to Scott, Wheeler was helped financially by a generous covenant from his close friend Viscount Furness. See Lloyds Bank to Wheeler, 11 April 1964. LDA, WDC, 10. William Anthony, 2nd Viscount Furness, was born in 1929. Educated at Downside, he was received into the Church at Westminster Cathedral in 1946 and was a Knight of Malta. Viscount Furness was a man of substantial and independent financial means. He died in 1995. See *Catholic Who's Who* and *Dictionary of National Biography*.

39 Scott, *The RCs: a report on Roman Catholics in Britain today*, pp. 183, 237–238. See also R. Finnigan, 'Bishop Wheeler' in R. Finnigan and J. Hagerty, *The Bishops of Leeds 1878–1985: Essays in Honour of Bishop David Konstant* (Keighley: PBK Publishing on behalf of the Diocese of Leeds, 2005), pp. 154–155.

40 *The Tablet*, 12 Feb 1966.

41 B. Bergonzi, 'The English Catholics' in *Encounter*, January 1965, p. 20.

Dobcross: Wheeler's birthplace

The young Wheeler with his mother

Student at Manchester Grammar School. Wheeler is on the front row, sixth from the left.

The Anglican Priest: Wheeler in December 1934

Student at the Beda with Cardinal Hinsley and other seminarians.
Wheeler is on the second row, second from the left.

Student in wartime: Wheeler (standing extreme right) and other Beda students with Mgr Charles Duchemin at Upholland in 1940

Administrator of Westminster Cathedral

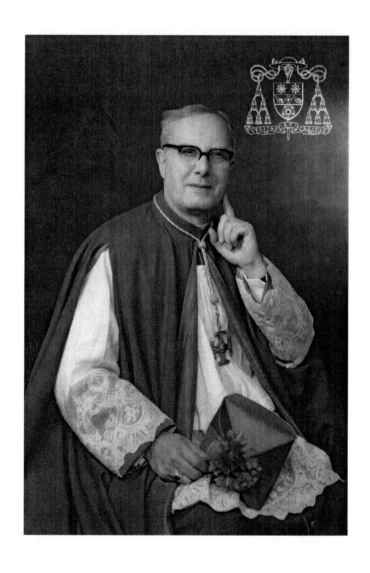

Wheeler as Coadjutor Bishop of Middlesbrough 1964

William Gordon Wheeler, Bishop of Leeds, 1966

Wheeler with his father following his consecration as Bishop of Leeds, 1966

Wheeler visiting the Leeds Diocesan Mission in Peru

12. Wheeler and Pope Blessed Paul VI

Wheeler with Pope Saint John Paul II

8 BISHOP OF LEEDS

Translation and Enthronement

Archbishop Francis Grimshaw of Birmingham died on 22
March 1965 and was succeeded on 21 December of the same year
by Bishop George Patrick Dwyer who had been Bishop of Leeds
since 1957. Wheeler was told by Archbishop Cardinale, the Apostolic
Delegate who had informed him of his appointment to Middlesbrough,
that the Holy See was 'in a dilemma' as to who should succeed Bishop
Dwyer. Cardinale said the Vatican thought that as Wheeler had some
experience as a Coadjutor and of Yorkshire, it might be best if he were
Dwyer's successor. Wheeler recalled that he was not enthusiastic about
the idea but, as before, said that he would comply with the wishes of the
Holy See.[1] His translation to Leeds on 3 May 1966 was not surprising:
twenty-six years a priest, he was very competent and had substantial and
successful pastoral and administrative experience. He had attended the
Second Vatican Council, his record in Middlesbrough was brief but
effective, he was loyal and orthodox, and he was a good communicator.
Wheeler became the second convert Anglican clergyman and second
former student of the Beda to become Bishop of Leeds—Bishop Henry
John Poskitt, bishop from 1936 to 1950, being the first.[2]

Despite there being only being six months between the appointment
of Dwyer to Birmingham and Wheeler to Leeds, his translation caused
some concern to Cardinal Heenan who wrote to the Apostolic Delegate
that 'The appointment of Gordon to Leeds raises in my mind again the
point of the long time it takes to fill a See in England and Wales'. He
asked if the nomination and appointment process could be accelerated.
The current procedure, he wrote, was cumbersome and the long delays
unhelpful. He suggested an end to the traditional *terna* and proposed that
the Hierarchy should quickly draw up and submit a list of candidates.
Archbishop Cardinale, however, could only work within traditional
domestic customs and the practices of the Holy See's Consistorial
Congregation.[3]

Bishop Brunner sent Wheeler his 'heartiest congratulations'. He wrote:
'You will be going to a larger diocese than Middlesbrough where you will
have more opportunities for God's work and the salvation of souls. You

will follow two bishops who have left their mark on the West Riding and I am convinced that you will do the same'. He was, however, sad that he was leaving:

> … you will be sadly missed in this diocese by the clergy and the laity and if I may say so, by myself… I am most grateful for all your help… I appreciate everything you have done for the diocese and for myself personally… I am only sorry that our partnership is to be dissolved… I hope and pray for many years of happy and successful work in Leeds Diocese for you and higher things even if it is the will of God.[4]

Archbishop Cardinale was delighted with the appointment. Wheeler had sent him a confidential memo on the state of the Diocese of Middlesbrough and warned him of the effect that the loss of a Coadjutor would have on Bishop Brunner. Middlesbrough, wrote Wheeler, was 'a very happy' diocese 'with few problems' but Bishop Brunner was old, the clergy needed vibrant leadership and encouragement, and the diocese as a whole needed more inspiration. While Bishop Brunner was very conscientious, he tended not to delegate and the organization of the diocese was 'haphazard'; it would be necessary for the next Ordinary to introduce many changes at all levels.[5] The Delegate answered that he would deal with Bishop Brunner's situation but '… As regards yourself, dear Gordon, more and more do I feel that this is God's will. No appointment ever went so smoothly of the many I have had to handle…' It would be good, he told Wheeler, to be 'THE Bishop' and 'you will be able to do things in your own image and likeness and set a wonderful example of government'. He concluded: 'Ecumenically, I am sure it will be a great success too'.[6] From Durban, South Africa, Archbishop Hurley sent best wishes and prayerful congratulations: 'Leeds has had quite a succession of pastors in the last ten years, so I don't quite know what to wish—"ad multos annos in Leeds" or translation, like Cardinal Heenan and Archbishop Dwyer to bigger things'.[7] Wheeler's two predecessors in Leeds sent their own congratulations. Cardinal Heenan wrote: 'Welcome to Leeds! You will find it strange at first but you will soon cease to pine for the loss of other Ridings…You will find the Diocese in splendid condition and your various officials all men of great ability and integrity…'[8] Meanwhile, Archbishop Dwyer wrote: 'I'm sure you are going to bring a most refreshing new touch to Leeds and that you will find them a most loyal flock eager to follow a lead'.[9]

Anglican prelates and clergy sent their congratulations. Archbishop Ramsey sent 'warmest wishes for this new venture' pointing out that 'Leeds was a great opportunity'.[10] Archbishop Donald Coggan of York sent his congratulations and prayers, adding that 'we shall miss you much in Middlesbrough'.[11] From Leeds, he received the congratulations of the Vicar Canon Fenton and those of the Leeds Council of Churches; from Wakefield, the best wishes of the Bishop and Clergy; while the Bishop of Hull sent good wishes and blessings adding: 'I am sure that you will maintain the high reputation in the succession'.[12] From the Archbishop of Canterbury's Commission on Roman Catholic Relations, he received good wishes 'and assurance of prayers'.[13]

Wheeler's enthronement as the seventh Bishop of Leeds took place at St Anne's Cathedral, Leeds, on 27 June, 1966, the Feast of Our Lady of Perpetual Succour, the Diocesan patroness. The ceremony, relayed on closed-circuit television to the congregation, was based on 'the ancient northern tradition as represented by the rite used in the pre-Reformation See of York'.[14] It began when the new Bishop was met at the west door of the Cathedral by the Provost and Canons of the Leeds Diocesan Chapter. He then processed into the nave under a canopy of cloth of gold carried by four Knights of Malta including Lord Craigmyle and Field Marshal Sir Francis Festing. The ceremony was conducted by Archbishop Cardinale and Wheeler concelebrated Mass with twelve diocesan priests. Bishop Dwyer had already slightly modified the sanctuary in line with Vatican II but Wheeler said Mass with his back to the congregation. Archbishop Beck of Liverpool conducted the enthronement and then the new bishop received the homage of the Cathedral Canons and other clerical representatives. The service concluded with the granting of a Plenary Indulgence and a papal blessing delivered by the Apostolic Delegate.

In his address, Wheeler referred particularly to his developing ideas on the episcopacy and to the current moral climate. If he presided at the *cathedra* or bishop's throne, he said, he did so as a symbol of a unity within the diocese 'in the one High Priesthood of Our Lord and Master whose true throne is the Cross and the altar…' Emphasising this unity in the office of the bishop, he repeated words he had used in Middlesbrough, that the Bishop must be something more than a chairman of an organization. He was required to be the chief administrator of such a big diocese but such work would be 'useless unless it was pastoral'. The unity of bishop, clergy and people, he continued, would be best illustrated by the frequent celebration together of the sacred liturgies and the protection of the young in the face of increasing secularization and the abandonment of moral absolutes: 'Only such action could call a halt to the disastrous abdication of parental responsibilities and the national loss of that regard for the true values which not surprisingly is depriving youth of the inheritance which is its due'.

In the congregation were Wheeler's eighty-six-year-old father and many of his friends including Lord Wicklow, godfather at his Confirmation; George Malcolm, Master of Music at Westminster Cathedral; Arthur Fleischmann, who had designed Wheeler's new crozier; and Lady Masham. A new dimension to the enthronement was the attendance of representatives of other Christian denominations and other faiths—John Moorman, the Anglican Bishop of Ripon, who had met Wheeler in Rome at the Vatican Council, was present as was J. W. Rutt, Moderator of the Leeds Free Church Federal Council, while Rabbi Solomon Brown, represented the Leeds Jewish community;[15] As with his appointment to Middlesbrough, Wheeler received many congratulations and letters of goodwill from his friends and former colleagues.[16]

Following the ceremony, the Apostolic Delegate again came in for criticism from Heenan and the Hierarchy, this time for speaking in the post-enthronement luncheon about the appointment of Wheeler in particular and bishops in general. Cardinale apologized for any misunderstanding he had caused and explained that he was replying to critics who felt the appointment process to be opaque and undemocratic. He made the point very strongly that at the last session of the Vatican Council, Heenan himself had suggested Wheeler for Leeds and that 'the final choice' corresponded 'with the overwhelming majority'. It seemed that the bishops also took exception to Cardinale consulting those outside the Church. Bishop John Moorman of Ripon had written to the Delegate expressing the hope that Dwyer's successor might be someone who would work in the spirit of Vatican II.[17] In a subsequent informal conversation, Cardinale had spoken unofficially to Moorman about who exactly he would like to see in Leeds to which Moorman replied: 'Gordon!' This response, asserted Cardinale, had not been allowed to influence his judgement and his subsequent advice to Rome.[18]

Despite some similarities in background, Wheeler was very different to his predecessor. Both were northerners, both were Oxbridge graduates and both were men of discerning intellect, yet they differed in upbringing, theological training, style and temperament. Born in 1908, Dwyer had grown up in an era when English Catholicism was led by the clergy and characterised by a largely introspective mentality. He had been schooled under Mgr Hinsley in the *Venerabile* tradition and his priesthood was of the obedient, missionary and ultramontane type.[19] He had gone up to Cambridge as a mature student and an ordained priest and therefore was not susceptible to the joys and influences of student life. He had a good record as a teacher at St Bede's College, Manchester, as a missioner with the Catholic Missionary Society, and was very friendly with Archbishop John Carmel Heenan of Westminster. As a bishop, he was very hard working and was respected by his priests but his brusque manner won him few friends among the laity. Most of the legendary stories about him revolved around his quixotic behaviour on the sanctuary and his frequent verbal challenges to all concerned, especially organists, yet he was totally dedicated to the service of his diocese.[20] Wheeler, on the other hand, had different roots and experiences. As a student, he had absorbed the Oxford social and religious scene and since then had cultivated influential acquaintances in Rome, London and elsewhere so that they had become firm and useful friendships. His social style was upper class English—gracious, courteous and polished—and his tastes were literary and aesthetic. His priesthood was traditionally orthodox yet wide-ranging, enthusiastic and creative. When he became a bishop, he had already been moulded by factors and experiences beyond the confines of the traditional English Catholic Church and its provincial dioceses and had been enthused by the influence of the Second Vatican Council.

Diocese, Priests and People

Geographically, the Diocese of Leeds was very extensive and scattered. It covered an area of 5,837 square miles and included the whole of the West Riding of Yorkshire and two parishes to the south of the River Ouse in the City of York. The diocese was divided culturally and economically into two parts—north and south. Located in the north was Wakefield, the administrative centre of the West Riding, but the biggest centre of population was the city of Leeds, dependent on a range of commercial, financial and industrial enterprises. The city of Bradford and other towns within West Yorkshire, such as Huddersfield, Halifax, Batley and Dewsbury were heavily reliant on the declining textile trade while towns like Castleford were connected with coal mining. To the north-west of the Leeds-Bradford conurbation were Harrogate, Skipton and Keighley. To the south of the diocese, the city of Sheffield, famous for its steelworks and the manufacture of cutlery, was the dominant urban area in the Hallamshire District while to its north were the Yorkshire coal mining and engineering towns of Barnsley and Rotherham and the railway nexus of Doncaster. Across the diocese, there were also extensive rural areas and huge tracts of outstanding natural beauty.[21] A Diocesan Curial report presented to Wheeler on his arrival informed him that because of the size and nature of the diocese, 'a reorganization of its territorial boundaries has been contemplated with a view to making a new diocese in the southern area of Sheffield and district'.[22] Wheeler noted that the Diocese of Leeds covered the same area as ten Anglican dioceses.[23] In the English and Welsh Hierarchy, it ranked sixth in size of Catholic population after the dioceses of Liverpool, Westminster, Southwark, Salford, and Hexham and Newcastle.[24]

Bishop Dwyer's legacy was one of growth and expansion. The Catholic population of the diocese rose from 230,000 in 1957 to 262,800 in 1965.[25] Most Catholics were working-class and middle-class although there had been substantial Catholic educational and social advancement since the Great War of 1914–1918. The building of local authority housing estates and the emergence of new Catholic communities on the outskirts of industrial towns and cities in the 1950s called for more priests and new parishes, churches and schools and Dwyer responded energetically. As Mgr Sharp has noted, thirty-two new churches and chapels were built in the diocese during Bishop Dwyer's episcopate: 'the rate of church building between 1957 and 1965 was unprecedented'. Mass attendance rose from 108,364 in 1958 to 135,753 in 1964 and conversions to the Faith exceeded 1,000 per year. The provision of schools in both primary and secondary sectors also increased: twelve new or replacement primary schools, twenty-two new secondary schools, and two special schools were opened by Bishop Dwyer. In line with Vatican II, Bishop Dwyer introduced liturgical changes, approved the re-ordering of churches and encouraged ecumenical relations, but he was never truly convinced about the wisdom of some of the Council's decisions and remained hesitant about both the nature and pace of change.[26] Whilst he admired Anglican scholarship, the liturgical sobriety of Anglican services and the Church of England's social conscience, he was less than certain of what Anglicans actually believed and for this reason was very cautious of close ecumenical involvement.[27]

Wheeler received 'a wonderful reception' in his new diocese. At the announcement of his translation in May 1966, the diocesan clergy were in conference at Myddelton Lodge, Ilkley. When told of the appointment, the priests greeted it 'with a spontaneous cheer'.[28] His reputation had obviously preceded him. For his part, he was aware that Heenan and Dwyer had been strong leaders with public profiles and that he had to follow them. In his first *Ad Clerum*, he wrote: 'It is with no little trepidation, humanly speaking, that I obey the Holy Father's request to be your bishop. I shall find it very difficult to live up to the examples of my predecessors' two of whom were 'still dynamically alive'. He added: 'I do promise that I shall do my utmost to be amongst you as one who serves…'[29] In his first Preface to the *Leeds Diocesan Directory*, he wrote of his joy at being translated to Leeds:

> I have been prepared for your great kindness by the two years I spent so happily in the Diocese of Middlesbrough. It had been a great joy to me to return to native Yorkshire and it seemed too good to be true. I am thankful that the move decided for me by the Holy Father, should not remove me from my beloved York-shire countryside and wonderful priests and people that I have encountered everywhere.[30]

The misgivings he had experienced over his translation to Middlesbrough and apparent exile seemed to have dissipated in what can only be described as this welcome promotion.

Wheeler inherited a vibrant diocese consisting of 173 parishes in twenty-six Rural Deaneries. 288 priests, over half of whom were native to the diocese, were on active duty in the diocese and were supported by seventy-five priests representing eleven religious institutes. Of the secular priests, 162 were parish priests and 126 were curates and within this cohort, there was a strong Irish contingent. Eighty-six parishes had more than one priest with some having two, three and even four priests. Eleven parishes were in the care of religious.[31] Foreign chaplains ministered to Polish, Lithuanian, Ukrainian, German, Italian Hungarian and Spanish communities. Eight priests were ordained for the diocese in 1966 and there were 143 candidates in the junior and senior seminaries. There were seventy-nine convents of twenty-five female religious orders. The number of churches and chapels had increased substantially and Mass was celebrated in 173 parish churches, eighty-five chapels of ease and Mass centres, and twenty private chapels. There were 199 schools—primary, secondary modern, grammar and special—serving 56,686 students. Included in these were Voluntary Aided, Direct Grant and independent schools. There were forty-two sodalities and societies ranging from the Union of Catholic Mothers to the Catholic Evidence Guild and from the Catholic Marriage Advisory Council to the Newman Association. Within months of his arrival, Wheeler opened two new churches (at Allerton in Bradford and Wilsden) and two new schools (St George's Secondary, Bradford, and St Cuthbert's Primary, Bradford), and noted that work had commenced on other churches and schools planned by Bishop Dwyer. In addition, extensions were being undertaken at schools in Bradford, Heckmondwike, Ilkley, Otley and Knaresborough.

Such developments may be described as traditional: since Catholic Emancipation in 1829, the Church in England and Wales had worked hard to provide priests, schools and places of worship but in his Preface Wheeler referred to new ventures more obviously related to the recent Vatican Council. Wood Hall near Wetherby had been acquired in 1966 as a Pastoral and Ecumenical Centre. The Catechetical Centre, formerly in the old Bishop's House in Leeds, was relocated to the College of the Blessed Virgin Mary in Headingley, Leeds, and another was opened at St Marie's in Sheffield. [32]A seminary hostel scheme was introduced in Leeds where sixth form boys in grammar schools who were considering the priesthood could live throughout the week and return to their homes at the weekend. This had been first mooted in 1963 when the lack of vocations was 'a cause of disquiet' but took firmer shape on Wheeler's arrival.[33] Finally, diocesan consultative and advisory councils, consisting of clerics and laity, were introduced. These innovations were to develop with varying degrees of success during Wheeler's episcopate. To those afraid of rapid change and 'fearful that the Church was passing through a crisis' he wrote, as he had done in Middlesbrough, that the Church remained the same 'albeit in a new garb'.[34]

Not all was well within the diocese, however, and a report prepared by Mgr Gerald Moverley, one of the Vicars General, gave Wheeler an early indication of some problems and challenges he would have to confront. Although the diocese was described as 'active and progressive' and was in a satisfactory financial state, there were some issues to address including the negative attitude of a small number of clergy towards ecclesiastical authority, the defection of priests over the issue of celibacy, the small proportion of seminarians reaching ordination, the reorganization of secondary schools, the leakage from the faith among many school leavers, and the nature and extent of spiritual care for Irish and other immigrant Catholics. The ecumenical outlook was slightly rosier but the 'general picture of ecumenical dialogue is becoming clearer as one of social co-operation rather than doctrinal discussion'. Concerns were also expressed that the needs of ordinary working-class Catholics might be overlooked in carrying out liturgical reforms, that over 4,000 Catholic children were being educated in non-Catholic schools because of the dearth of places in diocesan schools, that the Lay Apostolate needed to be well planned, and that the diocesan provision of social welfare had to be co-ordinated and expanded.[35] Finally, the Diocesan Curia, understaffed and of no fixed permanent abode for the past decade, had to be re-organised on a more efficient and effective basis.[36] As ever, with a new bishop, priests expected to be moved. Despite the well-publicised moves made by Bishop Heenan, three parish priests remained in the same parishes they had been in since the 1930s and eight others in the same parishes they had been in since the 1940s. There had been a huge annual movement of parish priests in the period 1951 to 1966, however.[37]

In Newman's Pulpit

One of Wheeler's greatest joys and a source of immense pride during his early years in Leeds was an invitation to preach at the University Church of St Mary the Virgin, Oxford. It was a unique occasion for Wheeler was the first Catholic priest to preach in the historic church since the Reformation.

Standing on the High Street, St Mary's is the spiritual heart of the university and has been the focus of Christian worship and debates about religion and politics for hundreds of years. It has witnessed historic events associated with people of very different theological opinions including Duns Scotus, Thomas Cranmer, and John Wesley and in 1555, during the reign of the Catholic Queen Mary, it was where Bishops Latimer and Ridley and Archbishop Cranmer were tried for heresy. In 1828, John Henry Newman became vicar of St Mary's and from the pulpit John Keble preached the Assize Sermon of 14 July, 1833, considered to have been the start of the Oxford Movement, an attempt to revive Catholic spirituality in the church and university. The influence of the Movement spread and affected the practice and spirituality of the Church of England. In 1843, disillusioned with Anglicanism, Newman resigned from St Mary's and two years later joined the Roman Catholic Church.

In November 1966, Wheeler received an invitation from the Vice-Chancellor 'to accept office as a select preacher in the University of Oxford for the academic year 1967–8'. He was required to preach a 'University Sermon' at St Mary's and then, as was customary, participate in a discussion about his sermon. Wheeler readily accepted knowing that it was a great honour to receive such an invitation and aware also that as a non-Eucharistic service it would cause no attendant problems.[38] It was, *The Tablet* recorded, a sign of the way things had developed both inside and outside the Catholic communion that someone who had followed the same path as Newman, moving from communion with Canterbury to communion with Rome, should be invited to preach from Newman's old pulpit in the university church.[39] Newman's spirit was manifest in the very fabric of the church itself and in Wheeler's makeup. It was to be a unique and memorable occasion for him.

Wheeler delivered his sermon on Sunday 15 October 1967 but, as he told Norman St John Stevas, it was 'not really a sermon, it is more like a paper on the renewal of the Church from an ecumenical viewpoint, in the context of the University'.[40] It was a conflation of Wheeler's long-held views originating in his reading of Newman, those crystallized during Vatican II, and those still in the process of formation. Wheeler's topic was Church renewal, as had frequently been Newman's from the same pulpit in the 1830s, and his title, appropriately, was 'Ecclesia Rediviva'.

Wheeler's text was taken from verse 10 of the 51st Psalm—"Renew a right spirit within me"—taken from the *Miserere*, 'the fourth and greatest of the penitential psalms'. This had been a favourite prayer of saintly individuals and the institutional Church throughout Christian history, he said, and in the age of Pope John XXIII, Pope Paul VI and Vatican II it had 'taken on a new significance in the shedding of triumphalism and the avowed return to the spirit of the gospels and the Infant Church'. Because of Vatican II there was now 'a sincere spirit of humility manifest in the Church's anxiety to establish communion with the world of our time', a position happily different, he said, from Giant Pope in *Pilgrim's Progress*. Bunyan's Christian had encountered Giant Pope who 'though he be yet alive, he is… grown so crazy and stiff in his joints, that he can now do little more than sit in his cave's mouth, grinning at pilgrims as they go by, and biting his nails because he cannot come at them'. The revival of Bunyan's Giant was neither to be expected nor desired, said Wheeler, but another form of triumphalism may be seen in the Apocalypse, the Revelation to St. John: 'I am the Alpha and Omega, says the Lord God, who is and who was and who is to come'. 'The growth of the Church to full stature, to valid gigantic proportions', he said, 'is the becoming of Christ'. It is this form of triumphalism that the Christian expects and desires.

Vatican II had taken the concept of 'the Pilgrim Church', 'the progress of the people of God', and particularly in *Lumen Gentium* had applied it to the modern world. Empowered by the Risen Lord, guided by the Holy Spirit and connected inextricably with the papacy, the Church, as always, was now renewing her life and structures while retaining its undiluted teachings. 'Excessive legalism and clericalism is at a discount in the true spirit of the Gospels', he said, but he carefully stressed that those 'historic structures which have assured validity even when they appeared cumbersome' and mismanaged by 'human frailty', were still 'essential structures rooted in the New Testament'. The Church, he asserted, possessed a unique quality of 'perennial adaptability' in response to the movements of the Spirit, and *aggiornamento* now compelled her to look outward and define her position in the modern world. The renewal of attitudes and practice made necessary in the Church's life by the enactments of Vatican II continued after the Council and the Church, often accused of torpor, 'shows herself to be dynamic at the very moment when her critics 'proclaim her to be merely static'.

The theological repercussions of renewal were considerable for the Church 'is now no longer seen as monolithic' but 'is in the process of becoming'. This process required much thought and dialogue but the outcome would be worthwhile for traditional 'definitions of doctrine expressed in clear, but sometimes out-dated philosophical formulae whilst retaining their usefulness and validity' will 'receive new insights and find new modes of expression'. Here the dialogue with scriptural and theological findings of other systems was mutually beneficial and John Henry Newman, he said, provided a clear example of this approach when combining his study of the great western theological tradition with the patristic and other insights of the East. Newman had applied his findings to the English setting and similarly Vatican II encouraged the development of local Churches within the context of the Universal Church.

Wheeler then came to the study of theology. It had been rightly said that theology, if it was to be a living theology, needed three things: a university setting, participation of the laity, and ecumenical dialogue. On the first Wheeler said that his own life, like Newman's, had been a tale of two cities—Oxford and Rome—'and I think that each is deeply enhanced by the other.' It was important that Theology—the most important of academic subjects—should be placed at the centre of university endeavour and that there should not only be academic study but academic dialogue. Stressing his long-held view, he continued that 'In this country we are concerned to bring about a closer approximation between our seminaries and the different universities' and here 'we must pay tribute to the religious orders who, in this university, have led the way' in the study of theology, facilitating meditation and responding to the call to holiness.

On lay participation he referred first to the Council's emphasis on the responsibilities of the Whole People of God and then to the Synod on the Laity currently meeting in Rome. 'This lay participation,' he said, 'must also be effected in the theological field, and the lay theologian, all too rare a phenomenon in the past, will become an ordinary feature in Catholic intellectual life.' But no individual, theologian or otherwise, lay or clerical, should over-estimate his own importance: 'For if the whole People of God have a part to play, under the Holy Spirit, in the development of doctrine, this is something which happens through the charisma of being a Christian and not by virtue of being a member of the intelligentsia.'

Regarding ecumenical dialogue, Wheeler said that although many individuals in the Oxford theological schools had long been engaged in dialogue with their opposite numbers in the Catholic world, routine dialogue should happen in every theological faculty, be something less haphazard and be more far reaching. It could play an inestimable part in the growth towards unity. There was no longer the need for separation. 'The concept of heresy', said the Bishop, 'has become, in a sense, outdated. Dissociation has taken the place of excommunication. There, must always be freedom for theological thinking in the Church'. He continued: 'I am deeply convinced that not only does theology need an ecumenical context, but further, that under God and through the workings of the Spirit in His Church, this theological dialogue between us can save this science by evaluating maturely the contribution of the existentialist and community insights—the death of God variations and the like—in the light of valid tradition. There are some startling discoveries among our own younger theologians nowadays, some valid, others not, which had become 'old hat' in Oxford when I was up nearly forty years ago'. Preaching in a seat of learning, he was anxious to emphasize that "there must always be freedom for theological thinking in the Church yet he added the rider 'There are limits to such rethinking and the Church has a right to dissociate herself from views divergent from essential Christian teaching'.

The true crisis of the times, he said, was a crisis of spirituality. It could be countered by the world placing spiritual values first, by contemplation and the example of the contemplative orders, by demonstrating love for man and the world, by concern for the wants and needs of the world, and for peace. Spirituality had to overcome materialism; 'He who cares more for the earthly welfare of humanity than for its sanctification has lost the Christian view of the universe'. He concluded with Newman's words: 'The Church aims not at making a show, but at doing a work. She regards the world, and all that is in it, as a mere shadow, as dust and ashes, compared with the value of a single soul. She holds that unless she can, in her own way, do good to souls, it is no use her doing anything...'[41]

The juxtaposition of Wheeler's topic and the location was heavy with meaning and symbolism for Wheeler had looked at Vatican II from Newman's insight and perspective. He had placed aspects of Newman's thought, speeches and writings—the rejection of triumphalism, dismantling church bureaucracy, spiritual renewal, reviving theology and church history, encouraging ecumenism and enabling an active laity—in the context of Vatican II. It was as if through the lens of Newman Wheeler had come to appreciate the full meaning of the Council's call for renewal.

Wheeler found the whole experience entirely satisfying. So many threads of his life were woven together in this one unique event. And that explains, in part, why the sermon when read today makes such an immediate impact. But far more than the threads of Wheeler's biography are at issue here for, as already noted, the sermon rings the changes on some of the main events of the Second Vatican Council. By studying Wheeler's sermon, something of the excitement and exhilarating momentum generated by that great event can be experienced. What he describes is wonderfully distilled and clear: the need for reform within the Church.[42]

The Diocesan Mission to Peru

The Leeds Diocesan Mission to Peru gave Wheeler the opportunity to look beyond the confines of his own episcopal jurisdiction, contribute specifically to the development of the universal Church, and implement Vatican II's call for justice and peace. He was appalled that inequality, famine, undernourishment and hopelessness prevailed in many parts of the world and was convinced that only economic and social justice would lead to security and peace. By supporting the Peru Mission, he was also following the example of Pope Paul VI who in 1967 had established an International Commission for Justice and Peace. Its aim was to enable the followers of Christ to be informed of the need for the spread of God's justice in the world as the only permanent and adequate answer to war, revolution and fratricide. Christians, said Wheeler, faced a great challenge 'to persuade governments on all levels, of the necessity of international justice as a prelude to peace.'[43]

The Peru Mission was one of a number of projects initiated by Bishop Dwyer and developed further by Bishop Wheeler. During an informal meeting with the Cathedral clergy in 1960, Bishop Dwyer spoke of his recent meeting in Ireland with the Superior of the Columban Fathers. They had discussed the Columban mission in the shantytowns (*barriadas*) of Lima, capital of Peru, and the possibility of extending their work into the rest of the country. The Bishop informed the clergy that he had decided to call for volunteers from priests in the Leeds Diocese to assist the Columbans. Thirty priests subsequently volunteered and from them Frs Tony Wilkinson and Sean Morrissey were chosen. Dwyer had responded to Pope Pius XII's 1957 encyclical—*Fidei donum*, the gift of Faith—in which the Pope spoke of the need to take the Church of God to the whole world and particularly to the 'boundless spaces of South America'. This missionary call was echoed in the Second Vatican Council where Wheeler had spoken on the Church's responsibility to the world's poorer countries.[44]

Frs Morrissey and Wilkinson arrived in Lima in November 1961. They were attached initially to Columban missions and very quickly began to appreciate the huge problems faced by the Church in Peru. The people of the shanty towns knew little about parish life as it was understood by the Irish and English priests, and the newly-arrived missionaries were astounded by the appalling physical conditions in which their 'parishioners' lived. As one priest recorded, 'It was all totally different from the West Riding!' Nevertheless, Leeds' priests continued to volunteer. Fr Joe Kearns, who arrived in 1962, was followed by Fr Hugh Curriston in 1963. Frs Gerard Hanlon and Gerald Burke replaced Frs Wilkinson and Morrissey in 1966, and Fr Peter Ward arrived in 1968. They worked alongside the sparse number of priests from the Archdiocese of Lima and the larger number of American, Irish, Australian and New Zealand volunteer clergy. For the hundreds of thousands struggling to live in the *barriada* communities they formulated pastoral planning, organised deanery meetings, and liaised with the local auxiliary bishops. In contrast with priests working in the richer residential areas of Lima, they became committed to the 'preferential option for the poor', the slogan of Liberation Theology. Like the Church in other parts of the world, the Church in Peru was going through a time of transition following Vatican II. Liberation Theology and its strong political dimension was a complicating factor in that transition.[45]

In February 1968, Wheeler visited the missionaries. He had flown from the United Kingdom via New York and Jamaica where he had stayed in Montego Bay. He wrote: 'It is a delightful experience to step out of winter into mid-summer and to enjoy the warm and colour of the Caribbean'.[46] His experience of the conditions in Peru was to be very different and he recorded that 'One's first reaction is of severe revulsion'.[47] A missionary recalled that the Bishop 'though always his charming self with priests and people and people…was daunted by conditions in the parishes where our priests were working'. On arrival, Wheeler, his secretary and the missionaries were herded on to a truck and accompanied by an armed guard were taken to the hotel. The city was in the throes of a general strike and once deposited in the hotel Wheeler's and his party were virtual prisoners.

On the first night with the Columban Fathers, he was woken by earth tremors. The next morning he arrived to say Mass dressed in 'full clericals with his breviary under his arm'. "Tell me", he said to one of the missionaries, "is the word 'gringo' a term of endearment? I decided to go out in the street and look for a church in which to say Mass when 'an Indian' called across the road and shouted "Go home gringo"'. He was advised that 'gringo' was definitely not a term of endearment and that he should stay in the hotel until called for. After Mass, Wheeler complained of a stomach upset and remained at the hotel while the others went off to see the Inca ruins at Macchu Picchu. On their return, they found him not in the hotel but having tea at the Columban Centre. Dressed always in episcopal attire, Wheeler completed his short visit to Peru and his tour of the 'Leeds parishes' and before leaving laid the foundation stone of Fr Curriston's new church. His visitation, noted a missionary, 'was not a great personal success' but he brought welcome funds with him, took Fr Curriston for a rest in the West Indies, and on his return to Leeds invited the parents of the priests to have tea with him at Bishop's House.[48] He later gave his views on the acute religious, social and economic problems of Peru but was careful not to express opinions that might have jeopardised the safety of his priests who were working there or embroil them in difficulties with the local Church.[49] He noted the concentration of wealth in the hands of a few families and the 'languid' way in which government operated. In the midst of squalor, inequality and inefficiency, his missionaries were setting up churches, schools and clinics—a political statement as much as religious witness. He acknowledged that the missionaries could not avoid the stark realities of life in their leadership of local Catholics: 'It is the role of the priest in these parts to lead them to social betterment and to fight many of their battles for them: battles for water, light, sanitation and health services. Having won their confidence in these ways, he can proceed to show them the ways of God'. It was 'a great apostolic field'.[50]

On his return to Leeds, his social sympathies for those in need sharply honed, Wheeler established the Peru Commission under a senior priest. Its principal task, according to the Bishop, 'was to quicken the interests and commitment of the whole diocese to the project of universal responsibility and to collect alms for its maintenance'.[51] He appointed that the First Sunday of Advent be set aside for his Pastoral on Peru and the annual diocesan collection for 'the Peru Mission'. The Bishop was totally committed and set about ensuring a steady supply of clerical volunteers and arranging for religious sisters to assist on the mission. On his return to Peru in autumn 1969, Fr Hanlon was accompanied by four Sisters of Mercy nuns from their convents in the diocese. Other priests continued the Leeds tradition with Frs Vincent O'Hara, Michael Ingwell, and Dan Harrison replacing those who returned.[52] Alongside the Peru Commission, in 1973 Wheeler set up a Diocesan Justice and Peace Commission, which he chaired, to stimulate an awareness of the need for justice both at home and abroad in the light of the Church's social teaching and to foster and encourage action for justice and peace at all levels of diocesan life. Justice and Peace Groups sprang up in the major towns and cities of the diocese, liaising closely with CAFOD and other international charitable organizations. The arrival of the Ugandan Asians in the autumn of 1972 enabled the diocese to respond to this call by collecting clothes and furniture and providing accommodation and transport for those displaced by the policies of Idi Amin.[53] The subsequent arrival of Chilean and Vietnamese refugees again gave the diocese an opportunity to put charity into action and again Wheeler ensured that their accommodation, linguistic and occupational needs were generously met. Addressing another Third World need, Wheeler saw to it that the diocese continued to collect funds for Pontifical Society of the Holy Childhood and the Society of St Peter the Apostle for Native Clergy.[54]

Ad Limina 1967–1972

In 1972, Wheeler submitted his first quinquennial *ad limina* report to the Vatican, a statistical statement of the diocesan position accompanied by personal reflections and comments.[55] He reported confidently that in the spirit of Vatican II diocesan structures had been established 'to ensure consultation and communication with all levels of the people and clergy' and that Commissions had been established to oversee a range of pastoral and administrative initiatives. Against these positive developments, however, he had to relate rather more depressing news regarding the fall in religious observance, the quality of seminary training, the state of vocations, and clerical defections. Wheeler recalled that he found his *ad limina* visits a source of encouragement and assurance, an occasion when he was able to gauge the effectiveness of his administration and pastoral leadership. Pope Paul VI was a good and sympathetic listener and, he wrote, 'I always came home refreshed and encouraged'.[56]

In terms of religious observance and practice, the picture was uneven, reflecting the impact and influence of the changes wrought by Vatican II and a general lessening of interest in and an adherence to religion. Wheeler reported that there had been a significant decline in baptisms reflecting, perhaps, the decline in the Catholic birth rate, but that Confirmations remained at a high level. The reception of Holy Communion had increased, perhaps due to a lessening of the obligation of fasting but attendance at the Sacrament of Penance had declined sharply. There was also evidence of a significant and worrying decline in Sunday Mass attendance with 117,465 attending in 1972 compared with 129,450 in 1968. The number of mixed marriages had increased while there had been a steady decline in the number of conversions.

The reduction in Church students and the rising costs of seminary training, he reported, was placing a heavy financial burden on Leeds and other dioceses. There had been some reorganization in provision with the Junior Houses at Ushaw and Upholland being amalgamated but it was expected that St Paul's Seminary Hostel in Leeds would address the work and formation previously covered in junior seminaries. Ordinations for the diocese remained relatively healthy. The number of priests ordained between 1967 and 1972 was as follows: 1967—thirteen; 1968—eleven; 1969—six; 1970—four; 1971—nine; and 1972—nine.[57] The expected number of ordinations for the coming five years was also very encouraging. Although the number of Church students was well down on the number stated in the last *ad limina*, Wheeler felt the situation was still promising. The decline, he claimed, was a phenomenon of the Western world. What he did find alarming, however, was that young men were being ordained without being able to say Mass in Latin. He wrote:

> Apart from being the prescription of the Church, it is very essential in this country that a certain amount of worship in Latin should be preserved in view of our penal times history and the consequent devotion to the international language of the Church.

> It would therefore be a great help if the Sacred Congregation could insist that every priest who is ordained must first prove to his Ordinary that he can celebrate the new rite of Mass in the Latin language.[58]

A more difficult problem was the loss, or defection, of ordained priests. The Vatican Council had overwhelmingly affirmed that celibacy was an obligation of priesthood, not for any pragmatic reason but for the spiritual dedication of the whole man to the service of God. Yet within five years of the Council, priests across the world had begun to leave their ministry at an alarming rate. The Dutch Hierarchy would not affirm Pope Paul's call for episcopal solidarity on the issue of celibacy while the English and Welsh Hierarchy felt the need to support the Pope. In February 1970, Cardinal Heenan offered guidance to the Westminster clergy. The Hierarchy, he said, re-affirmed its loyalty to the papacy and to clerical celibacy. He chastised 'the public cult of lapsed priests' and praised those who remained steadfast in their ministry. A desire to marry, he said, 'is almost invariably the motive for seeking release from priestly obligations' but 'the marriage bed is not a bed of roses'. The vast majority of priests, he concluded, remain faithful to their priesthood and chastity, both of which were God's gifts. He concluded: '... we must pray that the spirit of love and self-denial will grow in the hearts of those who have undertaken the sweet burden of the priesthood of Christ'.[59] For those priests and religious who had decided to leave the ministry, however, the

Hierarchy established a support mechanism called the Commission for Social Welfare.

The Diocese of Leeds, like others, was sorely affected by the defection of priests and in 1972 Wheeler reported to the Vatican that despite there being a good spirit among the clergy, 'we have had… our tragedies'. Fourteen priests had been laicised since 1967 while five had left without applying for a dispensation. The most difficult year, he wrote, was 1969 but since then 'there have been a decreasing number of problems' and defections.[60] He had lamented to one priest in 1969 that 'in some cases he had no inkling that anything was wrong'. 'These people', he wrote, 'all talk about the importance of communication and consultation, and yet the last person they consult is their father in God. By the time they come to him, everything is cut and dried with both a bride and a job'.[61]

Wheeler admitted later that like many other bishops, he suffered greatly over this trend but could not adequately explain it. It was, he wrote, 'a terrible sadness. I think in a sense that the years covered by the period of my Episcopacy, must have been one of the most distressing in the life of the Church. It certainly caused great sorrow to Bishops who couldn't understand why this was happening'. It was wrong, he wrote, to blame Vatican II. The mores of an increasingly permissive secular society may have had something to do with the defections, he wrote, but it would also be foolish to ascribe too much to these. A more telling reason may have been found in the circumstances in which seminarians had been trained during the period of Vatican II. Like other Church institutions, the seminaries were in a state of flux and uncertainty. Men training for the priesthood were taught predominantly by professors educated in a previous age who were themselves unsure and perhaps unwelcoming of Vatican II's attempts at renewal. Priests embarking on their ministry in the mid-1960s entered a Church and Catholic community shorn of the liturgical certainties and respectful attitudes towards bishops and clergy that had been there only a decade previously.

What was different about the losses of the late 1960s and 1970s was the publicity they generated. This had a huge unsettling impact on the Catholic community and on those priests who remained faithful to their ministry. Wheeler added that Pope Paul's willingness to grant priests dispensations from their vows contrasted with the sluggishness with which lay Catholic were granted dispensation from marriage vows.[62] This, he implied, did not help. At the end of his *ad limina* report, he concluded:

I hope here is no complacency or self-satisfaction in our report. Christianity is at a discount in our country today and there is a frightening drift from God. All the same, there are signs of a yearning for spiritual values. Our only prayer is that we may not be found wanting and for this we seek the support and blessing of the Apostolic See for which so many of our ancestors shed their blood.[63]

During his first four years in Leeds, Wheeler had done much to energise his extensive diocese in line with the pastoral demands of Vatican II. His dynamic efforts took a toll on his health, however, and in the summer of 1970, he suffered what was thought to be a mild heart attack. It was, in fact, coronary ischemia, a restriction of the blood flow to the heart. It slowed him down considerably but only for a short period and he went to rest at the Esperance Nursing Home in Eastbourne.[64] By September, he was recovering well, although he had lost weight and by October, he was undertaking light duties. By November, he was 'doing quite a lot' and was 'well on the mend'.[65]

The Forty Martyrs

An unfortunate result of Wheeler's illness was that he was unable to attend the canonization of the Forty English and Welsh Martyrs in Rome on 25 October 1970.

The martyrs of England and Wales were Catholic men and women executed for their faith between 1535 and 1679. Fifty-four had been beatified in 1886 and a further nine were beatified in 1895. Of these, Bishop John Fisher and Sir Thomas More were canonized in 1935. In 1929 another 136 martyrs were beatified. At Easter 1960, a cause was launched for the canonization of forty previously beatified martyrs. 'Our beloved martyrs' were very close to Wheeler's heart and he energetically supported the cause. The Dioceses of Middlesbrough and Leeds had strong connections with the Yorkshire Martyrs and Wheeler was anxious not only to witness their canonization and that of other martyrs but he was also determined to confront those of the opinion that the canonization process was somehow outmoded, at odds with the decrees and constitutions of Vatican II, and irrelevant in the modern Church. To Wheeler, the martyrs challenged modern Catholics to a deepening profession of their faith and the obligation to search for a new commitment to Christian unity.

In July 1967, in a lengthy and cogent article in *The Tablet*, he wrote that since the Council 'in trying to mature ourselves away from a "magical" use of the saints, we seem to have thrown the baby out with the bathwater'. The whole stress of the Council, he wrote, was Christocentric but the newly emphasized Christocentricity of the faith neither opposed nor contradicted anything that had gone before in the Church's official teaching relative to the communion of saints. Recalling *Lumen Gentium*, he continued that by reason of the fact that those in heaven are more closely united with Christ, they establish the whole Church more firmly in holiness, lend nobility to the worship which the Church offers on earth to God, and in many ways contribute to its greater development.

> For after they have been received into their heavenly home and are present to the Lord, through Him and with Him and in Him, saints do not cease to intercede with the Father rather they show forth the merits which they won on earth through the one Mediator between God and man, Christ Jesus. The saints served God in all things and filled up in their flesh whatever was lacking of the sufferings of Christ on behalf of His body which is the Church. Thus by their brotherly interest our weakness is very greatly strengthened.

If the role of the saints in Christianity were minimized or neglected, he wrote, it would not only be an impoverishment but also a failure to grasp the total concept which, while establishing the primary Christocentricity, follows on by indicating the importance of a new and deeper understanding of the meaning of "the communion of saints" and the interaction between the Pilgrim Church and the Church Triumphant. Those who participated in the Council, he continued, and who were specifically charged with its implementation, 'have always held the view that God the Holy Spirit speaks to the Church and the world of our time in the broad message of the conciliar decrees. Here, he contended, there was dissonance between the Conciliar Fathers and those who attributed the current spirit of unrest and uncertainty in the Church's life to the Council itself. 'On the contrary', he wrote, 'we are convinced that this is something characteristic of the world of our time to which the Church has an answer to bring'. Perhaps 'answer' was the wrong word, he claimed, for it was unfashionable to provide clear-cut answers, and 'whatever we may, think of some fashions they often have their own "insights". But Christ and His Church can and do 'give tranquillity in chaos. And tranquillity predicates balance. The Church, which is ever seeking fuller truth, can only attain its end when every considered stage of the development proceeds from a balanced implementing of her valid thinking. Therefore it would be wrong, on the one hand, to ignore the decrees of the Council and, on the other, to interpret them in an exaggerated or unbalanced manner'.

This was happening where one particular conciliar dictum or re-emphasis was observed at the expense of the total picture and this, Wheeler observed, was based on an inadequate interpretation or understanding of history. 'Our present age', he wrote, 'seems weak in its sense of history. But a true sense of history is essential, especially with regard to an objective viewing of an institution like the Church, which in the providence of God has developed or evolved in some part through the inter-play of historical (as distinct from political) pressures. Vatican II could not have spoken as it did unless Vatican I and Trent and the other eighteen General Councils of the Church, going right back to the Council of Jerusalem had preceded it. Vatican II is not an instrument of destruction but of a greater fulfillment'. Those who regarded the Church from outside may well interpret a lack of balance in this respect as 'a flight from the supernatural' and here they had something valid to say. The world never respected the worldly Christian. It looked to Christians for service but not merely for welfare work that can be done just as effectively by the good pagan. True Christian service had to be informed by fundamental Christian priorities—the conscious priority of God and spiritual values, both epitomized in the virtue of faith and a faith which is inseparable from hope and from love. These two important prerequisites, faith and a sense of the communion of saints, are epitomized in the martyrs. 'If enthusiasm for the canonisation of our English martyrs seems to be lacking, it is a sad reflection on our present state and symptomatic of a wrong order of priorities'. There are those, he concluded, who say that we should forget the past:

> It is true that sometimes the past is best forgotten. But the great heroes of the past must always be remembered and honoured. Our Lord Himself loved to speak of Abraham and Isaac and Jacob and Moses and David and the Prophets. These men were an inspiration to all of God's people. Today we specially need the example and the prayers of our martyrs, because people all around us are losing their faith. And we can only help them and ourselves by deepening and intensifying our own faith. There are those who think, quite mistakenly, that love for our martyrs leads to hatred of other Christian bodies. But they died with Our Lord's own words on their lips: "Father, forgive them for they know not what they do". Our attitude is, of course, the same. But anyhow, nobody holds the non-Catholic Christians of today in any way responsible for what

happened four hundred years ago. Indeed, there are many non-Catholics today who honour and venerate our martyrs. They realize that they died for their faith and are men for all seasons. And they realize further that, as faith is at such a discount today, we need their inspiration. If they do not always look to their own martyrs for a similar inspiration, it is no argument in favour of any neglect on our part. We shall fail to become mature Christians and to give the world the service that it needs, unless we place spiritual values first.[66]

In April 1967, Wheeler led the annual Tyburn Walk to commemorate the executions of the martyrs at Tyburn and arranged for a rally in York in July 1967 and a Mass at Hazlewood in June 1969 to promote the martyrs' cause. Fr George Bradley, who possessed unrivalled knowledge of the history of the diocese, was appointed as the diocesan representative on the national coordinating body and ultimately Bishop Moverley, twenty-eight diocesan priests and pilgrims joined with their counterparts from Middlesbrough and attended the ceremony in Rome. On 1 November 1970, over 10,000 people attended a martyrs rally held in York attended by Wheeler, Bishop Moverley and Bishop McClean of Middlesbrough.[67]

The canonization process was not without its difficulties especially at a time when Cardinal Heenan and the Hierarchy were intent on improving ecumenical relations with the Church of England. The Anglicans too had their martyrs from the time of the Marian persecutions and Archbishop Ramsey of Canterbury sought to play down and Heenan tried to avoid any Catholic triumphalism over the canonizations. Aware of the event's sensitivity, Pope Paul VI tried to assuage Anglican reservations when he said at the canonization: 'There will be no seeking to lessen the legitimate prestige and worthy patrimony of piety and usage proper to the Anglican church when the Roman Catholic church—this servant of the servants of God—is able to embrace her ever beloved sister in the one authentic communion of the family of Christ, a communion of origin and faith, a communion of priesthood and of rule, a communion of the saints in the freedom and love of the spirit of Jesus'. From beginning to end the ceremony was calculated to avoid any offence to the contemporary ecumenical spirit.[68] Ramsey himself was an advocate of ecumenism and had allowed the Catholic Hierarchy to celebrate Mass in the precincts of Canterbury Cathedral on 7 July 1970 to commemorate the eight-hundredth anniversary of the martyrdom of St Thomas Becket. Wheeler concelebrated at the Mass which was attended by approximately 8,000 people and which was conducted despite physical and vocal interruptions by extreme Protestants.[69]

Notes

1   B. Plumb, *Arundel to Zabi: A Biographical Dictionary of the Catholic Bishops and Wales (Deceased) 1623–1987* (Warrington, 1987); W. G. Wheeler, *In Truth And Love* (Southport: Gowland and Co., 1990), p. 85; *Catholic Herald*, 6 May 1966.

2   For Bishop Poskitt's appointment to Leeds in 1936, see *The Beda Review*, vol. 3, no. 6, Sept 1936.

3   Heenan to Cardinale, 6 May 1966. AAW, Heenan, HE1/A5.

4   Brunner to Wheeler, 24 April 1966. LDA, WDC, W2.

5   Wheeler to Cardinale, 24 April 1966. LDA, WDC, W2.

6   Cardinale to Wheeler, 28 April 1966. LDA, WDC, W2.

7   Hurley to Wheeler, 9 July 1966. LDA, WDC, W2.

8   Heenan to Wheeler, 3 May 1966. LDA, WDC, W2.

9   Dwyer to Wheeler, 28 June 1966. LDA, WDC, W2.

10   Ramsey to Wheeler, 14 May 1966. LDA, WDC, W2.

11   Coggan to Wheeler, 5 May 1966. LDA, WDC, W2.

12   Morley to Wheeler 5 May 1966; Shield to Wheeler, 11 May 1966; Bishop of Wakefield to Wheeler, 5 May 1966; Bishop of Hull to Wheeler, 5 May 1966. LDA, WDC, W2.

13   Tustin to Wheeler, 5 May 1966. LDA, WDC, W2.

14   If the enthronement was conducted according to an ancient rite, Wheeler was certainly breaking new ground with his crozier which was made out of Perspex by his friend the Hungarian-born sculptor Arthur Fleischmann. LDA, WPC, Enthronement 1966.

15   *Solemn Enthronement of the Right Reverend William Gordon Wheeler, Bishop of Leeds.* LDA, WPC, Enthronement 1966; *Yorkshire Post*, 28 June 1966.

16   *Solemn Enthronement of the Right Reverend William Gordon Wheeler, Bishop of Leeds.* LDA, WPC, Enthronement 1966.

17   M. Manktelow, *John Moorman: Anglican, Franciscan, Independent* (Norwich: Canterbury Press, 1999), p. 71.

18   Cardinale to Heenan, 20 Aug 1966. AAW, Heenan, HE1/A5(a).

19   Plumb, *Arundel to Zabi.*

20   W. G. Wheeler, *More Truth And Love* (Southport: Gowland and Co., 1994), pp. 34–35.

21   *QR*, 1967–1972.

22   'Views About the Diocese and its Special Problems' (1966). LDA, WDC, W2, Leeds Diocesan Curia.

23   R. E. Finnigan, 'Bishop Wheeler, 1966–1985' in R. E. Finnigan and J. Hagerty, *The Bishops of Leeds 1878-1985: Essays in Honour of Bishop David Konstant* (Keighley: PBK Publishing on behalf of the Diocese of Leeds, 2005), p. 156.

24   *Catholic Directory* (1966), p. 781.

25   *Catholic Directory* (1957), p. 222; *Leeds Diocesan Directory* (1967), p. 85.

26 B. Sharp, 'Bishop Dwyer, 1957–1965' in Finnigan and Hagerty, *The Bishops of Leeds 1878–1985: Essays in Honour of Bishop David Konstant*, pp. 133–149.

27 Dwyer to Heenan, 19 Jan 1964. AAW, Heenan, He1/L2.

28 Finnigan, 'Bishop Wheeler, 1966–1985', p. 155.

29 Wheeler, *Ad Clerum*, 18 May 1966. LDA, WDC, Wheeler Papers.

30 *Leeds Diocesan Directory* (1967), pp. 5–7.

31 LDA, WDC, Council of Clergy, 8 Jan. 1967.

32 *Leeds Diocesan Directory* (1967), pp. 5–7.

33 The seminary hostel was the idea of Mr B. Bruynseels, Headmaster of St Wilfrid's School, Featherstone. LDA, WDC, W38, Seminary Hostel and Catechetical Centre. Wheeler wished to name the hostel after Bishop Heenan but Heenan refused to let his name be associated with it. Heenan to Wheeler, 13 Aug 1966. AAW, Heenan, He1/L2.

34 The hostel for prospective seminarians was opened in 1968. LDA, WDC, W1, Memo on Vocations.

35 'Views About the Diocese and its Special Problems' (1966). LDA, WDC, W2, Leeds Diocesan Curia.

36 G. Moverley, 'Some Thoughts on the Organization of the Curial Offices', 18 Aug 1966. LDA, WDC, W2, Leeds Diocesan Curia.

37 'Parish Priests' (June 1966). LDA, WDC, W2, Leeds Diocesan Curia.

38 K. C. Turvin to Wheeler, 21 Nov 1966; Wheeler to Turvin, 24 Nov 1966. LDA, WDC, W43, Oxford Select Preacher.

39 *The Tablet*, 21 Oct 1967.

40 W.G. Wheeler to Norman St John Stevas, 20 Oct 1967. LDA, WDC, W43, Oxford Select Preacher.

41 W. G. Wheeler, 'Ecclesia Rediviva'. LDA, WDC, W43, Oxford Select Preacher.

42 Dining with the Vice-Chancellor at Oriel College, staying at the Randolph Hotel, saying Mass at St Benet's Hall and preaching in Newman's pulpit was 'a great joy' to Wheeler. Wheeler to Dom James Forbes OSB, 19 Oct 1967. LDA, WDC, W43, Oxford Select Preacher. *The Oxford Mail* published extracts from his sermon together with a photograph of him and the Vice-Chancellor and Wheeler suggested to Bishop Moverley that the photo, with an appropriate caption, might adorn the next issue of the *Diocesan Directory*. Wheeler to Moverley, 19 Oct 1967. LDA, WDC, W43, Oxford Select Preacher. To Norman St John Stevas he wrote that it was 'all a very delightful occasion' and was pleased to hear that his sermon would be printed in a forthcoming edition of *The Dublin Review*. Wheeler to St John Stevas, 20 Oct 1967; St John-Stevas to Wheeler, 24 Oct 1967. LDA, WDC, W43, Oxford Select Preacher.

43 W. G. Wheeler, 'Saturday Sermon–Justice and Peace' (n.d.). LDA, WPC, W68, Peru. The Leeds Diocesan Justice and Peace Commission established by Wheeler is dealt with in Chapter 14.

44 G. Hanlon, *In A Far Country - Leeds Diocesan Mission to Peru* (privately printed, 2011), p. 3; Wheeler, *In Truth And Love*, p. 123.

45 Hanlon, *In A Far Country*, pp. 47–54.

[46] W. G. Wheeler, 'Peruvian Journey' (Typescript, 1968). LDA, WPC, W68, Peru; Wheeler, *In Truth And Love*, pp. 123–125.

[47] Wheeler, 'Peruvian Journey'. LDA, WPC, W68, Peru.

[48] Hanlon, *In A Far Country*, pp. 58–61; Wheeler, *In Truth And Love*, pp. 123–124.

[49] *Novena*, June 1968, vol. xviii, no. 2.

[50] Wheeler, 'Peruvian Journey'. LDA, WPC, W68, Peru.

[51] *QR*, 1967–1972.

[52] Hanlon, *In A Far Country*, pp. 87–88, 114; *Leeds Diocesan Gazette*, Jan 1970.

[53] Wheeler, *Ad Clerum*, 10 Sept 1972. LDA, WDC, W43.

[54] *QR*, 1977–1982.

[55] An *Ad Limina Apostolorum* is the occasion for bishops to deliver a five-yearly report to the Pope on the state of their dioceses or territories. The visit 'to the threshold of the Apostles (Peter and Paul)' was made obligatory by Pope Pius X in 1909.

[56] Wheeler, *In Truth And Love*, pp. 119–120.

[57] *QR*, 1967–1972; *Leeds Diocesan Directory*.

[58] *QR*, 1967–1972.

[59] Cardinal Heenan, 'Catholic Priests and Celibacy', 25 Feb. 1970. LDA, WDC, Priestly Celibacy.

[60] *QR*, 1967–1972.

[61] Wheeler to Fr T. O'Shea, 6 Oct 1969. LDA, WDC, W69, Opus Dei.

[62] Wheeler, *In Truth And Love*, pp. 91–93.

[63] *QR*, 1967–1972.

[64] Bishop Moverley to Bishop Patrick Casey of Brentwood, 11 Aug 1970. BDA, Bishop Casey Papers.

[65] Correspondence between Wheeler and Bruno Scott-James, Sept–Dec 1970. LDA, WPC, Bruno Scott-James. Part of this correspondence relates to Wheeler's successful efforts to have Scott-James created a Domestic Prelate with the title of Monsignor.

[66] *The Tablet*, 8 July 1967. For an interesting discussion of the place of the saints in Catholic devotions following Vatican II see A. Harris, 'Undying Devotions' in *The Tablet*, 15 Dec 2012.

[67] LDA, WDC, W68, Forty Martyrs.

[68] LDA, WDC, W68, Forty Martyrs; *Catholic Herald*, 30 Oct 1970.

[69] LDA, WDC, W68, Forty Martyrs; *Catholic Herald*, 10 July 1970.

9 CHALLENGES TO AUTHORITY

Critical Opinions

THE YEARS OF Vatican II and the period immediately following were filled with tension. Some Catholics desperately wanted the Church to change; others expected change; some opposed change. Many did not know either what they wanted or what to expect. In this rather febrile atmosphere, a few took the opportunity of the new openness of expression to be highly critical of the Church, its structures and its leaders. In England, the Dominican Fr Herbert McCabe, in the *New Blackfriars* journal of February 1967, strongly criticised not only Church institutions but also the English and Welsh Hierarchy. This in itself was enough to raise the ire of the episcopate but it was not the first time McCabe had given cause for alarm: among other things, he had publicly supported Charles Davis who in December 1966 had very publicly left both the priesthood and the Church. Cardinal Heenan was distinctly unimpressed with McCabe who was subsequently dismissed from his editorship of *New Blackfriars* and temporarily deprived of his priestly functions by the Provincial of the Dominicans.[1]

While McCabe's view did not command universal respect, some Catholics were uncomfortable at the suppression of free speech and this galvanised opposition to the bishops. Wheeler received letters complaining about the Church authorities' handling of the affair and supporting McCabe. To some, McCabe's removal 'will silence a distinguished periodical, discourage creative theological thinking, cause scandal to some of our separated brethren, and it will be the last straw for some Catholics who have been thinking of following Charles Davis's example'.[2] Others felt that the bishops could have demonstrated tolerance and understanding by reinstating McCabe. Ian Gregor of the University of Kent was of the opinion that the affair 'identified clericalism with Catholicism in a way we thought had been ended by Vatican II' but he directed his criticism personally at Wheeler: 'It hardly needs saying, especially to you, that this authoritarian silencing accords ill with the virtues of intellectual integrity, self-criticism, and fair debate, which we like to think are a valuable part of university teaching'. Like some of his colleagues, Gregor felt that he could not contribute to forthcoming meetings of the universities and seminaries group for he had a view of the priesthood which, it seemed, was 'not shared by the Hierarchy'.[3]

McCabe was due to speak at the Leeds University Catholic Chaplaincy at the end of February 1967 but his suspension meant this had to be cancelled. It was something of an escape for Wheeler and he was spared the embarrassment of unwanted publicity.[4] In the diocese, however, petitions in support of McCabe were drawn up in school staff-rooms, by school governors and by Catholic teachers in the Leeds area. No one publicly supported McCabe's view that the Church was 'quite plainly corrupt' but they did oppose the suppression of free speech.[5]

Wheeler found it all rather depressing. He wrote to Cardinal Heenan in early February 1967 that he had been receiving 'the most tiresome letters from university teachers, who show great immaturity and seem to have gone berserk about the whole matter. They have even gone so far as to suggest withdrawing from the Commission regarding Seminaries and Universities'. He added, rather patronizingly: 'It sickens one with the whole lot of them, and makes one thankful for the simple Catholic faithful. Incidentally, I find the latter very disturbed and feel that we should be taking a stronger line, but what should we do?'[6] Guidance from Heenan was not immediately forthcoming but Archbishop Dwyer was deputed to respond to McCabe which he did in *New Blackfriars*.[7]

Another much-publicised critique of the Church came in *Objections to Roman Catholicism*, a collection of essays published in November 1964, when seven Catholic writers, including the Jesuit Archbishop Thomas Roberts, described the faults they perceived in the modern Church. *Objections to Roman Catholicism* was something of a landmark publication in that committed and constructive Catholics voiced their public criticism of an institution previously regarded as one of unassailable authority. Described as 'a witness to the rise of an informed and courageous laity', it was claimed that the book would have never seen the light of day had it not been for Pope John XXIII's *aggiornamento*. Other than Roberts, the authors were indeed all laypeople and included a well-educated housewife, a publisher, an author, an historian, a journalist, and a philosopher and essayist. Their topics ranged from the Church's emphasis on superstition and credulity in the veneration of the saints; the worldliness of the Church in its wealth and pomp; the Church's authoritarian nature and stress on conformity; the issue of censorship, freedom and the individual conscience; reactions against scholasticism; to contraception and war. The authors stressed they were not about to start 'a spiritual free-for-all' but they were dedicated to criticising an institution to which they all belonged. Their purpose was to begin a debate of among free minds which would lead to mutual understanding within the Church and with other Christian denominations outside it. The topics discussed and the terms used, however, were not designed to please the bishops and traditionalists.[8]

Humanae Vitae

One of the major problems facing Wheeler and other bishops during the late-1960s and early-1970s stemmed from Pope Paul VI's encyclical, *Humanae Vitae*, which in 1968 restated the Church's traditional teaching on artificial means of birth control, a practice made safer for women with the introduction of a reliable contraceptive pill. The pill could be used to remedy some gynaecological problems and the Church accepted its use in circumstances where less radical treatments were unavailable, but it remained contrary to the Church's teaching for Catholic women to use the pill with the explicit intention of preventing pregnancy. So too were Catholic men forbidden to use artificial means of contraception with the same intention. In his encyclical, Pope Paul was not, therefore, adopting a new position in reaction to scientific, medical or social developments but simply reaffirming Church teaching. Some Catholics welcomed the encyclical but others considered it an absolutist statement at odds with the demands of modern marriage and family life. The encyclical raised the ire of many Catholics, caused personal anxiety among priests and laity, and led to a crisis of ecclesiastical authority with bishops, priests and laity embroiled in a heated controversy. Some informed Catholics were appalled that the Pope had ignored the recommendations of the Commission on Birth Control. Priests who disagreed with the encyclical left their ministry while married people chose to interpret or disregard the teaching of the Church according to their consciences. Coming so soon on the heels of liturgical reforms, the debate rocked and confused the Church. Catholics who had seen their traditional liturgy dismantled to be more responsive to the modern world now heard an intransigent statement which appeared to leave the Church in a previous age.

In May 1964, the English and Welsh Hierarchy, of which Wheeler was now a member, issued a statement which unequivocally declared 'that contraception is not an open question for it is against the laws of God and of nature'. Maintaining that they would be failing in their pastoral duty if they remained silent, the bishops quoted St Augustine who wrote that sexual intercourse was unlawful 'where the conception of the offspring is prevented'. Pope Pius XII, they said, had spoken with equal bluntness: 'This precept is as valid today as it was yesterday, and it will be the same tomorrow and always, because it does not imply a precept of human law but is the expression of a law which is natural and divine'. It was not a statement without compassion, however, for the bishops recognized that sometimes there was an agonizing choice for married couples between natural instincts and the law of God. 'Our hearts are full of sympathy', said the bishops, 'but we cannot change God's law'.[9]

The Church's position was attacked increasingly, however, by those who doubted the validity of the natural law argument and saw no scriptural authority for outlawing contraception as a means of birth control. Non-theologians also took issue with the Church. In March 1965, a *Daily Telegraph* Gallop Poll showed that 60% of Catholics in England felt that the Church was wrong to ban contraception as a means of birth control. Alternatively, 19% were against change while 21% per cent were indifferent to the Church's pronouncements on the matter. In October 1965, a survey of the private opinions of Newman Association members indicated 'a probable majority' opposed to the Church's ban on contraception.[10] Opinion polls, however, do not decide the doctrine of the Church.

Pope John XXIII had removed the issue of contraception from the agenda of the Vatican Council and in 1962 had given it to a Pontifical Commission of clerical and lay members. In April 1966 a minority of the Commission's sixty-four members, 'acknowledged that they could not demonstrate the intrinsic evil of contraception on the basis of natural law and so rested their case on authority and the fear of possible consequences of change both to Authority and sexual morality'. This led Pope Paul VI to establish an Executive Committee of the Commission composed of sixteen cardinals and bishops to guide the Commission. This 'inner cabinet' was placed under the Presidency of Cardinal Ottaviani, Head of the Holy Office and guardian of orthodoxy, who was opposed to any change in the Church's teaching. Cardinal Heenan and Cardinal Doepfner of Munich were Vice-Presidents of the Executive Committee.[11] In June 1966, the Commission submitted a report to the Pope calling for artificial contraception to be allowed but a minority of the Commission was diametrically opposed to this view.[12] In October 1967, a meeting of the World Congress of the Lay Apostolate appealed to the Pope to allow Catholics to limit the size of their families in accordance with their consciences.[13]

By this time, the debate in England and Wales was in full swing and the Church under attack. Wheeler was asked but refused to associate his name with a pamphlet by the Catholic writer Rosemary Houghton entitled *Giving In On Birth Control?* He thought it defeatist and gave the impression that judgement had already been made. It was only right, he said, to wait for the Pope's pronouncement; meanwhile the teaching of the Church must be adhered to.[14] To personal and heart-rending letters from laity seeking counsel and from priests seeking clarification, he replied directly but sympathetically without giving false advice or contradicting the teaching of the Church.[15]

On 25 July 1968, in his encyclical *Humanae Vitae*, Pope Paul VI banned all means of artificial contraception and declared that every marriage act must remain open to life. It was a decision which led to the greatest split in the Church in modern times.[16] The English and Welsh bishops were unaware of the encyclical's impending publication and were caught completely unprepared. Wheeler was on vacation and his secretary, Fr John Dunne, was left to answer phone calls and enquiries, not all of which were pleasant.[17] Opponents of the encyclical quickly gathered force and claimed that the Pope could not issue an edict in this way and that his words did not constitute the solemn teaching of the Church. The encyclical gave rise to a huge crisis of authority with priests and laity publicly rejecting the Pope's letter.[18] It was, wrote Hastings, a 'powder keg' and as a result of it 'the sense of a grand and trusting alliance of bishops, theologians and laity united for the reform of Catholicism fell away'. The English and Welsh Catholic Church, docile and obedient for so long and accustomed to dealing with internal problems discreetly and privately, plunged into public ferment. The Hierarchy was caught off-guard by the scale and volume of disagreement and dissatisfaction aroused by the encyclical.[19] Vatican II may have encouraged many previously silent Catholics to express themselves publicly on aspects of the Church, but contraception became 'a turning point manifestly opening a gap between the bishops' doctrines and their flocks' actions'. It was an issue on which many 'first attained moral autonomy, rid themselves of supervision, and ceased to regard their religion as, in the moral sphere, the encyclopaedic rule book in which a clear answer was to be found to every possible question of conduct...'[20]

The publication of the encyclical, Wheeler recalled, led to 'loud protests' and 'widespread disobedience' which astonished and dismayed the Hierarchy.[21] Across the country, some priests refused to read their bishop's Pastoral on the encyclical; at some Masses, sermons were interrupted while at others congregations walked out. It led to a welter of attacks on the Pope, among the more notable being by Dominicans in Oxford and a member of the Papal Commission on Birth Control. A group of laypeople addressed a letter of protest to the Pope through the Apostolic Delegate while the Catholic historian Lady Antonia Fraser was 'passionately disappointed' at the Pope's decision. Others thought that young Catholics would be 'very angry' at the ruling. Anne Biezanek, a Catholic doctor who advised on birth control at a clinic on Merseyside, called the Pope's stand 'evil'. Comparing his encyclical with the recent Russian invasion of Czechoslovakia, she said that 1968 had been 'a great year for the Iron Fist.'[22] The Pope's defenders claimed that he was simply reaffirming Church teaching and that his approach was compassionate. Anglican bishops, meeting at the Lambeth Conference, saw the encyclical as a threat to ecumenism.[23]

On 29 July, Wheeler appeared with the Catholic Member of Parliament Norman St John Stevas and Lady Antonia Fraser on the BBC television programme *Panorama* to discuss the encyclical. St John Stevas described the encyclical as compassionate but inadequate 'in the sense of its disconnection from contemporary men and women'. The Pope's decision, he said, was 'partial, inadequate and propaganda, rather than rational theological argument'. Wheeler strongly opposed this opinion[24] and further developed his support for the Pope in *The Spectator* on 2 August. Again, St John Stevas felt obliged to disagree.[25]

Pastorals were hurriedly issued by the Hierarchy on the authority, purpose and content of the encyclical. Tension mounted among the 8,000 priests in England and Wales and fifty-five signed an open letter of dissent which stated that 'according to our consciences we cannot give loyal internal and external obedience to the view that all such means of contraception are in all circumstances wrong. As priests we feel that our duty towards Catholic people compels us to bear witness to the truth as we see it'. Alongside these objections were those of the laity and letters were signed by a large number of Catholics engaged in a variety of professions which were highly critical of the encyclical.[26]

Some of the priests who spoke out against the encyclical were suspended; a few, those who could not accept the encyclical, either resigned or walked out of their parishes. While Cardinal Heenan tried to defuse the situation, a minority of bishops publicly criticised disobedient priests and accused them of immaturity, disrespect for the Pope, and peddling false and mischievous advice. They demanded total acceptance of the encyclical and if was not forthcoming the offending priests were suspended.[27] The majority of the Hierarchy, however, took a more realistic line, seeing the encyclical as an ideal from which some backsliding may be expected. This group, which included Heenan, had refrained from suspending priests who spoke out. There was a much smaller group, however, including Bishop Butler, Auxiliary in Westminster, which pressed for a more liberal interpretation of the encyclical. He doubted that the Pope was speaking *ex cathedra* and later wrote to one correspondent that 'those who hold *Humanae Vitae* to be true should give equal freedom of expression to those who don't'.[28] Butler who had earlier written a draft response for the Hierarchy had stated that 'a statement which is not infallible is, at least in principle, reformable'[29] but this was toned down by Cardinal Heenan and the Statement issued by the Hierarchy in September 1968 supported the authority and validity of the Pope's teaching and called for self-discipline and mutual charity in 'this time of controversy'.[30] By October, however, following continued clerical outcries against the encyclical, the Hierarchy's attitude had hardened and it was agreed that an 'essential minimum will have to be asked of those priests who oppose the Encyclical'. Bishops would interview those priests who publicly rejected the encyclical and should a priest refuse to withdraw his opposition, then although he would not be prevented from celebrating Mass he would be forbidden to hear confessions. If his opposition continued, the priest would be maintained by the diocese until he found suitable alternative employment.[31]

Wheeler attended speedily to the diocesan reaction to the encyclical. He called his priests together for a frank but confidential discussion on the encyclical and thanked them for 'their loyalty, discretion and understanding in what has been a very difficult period'.[32] In his Pastoral on the issue, he wrote that 'Artificial birth control can only bring disaster on the human race. It leads easily to conjugal infidelity and the lowering of morality. It can lead to a lowering of respect for woman as an individual. It panders to selfish enjoyment'.[33] The encyclical, he wrote later, could not be detached from traditional Church teaching nor from the deliberations of Vatican II where the Fathers had debated 'many problems of special urgency in the context of contemporary society' including the population explosion and economic influences on family life. Vatican II had addressed the issues facing contemporary humanity but had seen no reason to change its doctrines. While debate was encouraged, submission to the Magisterium was not optional. He concluded that the encyclical stressed 'that man was primarily a spiritual being with a spiritual end and underlines the personal dignity of the individual'. He was of the view that although some will object to the encyclical and ignore it or leave the Church, the vast majority of Catholics would loyally accept the ruling as they had always done in the past and would not allow themselves to be upset by the criticism of those who had expected and hoped for a change. Too many, he wrote, had followed the clamour of the world and were naturally disappointed at the Holy Father's declaration.[34] To Cardinal Heenan he wrote in October 1968 that thirty Yorkshire laypeople had written a letter to *The Times* criticising *Humanae Vitae*. He was ignorant of the letter adding that such people were 'a few intellectuals being encouraged by the London group'. Most people, he claimed were 'completely and utterly loyal'. The same, however, was not entirely true of his priests. He had seen two 'rebels' who had guaranteed external assent to the Pope's encyclical. While there had been no public expression of clerical dissent, he expected to lose 'one or two of them'.[35]

In an address to the priests of the diocese, Wheeler placed the crisis in an historical perspective commenting that 'maybe the Church cannot flourish without one'. Up and down the country, priests had rejected the encyclical while others, though deeply troubled, had accepted the authentic teaching of the Pope. The encyclical, he said, was not a reversal of Church teaching but a confirmation of it and 'a great many theologians hold the teaching which it contains as the infallible teaching of the Church despite the fact that the Encyclical itself is not in the infallible form'. He called for a humble, responsible and balanced approach from the priests and if they disagreed, there had to be internal assent rather than external rebellion:

> No priest worth his salt is going to be so conceited as to imagine that he has been accepted by the Church and ordained by the Church to teach and preach his own private opinions. He has the mandate of the Church to teach the Church's doctrine. And it is

> consoling to see that even the most vociferous opponents of *Humanae Vitae* accept not only the fact that it is authoritative but also that they must not teach or preach publicly against it. Such people may often be said to withhold their internal assent but give an external one.

He hoped that there would be no hostile reaction among the priests, that they would accept the encyclical while simultaneously considering the right of an informed conscience, the use of the Confessional and the reception of the Eucharist. The sting, however, was in the tail of the *Address*. To those priests unable or unwilling to accept the encyclical or who publicly repudiated it, he offered to maintain them until they found suitable alternative employment.[36]

For some priests this was a very difficult time. Many were still coming to terms with the encyclical and the often hostile response it provoked among their parishioners. Wheeler summoned a small minority of priests to explain their views and pledge their obedience to him and orthodoxy. Some conformed but others considered their future to be outside the active ministry. Wheeler reported to Rome that 1969 was 'the most difficult year' regarding the laicization of priests but did not specify *Humanae Vitae* as a reason for the departures.[37] In August 1969 he wrote to Archbishop Cardinale, now Apostolic Nuncio in Brussels, that he had 'two bad kicks in the stomach' before he left for holiday in Sweden in 'the defections of two more priests whom I can ill afford to lose'.[38]

For Wheeler, the encyclical was fundamentally concerned with the dignity and value of life and the Sacrament of Marriage. It was, he wrote, 'a vital and essential proclamation' and the heart-of-the-matter was to preserve the authoritative teaching of the Pope and the worldwide episcopate was entirely behind him in this.[39] Like Cardinal Heenan and some other bishops, he maintained the right of Catholics to exercise the right of conscience but expected the conscience to be fully informed 'with the clear teachings of Christianity'. The priest, he wrote, should take all pastoral steps to prevent Catholics drifting away from the Sacraments and their faith. Above all, he was condemnatory of the mass media which attacked all the Commandments and exploited sex to such a degree so 'as to destroy the beauty of one of God's greatest gifts'. He sympathised particularly with the young 'who had a much harder time to get through adolescence than we had'. The departure from Christian principles in public life, he concluded, tricked and trapped people into moral degradation. A clear re-statement of the Church's teaching was the only antidote to this pernicious situation.[40]

When the diocesan Council of Priests met in October 1968, some priests expressed disapproval that they had to discuss *Humanae Vitae* yet again but as others pointed out, it was not simply a matter of the contraceptive pill but a serious matter of authority and conscience. Wheeler agreed and ensured it was on the agenda of Deanery Conferences for further discussion.[41]

Notes

1   *The Tablet*, 18 Feb 1967. For a detailed examination of the McCabe affair see J. Hagerty, *Cardinal John Carmel Heenan: Priest of the People, Prince of the Church* (Leominster: Gracewing, 2012), chapter eight.

2   A. H. Armstrong and R. A. Markus to Wheeler, 16 Feb 1967. LDA, WDC, W55.

3   I. Gregor to Wheeler, 17 Feb 1967. LDA, WDC, W55. There are no copies of Wheeler's replies.

4   Fr H. V. McAtamney to Wheeler, 24 Feb 1967. LDA, WDC, W55.

5   St Francis Junior Mixed and Infant School, Morley, 'Copy of School Letter', March 1967. LDA, WDC, W55.

6   Wheeler to Heenan, 2 Feb 1967. AAW, Heenan HE1/L2.

7   *New Blackfriars*, March 1967.

8   M. de la Bedoyere (ed.), *Objections to Roman Catholicism* (London: Constable, 1964).

9   *The Tablet*, 9 May 1964; ALA, GHC/S1/2/A/27; *Westminster Cathedral Chronicle*, June 1964, pp. 103–104.

10   *Daily Telegraph*, 26 March 1967; B. Sharratt, 'English Roman Catholicism in the 1960s' in A. Hastings (ed.) *Bishops and Writers* (Wheathampstead: A. Clarke, 1977), p. 141.

11   G. Noel, *The Anatomy of the Catholic Church* (London: Hodder and Stoughton Religious, 1980), pp. 78–79.

12   M. J. Walsh, *The Westminster Cardinals: The Past and The Future* (London: Burns and Oates, 2008), pp. 188–189; *The Tablet*, 15 Nov. 1975.

13   Noel, *The Anatomy of the Catholic Church*, pp. 79–80.

14   Wheeler to Dom Edmund Flood, 14 May 1967. LDA, WDC, *Humanae Vitae*.

15   LDA, WDC, *Humanae Vitae*.

16   Noel, *The Anatomy of the Catholic Church*, p. 82.

17   Personal testimony: Mgr John Dunne.

18   DAA, Butler Papers, D2.

19   A. Hastings, *A History of English Christianity 1920–1985 (London: Collins, 1968)*, pp. 574–576.

20   S. Lee and P. Stanford, *Believing Bishops* (London: Faber and Faber, 1990), pp. 67–68.

21   *Yorkshire Post*, 19 June 1978.

22   *Catholic Herald*, 2 Aug 1968.

23   *Yorkshire Post*, 19 June 1978.

24   *The Tablet*, 3 Aug 1968; *Yorkshire Post*, 19 June 1978. *The Yorkshire Post* was running a series '*Humanae Vitae* ten years on'.

25   *The Spectator*, 2 Aug and 9 Aug 1968.

26   *The Tablet*, 5 Oct 1968.

27   *Catholic Herald*, 16 Aug 1968.

28   Butler to V. G. Davies, 6 Sept 1980. DAA, Butler Papers, *Humanae Vitae*, C26.

29   *Sunday Times*, 6 Oct 1968; See also C. Longley, *The Worlock Archive* (London and New York: Geoffrey Chapman, 2000), pp. 360–370.

30   *Catholic Herald*, 2 Jan 1970, 'A Staff Reporter Looks Back' (at the past decade); Statement of the Bishops' Conference of England and Wales on *Humanae Vitae*, 24 Sept 1968. LDA, WPC, *Humanae Vitae*; W. G. Wheeler, *In Truth And Love* (Southport: Gowland and Co., 1990), pp. 105–107. For Bishop Butler's view see DAA, Butler Papers, C26 and G1 (*Humanae Vitae*) and G8 (Correspondence).

31   Wheeler, 'Address to the Clergy on *Humanae Vitae*', Oct 1968. LDA, WPC, *Humanae Vitae*.

32   Wheeler, *Ad Clerum*, 23 Oct 1968. LDA, WDC, Wheeler Papers.

33   Wheeler, 'Address to the Clergy on *Humanae Vitae*', Oct 1968. LDA, WPC, *Humanae Vitae*.

34   Wheeler, 'Why The Pope Has Not Taken The Easy Way Out'. LDA, WPC, *Humanae Vitae*; *Catholic Herald*, 9 Aug 1968.

35   Wheeler to Heenan, 30 Oct 968. LDA, WDC, The Cardinal.

36   Wheeler, 'Address to the Clergy on *Humanae Vitae*', Oct 1968. LDA, WPC, *Humanae Vitae*.

37   *QR*, 1967–1972.

38   Wheeler to Cardinale, 13 Aug 1969. LDA, WDC, W64. The defection of priests had begun before *Humanae Vitae*. It was estimated that excluding deaths but including ordinations there were 133 fewer priests in England in January 1968 than in January 1967. *National Catholic Reporter*, 12 June 1968.

39   Wheeler to the Apostolic Delegate, 4 Sept 1968. LDA, WDC, W34; *L'Osservatore Romano*, 14 Sept 1978.

40   Wheeler, *In Truth And Love*, pp. 105–107.

41   LDA, WDC, Leeds Council of Priests, 22 Oct 1968.

10 LITURGY, LATIN AND CHURCHES

Liturgical Commissions

THE COUNCIL OF Trent (1545-1563) decided that it was not expedient for the Mass to be celebrated in the vernacular. The thesis of those Council Fathers at Trent who favoured the use of Latin was that the Eucharistic Sacrifice is first and foremost the action of Christ Himself, and therefore its proper efficacy is unaffected by the manner in which the faithful participate. Some Fathers, however, felt that the Latin Mass failed to present a fully effective means of catechesis and communication. The essence of Vatican II was Church renewal and central to this was the introduction of the vernacular into the liturgy and the full participation of the faithful. To do this meant abandoning the 1570 Missal of Pope Pius V, often mistakenly referred to as the Tridentine Mass. Pius had authorised the printing and publication of the *Roman Missal* which brought liturgical uniformity to the Church of the West. The *Roman Missal* was a single volume containing the Order of Mass, the scripture readings and all the liturgical prayers of the Roman Rite. Several editions of the *Roman Missal* were approved over succeeding centuries with the last edition being as late as 1962. The *Roman Missal*, reformed according to directions set down in the Constitution on the Liturgy of Vatican II, was authorised by Pope Paul VI in his Apostolic Constitution of April 1969. Pope Paul issued this Constitution along with the reformed Order of Mass, published two years in advance of the complete reformed *Roman Missal*, and in the penultimate paragraph of this Constitution abrogated the *Roman Missal* of Pius V.[1]

In December 1963, the Council approved the Constitution *Sacrosanctum Concilium* paving the way, along with many other reforms, for the new *Lectionary* and the introduction of the vernacular in the Mass and other liturgical celebrations. *Sacrosanctum Concilium* was the first decree of the Council and an important manifestation of Pope John's call 'to impart an ever increasing vigour to the Christian life of the faithful.'[2] Towards the end of the Council's First Session, Archbishop Paul Hallinan of Atlanta had convened an informal group of English speaking bishops to consider the desirability of collaboration in the production of common liturgical texts. At the beginning of the Second Session in 1963, the meeting assumed a more formal character when episcopal representatives from the English speaking conferences met to discuss closer co-operation. From this came the International Episcopal Committee on English in the Liturgy and an International Advisory Committee on English in the Liturgy. Archbishop Grimshaw of Birmingham represented the English and Welsh Hierarchy on the Episcopal Committee while Fr Harold Winstone and Professor H. P. R. Finberg, both from England, were members of the Advisory Committee. From these two committees emerged the International Commission on English in the Liturgy, or ICEL, whose purpose was to prepare English translations of each of the Latin liturgical books and any individual liturgical texts in accord with the directives of the Holy See.

The English and Welsh Hierarchy, meanwhile, established a National Liturgy and Music Commission to prepare texts for domestic use. Archbishop Grimshaw chaired the group responsible for translating all the liturgical texts for which the use of English had been authorised.[3] The group's task was to produce an approved missal incorporating the approved English texts for Sunday and the greeter festival. Wheeler was a member of this group.[4] In their translations and presentations, both ICEL and the National Commission had to ensure that their documents were a witness to an unbroken tradition of doctrine and were accommodating to modern conditions[5] but each Bishops' Conference was given a large degree of freedom and flexibility by the Vatican.

In October 1970, Wheeler succeeded Archbishop Dwyer of Birmingham as Chairman of the National Liturgy and Music Commission and became an episcopal member of ICEL. He lamented to Canon Ronald Pilkington in Westminster: '... I badly need your prayers and help about the Liturgy. Things have gone so far that I am afraid I may be rather too late on the scene'.[6] Cardinal Heenan had expressed his reservations to Wheeler over the direction of liturgical change and particularly over ICEL: 'I have disliked it from the very beginning and I do not believe that our bishops have ever had an opportunity of making their views known.' He concluded: 'It would not be reasonable to break away from ICEL within the next year or so but after the trial period promised to the publishers I should be completely in favour of making our own translations.[7] Wheeler was in agreement. He was of the opinion that ICEL had to continue for the time being but was appalled by some 'ghastly' translations.[8] To Wheeler, this was the most serious of reservations for the texts of Mass were formative of the people: they were catechetical and contained the faith of the Church. The rapid movement from Latin to the vernacular did not, in his opinion, allow a balanced approach to change nor did it produce acceptable translations.

While the bishops in the USA and Canada were supportive of ICEL, the English and Welsh bishops pursued their own translations. In 1969, under Archbishop Dwyer, the National Liturgy and Music Commission published a revised *Ordo Missae* and *Lectionary*. This gave priests and people temporary translations of the Order of Mass and scriptural readings until more definite translations became available. In 1971, the Vatican released the new version of *Missale Romanum* and gave permission for this to be translated into the vernacular. The Bishops' Conference Liturgy Commission did not wait for the ICEL version of the translation but under Wheeler's chairmanship and with episcopal consent published its own version in 1973. It appeared with a Foreword by Wheeler but without the 'General Instruction' which determines the ethos of the Mass and sets out the importance and dignity of the Eucharistic celebration. The Vatican was not happy with the fact that the General Instruction had been omitted and gave the translation only interim approval.[9] No other English speaking Conference adopted the English and Welsh edition. The ICEL edition of the translated *Missae Romanum* appeared in 1974.

Wheeler's reservations about liturgical changes continued: his approach to ICEL was cautious and measured while his position on the National Liturgy and Music Commission was uncomfortable. While he could count initially on the support of Cardinal Heenan and Bishop Joseph Gray, Auxiliary Bishop in Liverpool, he increasingly differed from other bishops such as Derek Worlock whose liturgical views were more progressive. Wheeler's resistance to the vernacular, or more particularly to poor translations from Latin into the vernacular, was a battle soon lost; so too was his insistence on retention of the terms 'Thee' and 'Thou' in the Mass (with the exception of the *Our Father* and *Hail Mary*); and so too was the tendency to hold on to Pius V's *Roman Missal* during the critical period of adapting the Mass into the vernacular. By the end of his term of office as Chairman of the National Liturgy Commission in 1975, most of the liturgical reforms introduced by Vatican II had been implemented not always with his enthusiastic support.[10] He had, never-theless, to implement the changes in his own diocese.

Liturgical Reforms

Elodie Palloc has succinctly summarised Bishop George Patrick Dwyer's contribution to Vatican II and described his attempts to implement its Decrees and Constitutions in the Diocese of Leeds. In liturgical terms, much had been changed in the diocese prior to Wheeler's arrival in 1966.

Dwyer, a theologian and gifted linguist, frequently contributed to conciliar debates and became a familiar figure in the vast assembly. In theology and by training, however, Dwyer was a conservative Catholic[11] and Archbishop Worlock wrote that although he may have recognised the mood of the Conciliar Church 'temperamentally he did not seem to like such disturbances himself'; he was 'very much a creature of the Church before the Council, a far more static model'. Yet, continued Worlock, Dwyer 'had no doubts that Vatican II had correctly read the signs of the times, and that it was his task to see the prescriptions applied. He had no time for movements in the Church which were disobedient or reactionary, though he had some sympathy with those who found change hard to accommodate'.[12]

Between 1963 and 1965, Dwyer prepared his diocese for the radical changes introduced by the Council and sought to implement some of them even before the Council had ended. *Sacrosanctum Concilium* allowed for liturgical renewal and the introduction of the vernacular into the Mass and a Council for implementing the Constitution was established by Pope Paul's Motu Proprio *Sacram Liturgiam* of January 1964. The vernacular was introduced into some parts of the old Order of Mass—the readings, the Prayer of the faithful and the 'Common' parts of the Mass—the *Kyrie, Gloria, Sanctus-Benedictus, Agnus Dei* and *Pater Noster*.[13] Within two years, the old Roman Rite practised for centuries in Latin had begun to change and was accompanied by the physical reordering of sanctuaries to accommodate the new liturgical approaches. This rapid transformation appeared completely out of character with the Church's traditionally ponderous and bureaucratic approach to any reform.

Liturgical changes were the most obvious and immediate—significant parts of the Holy Mass were now celebrated in the vernacular with, where possible, the priest facing the people from behind an altar placed in the middle of the sanctuary. In older churches, temporary altars were erected but new churches generally met the architectural requirements of the new liturgy. For a time, the renewed liturgy was celebrated in churches ill equipped for it.[14] The Sacred Heart Church, Ilkley, for example, was reordered in 1963 'to allow the priest to say Mass facing the congregation' but the new Church of St Brendan, Bradford, opened in 1964, already 'accommodated recent liturgical reforms'.[15] In April 1963, Bishop Dwyer commenced the 'modernization' of St Anne's Cathedral by improving the spatial effect of the sanctuary and relating it more closely with the nave. This involved removing the old high altar from beneath the reredos and taking away two flights of steps and low screen walls at the entrance to the sanctuary. A new high altar with tabernacle was now free standing on a more spacious sanctuary. The canons' stalls were fixed beneath the reredos and behind the new altar and new altar rails were installed. The celebration of Mass became more visible to worshippers but, for now, the priest was still celebrating *ad orientem* with his back to the congregation. A consequence of the remodelling was that some furnishings and fittings of historic and artistic significance, such as the Bishop's throne, frescoes on the sanctuary and in the Blessed Sacrament Chapel, and the communion rails, were lost. The results did not please everyone.[16] Elsewhere, there were examples of church architecture introduced to accommodate the new liturgy running alongside traditional approaches. The Holy Family Church at Chequerfield, opened in 1964, and the Scared Heart, Leeds, opened in 1965, were ultra-modern in line with new architectural concepts, designs and materials whilst the Church of St James, Huddersfield, opened in 1964, was built with the pre-Conciliar liturgy in mind.[17]

Never an enthusiastic ecumenist, Dwyer opened a dialogue with those of other Christian traditions and encouraged his priests to do the same. He also began to establish diocesan structures more responsive to the modern world and the modern Church.[18] He was aware, though, that there were many like himself who remained unconvinced by the changes brought about by Vatican II. He acknowledged that some Catholics were bewildered, disturbed and anxious about the changes because the comfort of familiarity had disappeared and traditional practice had changed overnight without the laity being consulted. While most Catholics did not understand Latin, for example, there was a strong historical, devotional and emotional attachment to it. The title of one of Dwyer's Pastorals dealing with change—*Weathering the Storm*—gave an indication of his own feelings as he likened contemporary Catholics to the Apostles sitting alongside Jesus in the storm-tossed boat.[19]

As Scott had noted, Wheeler was perceived as a 'modern bishop'—'a progressive'—and arrived in Leeds with that reputation. He inherited the changes initiated by Dwyer but, like Dwyer, was unenthusiastic and quite unprepared for their radical nature. He 'found it a difficult period, especially when the liturgical changes happened' and when the Latin Mass according to the pre-Conciliar liturgy was phased out. He thought many changes were unnecessary and implemented them not out of any strong personal conviction but because he would not depart from the requirements of the Universal Church.[20] He may have been inspired by Vatican II 'and the wealth of prescribed thought and action' in the Constitutions and Decrees but putting all this into practice was not going to be easy.[21] In Advent 1966, he told the diocese that 'we have to reconcile ourselves to many changes whether we like them or not' but he added that 'change is not necessarily decay' and 'there is a great new life invigorating the whole of God's Church…and we should all welcome it and take part in it'.[22] Addressing the Catholic Missionary Society's Easter Conference in April 1967, he acknowledged that there was now a sense of renewal and a sense of purpose in the Church but warned that there also had to be 'a sense of providence in the face of agonised impatience'.[23] Nonetheless, he set about his reforming task with single-mindedness.

In July 1969, Wheeler established a Diocesan Liturgy Commission to encourage and promote the renewal of liturgical life and to ensure orthodoxy. It was an important decision as the use of the vernacular, for example, was not simply applied to the Mass but to all rites of the Church. There was a huge amount of work to undertake as translations were made and remade before final approval was given by Rome. Through letters and instructions to the clergy and Pastorals to the faithful, Wheeler embarked on the transformation of diocesan liturgical practice. Nothing was left to chance and changes were introduced according to detailed episcopal instructions. Keeping the clergy, faithful and schools abreast of the new rite of Mass with its frequent translations was especially difficult. In Advent 1966, he wrote: 'You were used to the new form of Mass and there it is changed again'.[24] As Hebblethwaite noted: 'liturgical change was the one that most Catholics could easily see if not entirely understand'. It 'touched most people immediately' and 'caused deep foreboding about the future'.[25] In 1967, Wheeler gave permission for new English and Latin translations to be used in the Breviary and in the Mass. Further liturgical changes followed in 1969 when the new or 'Normative' Order of Mass in the vernacular was introduced and in Advent 1971 when public celebration of the Latin Mass according to the Roman Rite of 1570 ceased. This familiar act of adoration and thanksgiving, so precise, mystical and formulaic, disappeared as did many cherished forms of devotion. Newly translated Canons of the Mass appeared, significant sections of the Mass were recited in English, bidding prayers were introduced, and items of clerical vestments such as the maniple and biretta traditionally worn in the old Mass disappeared.[26] They were developments not always welcomed by Wheeler. Above all, he was saddened by the loss of Latin for no matter what contingencies were put in place to preserve it, Latin would disappear once the vernacular had been introduced. In 1969, he had written to the diocese: '... I would like to point out that the definitive form of the new order of Mass is in Latin' but added 'it is my hope that a tradition of Latin as well as English will remain, and that priests, religious and people alike will familiarize themselves with the new forms in both languages'.[27] It was a forlorn hope.

For many Catholics the end of the old Mass was sad and bewildering, leaving them with a huge feeling of loss. Some saw it as symptomatic of a sad transformation of the Church and they disapproved intensely. The Latin Mass Society, founded in 1965, waged a persistent campaign against the loss of Latin and 'the devaluation of the Mass' now 'almost entirely unrecognizable'.[28] The traditionalist Wheeler was not exempt from this feeling and later wrote that

> ...for me personally the liturgical reforms went against the grain, and were one of the hardest things I had to do: returning to the vernacular after saying Mass for more than a quarter of a century in Latin. Latin was understandably for me a symbol of the gift of the fullness of the faith.[29]

There was no fear, however, of Wheeler contradicting the prescriptions of the Holy See regarding the celebration of Latin Mass. To a member of the Association for Latin Liturgy he wrote that he was glad that a body had arisen to help preserve Latin in the Liturgy 'without impugning either explicitly or implicitly the Holy Father's proclamation of the new Rite of Mass'.[30] He himself celebrated in his own chapel Mass in the New Order in Latin and at the cathedral on Holy Days of Obligation and at Easter and Christmas.

Some priests dispensed with the pre-Conciliar Mass as soon as possible and many Catholics thought that Latin and the Latin Mass were gone forever. Afraid that this would indeed be the case, Wheeler told his priests in 1970 that Mass in the new form should be celebrated weekly in Latin and that children must learn prayers in Latin. Mass in the vernacular had become the norm by this time but according to Wheeler 'that does not liberate us from our duty of preserving the great inheritance, liturgically, spiritually and musically of the Latin Mass and we ask you to do all in your power to preserve it'. He was of the opinion that if the laity were given the option of more frequent Latin Masses 'there would have been less nostalgia for the "old Mass"'.[31] Preserving the Old Mass in contradiction to the mind of the Council, however, was unacceptable and he condemned Archbishop Marcel Lefebvre and those traditionalists who refused to abandon Pope Pius V's Latin Mass and openly disobeyed the 'the divinely appointed Hierarchy of Pope and bishops'.[32] Following Lefebvre's suspension by Pope Paul VI in 1976, Wheeler told the diocese that the Council had not changed 'any doctrine of our Faith' but that it can be expressed in new ways. Lefebvre, he wrote, disapproved of the Council and had continued to celebrate 'the old form of the Mass commonly known as the Tridentine Mass which is, of course, entirely in Latin'. There could be no association with the Lefebvrists, he wrote, because they defied the Council. 'We all have a certain sympathy for those who prefer the old style of Mass', he continued, for 'it was the Mass the martyrs knew and the one which older Catholics knew and loved so well. But there is not one of those martyrs who would have stood against the directives of the pope and Bishops'. There were, he concluded, 'many different ways of participating in the Holy Sacrifice of the Mass and the Church provides for all types. The important thing is that we offer it in union with the whole Church. And that means in unity with our Holy Father the Pope and all the Bishops and the whole faithful people of God'.[33] Yet Wheeler loved the old Mass and wrote in 1973 that 'I try to keep the right balance in... different kinds of liturgy. In particular, I do my utmost to see that Latin is preserved'.[34] In 1969, the Latin Mass was celebrated in eighteen parishes[35] and he was asked by some priests why he persisted in allowing the Tridentine Mass. He replied that 'with permission there was nothing wrong with the Tridentine Mass. The Holy Father had allowed bishops to grant permission'. He concluded: 'Why be less generous than the Holy Father'.[36]

There was, however, a difference of opinion within the Bishops' Conference on the celebration of the old Latin Mass. In October 1971,

Cardinal Heenan had secured a special Indult, issued by the Prefect of the Congregation for Divine Worship, to allow the old Order of Mass in England and Wales to be celebrated under certain conditions. For Wheeler this was 'the saving of the situation'.[37] It was not, however, a view shared by all of his episcopal brethren and an informal poll of bishops in early 1976 showed that a substantial minority wished the Indult to be withdrawn. Within months of Heenan's death the Bishops' Conference agreed that the 'so-called "Tridentine Mass Indult" be phased out gradually by the bishops in their dioceses rather than withdrawn by the Holy See'.[38] Before visiting Rome in 1977, Cardinal Hume wrote to Wheeler: 'Frankly, one of the problems is that I cannot speak on behalf of all the English bishops, since several of them would not wish to see any extension of the provision to use the Tridentine Mass'.[39] Division and confusion were frequent and exacerbated by a claim of those struggling to retain the Tridentine Mass that they alone were fighting to preserve the true Catholic faith. On hearing that the Indult might be withdrawn, Wheeler immediately advised the Papal Secretary of State 'that such action could provoke... a great hostile outburst in this country'. He felt the Indult showed great compassion for some, such as elderly priests and religious, but the infrequency of the Latin Mass deprived others.

There was no fear that the Tridentine Mass mentality would supersede the new Normative Rite which had been welcomed by the vast majority of Catholics, but the withdrawal of the Indult would have damaging consequences. The press would imply the persecution of a minority by Rome, supporters of the Tridentine Mass would be driven underground and become schismatics, the Tridentine Mass would be lost forever, the bishops would lose control over the celebration of the Tridentine Mass, and the Latin Mass Society, 'a minority on the wane' would begin to recruit those favouring individual liberty.[40] Cardinal Benelli replied that Cardinal Hume, recently in Rome, had received a Pro-memoria from Cardinal Knox stating that the English and Welsh bishops had to issue an unequivocal statement about the continued use of the Indult, reveal the riches of the renewed liturgy, and make available systematically for all the faithful 'the celebration of the new liturgy in Latin with vernacular readings'. If these directions were followed, 'the question of the Tridentine Mass will solve itself without notable difficulty'.[41]

Despite sympathizing with supporters of the Latin Mass there was, in truth, little Wheeler could do to preserve the Mass in its pre-Conciliar form. The bishops recognised that the pre-Conciliar Mass would eventually fade out and Wheeler told Hume that 'humanly speaking... it was a terrible error of judgment to prescribe the old Rite. As you know, I have always been entirely loyal to the Holy See in the matter' but he wished that the Indult had been universally granted.[42] Those in favour of the Old Order of Mass did not lose their determination to have it restored and Wheeler remained a conduit through which they hoped to reach the Hierarchy and the Vatican and effect a change.[43] Hume had some sympathy with those seeking to restore the Latin Mass. In 1978, he wrote to Wheeler: 'I really think we probably ought to give a big shove in the direction of helping them'.[44] The *Catholic Herald* reported that the Diocese of Leeds was 'gently tolerant of Tridentine enthusiasts'.[45]

Another development which caused Wheeler great unease was the suggestion that the Blessed Sacrament might be placed directly into the hands of those receiving Holy Communion. Wheeler wrote to the Pope that there was a danger that such a development would diminish the reverence of the Sacred Species and with other changes such as the reordering of sanctuaries and standing rather than kneeling to receive Holy Communion, he felt that 'transubstantiation is being played down'. In England, there was a particular historical aspect not always understood elsewhere. After the Reformation and in Reformed Churches, he wrote, 'standing for Communion showed and proclaimed a disbelief in the Eucharistic Presence'. He feared that reception in the hands would lead Catholics to think 'that the doctrine of transubstantiation is an old fashioned and outworn belief'. He and many priests in his diocese were of the opinion that there was too great a liberty being taken with regard to the Blessed Sacrament. Manual reception, he wrote, would be a scandal to many Catholics and to High Anglicans who received Holy Communion directly on to the tongue. His diocese, he wrote, had accepted *Humanae Vitae* and the Pope's lead on morality; so too would they welcome his lead and guidance on liturgical matters and an end to experimentation: 'They feel angered that people who experiment seem to be able to force a pace which is scarcely consonant with Catholic doctrine as they understand it'. It was his view too.[46] His letter was transmitted to the Council on the Sacred Liturgy[47] and later the Bishops' Conference received notification from the Vatican that 'Communion in the hand is not to be introduced'.[48] The matter did not end there, however, and the practice became common in parishes and university chaplaincies in defiance of Vatican and episcopal edicts.

Wheeler told Bishop Casey of Brentwood that 'I would never give permission for a thing like communion in the hand'[49] and in May 1971 he told the priests of the diocese that it was not permissible to give or receive the Sacred Host in the hand.[50] Eventually, Wheeler eventually did allow Holy Communion to be received under both kinds but only in accordance with the Vatican directive that it be confined to Sundays and Holy Days. By 1976, he had also modified his view that the Sacred Host could be received on the hand[51] but was unhappy with what he considered a trend 'not of Vatican II'.[52]

It was not only the loss of Latin and other liturgical developments that disturbed Wheeler: the more relaxed atmosphere in Mass and other services had led to an increasing lack of reverence and he told Catholic teachers that 'De-fossilisation should not mean 'de-sacralisation'.[53] He was adamant that clergy and religious maintain their distinctive dress code for it had become fashionable for priests and nuns to cast off the traditional Roman collar and habits. In 1968, he wrote that he was 'depressed and discouraged' by the tendency among clerics and religious 'to wear Carnaby Street shirts and ties and to bear no witness to the religious life whatever...'[54] In 1970 he asked Cardinal Wright at the Sacred Congregation for the Clergy for advice on the issue. 'One cannot help feeling', he wrote, 'that the general relaxation in this matter is symptomatic of the prevalent uncertainty as to the priestly role in the world of our time'. While he acknowledged that there could be no universal norm, he feared the secularisation of clerical dress and remarked that Cardinal Heenan, surprisingly, was quite 'open-minded' about it. For Wheeler, 'laicisation' of the clergy had gone too far and should be arrested.[55] In 1971, in reply to someone complaining about nuns abandoning their traditional habits, he wrote, 'I will refrain from speaking about the new habits of nuns' but nevertheless he continued: 'They are neither bearing witness to the religious life or attracting other vocations when they wear these absurd garments or go into secular dress...' They were 'foolish' he concluded, in 'trying to laicise themselves'.[56]

Reordering the Churches

New churches built and opened during Wheeler's episcopate were designed according to the new liturgical requirements but sanctuaries in the more historic churches did not easily facilitate such changes and had to be reordered. The building of new churches such as St Anthony's,

Windhill, in 1966, St Michael's, Wombwell in 1967, St Joseph's, Hunslet, in 1968, English Martyrs, Huddersfield in 1970, St Patrick's, Birstall, in 1970, St Peter's, Doncaster, in 1973, St Margaret Clitherow, Grassington in 1973[57] and the Chapel of Christ the King at the Army Apprentices College, Harrogate, in 1968,[58] enabled the Bishop, priests and architects to prepare from the inception a liturgical space fully adapted to a corporate act of worship in line with conciliar changes. In such cases, architects took every opportunity to introduce new designs and use less traditional materials for altars, statues, windows and paintings. Angular shapes, wrought iron furniture and sculptures, abstract paintings and modernist stained glass designs, however, were not to everyone's taste. Further and more extensive developments occurred only as existing churches were remodelled. This process was not undertaken rapidly; some churches, including those built and opened in the late 1950s and early 1960s were not reordered until the early 1980s.[59] Among some senior and more reactionary parish priests, there was both a liturgical and financial reluctance to remodel their churches while younger priests of a more radical disposition had to wait until they acquired a parish before they could introduce liturgical modifications according to their interpretation of Vatican II. Meanwhile, alterations to churches that were listed buildings involved liaison with civic authorities and preservation societies.[60]

The remodelling and modernization of some of the diocese's older and highly decorated churches and chapels was controversial and caused much anxiety for priests and many traditional Catholics. Within the diocese, twenty-seven churches and chapels were built between the thirteenth and nineteenth centuries and some were of great historical and architectural merit.[61] Some were chapels attached to the houses of the Catholic gentry while others belonged to religious orders or were within convents. The Diocesan Sites and Building Commission was frequently called upon to advise Wheeler on the reordering the sanctuaries in such churches and chapels and he was anxious to retain as far as possible the historic features of older buildings. To facilitate circulation on the sanctuary some priests were confronted with the problem of retaining existing and ornate features while removing what they termed 'Victorian clutter'.[62]

Of importance to Wheeler was the provision of a Blessed Sacrament Chapel where people might engage in private and quiet devotion. There were Blessed Sacrament Chapels in some churches but the reordering of sanctuaries and in accordance with the recommendations of Vatican II meant that it became a problem especially in older and smaller churches where it was not always easy to accommodate a new chapel. Wheeler decided that the tabernacle, if removed from the main altar, had to be repositioned in a place visible to the congregation and not obscured by the celebrant. Requests came to him from priests with responsibility for older churches for permission to have ornate altars, reredoses and communion rails removed, pulpits dismantled and rood screens taken down. Wheeler took a close interest in every scheme.[63]

In some cases, parishioners were consulted by the clergy; in others, the clergy, as was the tradition, made unilateral decisions. Occasionally, priests made alterations without recourse to either the Sites and Building Commission or the Bishop. While they were about reordering the sanctuary, some parish priests took the opportunity to make extensive renovations to their churches and sometimes presbyteries. Either way, someone was bound to be upset by the changes and consequently disaffected as they nostalgically observed the churches of their childhood and youth being tastelessly modified for a modern liturgy they did not want. At St Patrick's, Bradford, built in the 1850s, a major adaptation and simplification of the sanctuary was completed in 1970 after the clergy had told the parishioners in 1968 that 'the church would have to be modernised'.[64] The parish priest informed the local newspaper that 'churches must now be simple with an altar brought forward so that the priest can face the people'. He continued: 'our present high altar and tabernacle which is the biggest and most fancy I have ever seen will have to go.' He rightly concluded: 'I think that is the thing that will upset most people...' Indeed it did, as over the next twelve months parishioners saw the high altar, tabernacle, communion rails, rood screen, baptistery, nuns' tribune and statues dismantled and disappear. To clear away and replace Victorian features cost over £20,000. According to the parish priest, St Patrick's now had a church 'fit for the new liturgy without destroying its atmosphere'. Many found his claims less than convincing.[65]

The reordering of churches such as St Patrick's, Leeds, St Marie's, Sheffield, St Mary's, Halifax, St Paulinus, Dewsbury, St Robert's, Harrogate, St Mary's, Selby, and St Cuthbert's, Bradford, may, in the opinions of some, have enhanced the quality of worship but did much to damage venerable churches. Opponents were not slow to air their views. When parishioners at St Robert's, Harrogate, took their grievances to the press calling the diocese high handed and heartless in its determination to replace the familiar with the clinically modern, Wheeler informed Canon George Collins, the parish priest, that the re-ordering was splendid and he felt sure that people would come to appreciate it.[66]

Reordering was also costly. For example, to take down the reredos and screens, provide a new tabernacle and altar and make other improvements at St Mary's, Halifax, cost over £24,000.[67] The Bishop would have noticed such transformations at consecrations and on Visitations. Possessing an acute sense of history and taste, he remarked in his memoirs that 'people started playing about with very historic and wonderful buildings. Such happenings were never intended and should never occur'. The changes were, to his conservative nature, 'a sort of vandalism that could happen and did happen'.[68] As far as the Cathedral was concerned, he had little room for manoeuvre. Bishop Dwyer's modifications had proved liturgically unsuitable but so recent and costly were the changes that Wheeler could undertake no immediate remedial action.[69]

Notes

[1] I am indebted to Mgr Anthony Boylan for his expert guidance on this chapter. Mgr Boylan was Secretary of the Bishops' Conference National Liturgy Commission during Bishop Wheeler's chairmanship.

[2] *International Commission on English in the Liturgy, Reflections on the Constitution on the Liturgy 1963–1978*. LDA, WDC, Liturgy.

[3] *The Tablet*, 27 June 1964.

[4] *Catholic Herald*, 31 July 1964.

[5] Catholic Bishops Conference of England and Wales, *General Instruction of the Roman Missal* (London: CTS, 2005), pp. 3–6.

[6] Wheeler to Canon Pilkington, 30 Oct 1970. LDA, WDC, W68, Forty Martyrs.

[7] Heenan to Wheeler, 8 Oct 1970. LDA, WDC, Liturgy.

[8] Wheeler to Heenan, 9 Oct 1970. LDA, WDC, Liturgy.

[9] *Roman Missal: English Translation of the 1971 Missale Romanum* (Alcester and Dublin: Goodliffe Neale, 1971). Wheeler wrote the Foreword.

[10] I am indebted to Mgr Anthony Boylan for his guidance on this section.

[11] E. Palloc, *Une Eglise En Marche: Vatican II dans Le diocese de Leeds (Angleterre) 1959–1980* (unpublished memoire de maîtrise, Université Lyon II Lumière, 1992). p. 56.

[12] *The Times*, 18 Sept 1987.

[13] G. Alberigo, *A Brief History of Vatican II* (Maryknoll, New York: Orbis Books, 2008), pp. 59–136.

14   A. Flannery and M. Harty, 'Changes in Low Mass' in A. Flannery (ed.), *Vatican II: The Liturgy Constitution* (Dublin: Scepter Books, 1965), p. 164.

15   *Leeds Diocesan Directory* (1966), pp. 149, 150–151; *Catholic Building Review* (1965), pp. 138–139 and (1966), pp.110–115.

16   R. E. Finnigan, *The Cathedral Church of St Anne, Leeds: A History and Guide* (London: Universe Publications Company Ltd., 1988), pp. 49–52; R. E. Finnigan (ed.), *St Anne's Centenary: Leeds Cathedral 1904–2004* (Keighley: PBK Publishing Ltd., 2004), pp. 33–34; *Catholic Building Review* (1964), p. 126.

17   *Catholic Building Review* (1965), pp. 110–115, 125–127, 138–141.

18   Palloc, *Une Eglise En Marche: Vatican II dans Le diocese de Leeds*, pp. 74–75.

19   Dwyer, Lenten Pastoral, 1965, 'Weathering the Storm'. LDA, Dwyer Papers.

20   W. G. Wheeler, *In Truth And Love* (Southport: Gowland and Co., 1990), p.75.

21   R. E. Finnigan 'Bishop Wheeler, 1966–1985' in R. E. Finnigan and J. Hagerty (eds.), *The Bishops of Leeds 1878–1985: Essays in Honour of Bishop David Konstant* (Leeds: PBK Publishing on behalf of the Diocese of Leeds, 2005), p. 155.

22   Wheeler, Advent Pastoral, 1966. LDA, WDC, Wheeler Papers.

23   *The Tablet*, 8 April 1967.

24   Wheeler, Advent Pastoral 1969. LDA, WDC, Wheeler Papers.

25   P. Hebblethwaite, *The Runaway Church* (London: Collins, 1975), p. 27.

26   Palloc, *Une Eglise En Marche: Vatican II dans Le diocese de Leeds*, p. 92.

27   Wheeler, Pastoral on 'The New Order of Mass', 1 Nov 1969. LDA, WDC, Wheeler Papers.

28   Pyne to Wheeler, Passion Sunday 1968. LDA, WDC, W33, Latin Mass Society.

29   Wheeler, *In Truth And Love*, p. 101.

30   Wheeler to R. H. Richens, 10 Oct 1969. LDA, WDC, W44, Latin Mass.

31   Wheeler, *Ad Clerum*, April 1970. LDA, WDC, Wheeler Papers.

32   Quoted in Palloc, *Une Eglise En Marche: Vatican II dans Le diocese de Leeds*, pp. 116–117.

33   Wheeler Pastoral, 5 Sept 1976. LDA, WDC, Wheeler Papers.

34   Wheeler to J. F. Diamond, 12 April 1973. LDA, WDC, W44, Latin Mass.

35   *Leeds Diocesan Directory* (1969), p. 86.

36   LDA, WDC, Council of Priests, 26 Oct 1976.

37   Wheeler to Hume, 11 Aug 1976. LDA, WDC, Cardinal Hume.

38   LDA, WDC, *ACTA* Papers, April 1976.

39   Hume to Wheeler, 28 Sept 1977. LDA, WDC, Cardinal Hume.

40   Wheeler to Cardinal Benelli, 18 Feb 1976. LDA, WDC, *ACTA* Papers, 1976.

41   Benelli to Wheeler, 11 March 1976. LDA, WDC, *ACTA* Papers, 1976.

42   Wheeler to Hume, 11 Aug 1976. LDA, WDC, Cardinal Hume.

43   LDA, WDC, W62, Latin Mass contains numerous letters and petitions sent to Wheeler throughout the 1970s.

44   Hume to Wheeler, 25 April 1978. LDA, WDC, Cardinal Hume.

45   *Catholic Herald*, 27 Aug 1976.

46   The consultation document on the reception of Holy Communion was issued by the Vatican on 28 October 1968. Wheeler wrote to the Pope on 20 November 1968. LDA, WDC, W68, Sacred Congregation: Reception of Holy Communion.

47   Cardinal Cicognani to Wheeler, 3 Jan 1969. LDA, WDC, W68, Sacred Congregation: Reception of Holy Communion.

48   Bishop Patrick Casey to Wheeler, 16 June 1969. LDA, WDC, W68, Sacred Congregation: Reception of Holy Communion.

49   Wheeler to Casey, 29 May 1970. BDA, Casey Papers.

50   Wheeler, *Ad Clerum*, 25 May 1971. LDA, WDC, Wheeler Papers.

51   Wheeler *Ad Clerum*, 4 Aug 1976. LDA, WDC, Wheeler Papers.

52   Wheeler to Bishop Gray, 21 Feb 1979. LDA, WDC, *ACTA* Papers 1979.

53   Quoted in Palloc, *Une Eglise En Marche: Vatican II dans Le diocese de Leeds*, p. 117.

54   Wheeler to Illtud Evans OP, 6 Sept. 1968. LDA, WDC, W2.

55   Wheeler to Cardinal Wright, 14 April 1970. LDA, WDC, W10.

56   Wheeler to Sr Malachy, 9 June 1971. LDA, WDC, W2.

57   *Catholic Building Review* (1966), pp. 110–115, 120; (1967), pp. 98–99; (1968), pp. 76–77; and (1971), p. 131. *Leeds Diocesan Directory* (1974), pp. 131, 133.

58   *Catholic Building Review* (1968), pp. 89–91.

59   St Mary's, Penistone, was reordered in 1966; St Clare's, Bradford, opened in 1955 was reordered in 1967; the Immaculate Heart of Mary, Leeds, built in 1956, was reordered in the late-1980s. See *Catholic Building Review* for descriptions of these churches. St Theresa's, Cross Gates, Leeds, built in 1953 was reordered in 1980 when it was claimed 'that shortcomings in the way it worked as a place of worship had become apparent'. *Leeds Diocesan Directory* (1981), p. 133.

60   Personal testimony: Mgr John Dunne.

61   The chapel at Hazlewood Castle dated from 1290; St Joseph's, Bishop Thornton, dated from pre- Emancipation days.

62   Fr A. Davies, St Anne's, Bradford, to Wheeler, 14 Sept 1972. LDA, WDC, W24, Sites and Buildings Commission. By 1976 Wheeler had established the Leeds Diocesan Scheme of Quinquennial Inspection of Church Premises and a Diocesan Liturgical Sub-Commission for Art and Architecture to advise him. See LDA, WDC, W43.

63   LDA, WDC, Sites and Building Commission, 1967–1971.

64   *Leeds Diocesan Directory* (1971), pp. 134–135. *St Patrick's Church, Westgate, Bradford. Re-opening of Church and Consecration of New Altar, 5 June 1970.* LDA, WDC, W68.

65   B. Parry, *From Erin's Green Valleys: A Celebration of 150 years of St Patrick's Bradford 1853–2003.* (Bradford: 2003), pp. 39–40.

66   Wheeler to Collins, 10 Dec 1970. LDA, WDC, W68.

67   LDA, WDC, W43.

[68] Finnigan, 'Bishop Wheeler, 1966–1985', p. 175. When, in retirement, Wheeler was asked about the 'unfortunate consequences' that the architectural changes of the 1960s had on the older churches and particularly on the loss of their historic features, he sidestepped the question and spoke of the loss of popular devotions: it seemed to be a development he would rather forget. See Wheeler, *In Truth And Love*, p. 103.

[69] Finnigan, *The Cathedral Church of St Anne, Leeds: A History and Guide*, p. 52.

11 A DIOCESE TRANSFORMED

The Wood Hall Experiment

A FUNDAMENTAL ASPECT OF Wheeler's implementation of Vatican II at the local level was his emphasis on renewal, catechesis and ecumenism. In 1966 he wrote that 'my feeling was that the enrichment shared by those of us who had been at the Council itself had not... really percolated through either our clergy or the laity. This was understandable but I wanted to ensure that the spirit of renewal was communicated to all our people'.[1] Accordingly, he proceeded to remedy this deficiency. He transferred the Diocesan Catechetical Centre to the Headingley campus but his major initiative was the opening of the Diocesan Pastoral and Ecumenical Centre at Wood Hall, a Grade II listed Georgian mansion near Wetherby, which was blessed on 29 April 1967 by Archbishop Cardinale, the Apostolic Delegate, in the presence of senior leaders from other Churches. It was the first centre of its kind in England and Wales. The Shrine of Our Lady at Wood Hall was designed and executed by Arthur Fleischmann and according to Wheeler Wood Hall was to do for priests what the Vatican Council had done for the bishops. It was to transmit the pastoral and ecumenical message of Vatican II and become the symbol for renewal in the diocese. Priests could 'bring the decrees of the Council and the renewal of the Church's life to the people of the diocese and enable them in turn to play a fuller part in the Church's life'. In a warning to those who thought they might be able to force the pace of reform, however, he wrote that Wood Hall was to be 'an experiment in the light of Vatican II. If it is to succeed, it must be a balanced experiment. It will not confuse progress with licence; it will always give primacy to the spiritual. It will, I hope, generate apostolic activity: but it will fail to do so if it is merely activist'.

Led by Mgr Michael Buckley, who was aided by Sisters of the Holy Family of Bordeaux, Wood Hall quickly became famous for its residentials on theology and practical Christianity for priests, youth leaders, schools, universities, and prayer groups of different denominations.[2] Father Buckley saw each parish as a miniature Vatican II: to him Church renewal essentially meant parish renewal.[3] Such was Buckley's enthusiasm and the Centre's immediate popularity that Wheeler had to temper his efforts: 'I am very anxious that we should not appear to be making a "takeover" bid of any kind. Liverpool might think we were becoming the Metropolitan See.'[4] Not all those who attended the courses were pleased with the Centre's facilities, the course content, the 'dialogue with communists' or Buckley's leadership but Wood Hall was a huge success. Bishop Christopher Butler wrote to Wheeler that 'you have set the rest of the country an example here, and I hope it will be more and more followed'.[5]

There were some, however, who saw another side of the initiative. In its report on a meeting of the Converts' Aid Society, the *Catholic Herald* claimed that Wheeler

> cut splendid figures of eight over some rather thin ice, for it is ironical to some that the most ecumenical of the bishops, who has just founded a special centre in Leeds to foster ecumenism, is also the chairman of this society which, from the time of Leo XIII, has looked after convert clergymen and is doing so as strongly as ever. The bishop found no difficulty: ecumenism is a fine thing creating a much better atmosphere, but individual conversions are also fine things. Men must follow their consciences even when that leads them into the Catholic Church.[6]

There were few other detractors and Wood Hall's ecumenical activities got off to an impressive start in June 1969 when an array of senior representatives from the Catholic and Anglican Churches gathered to discuss spirituality in the modern world and participate in an ecumenical service especially composed to emphasize the closer links which now existed between the Christian Churches. *The Tablet* called it 'the most important meeting between Catholics and Anglicans ever to be held since the Reformation'. The Catholics were led by Cardinal Gray, Archbishop of St Andrews and Edinburgh, and included Bishop Wheeler, Bishop Butler, Auxiliary of Westminster, Abbot Hume of Ampleforth, Mgr Buckley, Warden of Wood Hall, and Fr Dalrymple. From Rome came Mgr Moeller, of the Congregation for the Doctrine of the Faith and Canon Purdy of the Secretariat for the Promotion of Christian Unity. The Anglicans were led by the Archbishop of York, Dr Coggan, and included the Bishops of Ripon, Coventry and Selby supported by the theological expertise of the Dean of York, Canon Cant of York Minster, and Professor Hanson of Hull University.[7]

In 1970, Wood Hall hosted the first National Conference of Priests convened by the English and Welsh Hierarchy. Cardinal Heenan informed the priests they had not been called 'to settle a crisis' but to discuss matters of common concern to the Catholic community. The conference was characterised by strong feelings and lively debates on topics such as celibacy, married priests and forging partnerships with the laity.[8] Within five years, nearly 10,000 people had attended courses at Wood Hall, some of which included leading national and international Catholics and Anglicans speaking on a wide range of topics. Mgr Buckley's tendency to be outspoken, however, regularly caught Wheeler on the hop and his cherished hope of Wood Hall being a beacon of pastoral renewal and ecumenical co-operation gradually became a problem which largely devolved on the Warden. Buckley's frequent appearances in the press and on television gave him many opportunities to voice his opinions. In 1974, he wrote that compared with Catholics in continental Europe those in Britain lived 'behind a curtain of clerical conservatism'. European Catholics, he continued, had a different view of priestly functions and displayed none of 'the apathy we have come to accept in matters ecclesiastical in this country'. The 'fire and power of the first Pentecost', he concluded, was absent from English Catholicism.[9] In 1975, Buckley castigated the Church's attitude to women as misogynist and wasteful of much talent and commitment. On television, he announced that he differed from the Pope on the issue of women priests.[10]

In addition to these challenges to ecclesiastical authority, Buckley's increasing shift to the 'activist' model and his involvement with the Peace Movement began to cause Wheeler further anxiety. The newly formed Peace Movement was the mainland equivalent of the Peace People of Northern Ireland to whom it gave moral and financial support. In February 1977, as the violence in Ulster continued, Buckley, with Wheeler's approval, convened a meeting at Wood Hall to establish a secretariat for the National Peace Movement under the presidency of Jane Ewart-Briggs, widow of Christopher Ewart-Briggs, the recently assassinated British Ambassador to Ireland. At that meeting were Betty Williams and Ciaran McKeown of the Peace People of Northern Ireland.[11] While supportive of the Peace Movement and happy for it to hold meetings at Wood Hall, Wheeler was aware that too close a political affinity with them could cause problems for him and the Catholic Church in England. Buckley's public comments on Ulster and on some of its key political and religious personalities became far too sensitive for the Bishop and the Hierarchy and Wheeler felt obliged to remove Buckley in late

February 1977. There followed much bad press for the Bishop who was unfairly accused of being unsympathetic to both the Peace Movement and the Warden who was inevitably dubbed 'a turbulent priest'. One of the Peace Movement's leaders said that they were fighting the Provisional IRA and the Hierarchy as well. Buckley himself was upset over the way he had been treated by Wheeler and went public with his comments. He had been notified of his transfer by a brief letter from the Bishop on Ash Wednesday and had no means of appeal. He commented: 'The whole case is a typical example of non-communication which in the end can only damage the Church. Our main task is to pray that healing will follow and that the Church's image will be for peace'.

However, Buckley saw Wheeler on 14 March, accepted his decision and thereafter praised the Bishop's support for him, the Centre and the Peace Movement.[12] Wheeler refrained from public comment save to say that Buckley had not been sacked but merely transferred after a decade of high powered activity. Privately, he wrote that ten years at the very public helm of Wood Hall had taken a physical and emotional toll on Buckley who was replaced by Fr Gerard Spelman.[13] Wheeler wrote that 'it is a tragedy the way the press interpreted' the removal of Buckley and told Tom Burns of *The Tablet* that it had nothing to do with the Peace Movement.[14] To Dom Alberic Stacpoole he wrote that the press 'did us a great disservice in associating the transfer (of Monsignor Buckley) with the Peace Movement which I have always supported and will continue to support'.[15] To Sheila Peppiatt attending a peace conference in Enniskillen, he wrote: 'I have always supported the Peace Movement and will continue to do so...' He sent a small donation to the meeting.[16] At a later event to celebrate the tenth anniversary of Wood Hall's opening, Wheeler praised Buckley's huge contribution to the centre. He had, he said, encouraged and supported Buckley in all his endeavours but felt the time had come for the Warden to rest from the intensive work that Wood Hall demanded. In return, Buckley paid generous tribute to Wheeler for his vision, courage and determination in establishing Wood Hall and for giving him 'ten glorious years of priestly apostolate'.[17]

Wheeler successfully persuaded religious institutes to enter the diocese in order to develop and consolidate spiritual renewal. A Carmelite convent was established next to Wood Hall and in 1967, at Wheeler's invitation, Carmelite Friars purchased Hazlewood Castle near Tadcaster, the home of the recusant Vavasour family. The Carmelites who had originally established a priory in York in 1253 thus returned to Yorkshire for the first time since the Reformation.[18] Wheeler envisaged Hazlewood as the 'Aylesford of the North'—a northern shrine of Our Lady and the English Martyrs—and eventually, restored and renovated, it opened in 1972 to accommodate retreat groups, pilgrimages and residential courses supplementing the long-established Passionist retreat house at Myddelton Lodge, Ilkley and the recently established Wood Hall.[19] To those who doubted the wisdom of opening so many centres, the Bishop replied that 'there was almost an infinite need for places of this kind, where people can find spiritual refreshment and be developed in prayer and the appreciation of the things that really matter, according to the mind of God and His Church'.[20] The restoration of ancient Catholic properties such as Hazlewood and Myddelton appealed to Wheeler and he saw these alongside Carlton Towers, Broughton Hall, Ripley Castle, Rudding Park and Markenfield Hall as beacons preserving the blessed memory of persecuted Catholicism.

With courses for priests at Wood Hall, Hazlewood Castle, Myddelton Lodge, Ushaw and the Upholland Northern Institute, Wheeler made every effort to bring the spirit of Vatican II into the diocese. He hoped that the courses for the clergy would lead to similar in-service for the laity but it was clear, he recalled, that he was expecting a great deal in a short time.[21] It was not easy nor was it always undertaken with willingness or strength of purpose. In 1973, at the conclusion of a Priests' Conference designed to inspire clerical confidence in Vatican II and Pope John's *aggiornamento*, Wheeler said:

> The rapid and continuing pace of change in the world makes such courses essential in the Church as in all branches of industry. We are in this changing world even though not of it. Every priest is conscious of the vast changes that have taken place. To some it is exciting; to others it is a little bewildering. But all of us have to live with it and must accept the challenge if the Church is to live in this country.[22]

It was hardly a ringing endorsement of the changes put in motion by Pope John but Wheeler had been determinedly faithful to the Pope's message and the intentions and the spirit of Vatican II.

Diocesan Structures

By 1970, new organizational structures were in place to facilitate diocesan administration and communicate and percolate Conciliar thought and practice. Wheeler was fortunate in that he was able to locate many diocesan facilities near or in the College of the Blessed Virgin Mary in Headingley, Leeds, a former Wesleyan College owned by the Little Sisters of the Poor. The pre-war Diocesan Curia had occupied the former Bishop's House adjacent to the old Leeds Diocesan Seminary of St Joseph. The house had been commandeered by the military during the Second War and was not released to the diocese until the mid-1950s. New Curial Offices were subsequently opened by Bishop Heenan in February 1956 at Hyde Terrace. In 1969, Wheeler moved the Curial Offices to Brotherton House, the former Toc H headquarters adjacent to the College of the Blessed Virgin.[23] Unlike Heenan and Dwyer, he chose not to live in Roundhay near the centre of diocesan administration and in autumn 1966 purchased from Lord Mexborough what could be best described as a very comfortable gentleman's residence in sixteen-and-a-half acres of land at Eltofts near Thorner on the outskirts of Leeds.[24] It was, he told his priests, 'a farmhouse' on the outskirts of Leeds.[25] There he entertained many guests, his family and friends and lived in style with his collie dog Finn and cat Sweetie, all of whom were well cared for by attentive Franciscan nuns. The nuns, who now had better sleeping quarters than they had at Bishop's House, stayed with Wheeler until his retirement and were instrumental in maintaining high quality living at Eltofts.

The Bishop paid close attention to diocesan structures, seeing them as important factors in cascading Vatican II's ideas and in the collaboration between clergy and laity in the effective administration of the diocese. He did not see the Apostolate of the Laity, however, simply in terms of doing jobs for and with the clergy. In February 1967, he told students at the University Chaplaincy in Manchester that it had a deeper theological aspect—'to bring Christ into the World of our time'. The laity's closer intellectual and theological partnership with the clergy, he said, must be activated by charity to bring Christ to the notice of man.[26] In reality, the practice was not to be so clear-cut. First, Wheeler had to establish his Curia and central offices. In December 1967, Fr Bryan Sharp, recently returned from studies in Rome, was informed by Wheeler that he was to replace Bishop Moverley as Chancellor of the Diocese with responsibility for matrimonial cases. To enhance his status, he was appointed a parish priest before his due time. Wheeler, Mgr Sharp recalled, allowed men to do jobs once he had delegated responsibility.[27] In 1968, once the Diocesan Chancery had been reorganised, Diocesan Commissions were established for Finance, Schools, Liturgy, Ecumenism and for Peru; subsequently a Justice and Peace Commission and a Vocations and Adult Religious Education Commission were added to this list. By 1970, there was a Diocesan Pastoral Council composed of representatives from the Council of Priests and the Council of Laity. Parish Councils fed delegates into thirteen Area Pastoral Councils which in turn sent representatives to a Council of Laity while the clergy elected representatives to the Council of Priests.[28] Such bodies were meant to be manifestations of healthy discussion, mutual support, co-operation and guidance. Above all, the role of the laity was to be enhanced: 'the laity will be called in to advise us on many levels and on many Commissions', wrote Wheeler, and many lay representatives were either co-opted or elected on to diocesan bodies. 'Co-responsibility', he wrote, 'is our theme'.[29] In 1977, to achieve more effective communication and joint action, Wheeler refined the consultative structures by replacing the Area Pastoral Councils with twenty-eight Deanery Pastoral Councils. Each deanery Pastoral Council then sent a priest and a lay representative to the Diocesan Pastoral Council while the priests of each deanery sent a priest to the Council of Priests.[30]

Wheeler began to develop these structures soon after his arrival from Middlesbrough. In December 1966, he asked parish priests to convene meetings of their interested parishioners to consider 'The Apostolate of the Laity' and its share in the mission of salvation. Such structured discussions, he hoped, would lead to the formation of parochial, deanery and diocesan organizations to collaborate with the clergy.[31] The meetings generated great enthusiasm and over 270 people gathered with the Bishop at Notre Dame College, Leeds, in April 1967 to discuss issues raised and take steps towards the formation of parish and area councils. [32] Wheeler encouraged his flock to develop more consciously into a community through participation in diocesan affairs and make use of the new diocesan Pastoral and Ecumenical Centre at Wood Hall.[33] In 1968, he convoked the first meeting of the Diocesan Pastoral Council.[34]

In November 1966, Wheeler informed the clergy of his intention to convene a Council of Priests based on Pope Paul VI's Motu Proprio, *Ecclesiae Sanctae*, which promulgated norms for the execution of the Council's decrees on The Office of Bishops, The Ministry and Life of

Priests, Renewal of Religious Life and the Missionary Activity of the Church. Wheeler had set up a small working party to consider the possibilities and the first meeting of the diocesan Council of Priests assembled at the Immaculate Heart of Mary Church, Leeds, on 27 February 1967. There were seeds for confusion in the terminology. In his *Ad Clerum* the representative 'Council of Priests' was also termed 'Council of Clergy' and there was a 'Senate or Committee of Priests' which was also described as 'representative of the clergy'. There was room for further confusion in that the Chapter was retained as an 'existing consultative entity' to the Bishop.[35] Sixty-eight priests attended the first meeting including seventeen who had been ordained over twenty-five years, eighteen who had been ordained between twelve and twenty-five years, and eighteen who had been ordained under twelve years. In addition, there were representatives from religious orders, Chapter representatives, the Vicars General, a representative from Ushaw College, four *periti*, two secretaries and the Bishop. It was, as Wheeler intended, all highly redolent of the Vatican Council with the meeting considering forty-five propositions contained in seven schemas. However, while some propositions focussed on the Priestly Life, the Liturgy, the Sacraments and Pastoral Care, others, at the first and later meetings, were directed towards more prosaic issues such as clerical stipends, pensions, school admissions, lapsed Catholics, finance, and presbyteries. By its very nature, such a large and representative gathering could only be consultative and indeed that is what it was.[36] Eighteen meetings took place between February 1967 and April 1974 and each had a substantial agenda. Consequently, meetings were unwieldy and business was rarely concluded.[37]

Representative councils of both priests and laity inevitably set up working parties and sub-committees to consider a wide range of issues and the whole apparatus became cumbersome. The Area Pastoral Councils, for example, were very large and were soon bogged down in constitutions, rules, responsibilities and representation. Over forty representatives of twenty-four Bradford Parishes attended the Area Pastoral Council in June 1969 while sixty-three attended the Leeds Area Pastoral Council in January 1970.[38] Such huge gatherings could not be effective and were usually driven by cliques of articulate middle-class Catholics bent on change and reducing clerical control. Some tried to influence Wheeler. The Rotherham Area Pastoral Council thanked the Bishop for his 'encouraging directive' that priests should face the people when celebrating Mass but felt that it needed authority to have the practice adopted everywhere.[39] Wheeler wished· the Lay Councils to be outward looking and to some extent they were but they became enmeshed in immediate issues such as the reorganization of schools and youth clubs. Many priests, long accustomed to being the sole fount of authority in parishes, found such structures unwelcome and interfering; to most working-class Catholics, used only to participating in ritual, they were irrelevant. A recurring theme at the Council of Priests was that the various diocesan Councils appeared to be running in parallel and that Councils actually kept clergy and laity apart. Some priests dragged their feet over the formation of parish councils while others felt that the whole structure was unworkable and asked how Deanery Conferences fit into the new system. Some asked the Bishop if Deanery Conferences should be abolished. It was not a suggestion that appealed to him.[40]

Wheeler later reflected that the structures he introduced did not really serve the purpose for which they were intended, that a top down model had not been the most effective, that enthusiasm for such consultative processes was uneven and that in some cases it was opposed. The problem, he admitted, lay in the failure of many parishes to establish their representative councils or committees. In 1973, six years after he had called for parish councils to be set up, Wheeler was informed by one correspondent that his parish priest had not bothered to convene a parish council but instead relied upon chosen acolytes to attend diocesan meetings and report directly to him not the parish. Wheeler's reply was non-committal; he refused to criticise the priest publicly.[41] Yet he was aware of the problem. 'With…hindsight', he wrote, 'I would want to have begun with a patient but insistent creation of a parish community in each place'. This together with communication and cooperation between all interested groups would have provided a more solid structure upon which to build other levels of deliberation and decision. Without the foundation of a parish community, he wrote, the richness of enlightened progress was lost.[42] Citing the Priests' Council, Mgr Sharp recalled that although Wheeler encouraged participation, his own subsequent involvement was at arms-length and consequently he never influenced agendas or specified deliberation or action.[43] This inevitably led to a dissipation of focus and effort and a lack of concrete achievements. It also allowed reactionary parish priests to maintain the status quo and their undisputed authority. In 1974, disappointed with the lack of progress on a variety of issues and of the general opinion that there was much duplication of effort, the Council of Laity voted itself out of existence.[44]

The Celibate Priesthood and the Permanent Diaconate

Wheeler's ordination of permanent deacons marked him out as a progressive among the English and Welsh bishops yet his actions were in line with the vision of Vatican II. He was certainly not in need of deacons for his diocese was well stocked with priests and there was a healthy cohort of seminarians. In the permanent diaconate, however, Wheeler saw the possibility of engaging and involving a minority of laymen in the sacramental life of the Church in accordance with the decrees of Vatican II. It was a unilateral decision made with the knowledge of the Hierarchy but not necessarily with its approval.

The office of deacon had its origins in the early Church but Vatican II restored the diaconate as a proper and permanent ordained rank in the hierarchy of the Church which could be conferred upon married men to assist the priest and serve the community. The Dogmatic Constitution *Lumen Gentium* stated that:

> At a lower level of the hierarchy are deacons, upon whom hands are imposed 'not unto the priesthood, but unto a ministry of service.' For strengthened by sacramental grace, in communion with the bishop and his group of priests they serve in the diaconate of the liturgy, of the word, and of charity to the people of God. It is the duty of the deacon, according as it shall have been assigned to him by competent authority, to administer baptism solemnly, to be custodian and dispenser of the Eucharist, to assist at and bless marriages in the name of the Church, to bring Viaticum to the dying, to read the Sacred Scripture to the faithful, to instruct and exhort the people, to preside over the worship and prayer of the faithful, to administer sacramentals, to officiate at funeral and burial services.[45]

Originally, deacons supported the apostolic ministry by distributing alms, preaching and baptising. Later they assisted priests at Mass by pouring wine into the chalice, replacing and removing the pall, receiving the Sign of Peace and passing it to others, and distributing Holy Communion. In modern times, the diaconate had come to be recognised as the third level in the Sacrament of Holy Orders and a stage on the path to ordination but in the early life of the Church some ordained men, married and unmarried, remained deacons throughout their lives. Vatican II decreed that just as the Apostles had recruited men to be deacons, so now could their successors:

> It pertains to the competent territorial bodies of bishops, of one kind or another, with the approval of the Supreme Pontiff, to decide whether and where it is opportune for such deacons to be established for the care of souls. With the consent of the Roman Pontiff, this diaconate can, in the future, be conferred upon men of more mature age, even upon those living in the married state. It may also be conferred upon suitable young men, for whom the law of celibacy must remain intact.[46]

The ordination of married men to this state opened up the wider participation of the laity in the sacramental and pastoral life of the Church. However, before he was allowed to preach, administer the Sacrament of Baptism, bring *viaticum* to the sick, or officiate at funerals and burials, a deacon had to undergo training in Dogmatic and Moral Theology and undertake work in a parish.[47]

In June 1967, Pope Paul's *Motu Proprio, Sacrum Diaconatus Ordinem,* gave further impetus to the restoration of the permanent diaconate when he gave bishops the freedom to decide, with the approval of the Holy See, whether they wished to ordain permanent deacons.[48] In May 1970, the Hierarchy submitted a paper prepared by Wheeler on the Restored Diaconate to the Holy See and requested permission to proceed with the preparation of suitable candidates. The request was approved.[49]

Wheeler had been a prime mover in this development and his personal initiative came to fruition on 2 May 1971 when he ordained two married men, Maurice Pearce and Anthony Winn, who were not convert clergymen, to the permanent diaconate. He thus became the first bishop in the British Isles to implement the Council's decree to restore the office of permanent deacon. The *Catholic Herald* described the ordination as 'a memorable occurrence whose significance it is difficult to exaggerate'. The permanent diaconate, it continued, 'had a self-contained character independent of any exclusively and strictly sacerdotal function. It is, in other words, emphatically not a half-way house toward a married clergy. It in no way implies that the vow of celibacy for priests will or should be modified in the foreseeable future'. Neither, the report continued, was the married diaconate 'a sudden innovation; it is something very old, as well as very new; a restoration in fact of a vital part of early church life to meet modern needs'. The second point, the report stressed, was that

Wheeler's initiative was experimental and exploratory: 'It is now up to the ordinary clergy to see and say how much further the experiment should be taken, and how soon'.[50] Subsequent developments, however, which allowed others, both male and female, to become commissioned Eucharistic Ministers rather took the impetus out of the ordination of permanent deacons for one of their most important functions was to assist at the distribution of Holy Communion.

When Wheeler informed the Council of Priests in 1967 of his intention to introduce permanent deacons, his pronouncement was met with less than enthusiasm. It was, he said, a state to which married and unmarried Catholic men and married convert clergymen could aspire but while some priests accepted the idea others felt that it was 'foreign to our needs'. Wheeler did not force the issue and throughout his episcopacy, the permanent diaconate remained but a limited experiment.[51] Between 1971 and 1985, despite the fact that priestly ordinations declined, there were never more than three permanent deacons. There was no way in which Wheeler would ever give the impression that the sacrifice of the Mass could be celebrated by anyone other than a priest[52] nor would he wish to arouse the wholesale opposition of his clergy to the idea of the permanent diaconate.

The ordinations caused minor controversy and Wheeler received letters of protest from those who disagreed with him and from those who misunderstood the nature of the permanent diaconate. One Catholic correspondent accused him of 'dealing in gimmicks and seeking the limelight'. Deacons were yet another addition to the disruption in the Catholic Church' and the Bishop of Leeds, having turned his back on the Anglicans to become a Catholic priest, was now adopting a Protestant order.[53] Nevertheless, he received letters from all over the world from men asking to be taken on as candidates for the diaconate. Mgr Tomlinson wrote to congratulate him and he hoped that 'other bishops will follow the trail you so courageously blazed'.[54]

Inevitably, there were comments that while Wheeler was prepared to accept married deacons, he was not disposed to dispense with priestly celibacy.[55] Lest anyone should think that the permanent diaconate was a significant milestone on the road to married priests and a rejection of celibacy, Wheeler was anxious to disabuse them and especially those who considered the celibate life to be unnatural and one of sexual frustration. 'There can be nothing unnatural about celibacy', he wrote, 'because otherwise you would be calling Our Lord himself unnatural and many of the great saints who followed Him'.[56] Wheeler thus repeated Pope Paul who in his 1967 encyclical *De Sacerdotali Caelibatu* ensured that the married diaconate would not be an advance towards married priests.[57] Two years later, a lay group in the diocese wrote to Pope Paul asking him to change his mind over the issue of clerical celibacy. The Vatican Secretariat of State returned the petition to Wheeler to deal with as he saw fit. Wheeler ignored it.[58] Aware that people would see the Permanent Diaconate as an advance toward married clergy, he wrote:

> Some people—especially in the mass media—seemed to think that this was another step towards a married priesthood. It may be that one day certain categories of mature married men may be raised by dispensation to the priesthood: as has already happened in a small way in other parts of the world. The permanent diaconate is, however, in the mind of the Council and the Bishops something quite apart from and certainly independent of the question of priestly celibacy. It is an experiment which we believe may prove useful in its own right. But we must not prejudge the matter. Time will tell.[59]

Wheeler's attitude to priestly celibacy never changed nor did his opposition to the ordination of women. While he may have considered marriage as an Anglican clergyman, the thought was banished from his mind on his entry into the Catholic priesthood. Free from the constraints of marriage, the Catholic priest for Wheeler

> … is free to do, as we understand it, what God wants him to do: to stay where God wants him to stay, or for that same reason to move elsewhere. By God's grace, I would say that celibacy is the ideal. Of course, there will always be scandals. A priest is a man and God has built his priesthood on manhood. It is, however, a manhood that is engraced in a special way: not by way of destruction but by the gradual transformation tempered by humility and love. [60]

In November 1968, Cardinal Garrone sought Wheeler's views on 'the very person of the priest with special reference to ecclesiastical celibacy' and the factors which affected the priestly life.[61] Wheeler responded by saying that young priests thought of 'service' in material rather than spiritual terms. This, he claimed, had the effect of postponing indefinitely direct spiritual aid and the cultivation of spiritual powers in the priest. Increasingly, young priests failed to understand the true meaning of

Sacrament of Orders which led therefore to a spiritual crisis. There had
to be, he wrote, 'an intense spiritual apprenticeship' where prayer and the
Divine Office were seen to be essential aspects of the priestly life and not
occasionally undertaken for personal edification. Other unfortunate
features of the current climate were the rejection of clerical dress and
private prayer. All these issues, he contended, made for a serious lack of
commitment and balance in the clerical life and doubts over the priestly
identity. Immature and self-assertive priests, he claimed, did not see the
value of celibacy in a material and secular world whilst their congregations
did. Such priests were a problem and left the ministry out of frustration
and insecurity. More mature and better-educated priests were required.
Discussions and courses on Vatican II, he concluded, had brought older
and younger priests together and broken down barriers between them.
Generations of priests had to collaborate in finding the solutions to
common pastoral problems.[62]

The retention of celibacy was not a position held by all priests and
discussion continued in the midst of defections and a lack of vocations. The
National Conference of Secular Priests discussed the issue at Wood Hall
and, in September 1971, at Liverpool. In among a call for the reduction to
the minimum of 'obligatory laws' and 'more autonomy in liturgy and
expressions of Faith', some priests noted that the link between celibacy and
the priesthood was 'not dogmatic'. To some priests, celibacy was 'a legal
intrusion into personal rights' and they would welcome a debate about
married clergy. If the Church was prepared to ordain married men as
deacons, then why should there not be married priests, some asked. A motion
proposing that priests should be able to marry after ordination, however, was
not carried.[63] For many bishops and priests, celibacy was not just a matter of
discipline but part of the important theology of priestly asceticism.

With regard to the ordination of women, Wheeler adhered to the
orthodox line. God took on human nature as a man, he wrote, but paid
the highest tribute to womanhood 'in choosing the Blessed Virgin Mary
as the vehicle of the birth of His son and her son'. The important events
in Christ's subsequent ministry were 'masculine' events because the actions
the Apostles and their successors were to perform 'involved total identification with Himself'. The Catholic priesthood from the start, in this
identification with the manhood of Christ, was something entirely
different from 'ministry'. Christ 'liberated' women to assist him in His

mission in all ways but one—the priesthood. Not even His mother was accorded that privilege.[64]

Dividing the Diocese

Soon after he had arrived in Leeds, Wheeler became convinced by his own observations and the views of others, that the geographical extent of his diocese was a limiting factor in the provision of adequate pastoral care and the maintenance of a diocesan ethos. Priests and parishes were scattered and the small diocesan curia struggled to cope with the myriad of local councils across Yorkshire in the planning processes for churches, presbyteries, schools and welfare facilities. To Wheeler it seemed clear that a resident bishop was needed in the southern part of the diocese.

In his *Ad Limina* of 1972, Wheeler wrote: 'it was soon evident to me that to care adequately for the Faithful in such a large diocese there must be another Bishop'[65] and one of his first moves after arriving in Leeds was to secure the appointment of an Auxiliary. In January 1967, he requested the Apostolic Delegate to submit his petition to Rome for an Auxiliary Bishop as he could not manage his role as Ordinary and simultaneously be on four Hierarchy commissions.[66] This appointment was to lead later to a consideration of the diocesan structure in Yorkshire, Lincolnshire, Nottinghamshire and the North East of England but still within the Province of Liverpool.[67]

Leading figures in diocesan administration were the Vicar General Mgr John Joseph Kelly and Mgr Gerald Moverley who had been Bishop Heenan's secretary and was Chancellor of the Diocese. Mgr Kelly had acted as Vicar Capitular during the interregnum between Dwyer and Wheeler. On his translation, Wheeler consulted his two immediate predecessors and concluded that administratively it was a good idea and that it was 'an obvious necessity' in line with Vatican II's call for smaller dioceses and greater pastoral efficiency. Visits to the Sheffield area convinced him that it was 'of a very different character from the northern parts of the diocese, and it did seem that there was something to be said for a sub-division of this great Diocese of Leeds'. Congregations in the south of the diocese did not look north to Leeds but to Sheffield and Hallam. As a first step in the reduction of his own workload, Wheeler applied successfully to the Holy See for an Auxiliary Bishop and Mgr Moverley was consecrated at St Marie's Church, Sheffield, on 25 January 1968, taking the title of Bishop of Tinisa in Proconsulari. He became

Vicar General for the southern part of the diocese and took up residence in Sheffield. It was said, incorrectly, that Wheeler regarded Moverley as 'an episcopal curate' but Wheeler gave his Auxiliary every possible jurisdiction; the two signed all pastorals and Wheeler allowed Moverley to act with power as an area bishop. In 1971, following Mgr Kelly's illness, Wheeler recalled Fr Kevin O'Brien from his position as Superior of the Catholic Missionary Society to be Vicar General alongside Bishop Moverley who since 1969, had been Vicar General with Mgr Kelly.[68] Reflecting on his management style, Wheeler wrote that he had learned from his earlier providential placements and from the Cardinals and bishops he had encountered at Westminster. At Middlesbrough, he had learnt the important lesson that there had to be 'a relationship of a loving friendliness between a bishop and his priests and between priests and one another...' To him this was more fundamental than administrative efficiency but he was too much of a realist to know that administrative inefficiency would hinder diocesan development. The underlying principle of his management style, he recalled, was 'to delegate but never to abdicate'.[69] His relationship with Bishop Moverley, however, was always correct and formal rather than a friendly, instinctive partnership.

Wheeler proceeded with plans to divide the diocese but the pace of change was desperately slow and complicated. After Vatican II, Wheeler and the Bishops of Middlesbrough and Hexham and Newcastle began discussions on the restructuring of their dioceses into smaller ones. Leeds, Middlesbrough and Hexham and Newcastle would be reduced in size and three new dioceses would be created based on Cleveland, South Yorkshire and Humberside. The creation of a diocese in South Yorkshire would, however, necessitate the co-operation of the Bishop of Nottingham.[70] The guiding principles for the division of the dioceses were based on Conciliar documents such as *Lumen Gentium* and the Franciscan Fr Ignatius Kelly produced a discussion paper on 'The Theology of the Local Church and the Place of the Bishop'. This emphasised that a diocese was the full presence and manifestation of the Church of Christ in a particular place and not just an administrative unit of the Universal Church. A diocese, in other words, was a sacramental reality concerned with people not territory.[71]

Beyond Leeds and Wheeler's immediate concerns, the Hierarchy had been studying demographic trends and diocesan management. In 1966, the Bishops' Conference established a commission to study the possible restructuring of dioceses and in 1968 set up a National Commission for

Population Study to report on present and future population trends of the Catholic community and their impact on the number, manageability and effectiveness of dioceses. Developments were deferred, however, until after the Re-organization of Local Government in 1972 which led to new local authorities in 1974.[72] As a result, the Diocese of Leeds now included parishes in the Metropolitan Counties of West Yorkshire, South Yorkshire and Greater Manchester; in the Non-Metropolitan Counties of North Yorkshire and Lancashire; in the Metropolitan Districts of Leeds, Bradford, Calderdale, Kirklees, Wakefield, Doncaster, Rotherham, Barnsley, and Sheffield; and in the Unitary of Authority of York.[73] The effects of such a radical overhaul of local government on the diocese had been addressed by the Bishops' Conference in June 1974 when it discussed *Groundplan* which suggested, among other things, a structural re-organization of the Leeds Diocese and the erection of new Dioceses of Hallam and Humberside.[74]

Proposals were subsequently discussed at Deanery meetings in Leeds in November 1974 and at Pastoral Council meetings. In Lent 1974, Wheeler visited the seven deaneries in the south of the diocese to discuss the proposals and in January 1975 Bishop James McGuinness of Nottingham discussed with his clergy the effects of the proposed division of Leeds and the formation of a new diocese based on parishes from the Dioceses of Leeds and Nottingham. While the laity in general favoured the creation of a new diocese, the clergy had reservations because of their loyalty to the diocese for which they had been ordained. Priests also expressed concern that if they volunteered for the new diocese their apostolic experiences would be curtailed due to a lack of cultural and topographical variety and that the new and small diocese might not be financially viable. At its meeting in 1975, the Hierarchy approved the formation of the new Diocese of Hallam and Humber but not a separate Diocese of Humberside.

The proposal was that a new Diocese of Hallam and Humber would cover the Metropolitan County of South Yorkshire, its proximate commuter areas and the district of South Humberside. This meant that it would take fifty-two parishes, seventy-one diocesan priests and 67,300 Catholics from the Diocese of Leeds and sixteen parishes, twenty-one diocesan priests and 6,600 Catholics from the Diocese of Nottingham. The new diocese, although small in resources was 'clearly viable and eminently desirable so that a living Church with a sense of identity can come into being from areas which suffer from being at the extremities of their present existing dioceses'. The Diocese of Leeds had continued to grow: in 1977, it had a Catholic population of 270,000 served by 181 parishes, fifty-eight chapels of ease and thirty-six Mass centres. The loss of fifty-two parishes would still leave the Diocese with over 200,000 Catholics and a reduced diocese would become much more manageable in the terms of *Christus Dominus*, Vatican II's Decree on the Bishop's Pastoral Office.[75] The overall plan—to re-organize the Dioceses in the North East—did not reach fruition, however. In November 1977 the Hierarchy's Committee for the Review of Diocesan Boundaries rejected a proposal that a new Diocese of Cleveland, and a new Diocese of Beverley, Hull and York be erected. Such dioceses, the commissioners opined, would not be viable.[76] Subsequent discussions, therefore, focussed on the division of the Leeds and Nottingham dioceses and the creation of a new diocese centred on Sheffield.

In February 1978, the proposal for the creation of a new diocese in the south was modified yet again with the addition of the High Peak District of Derbyshire. Nottingham now provided twenty-eight parishes, thirty-five priests and just over 17,000 Catholics. The proposed diocese was to be called the Diocese of Hallam and Axeholme[77] but further consultation with clergy and laity led to a rejection of the proposals.[78] Wheeler disconsolately wrote to the Apostolic Delegate that it would be folly to proceed with the plan in its present form and that there 'will have to be a rethink about the whole question'. Archbishop Heim replied that 'the Church is not a democracy' and that Wheeler and his brother bishops had already engaged in long and careful consultation. He continued: 'The news is very sad and I think priests are inclined to be moved by precipitous and perhaps sentimental reasoning which has no relevance for their successors'.[79] Heim may have been correct but to priests and laity it was a natural reaction. Wheeler was on dangerous ground and many suspected his motives to be based on personal ambition rather than on pastoral or even managerial criteria. He admitted to McGuinness that he was taken aback by the tone of the Delegate's letter.[80] There was continued opposition to the plan and cries that it was a 'done deal'.[81] In December 1979, Wheeler and McGuinness informed their dioceses that consultations had ended.[82] *A Petition for the Creation of a New Diocese from Parts of the Dioceses of Leeds and Nottingham in England* was submitted to the Holy See in January 1980.[83] Opposition took a new twist when some priests came out openly against Moverley being the Ordinary of the new diocese. They wanted a man who was new to the situation and who would bring fresh ideas 'at the start of this new step in history'.[84] To Wheeler these 'malcontents' ignored Moverley's experience and skills.[85] Nevertheless, it could be argued that consultation over the appointment of the new bishop was something of a sham.

On 10 June 1980, the new Diocese was erected with St Marie's, Sheffield, as its Cathedral Church. Bishop Moverley was appointed by Pope John Paul II as the first Bishop and was installed on 3 July. Hallam's geographical extent covered the County of South Yorkshire including Sheffield, Barnsley, Rotherham and Doncaster part of the High Peak District of Derbyshire including Chesterfield; and the Bassetlaw District of Nottinghamshire. It took fifty parishes from the Leeds Diocese and sixteen from the Diocese of Nottingham and had ninety-four secular priests, of whom eighty-six were on active ministry in the diocese, and twenty-two from religious orders. Its Catholic population stood at almost 79,000 while that of Leeds was 199,825. The *Leeds Diocesan Directory* described it 'as a remarkable unity in area and an example of the kind of pastoral planning prescribed by Vatican II'.[86] Leeds was now a significantly smaller diocese becoming the eighth largest of the twenty-one bishoprics in England and Wales. Geographically it included West Yorkshire and parts of North Yorkshire, Cumbria, Greater Manchester, Lancashire and Humberside. The reduced diocese comprised 133 parishes, 260 diocesan priests and forty-four religious, fifty-two convents, and 128 schools. To complete the re-organization, in 1981 two Leeds parishes south of the River Ouse in the City of York were ceded to the Diocese of Middlesbrough.[87] Wheeler now had a smaller diocese to care for but the administrative and pastoral demands on him did not lessen. His health was not strong and he was beginning to feel physical stress. Accordingly, in February 1981 he petitioned Rome for the appointment of an auxiliary bishop to replace Bishop Moverley. His request was unsuccessful.[88] 'The division of the diocese had been 'a traumatic experience for me', he told Archbishop Worlock. He added: I am afraid that I may go down in history as the Bishop who decimated the Diocese'.[89] Some would have agreed with this sentiment.

There were now four dioceses east of the Pennines and it has been suggested that if the proposed Humber diocese had materialised Wheeler would have been the obvious candidate as a new Metropolitan in the North East with the possible title of 'Archbishop of Beverley'. Wheeler would have welcomed the added status for the northern dioceses east of the Pennines and be free of the authority of the incumbent northern Metropolitan, Archbishop Worlock of Liverpool, although Worlock was in no way obstructive regarding the erection of Hallam. There was rivalry between the two men dating from Westminster days when both were at the centre of power and Wheeler's part in the appointment of Abbot Basil Hume to succeed Cardinal Heenan as Archbishop of Westminster in 1976 would hardly have endeared him to Worlock who had high expectations of the job.[90]

Ad Limina 1972–1977

Wheeler's report to Rome in 1977 reflected a developing diocese striving to implement the decrees of Vatican II while coming to terms with a variety of debilitating influences frequently beyond the Bishop's control.

Diocesan Councils remained but had been refined in order 'to achieve more effective consultation and joint action'. The Diocesan Pastoral Council, the Priests' Council, Area Pastoral Councils and Parish Councils remained unchanged but Deanery Councils had been increased to twenty-eight. 'The success of such arrangements', wrote Wheeler, 'depends ultimately, of course, on the effectiveness of the parish council, and the willingness of the parish priests to establish one'. It was obvious that some parish priests were reluctant to co-operate for, he wrote, 'this is a gradual development but one which is taking place'.

The supply of priests remained healthy with 297 diocesan priests on duty in the diocese and another twenty-five working elsewhere. Fifty-nine religious priests were also ministering in the diocese. Over the past four years, thirty-six priests had been ordained for Leeds but during the same period, eighteen priests had left the active ministry. A significant feature was that of those who had left the majority were amongst those who had been ordained in the last ten years. Wheeler reported that in most cases 'involvement with a woman has been a major factor in the decision to leave' but he added 'underlying this involvement is often a lack of maturity sufficient to cope with the increased pressures of the world in which they are called to exercise their priesthood'. Fifty-eight diocesan students were in training for the priesthood and Wheeler estimated that over the next five years that thirty-two men would be ordained. This represents, he wrote, 'a decline in overall numbers, but in the present climate, it is no way discouraging, particularly since there continues to be an increase in the number of applicants in the 20–30 age group'. Considerable efforts were being made, he concluded, to foster interest among the young and he referred to the Vocations Weeks held in the schools, the traditional source of vocations.

The numerical bedrock of the Faith in the diocese was seriously weakening. The drop in infant Baptisms was 'dramatic' and this was Wheeler's 'greatest cause of concern'. The number of baptisms in 1976 was only half that of 1966 and had dropped from 6,275 in 1972 to 4,136 in 1976. Figures for marriages, conversions, and Mass attendance too were all significantly down on the previous report. The number of marriages had fallen from 2,448 in 1972 to 1,852 in 1976. Whereas the diocese had welcomed over 1,000 converts per annum fifteen years ago, it was now receiving just over 200 per year. In 1974, the number attending Mass on a specified Sunday had been 119,962; in 1976, this had fallen to 110,435. Much effort had been invested into the New Rite of Penance and the fall in attendance appeared to have stopped. While communicants had increased at morning Mass on Sunday, there remained 'a hard core of those attending Evening Masses who rarely receive the Eucharist'.

The drop in baptisms had begun to affect diocesan primary schools while at secondary level the introduction of the comprehensive school demanded an end to the traditional grammar-secondary modern divide while at the same time involving considerable extra expense. As Wheeler noted, 'a high percentage of our income goes in paying for our schools'. Beyond the age of compulsory education, now raised to sixteen, the diocese provided successful catechetical and teacher training courses and adult formation in the Faith.

Wheeler reported that during the past five years the Diocesan Liturgical Commission had promoted the renewal of the liturgical life of the diocese and had sought to bring about a fuller understanding of the liturgy and its place in the life of the Church. The Tridentine Mass was still allowed, at the discretion of the Bishop, 'to keep in touch with the Church's inheritance' but 'there is very little support for the movement of Archbishop Lefevbre' although one diocesan priest had left to join the Archbishop's society.

Among the other Diocesan Commissions, the Justice and Peace and Peru Commissions were particularly active with the former raising awareness and the latter raising funds. Parish Justice and Peace groups had developed, a joint diocesan Co-ordinating Council had been formed, and a Columban Father had been appointed as full-time 'animator of this apostolate'. The Justice and Peace Commission were witness to action for justice and participation in the transformation of society and they zealously pursued this aim across the diocese, notably among young people and the schools. 'Third World' issues were also addressed through a prayerful and financial commitment to CAFOD and the Peru Commission which Wheeler supported with priests and the diocese continued to finance through voluntary contributions. On the domestic front, the diocese's own Rescue, Protection and Child Welfare Society was very active and successful and there were many lay associations and organizations involved in charitable work.

Despite his concern over some issues, Wheeler reported many encouraging developments and noted that in spite of contemporary society's materialism there was a yearning for spiritual values among people. He saw hope and optimism in the young. 'They are concerned', he wrote, 'about justice and charity and they feel the need of prayer; and it is good that this is evident among young people. Their Faith is real, they are keen to know it and to live it, and their attentive at Mass and the Sacraments is attentive and devout'.[91]

Notes

[1]   W. G. Wheeler, *In Truth And Love* (Southport: Gowland and Co., 1990), p. 86.

[2]   *Wood Hall Programme of Courses March-May 1967*. LDA, WDC, W2; R. E. Finnigan, 'Bishop Wheeler, 1966–1985' in R. E. Finnigan and J. Hagerty, *The Bishops of Leeds 1878–1985: Essays in Honour of Bishop David Konstant* ((Leeds: PBK Publications on behalf of the Diocese of Leeds, 2005), pp. 160–162; E. Palloc, *Une Eglise En Marche: Vatican II dans Le diocese de Leeds (Angleterre) 1959–1980* (unpublished memoire de maîtrise, Université Lyon II Lumière, 1992), p. 97; Wood Hall was set in beautiful and extensive grounds.

[3]   Buckley to Wheeler, 3 Feb 1967. LDA, WDC, W2.

[4]   Wheeler to Buckley, 31 Oct 1967. LDA, WDC, W2.

[5]   Butler to Wheeler, 6 Feb 1969. LDA, WDC, W2.

[6]   *Catholic Herald*, 8 July 1967.

[7]   *The Tablet*, 7 June 1969.

[8]   Wheeler to Scott-James, 4 May 1970. LDA, WPC, Scott-James. Wheeler told Scott-James that Buckley and the Hierarchy had organised the conference to offset attempts by 'the Dutch' to get 'innumerable groups of young clergy on their side in this country'. He wrote: 'I would be glad if it were elsewhere'. See also *Official Report of the First National Conference of Secular Priests of England and Wales*; *Catholic Herald*, 5 June 1970. LDA, WDC, W43.

[9]   *Catholic Herald*, 17 May 1974.

10   *Catholic Herald*, 21 March 1975.

11   LDA, WDC, W63, Peace People.

12   *Catholic Herald*, 4 and 11 March 1977; *Yorkshire Post*, 1 March, 1977.

13   Finnigan, 'Bishop Wheeler, 1966–1985'; pp. 161–162.

14   Wheeler to Riddle, 18 March 1977; Wheeler to Burns, 9 March 1977. LDA, WDC, W2. On leaving Wood Hall, Buckley aired his views on the Ulster problem. See his article on 'The Ulster Vacuum' in *The Tablet*, 15 May 1977. In 1986, he said he had been removed from Wood Hall because he was 'a hot potato' due to his support for the Peace Movement. *Yorkshire Evening Post*, 2 Feb 1986. Wheeler considered the accommodation of Vietnamese Boat People from 1979 to 1981 as a humanitarian intervention rather than a political gesture. See Finnigan, 'Bishop Wheeler, 1966–1985', pp. 161–162.

15   Wheeler to Stacpoole, 23 March 1977. LDA, WDC, W1.

16   Wheeler to S. Peppiatt, 30 March 1977. LDA, WDC, W63, Peace People.

17   *Ampleforth Journal*, Summer 1977, vol. LXXXII, Part II, pp. 46–54.

18   *The Tablet*, 13 May 1967.

19   Finnigan, 'Bishop Wheeler, 1966–1985', p. 162; *Leeds Diocesan Directory* (1968), p. 5.

20   Quoted in Finnigan, 'Bishop Wheeler, 1966–1985', p. 162.

21   Wheeler, *In Truth And Love*, pp. 86–87.

22   Palloc, *Une Eglise En Marche: Vatican II dans Le diocese de Leeds*, p. 96.

23   G. Moverley, 'Some Thoughts on the Organization of the Curial Offices'. LDA, WDC, W2.

24   Wheeler, *In Truth And Love*, p. 113. According to the *Catholic Herald*, Eltofts was a 'comfortable stone mansion which had once been a mushroom farm'. *Catholic Herald*, 10 Aug. 1973.

25   Wheeler, *Ad Clerum*, 30 Aug 1966. LDA, WDC, Wheeler Papers.

26   Wheeler, 'The Apostolate of The Laity', Manchester, 11 Feb 1967. LDA, WDC, W55. The concept of the Lay Apostolate was not new. The First World Congress of the Lay Apostolate was held in Rome in 1951. Cardinal Griffin convened twice-yearly meetings of representatives of lay societies which became the consultative National Council in 1962. By 1964 it was discussing issues such as nuclear disarmament and contraception.

27   Personal testimony: Mgr Bryan Sharp.

28   *Catholic Directory* (1973), pp. 186–187; *Ibid.*, (1977), p. 198–199; *Ibid.*, (1977), p. 222.

29   LDA, WDC, Wood Hall; *Leeds Diocesan Directory* (1967), p. 6; (1970), pp. 30–33; Palloc, *Une Eglise En Marche: Vatican II dans Le diocese de Leeds*, pp. 102, 110–11; *Leeds Diocese and the Future*, 1969.

30   Finnigan, 'Bishop Wheeler, 1966–1985', pp. 165–167.

31   Wheeler, *Ad Clerum*, 'The Apostolate of The Laity', 8 Dec 1966. LDA, WDC, Wheeler Papers.

32   Wheeler, *Ad Clerum*, 'The Church in the World of Our Time', May 1967. LDA, WDC, Wheeler Papers.

33   Wheeler, Pastoral, 'The Christian Community', 21 Nov 1967. LDA, WDC, Wheeler Papers.

34   B. Quinn, 'Position Paper, Diocesan Pastoral Council', (n.d. 1980?). LDA, WDC, W12.

35   Wheeler, *Ad Clerum*, 13 Jan 1967. LDA, WDC, Wheeler Papers.

36   LDA, WDC, Leeds Council of Priests. 27 Feb 1967.

37   LDA, WDC, Leeds Council of Priests, Minutes, 1967–1974.

38   Area Pastoral Councils, Bradford Minutes, 3 June 1969; Leeds Minutes, 12 January 1970. LDA, WDC, 42.

39   Area Pastoral Councils, Rotherham Minutes, 20 June 1969. LDA, WDC, 42.

40   LDA, WDC, Leeds Council of Priests, Oct 1968.

41   J. Grace to Wheeler, 3 Oct 1973; Wheeler to Grace, 5 Oct 1973. LDA, WDC, W5. Canon Law requires that each parish has a Finance Committee but not a Parish Council.

42   Wheeler, *In Truth And Love*, p. 88.

43   Personal testimony: Mgr Bryan Sharp.

44   LDA, WDC, Leeds Council of Priests, April 1974; B. Quinn, 'Position Paper, Diocesan Pastoral Council', (n.d.; 1980?). LDA, WDC, W12.

45   See Vatican II, *Lumen Gentium*, Chapter 3, section 29.

46   *Ibid.*

47   Wheeler, *In Truth And Love*, pp. 96–97.

48   Wheeler set out the meaning and implications of this pronouncement in *The Tablet* on 5 August 1967.

49   Wheeler to Hierarchy, 6 May 1970; Apostolic Delegate to Heenan, 5 Nov 1970. LDA, WDC, W52, Married Diaconate.

50   *Catholic Herald*, 7 May 1971.

51   LDA, WDC, Leeds Council of Priests, Oct 1967.

52   Wheeler, *In Truth And Love*, pp. 93–94.

53   M. S. Walsh to Wheeler, (n.d.). LDA, WDC, W52, Married Diaconate.

54   G. A. Tomlinson to Wheeler, 3 May 1971. LDA, WDC, W52, Married Diaconate.

55   L. J. Mayne to Wheeler, 11 May 1971. LDA, WDC, W52, Married Diaconate.

56   Wheeler to Roger Peel-Yates, 9 July 1968. LDA, WDC, W55.

57   *Catholic Herald*, 30 June 1967.

58   Secretariat of State to Wheeler, 28 June 1969. LDA, WDC, W10.

59   *Leeds Diocesan Directory* (1972), p. 8.

60   *Ibid.*, pp. 94–95.

61   Garrone to Wheeler, 22 Nov 1968. LDA, WDC, W68.

62 Wheeler to Garrone, 12 Dec 1968. LDA, WDC, W68. Wheeler had made the same point about priestly identity to Archbishop Cardinale in August 1969. See Wheeler to Cardinale, 13 Aug 1969. LDA, WDC, W64.

63 'Celibacy: Points in the Celibacy Debate'. Report of the National Council of Priests Meeting, Liverpool, Sept 1971. LDA, WDC, W10.The National Council of Priests suffered from some internal dissension and not all priests associated themselves with it. On certain issues, some NCP members were far more radical than many priests would tolerate.

64 Wheeler, *In Truth And Love*, p. 95.

65 *QR*, 1967–1972.

66 Wheeler to the Apostolic Delegate, 18 Jan 1967. LDA, WDC, W34, Auxiliary Bishop.

67 LDA, WDC, W31, New Dioceses.

68 Wheeler, *In Truth And Love*, pp. 110–112; *Leeds Diocesan Directory* (1969), p. 5; *Catholic Directory* (1973), pp. 186–187.

69 Wheeler, *In Truth And Love*, pp. 109–110; Finnigan, 'Bishop Wheeler, 1966–1985', p. 160.

70 *Bishops Propose Renewal of Church Boundaries in North East*. LDA, WDC, W63, Groundplan; LDA, WPC, Hallam.

71 I. Kelly OFM, 'The Theology of the Local Church and the Place of the Bishop' (undated typescript). LDA, WPC, Hallam.

72 *The Installation of the First Bishop of Hallam, The Right Reverend Bishop Moverley JCD*, 3 July 1980. LDA, WPC, Hallam.

73 *Local Government Act 1972; Metropolitan and Non-Metropolitan Counties of England*.

74 *Groundplan; A Suggested Scheme for Roman Catholic Diocesan Boundaries* (Pinner: Catholic Information Office, 1974).

75 'A Proposal for the Creation of a New Diocese in South Yorkshire and South Humberside', Sept 1977. LDA, WPC, Hallam; Finnigan, 'Bishop Wheeler, 1966–1985', p. 159.

76 Lawrence to Wheeler, 10 Nov 1977. LDA, WPC, Hallam, Committee for the Review of Diocesan Boundaries.

77 A Proposal for the Creation of a New Diocese in South Yorkshire, South Humberside and High Peak', Feb 1978. LDA, WPC, Hallam.

78 *The Tablet*, 22 April 1978.

79 Wheeler to Heim, 12 April 1978; Heim to Wheeler, 15 April 1978. LDA, WPC, Hallam.

80 Wheeler to McGuinness, 20 April 1978. LDA, WPC, Hallam.

81 Wheeler to Cardinale, 5 Jan 1979. LDA, WDC, W1. Wheeler told Archbishop Cardinale that Bishop Moverley faced 'much opposition and misunderstanding' in South Yorkshire. Some of it, Wheeler said, was due to Moverley's bluntness of manner which 'puts people's backs up'. Wheeler said that he appreciated such an approach.

82 Correspondence to Bishop Wheeler re the Division of the Diocese. LDA, WPC,

Hallam; LDA, Wheeler and Moverley, *Ad Clerum*, 5 Dec 1979. LDA, WDC, Wheeler Papers.

83 *A Petition for the Creation of a New Diocese from Parts of the Dioceses of Leeds and Nottingham in England.*LDA, WDC, W31, New Dioceses.

84 Clergy of the Rotherham Deanery to Wheeler, 15 Dec 1979. LDA, WDC, W31, New Dioceses.

85 Wheeler to Worlock, 24 Dec 1979. LDA, WDC, W31, New Dioceses.

86 *Leeds Diocesan Directory* (1981), p. 5; *Hallam Diocesan Year Book* (1981), pp. 9, 38. News of the Vatican's approval was received on 28 April 1980.

87 Finnigan, 'Bishop Wheeler, 1966–1985', pp. 159–160.

88 Wheeler to Cardinal Prefect of the Sacred Congregation of Bishops, 9 Feb 1981. LDA, WPC, Wimbledon Letters.

89 Wheeler to Worlock, 4 Dec 1981. LDA, WDC, W31, New Dioceses.

90 Worlock to Wheeler, 1 March 1980. LDA, WDC, W31, New Dioceses. As Metropolitan, Worlock had to oversee the consultation process regarding the new dioceses. For this, he told Wheeler, he had 'been getting the stick'. The appointment of Abbot Hume to Westminster is examined in a later chapter.

91 *QR*, 1972–1977.

12 CATHOLICS AND OTHER CHRISTIANS

Problems and Possibilities

D ESPITE THE UNIFYING ecumenical vision of Vatican II, there were still huge obstacles across the path to Christian unity. Except for vociferous fringe elements, rancour had largely disappeared from the dialogue between Catholic and other Christian Churches, especially in England, but there remained serious points of difference. Anglicans still rejected transubstantiation and papal supremacy was a grave barrier to non-Catholic Christians. Nor were recent ecumenical developments welcomed by all Catholics. Some priests and laity shunned all ecumenical contacts while others were indifferent to inter-faith collaboration.

Wheeler's spiritual roots and formative education in the Anglican tradition and his intimacy with senior figures in the Established Church meant that he was not confined within the limits of historical Catholic suspicion which prevented genuine cooperation with the Church of England. Like Bishop Moorman of Ripon, he was convinced that ignorance was at the root of so many ecumenical misunderstandings in England and the cause of insensitive continental Catholic interference in English Church affairs.[1] His personal contacts with Anglicans at Westminster, in Yorkshire and elsewhere were friendly and fruitful and his public utterances on ecumenical relations were never strident or condescending particularly with reference to the Anglican Church. As he had written in the 1930s so too did he in the 1960s:

> The Church of England has in its possession many of the fundamental truths of Christianity. The Church of Rome, however, has the greatest fullness. Anyone who realises this has the gift of the Faith and should embrace the Catholic Faith. There is no conflict here with ecumenism. All those people who are in good faith must remain where they are, but those who catch a glimpse of something greater must pursue it.[2]

Having knowledge of both sides but being clear on which side he now stood, he entered into the ecumenical dialogue after Vatican II with some enthusiasm and the clear support of his Church.

Senior Vatican figures had given an added impetus and strong support for further ecumenical developments following the Heythrop Conference of 1962. Wheeler had emerged from this with some credit but as Abbot Christopher Butler pointed out to him two years later, 'you will have a hard task to teach your brethren the elements of ecumenical theology'. Genuine ecumenism, noted Butler, was not a natural position for the Hierarchy.[3] From Heythrop came the understanding that the essential principles underlying genuine ecumenism lay in the writings of St Paul and were based on truth and love but it was recognised that the path to union would be arduous and difficult. Vatican II had further strengthened the idea of ecumenism when Pope John XXIII emphasised the ecumenical nature of the Council and invited observers from other religions to Council meetings. After this breakthrough, there could be no burying of heads in the sand or pretending that other Christian denominations and non-Christian faiths did not exist, but this did not mean ceding ground on matters of doctrine.

In early 1966, Wheeler wrote in *The Tablet* that as priests and people gathered together to explore possibilities and to formulate plans for the renewal of the Church's life after Vatican II, the post-conciliar outlook would inevitably form itself and one aspect of *aggiornamento* would be the move towards Christian unity. It was not surprising, he wrote, that the ecumenical decree, *Unitatis Redintegratio*—and the ecumenical undertones of all the decrees—should find a special development of expression in this country where the presence of the Church of England (singled out in the decree) added a particular dimension. It seemed certain that a new movement of mounting proportions was under way and that there would be a redressing of those deficiencies among Catholics which had often driven Anglicans to the continent of Europe for any under-standing of ecumenical relations with Catholics. He was of the opinion that the emerging theme was that of the different contributions which the individual ecclesial bodies could bring to the fullness of Christ's Church. The suggestions as how this might be achieved, however, were many and varied but of critical importance was what the Roman Church might bring to the process of unity. To other denominations, it was striking how often the stress was less on unity, catholicity, or apostolicity, than on holiness and prayer and this was his central message—that the most effectual means of unity was to be found in prayer, not merely intercessory but in the adoration and glorification of the Father.

While there was 'a crisis of authority', he found that profound difficulties entered into that debate when theologians and other critics were so preoccupied with their own egos that they lose all objective standards and became self-centred instead of God-centred. He was convinced that the real crisis was not so much a crisis of authority as a crisis of spirituality. The two were not unconnected for preoccupation with self instead of with God, or one's neighbour, were at the heart of both. In recent years, he continued, there had been a stress on personal edification in the spiritual life rather than the objective worship of God. However, the Church in her wisdom was always redressing balances and had passed through an age when it was perhaps important to stress pure worship at the expense sometimes of understanding. The new legislation on the vernacular had remedied this by familiarizing the People of God daily with a wealth of scriptural understanding. By enabling articulate participation as well as understanding it had brought the liturgy to life and the edification derived was the means of spiritual renewal which of itself possessed ecumenical value.

Wheeler saw many signs of encouragement: the maintenance of the great cycle of Christ's own prayer by priests, monks and nuns and other religious throughout the world; the preservation in Anglican cathedrals, abbeys, monasteries, churches and religious orders of an objective worship directed primarily to the God-head. It was a consolation as well as a strength to the major part of God's people as they went about their business in the world that in isolated places His worship continued, in the name of all whether physically present or not. These dedicated souls were not necessarily interceding chiefly for unity but by giving to the Father that adoration which is the prayer of Christ they were obtaining for His people a growing together with Him whose end was the same. He concluded that the common pursuit of objective worship, which was the same thing as an identification with Christ praying, could do more than anything else for Christian unity. There was no better guide to *aggiornamento*.[4] It was an article which gave encouragement to many.

His stance was consistent in that the Catholic faith was the one true faith and that other faiths were imperfect but the quest for unity must continue. In 1969, he wrote:

The Council describes the Church in the New Testament terms as the people of God. This Church will attain her full perfection only in the glory of Heaven. But she already possesses a fullness surpassing that of any other body. And so the greatest gift in this life is to be a member of the Catholic Church. Once a man sees this, he must in conscience become a Catholic. Members of other Christian bodies, believing that Christ is God, and baptised in His name, are brought into a certain, though imperfect, communion with the Catholic Church. It is our privilege to accept them as brothers with respect and affection. They possess insights from which we may learn. They stand with us, proclaiming Christ in the face of a pagan world. The differences between us are far less that the agreements. It is Christ's will that we should all be one. This does not mean the glossing over of differences or the watering down of Faith. We can only grow together through truth and love; these two together, for truth without love is intolerance, and love without truth is often just sentimentality.[5]

Conversion, Anglican Orders and Public Collaboration

The Second Vatican Council's Decree on Ecumenism made it clear that there was no contradiction between the reception of individual converts into the fullness of the true faith and the continuing progress of institutional ecumenism—a position held and expounded by Wheeler at Heythrop and subsequently. It was, he said, a question of conscience: when one knows that one is ready to accept 'the greater fullness', then it must be embraced. He saw no incompatibility between accepting individuals who had embraced the faith while working at the same time for the unity of Christendom; such actions need not be mutually exclusive. His priests continued to accept individual converts but he had invited other Church leaders to his consecration and to participate in the opening and on-going activities of Wood Hall. As the Council advocated a 'common Christian front' in the 'pagan world of today', so too did Wheeler. In an interview with George Scott, he had said that 'Living in an increasingly secular and materialistic world and in view of this tremendous pressure on the Christian Churches which will go on mounting, we have got to join together'.[6] How this was to be achieved was another matter, however, but within this process he had no intention to diminishing 'one iota of fundamental Catholic teaching in our attitude to ecumenism'. In this, he was adopting the stance of Heenan and other senior Catholic leaders. Unity, he said would come in God's time not man's. In the meantime, there had to be prudence and prayer and sincere cooperation and collaboration between Christian denominations. He was especially critical of those who sought to increase the speed to unity by means of intercommunion. 'Intercommunion', he wrote, is the crown of unity achieved and far from being the means to this end it could frustrate that organic unity intended by the Church.[7]

As demonstrated at Heythrop in 1962, Wheeler's tactics, if not his strategy, on ecumenism differed from Heenan and the Cardinal recognised this. Heenan was suspicious of Cardinal Bea and Mgr Willebrands involving themselves in English affairs and on hearing second hand that Archbishop Ramsey of Canterbury was to visit Rome in March 1966, he suspected that he was being frozen out of the arrangements. He was amazed that he had not been informed and expressed his discontent to Bea. Conscious of what he perceived to be a lack of understanding in the Roman Curia of English ecclesiastical history, he was afraid that the intrusion of the Secretariat for Promoting Christian Unity would harm the efforts of the Hierarchy to establish harmonious relations with the Anglican Church on its terms. He wrote to Bishop Holland of Salford suggesting that he should accompany the Archbishop's party and added that he did not want Wheeler, still Coadjutor in Middlesbrough, to go. 'I am quite sure it would be a mistake to send an ex-Anglican in the party', he wrote.[8]

Yet later, in October 1966, at the request of the Hierarchy, Wheeler attended the fortieth anniversary celebrations of the Malines Conversations, an event which highlighted the traditional gulf between Anglicans and English Catholics and presented Wheeler with an embarrassing situation. The Malines Conversations were a series of informal discussions held in the Belgian primatial see of Malines from 1921 to 1927 when Belgian but not English Catholics explored the possibilities of corporate reunion between the Roman Catholic Church and the Church of England. The Conversations were the initiative of Cardinal Mercier with support from the Vatican and the Archbishops of Canterbury and York. The Anglicans were represented by Lord Halifax, Bishops Frere and Gore and Armitage Robinson, the Dean of Wells. The Catholic participants included Mercier and his successor Cardinal van Roey who wound up the conversations in 1927. Van Roey was less disposed to the idea of unity than his predecessor and Cardinal Bourne of Westminster successfully urged the Vatican to withdraw its encouragement, in line with Leo XIII's bull *Apostolicae Curae* (1896), which denied the validity of Anglican orders.

It was the invalidity of Anglican orders that led to Wheeler's embarrassment at the commemoration. Unknown to Wheeler, Cardinal Léon-Joseph Suenens, the current Cardinal-Archbishop of Malines, and the Anglican dignitaries had arranged an Anglican Eucharist. To attend the service indicated recognition of Anglican orders and Wheeler told Suenens why he could not participate. As host, Suenens felt he could not refuse and knelt throughout the ceremony. In his report to Heenan, Wheeler explained the incident and asked the Cardinal not to mention it to Suenens.[9] To Heenan, however, it was more evidence of the continental hierarchies' inability to understand the English ecumenical situation. 'What a pity', he wrote, that 'the Anglican Eucharist was arranged. It is one more proof that enlightened people like Cardinal Suenens do not really understand the issues as they appear on our little island.'[10] To be fair to Suenens, he could not be the discourteous host but Wheeler felt seriously compromised and wrote that 'the less said about it the better'.[11] To Archbishop Cardinale, Wheeler explained his actions and those of Cardinal Suenens, but felt that 'the whole thing had been a great success and went very beautifully and circumspectly'.[12] In a letter to Suenens, Wheeler thanked the Cardinal for his hospitality and expressed his pleasure to be able 'to see so historic a place on such a significant occasion' but chose not mention the Anglican Eucharist.[13] Nevertheless, those Anglicans who attended the commemoration felt that Wheeler's presence had given them encouragement.[14]

When Suenens paid a return visit to York in April 1969 there were still significant differences between him and his English co-religionists. After staying with Wheeler at Eltofts, Suenens visited the Community of the Resurrection at Mirfield and a day later attended Matins in York Minster. Wheeler was present as were the Bishop of Middlesbrough, descendants of Lord Halifax, the Cardinal's entourage and the Archbishop of York and diocesan clergy. In his sermon Suenens said that 'the unity we are aiming at is not a human affair; not a diplomatic compromise. We need to discover the will and commandment of the Lord'. Through dialogue, he said, Christians learn to pray together and discover that all are the sons of the same Father. These were sentiments with which Wheeler could agree. However, while Suenens concelebrated Mass at the Bar Convent in York, the Cardinal was personally represented by Mgr

Theeuws and Canon Dessain at Solemn Eucharist in Minster. There is no record of Wheeler's reaction to this but in his assessment of the Cardinal's visit, he wrote that 'Whilst differing from the Cardinal is some matters, we all have a great regard for his dynamism and his gifts of leadership. Ecumenically, his actions have spoken even louder than his words ...' Thanks to Pope John XXIII and Pope Paul VI, he continued, relations between Rome and Canterbury were much easier and friendlier but he concluded: 'In God's time—and not ours—the unity for which Christ prayed will happen'. It had to be pursued in prayer and dialogue and in truth and in love.[15]

Practical Commitment

Wheeler's contribution to ecumenism and inter-faith relations within the geographical limits of his diocese was sincere and significant. He acknowledged that the new ecumenical momentum was a cause of surprise and bewilderment among Catholics long accustomed to being told to shun other Christians but told his diocese that 'this is assuredly the work of the Holy Spirit'. There was, he said, a call for renewal, an acceptance of the fact that more united Christians than divided them, and a need to grow closer to others in an increasing love for God. He pointed out, however, that other Christian beliefs about the Blessed Sacrament and priesthood 'are usually very different from ours' and 'even when they seem to be very close, their clergy do not possess the powers of the Catholic Priesthood'.[16]

His practical commitment to ecumenism was evident in his ministry. He ensured that the diocese was represented on Leeds Council of Christians and Jews[17] and that the annual Octave of Christian Unity was observed. Soon after his arrival in Leeds, he set up a Diocesan Ecumenical Commission and a number of practical ventures were undertaken with other faiths such as 'The People Next Door Project' in 1967, 'The Call to the North' in 1968 and anti-abortion rallies. In January 1968, during the Octave of Christian Unity, Wheeler became the first Catholic bishop to preach in Leeds Parish Church and Canon Fenton Morley, Vicar of Leeds, preached in St Anne's Cathedral on the following night.[18] In the Parish Church, Wheeler said: 'Together we have to go out to the world of our time, bringing the love of God and the love of Christ to the world today'. That world, he said 'was hungry for spiritual values' and 'our own country is starving spiritually'. Ecumenism, he concluded, made people better Christians, no matter what their denomination might be. A few days later, he gave the University Sermon in the Emmanuel Church, Leeds.[19]

In his 1972 *ad limina*, Wheeler reported that 'We do everything possible to encourage the Mind of the Church regarding Ecumenism. But all the rules of the Holy See are scrupulously followed and no aberrations are permitted'. He found experiments in other countries such as the USA to be a great disadvantage as they ran counter to the Church's regulations.[20] In his 1977 *ad limina*, he reported the success of the Pastoral and Ecumenical Centre at Wood Hall in developing ecumenical relations and the good work being done at area levels but the increasing divergence of views between Catholics and other Christians on social and moral issues was becoming more apparent. Moreover, some priests did not welcome ecumenism while others, far fewer, wished to go quicker than the Church wished or allowed. Progress, he concluded, was gradual but steady.[21] One reason, as John Dennis, Anglican Bishop of Knaresborough pointed out to Wheeler, was that the practical possibilities of ecumenism were hampered by confusion over Anglican and Roman Catholic diocesan boundaries, jurisdiction and spheres of influence.[22] This did not prevent Wheeler and the Anglican bishops of Ripon, Bradford and Wakefield backing The People's March for Jobs in 1981.[23]

Wood Hall was the diocesan centre for prayer and discussion on Vatican II and ecumenical initiatives and there Wheeler had built an Ecumenical Chapel of the Good Shepherd. This was for joint use in non-Eucharistic services involving Catholics and those of other faiths and by Anglicans and Methodists for their own services, including the Eucharist, which Catholics attended. As Finnigan writes, 'The building gave tangible expression to Wheeler's commitment to ecumenism within his programme to implement Vatican II'.[24] Of Wood Hall, The Bishop of Pontefract wrote: 'What an imaginative venture on the part of your diocese to start such a place as that'. It was, he continued, a 'highly significant contribution to the cause of unity'.[25] Wheeler's enthronement had been attended by leaders of other faiths, itself an innovation and he was always ready to preach where appropriate and possible at non-Catholic services. It was at the personal and social level, however, where he had the biggest influence in forging links and lessening difficulties. His correspondence with the Archbishop of York and other Anglican bishops in Yorkshire was particularly warm and intimate and through frequent lunches, dinners and other social contact he developed a network of amicable and collaborative relationships with these and other religious leaders. He was especially close to Bishop Moorman of Ripon who found him to be a congenial colleague. They shared platforms during Weeks of Prayer for Christian Unity and preached in each other's churches; in 1973, they established the Associated Sixth Form of St Aidan's Church of England High School and St John Fisher Catholic High School in Harrogate. An attempt to unite the Leeds University Chaplaincies did not materialise but the ascetic Moorman was impressed with the five-course lunch he received at Eltofts during exploratory discussions.[26]

In 1982, in his final *ad limina*, Wheeler expressed satisfaction in the continued use of Wood Hall and in other diocesan ecumenical initiatives. There were now regular meetings with leaders and workers of other faiths and a Diocesan Ecumenical Officer had been appointed. Greater use was being made of the media to transmit the Christian message and there were practical ecumenical projects in hospitals, prisons, universities, and a range of housing and social welfare programmes. The Leeds Metropolitan Council of Churches, Neighbourhood Councils of Churches, Clergy Fraternals and the Yorkshire Council of Social Service had all served to lower the barriers between faiths, Christian and non-Christian, in the pursuit of the common good. 'Much more', he wrote, 'is happening in the ecumenical field' but unity was still 'fragile'.[27] By the late-1970s and early 1980s, discussions about the ordination of women priests in the Anglican Church began to force the Catholic Church back on the defensive in ecumenical relations. In 1976, a Vatican declaration had reiterated that the Church did not consider itself authorised to admit women to priestly ordination.[28]

The visit of Pope John Paul II to Great Britain in 1982 came at a propitious time for the ecumenical cause and expectations were high. Following three years preparatory work, the Anglican-Roman Catholic International Commission (ARCIC) was established in 1970 to explore specific problems of division—Eucharistic Doctrine, ministry and ordination, and authority in the Church. While acknowledging the significant differences between the two Communions, ARCIC felt able in 1976 to invite their leaders to consider 'closer sharing... in life, worship and mission'. In their Common Declaration, Pope Paul VI and Archbishop Donald Coggan of Canterbury accepted this invitation and a subsequent statement pronounced that a joint communion stood at 'the centre of the Christian witness to the world'. ARCIC presented its final report to Rome in 1981 and the Congregation for the Doctrine of the Faith published its observations in March 1982.[29] The Congregation recognised the positive aspects of ARCIC's report and acknowledged the Commission's patient and thorough investigations and exemplary ecumenical dialogue. Of particular note was the quality of doctrinal rapprochement achieved and the attention given to previous observation made by the Congregation. However, in the opinion of the Congregation, there were ambiguous statements in the Report and potential for the misinterpretation of fundamental issues. The Congregation invited ARCIC to continue its dialogue, address the points made by the Congregation, and extend the dialogue to 'new themes, particularly to those which are necessary with a view to the restoration of full church unity between the two Communions'.[30] The General Secretary of the British Council of Churches was realistic about the Vatican's reception of the Report and was of the view that the Pope would make no major ecumenical announcement during his visit. All he could hope for was general encouragement from His Holiness.[31] Catholic Anglicans were more willing to see the Pope as the symbol of authority and unity rather than a dangerous foreigner trying to subvert the national religion and the *Church Observer* of Spring 1982 included very positive articles by eminent Catholic Anglicans. Its editor was ready to 'welcome John Paul Our Pope'. Divisions remained and there were opponents of unity in both if not all Communions but at Canterbury Cathedral, in a service rich in history and symbolism, Archbishop Robert Runcie and the Pope called for an end to historical quarrels 'which have tragically disfigured Christ's Church' and further dialogue which will lead 'to the day of full restoration of unity in faith and love'.[32]

Although Wheeler made every effort to advance the cause of ecumenism, he was under no illusions over the inherent difficulties or the length of time it would take to reach fruition. He was never less than honest in his dealings with those of other faiths and repeated frequently that it was 'absolutely essential that we do not diminish one iota of fundamental Catholic teaching in our attitude to ecumenism'. 'Humanly speaking', he wrote, 'it is always difficult to see how unity can happen' for it could only materialise through God's providence. It was for God to decide when 'His unity...shall happen'. Wheeler was impatient with those who laid down timed targets for unity—that was not how God worked—and he castigated those who, for example, advocated intercommunion as a quick way to unity. This would not, he argued, achieve organic unity. Nevertheless, in a pagan world it was essential that there was a common Christian front derived from the joint efforts of 'the whole People of God in truth and love'.[33]

Notes

1   Moorman to Wheeler, 7 Dec 1964. LDA, WDC, W48, Ecumenism.

2   Wheeler to R. Peel-Yates, 8 July 1968. LDA, WDC, W55.

3   Butler to Wheeler, 13 Feb 1964. DAA, Butler Papers.

4   *The Tablet*, 12 Feb 1966.

5   Quoted in R. E. Finnigan, 'Bishop Wheeler, 1966–1985' in R. E. Finnigan and J. Hagerty, *The Bishops of Leeds 1878–1985: Essays in Honour of Bishop David Konstant* (Keighley: PBK Publishing on behalf of the Diocese of Leeds, 2005), pp. 162–163.

6   G. Scott, *The RCs: a report on Roman Catholics in Britain today* (London: Hutchinson, 1967), p. 267.

7   W.G. Wheeler, *In Truth And Love* (Southport: Gowland & Co., 1990). pp. 88–90.

8   Heenan to Holland, 5 Jan 1966. AAW, Heenan, He3/77.

9   Wheeler to Heenan, 31 Oct 1966. LDA, WDC, W41.

10 Heenan to Wheeler, 4 Nov 1966. LDA, WDC, W41.

11 Wheeler to R. Slade, 16 Nov 1966. LDA, WDC, W41.

12 Wheeler to Cardinale, 1 Nov 1966. LDA, WDC, W41.

13 Wheeler to Suenens, 31 Oct 1966. LDA, WDC, W41.

14 Bishop of Winchester to Wheeler, 2 Nov 1966. LDA, WDC, W41.

15 *The Visit of Cardinal Suenens to York Minster 27th April 1969*. LDA, WDC, W48.

16 Wheeler, Pastoral, 'Christian Unity', Jan 1968. LDA, WDC, Wheeler Papers.

17 Leeds Council of Christians and Jews. LDA. WDC, W23. Wheeler was committed to this initiative although he played little part in its activities.

18 *Yorkshire Post*, 10 Jan 1968.

19 *Yorkshire Evening Post*, 1 Jan 1968.

20 *QR*, 1972.

21 *QR.*, 1977.

22 Dennis to Wheeler, 18 Nov 1982. LDA, WDC, W64, Anglican Bishops Miscellaneous.

23 *Catholic Herald*, 17 April 1981.

24 Finnigan, 'Bishop Wheeler, 1966–1985', p. 162.

25 Bishop of Pontefract to Wheeler, 20 Sept 1976. LDA, WDC, W10, Anglican Bishops 1966–1976.

26 M. Manktelow, *John Moorman: Anglican, Franciscan, Independent* (Norwich: Canterbury Press, 1999), p. 71.

27 *QR*, 1982.

28   K. Robbins, *Oxford History of the Christian Church: England, Ireland, Scotland, Wales: The Christian Church 1900–2000* (Oxford: Oxford University Press, 2008), p. 442.

29   The Roman Catholic Ecumenical Commission of England and Wales, *Bulletin 41*, Spring 1982.

30   Sacra Congregatio Pro Doctrina Fidei, 'Observations on the Final Report of ARCIC', 29 March 1982. LDA, WDC, ARCIC.

31   The British Council of Churches, General Secretary's Introduction to the Assembly, Spring 1982. LDA, WDC, ARCIC. In 1974, the Bishops' Conference rejected a proposal to join the British Council of Churches.

32   *The Tablet*, 5 June 1982.

33   Wheeler, *In Truth And Love*, pp. 90–91.

13 THE EASTER PEOPLE

Abbot Hume and Westminster

I N FEBRUARY 1976, Basil Hume, Abbot of Ampleforth, was appointed
to succeed Cardinal John Carmel Heenan as Archbishop of Westminster.[1] To many, it was a huge surprise. The *Daily Express* named
him 'The long-shot Archbishop' and reported that 'most of the bishops'
were 'shattered' by the appointment.[2] Wheeler, however, was not shocked
for he had worked behind the scenes to secure the Benedictine's preferment.

Cardinal Heenan, who died on 7 November 1975, had already placed
his resignation with the Pope and had announced to his clergy and laity
that a more democratic system of choosing the next archbishop would be
introduced. He believed that to be fully effective a bishop must have
widespread support among priests and people and therefore they should
be fully consulted before a decision was made.[3] The traditional method
was for the Canons of the Cathedral Chapter to tender three names, called
a *terna*, to the Vatican but more recently the Apostolic Delegate had taken
control of the procedure whereby bishops and archbishops were
appointed. Archbishop Heim invited public consultation and added his
views and those of senior clergy and nominated laypeople to the names
submitted by the Canons. For such an important post as Westminster,
the *terna* would inevitably be supplemented by the opinions of the
Hierarchy and leading Catholics and because of this, and Heenan's
announcement, Heim was faced with ninety-five names.[4]

Press and media interest in the appointment of the new Archbishop
soon hit fever pitch. The *Catholic Herald* reported that 'Christians in this
country seem to be seeking some charismatic figure who will restore the
faithful to their pews and the priests to their altars, who will re-pack the
confessionals, cure the ill-mannered dissensions within the Catholic
Church in England and Wales, and restore that in-gathering of intellectuals who once sought, not a refuge, but a solid foundation upon the
ancient certainties of the Church'. The new archbishop would be
expected, among other things, to instil loyalty, be a political operator, and
not be impatient of ceremony. In other words, superhuman qualities were
needed.[5] According to Schofield and Skinner, it was felt in many quarters
that a different style was needed after the Heenan era.[6] Hastings wrote

that there was a sense of tension and drift among the various post-Conciliar strands of Catholic in the English and Welsh community and a new lead was required.[7]

Archbishop Heim had played a significant part in Bishop Thomas Winning's appointment as Archbishop of Glasgow and demonstrated that he was capable of being unconventional. As a papal diplomat, he possessed an international outlook and it was felt that he wished the English and Welsh Church to look beyond its traditional historical, theological and intellectual frontiers. Heim did not have to nominate one of the more automatic choices but, nevertheless, the obvious episcopal names were put before him: Bishop Worlock of Portsmouth, Bishop Clark of East Anglia, Bishop Butler, Auxiliary in Westminster, and Archbishop Dwyer of Birmingham. The retirement of Archbishop Beck of Liverpool further complicated the situation as that See would also have to be filled.[8] *The Sunday Times* ran an article listing the advantages and disadvantages of all the obvious candidates but interestingly added the names of Basil Hume, Abbot of Ampleforth, and Fr Michael Hollings, a parish priest in Southall.[9] Bishop Worlock, the most active, energetic and experienced among the candidates, was respected but not particularly well liked by his episcopal brethren. None of the Hierarchy, it seemed, wanted Worlock at Westminster but no obvious alternative emerged.[10]

As is traditional in these cases, lobby groups, clerical and lay, wielded considerable influence and power. In late 1975, the most important group among the Catholic laity included the politicians Norman St John Stevas and Shirley Williams, William Rees-Mogg, editor of *The Times*, and Miles FitzAlan-Howard, 17th Duke of Norfolk and Premier Earl of England whose home at Arundel Castle became a centre for the discussion of suitable successors to Heenan. Initially, Norfolk had supported the cause of Fr Hollings, a charismatic parish priest and like Norfolk, a former Guards officer. Hollings, however, was diametrically opposed to his name being put forward. Norfolk (an old Amplefordian) immediately switched his interest to Basil Hume, the Abbot of Ampleforth, and went to see the Apostolic Delegate to further Hume's candidacy.[11] Other supporters went to Rome to press the Abbot's cause.[12] Arthur Wells wrote that Bishop Christopher Butler had 'without doubt' paved the way for Hume's preferment.[13]

Clearly there were forces at work in support of the Abbot's candidacy but Cardinal Cormac Murphy-O'Connor, who was Rector of the Venerable English College, Rome, in 1976, claimed that Wheeler's intervention was instrumental in Hume's appointment. It was felt that Rome wished the efficient and experienced Bishop Worlock to succeed Heenan but Murphy-O'Connor has suggested that Wheeler's influence over Archbishop Heim proved decisive. Hume was not particularly well known by the Hierarchy but to Wheeler he was an associate and a friend. Wheeler was also close to the Apostolic Delegate. Heim, recalled Murphy-O'Connor, liked his men to be out 'of the top drawer' and Hume had all the right spiritual, academic and social qualifications. The son of a knight, educated at Ampleforth, Oxford and Fribourg, an experienced abbot, and with contacts in the higher reaches of society and government, Hume possessed the right credentials. Murphy-O'Connor recalled that Wheeler and Bishop McLean of Middlesbrough suggested Hume's name to the Delegate and cultivated the support of the Norfolk faction, the old Amplefordians Hugo Young at *The Times* and Andrew Knight at *The Economist*, and Rembert Weakland, the American Benedictine Abbot President in Rome.[14] It was a formidable alliance. Anthony Howard claimed that Wheeler 'strongly influenced' the Apostolic Delegate in favour of Hume and that until he retired in 1985, Wheeler 'remained closer to Hume than any other member of the Hierarchy'.[15] Eventually, Bishop Worlock was announced as Archbishop Beck's successor at Liverpool on 11 February 1976 and a few days later Abbot Hume was named Archbishop of Westminster. The supporters of Bishop Worlock of Portsmouth claimed that their man had been 'dished by the Arundel and Brighton blue-blood set' apparently unaware, at the time, of Wheeler's involvement.[16] *The Tablet* expressed the view that Hume's appointment was 'a sagacious and imaginative decision on the part of the Holy See' and welcomed it unreservedly.[17]

Correspondence between Wheeler and Hume was much more intimate than that between Wheeler and Heenan and in the Abbot's early days at Westminster, Wheeler offered him much practical advice. A further mark of their closeness was that Wheeler was the only English bishop in attendance when Hume received the cardinal's Red Hat from Pope Paul VI in May 1976. It was an occasion, he told Hume, 'I would not have missed for anything'.[18] He was also present when Hume took possession of his titular church, San Silvestro in Capite.[19] In his memoir Wheeler judiciously revealed nothing of his involvement in Hume's appointment but instead chose to give some reasons why the Abbot had been selected. There was no obvious candidate of the right age, he wrote, and there was also a feeling that 'a new image' was needed. Given these two lines of thinking the Abbot of Ampleforth was a fairly obvious choice. 'His strong spiritual background and gift of leadership were alike well-known and combined with a typical English understatement have surely produced an inspired appointment'.[20] He omitted to mention his long friendship with the Abbot, that Hume's brother-in-law was the Cabinet Secretary, and that the new Archbishop was relatively well-known in the country's higher social and political echelons.[21] Hume's Scottish-French background also contrasted with the Anglo-Irish lineage of many other bishops and this too, particularly in the context of contemporary problems in Ulster, may have been a more comforting prospect in the eyes of the British government.

There were two unprecedented features to Hume's appointment: he became the first monk to be appointed to Westminster and only the second Archbishop of Westminster who was not previously a bishop, the other being Cardinal Manning.[22] In the local press Wheeler was anxious to alleviate the concerns of those who felt that a man who had spent his life in monastic environment might not be able to tackle the challenging job at Westminster and lead the national Church. Abbot Hume, he wrote, 'has eminent qualities of leadership in many different fields. Above all, he will doubtless prove a great spiritual guide and inspiration where there is a need and hunger for the things of God'. Like Archbishop Donald Coggan of York, the former neighbour of both Hume and Wheeler and recently appointed Archbishop of Canterbury, Hume was now going south and 'their longstanding friendship will doubtless help the growth towards Christian unity'.[23] Elsewhere, he wrote that Hume was an 'inspired' choice for he was an outstanding leader, a man of great charm, compassion and erudition, and 'a wise and balanced ecumenist'.[24] To Archbishop Giovanni Benelli at the Secretariat of State, he wrote: 'As you will know, he is a great personal friend of mine and I am delighted about the appointment, which has certainly been wonderfully well received and with acclamation in this country'.[25]

The National Pastoral Congress

In May 1980, a National Pastoral Congress was convened in Liverpool. It was conceived as an opportunity for Catholics in England and Wales to apply the findings of the Second Vatican Council to the life of the Church in the latter part of the twentieth century. Two thousand people—priests and laity—discussed issues of relevance and concern to the Church in England and Wales and produced a joint pastoral strategy. It was the first time that the laity and clergy had met together in such a gathering with such an objective and the Congress was seen as an opportunity for the laity 'to stake their claim to be authentic leaders of their Church, as much 'the people of God' as the clergy'.[26] As Longley writes, however, the Congress became an 'official venture of the Bishops Conference' and was controlled by them. There were some who denounced the whole idea and made formal objections to Rome.[27]

In 1972, a joint working party of bishops, diocesan priests, religious and laity had been convened to consider in depth the pastoral situation in England and Wales. Sponsored by the Hierarchy and the National Conference of Priests, the joint working party produced two reports— *Church 2000* (1973) and *A Time for Building* (1976)—the latter proposing that 'a national conference' be convened 'to determine the broad outlines of a national pastoral strategy'.[28] 25,000 copies of *Church 2000* were circulated but it generated a disappointing response; *A Time for Building* provoked more interest.[29] Some bishops were concerned that the whole exercise would be dominated by discussions on *Humanae Vitae* but Archbishop Worlock and his episcopal steering committee directed the Congress firmly towards topics other than birth control.[30]

20,000 people replied to a consultation paper requesting suggestions for themes to be discussed. Eight were chosen—Marriage and the Family, The World of Work, Growing in Faith, You and the Church, A Question of Justice, Young People in the Church, Unity among Christians, and Catholic Education. Discussion papers were drawn from these themes and circulated to parishes. Subsequently, in a period of sixteen months, 70% of parishes submitted reports to diocesan co-ordinators. From these, seven themes were chosen for the Congress agenda—The People of God: Co-responsibility and Relationships; The People of God: Ministry, Vocation, Apostolate; Family and Society; Evangelization; Christian Education and Formation; Christian Witness; and Justice—and discussion papers were circulated to the dioceses.[31] Among the laity, expectations were high and enthusiasm was almost unbounded. Robbins wrote that 'The Congress was to be an expression of the notion that the church existed in dialogue'.[32] Hastings wrote: 'Now at last, the teaching and spirit of Vatican II were to be deliberately adopted by, and adapted to, the Church in this country. It was a long awaited moment...' Since well before

227

Vatican II, he continued, the English Catholic laity had become much more outgoing and confident, 'so central to the life of the nation, so rich with distinguished people in its ranks'. The laity gathered at the Congress was to reflect this confidence.[33] There was indeed hope in the air but some cautioned realism. Reflecting on the Congress, the editor of the *Catholic Gazette*, organ of the Catholic Missionary Society, asked if 'the new spring begun by Vatican II would burst into new openness in our country through the Congress?' There was opposition to the Congress within the ranks of both Catholic traditionalists and progressives and what was needed for the Church was 'not a middle class, institutionalised organization, not more structures, not a strengthening of the fortress, but a more open attitude to the world and its problems'. The impact of the Congress, the editor feared, would reach only a few people.[34]

Such reservations did not adversely affect diocesan planning. Wheeler appointed Fr Arthur Roche to be a member of the Congress Committee and co-ordinator of the Leeds diocesan preparations. By early 1979, deanery and other meetings had been convened to discuss Marriage and the Family, the World of Work and Unity with Other Christians.[35] One hundred diocesan delegates assembled at Trinity and All Saints Colleges, Leeds, on 24 November 1979 when Wheeler told them they would 'be asked to examine how faithfully the Church is carrying out the message given to it by Christ, to assess the strength and weakness of our spiritual lives; and to point the way ahead'. The bishops, he told them, 'have already arranged to meet in July to assess your findings and to see how best they can be implemented'. Fr Roche reminded delegates that they had been fortunate 'in having strong encouragement and leadership' from the Bishop and invited them to study more closely the themes before them and prepare themselves through discussion, prayer and reflection for the meeting in Liverpool.[36] The Hierarchy hoped that the Congress would lead to 'a stirring of new life, under the Holy Spirit, a kind of spiritual resurrection'.[37]

The Congress opened in the Metropolitan Cathedral of Christ the King on Friday 2 May 1980. Pope John Paul II sent his prayers and good wishes:

> Your two thousand delegates—drawn from every part of England and Wales, and including priests, deacons, men and women religious, and laity—have gathered at the invitation of your Bishops and under their guidance. As members of the Pilgrim Church, you come together to share information and to take stock

of what has so far been done, in fidelity to the Gospel, to implement the decrees of the Second Vatican Council. In this, you are following my declared intention when I was made Pope: to be faithful to the Council and to strive to bring it to fruition. May God bless and guide you in this important resolve.

I have been informed of how you have made careful preparations in your dioceses and religious congregations and organizations for this special occasion. Your desire is to achieve a deep spiritual renewal of your lives. You wish to strengthen your common commitment to the mission which our Lord Jesus Christ entrusted to his Church, a mission in which all the People of God share through Baptism and Confirmation. I pray that your work together in these days will bear great fruit... I invite you to place all your trust in God whose power, working in us, can do infinitely more than we can ask or imagine.[38]

Expectations ran high among the delegates and there followed four days of earnest and prayerful discussion. The delegates tackled a dauntingly ambitious agenda and even though the seven themes were broken down into topics and smaller discussion groups, there were severe constraints of time.

Wheeler himself attended the Congress and participated in the discussions on Public and Civic Life within the sector devoted to Christian Witness. The report of his group included all the elements of lay involvement he had long aspired to—a politically informed laity, Catholics fulfilling civic obligations, an active apostolate on statutory and voluntary bodies, finding social and political solutions acceptable to the Christian conscience, and a strong commitment to the common good. His group also recommended that seminaries should ensure that priests were equipped to understand and react to 'the political structure' and that Church organizations should know and be able to exploit the skills and talents of parish and diocesan communities.[39]

In his closing declaration, Cardinal Hume summarised the work of each sector and said that the delegates had tried to represent faithfully the Church in England and Wales. Under the guidance of the Holy Spirit, they 'had shared freely with each other their hopes and anxieties and had together sought the will of God'. On returning to their dioceses, they would have to share the joy they had experienced at the Congress and reflect more deeply on their commitment to God and on the practical implications of that commitment. It was for the bishops, he concluded pointedly, to study the recommendations of the sectors and their guidance for future pastoral action: 'It will be for them to discern the way forward'.[40] It was a huge task: at the end of the Congress, the seven sectors submitted reports which included over 200 recommendations, proposals or suggestions covering an astonishing range of issues relating to Catholic life, morals and belief.[41] The reports were drawn together by a drafting committee chaired by Archbishop Worlock and the result was published in 1980 under the title *The Easter People*. The final section of *The Easter People* was concerned with the process of pastoral planning and laid out stages of development based on the principles 'See, Judge, Act'.[42]

After the exuberance of the Congress, delegates returned to their dioceses aware that its success or failure depended on the effectiveness of diocesan structures to facilitate development and their own ability to communicate its messages to the people they represented. They carried with them an encouraging but uncomfortable mandate: to tell their dioceses that the survival and growth of the Church in England and Wales country depended on the wholehearted acceptance of the priorities of the Gospel but that this could not be enforced by ecclesiastical decree. The *Catholic Herald* noted with pleasure that the Congress, an experiment in shared responsibility, avoided the predicted pitfalls of polarization and commentators looking for an English rebellion against Rome or for a split between traditional and progressive groupings went away disappointed: 'There was honest dissent and caring criticism but a minimum of destructive posturing'. The very decision to hold the Congress showed that the bishops had faith in shared responsibility but the Hierarchy now faced the challenge of how far it would be prepared to relinquish control over the running of the national Church.[43] There was little chance, however, that it would cede much if any of its power. For individual Catholics, the final test of the Congress would depend on their willingness to preach the gospel through their own lives and become involved at grass roots level.

Wheeler appeared anxious that the messages of the Congress were disseminated and that the strategy for pastoral renewal and development outlined by the bishops in *The Easter People* should be undertaken immediately. In September 1980, he told a meeting of the Diocesan Pastoral Council that *The Easter People* was an 'absolute must' for it set out a pastoral strategy for the next decade. Fear of the size of that task 'must be disarmed', he said, and developments should begin at the deanery level.[44] In October 1980, he convened a three-day meeting of over 200 clergy at Hazlewood to reflect on the Congress and consider their own priestly lives, the life of their parishes and the life of the diocese.[45] In his opening address, he emphasised the importance of their sacred ministry and the value of the Congress in helping them to reach the full fruition of that calling with the assistance of the laity. At the Congress, he said, 'there came to us loud and clear not only a deep appreciation of our priesthood on the part of the laity, but a longing on their part also for us to become of even greater service'. *The Easter People*, he said, was 'a frightening document' and could easily lead to dismay. The answer, he suggested, was to further enlist the collaboration of the laity and consolidate on gains already made and developments being undertaken. Priests and laity, he said, had to share and collaborate fully in systems of mutual support and confidence. He asked them to guard against 'an entirely irrational fear of the laity' and warned against cynicism and apathy for they serve to 'erode the spirit of hope which every Christian must have'. Wheeler felt that the Congress had reinvigorated the diocesan councils which he had established. He remarked: 'Even if the event in Liverpool had not been a success, the preparation work would have given new life to the spiritual and pastoral life of the diocese. The Congress at Liverpool...was a very remarkable success and gave new inspiration to everybody present'. However, one of the priests, Fr Arthur McCrystal, while welcoming the laity's interest in his priestly ministry and in other developments, thought *The Easter People* was too prescriptive in terms of the laity's demands and expectations.[46]

Wheeler had spoken earlier of the differences in vocation and mission between priests and laity at a seminar on priestly spirituality organized by the Rome-based *Centro Romano di Incontri Sacerdotali* which had been started by priests of Opus Dei as a pastoral exchange for priests from different countries. Speaking in August 1980 to more than sixty diocesan priests at Maria Assumpta College, London, he quoted from the bishops' response to the Pastoral Congress due to be published later in the month. 'Priests are not required of necessity to be expert in all the secular concerns which are the primary sphere of the apostolate of the laity', he said, 'but lay men and women will expect a priest to help them to set their problems which challenge our lives today, within the light of the Gospel'. Wheeler said that the Pastoral Congress had set the Church in this country on the brink of a new facelift and the priests would find their response outlined in Pope John Paul II's Holy Week letter to priests which contained the whole essence of Vatican II's message, notably *Lumen Gentium*. A priest committed to sacramental service of the community, Wheeler said, needed constantly to renew himself spiritually. The Church needed a new priestly dynamism. People may feel they want to celebrate the Eucharist, but priests also had to follow Christ in washing another's feet.[47]

The Diocesan Pastoral Council decided to initiate the programme of pastoral planning outlined in *The Easter People* but the exercise meant that another 100 people attended the DPC's meetings and it became oversubscribed. Wheeler's exhortations and desire for diocesan involvement, however, did not meet with a uniformly positive response for there were some deaneries and parishes where inertia or opposition reigned. Some deaneries and parishes were thus not represented on the DPC.[48] Wheeler set up a working party to decide on the way forward and ensure that the twenty-one deaneries fed in representatives to the DPC but there is little evidence that his personal intervention led to a vigorous implementation of *The Easter People*. He was still stressing the importance of Area Pastoral Councils in 1982.[49]

Many diocesan initiatives reflected much of what was contained in *The Easter People* and were a continuation of what Wheeler had begun with discussions on the Apostolate of the Laity in 1966 and his formation of diocesan commissions. He wrote that 'we now have the task of implementing all that emerged from the Congress for doing so is very clearly outlined in...*The Easter People*'[50] but his conservative nature probably outweighed his willingness to further extend lay involvement and, more importantly, cede clerical control in particular circumstances. One of Wheeler's first post-Congress decisions was to introduce, in November 1980, a diocesan monthly newspaper—*The Catholic Voice*—to maintain the momentum of the Congress, communicate developments within the diocese, and impart news and views.[51] In January 1981, he began a tour of the deaneries to talk to priests about pastoral matters and new initiatives undertaken following the Congress.[52] The many vibrant lay groups and organizations in the diocese had already begun to work out the implications of the Congress but there is little evidence to show that they changed significantly.[53]

An important feature of the Congress was that the laity, in Leeds and elsewhere, challenged the episcopate on a variety of sensitive issues and called for a more radical social and political commitment. *The Easter People* was the written manifestation of this approach and demands. One strong expression of lay discontent was with the Church's teaching on contraception and its treatment of divorced Catholics and those seeking annulments. When Cardinal Hume and Archbishop Worlock attended the Bishops' International Synod on the Role of the Christian Family in the Modern World in Rome in August 1980, they presented Pope John Paul II with a copy of *The Easter People*. Hume asked for a fresh look at *Humanae Vitae* and the exclusion of divorced and remarried Catholics from Holy Communion. Stourton, Stanford and Longley claim that Pope John Paul II rejected both the report and the Cardinal's request[54] thus denting many of the hopes generated by the Pastoral Congress.[55] At its first meeting after the Synod, the Hierarchy discussed the Pope's response. It took pains not to criticise the Pope and diplomatically concluded that the Synod 'had not yet evolved the right machinery for its discussion'.[56] There was more to it than that, however. Pope John Paul II had made it very clear that he had limited Pope Paul VI's Vatican II concept of episcopal collegiality. He had begun to curb the liberal elements in the Church, including as he saw it, the contemporary English and Welsh Hierarchy and return control to the more conservative bastions of the Roman Curia.[57]

Pope John Paul II's action may have been a signal to Wheeler to be circumspect for his 1982 *ad limina* contained few references to the Congress. He recorded that 'the entire presbyterium' met at Hazlewood to study the Congress reports and 'devise methods of implementing them as widely as possible in all the parishes of the diocese'.[58] Reports on diocesan Pastoral Commissions, however, were not placed in the context of the Congress and its impact and influence appeared diffused. For example, on Catechesis, he wrote:

> During the last 12 months, the people of the diocese in a follow up to the National Pastoral Congress have been involved in catechesis of a very different kind. The laity are learning their responsibilities through the process of involvement, as they choose priorities for their parish and diocese. Initially they began discussions on the three areas of Mission, Community and Work, always with an eye to choosing significant areas of concern that could become diocesan priorities.
>
> The experience of those taking part has been their growth and understanding of what it means to be an active layperson in the local Church. They understand much more now how they have

co-responsibility with their clergy and Bishop in living out the truths of the Gospel.[59]

Activists who attended the Congress could be forgiven for seeing this as a slightly patronising and outmoded comment. The *ad limina* may have contained scant reference to the Congress yet lay activity in diocese was widespread, purposeful and generally effective.

The Congress was not welcomed by all Catholics across England and Wales nor did its outcomes please everyone. Fr James Pereiro has written that by failing to dedicate a particular section of *The Easter People* to the role of laity, who made up the majority of the Pastoral Congress, the Bishops missed the opportunity 'to address this fundamental topic in a systematic and organic way.' The lasting effects of the Congress, he writes, 'were disappointing.'[60]

Whatever the outcomes, The National Pastoral Congress was a key event in the life of the post-Conciliar Catholic Church in England and Wales and Wheeler encouraged and supported it. In essence, it provided the domestic Church with a development plan for the future but its momentum was dissipated and attempts at its implementation were overtaken by the visit of Pope John Paul II to Great Britain in 1982.[61]

The Papal Visit

In 1982, Pope John Paul II made a visit to Great Britain, the first by a reigning pontiff. It was an historic event for the Catholic community but there was a very real danger that it would be cancelled because of the Argentine invasion of the Falkland Islands and the despatch of a British Task Force a few weeks before the Pope was due to arrive. Aware that the Pope could not be seen to siding with either Great Britain or Argentina, the Hierarchy stressed that his visit would be primarily a pastoral event with an ecumenical dimension. The Pope decided to come precisely on those terms.

Cardinal Karol Wojtyla, the Archbishop of Krakow, had succeeded to the papacy in October 1978 following the sudden death of Pope John Paul I. Wheeler had met Wojtyla, who took the name John Paul II, in March 1979 when he was received in private audience by the Holy Father. He was impressed with the man from Poland, the first non-Italian pope for 455 years. The Pope, he wrote, 'has a massive frame and gives the impression of bursting with health and *joie de vivre*...His every movement is that of a man much younger than his years. There is a great toughness which will carry him through many obstacles'. 'At the same time', he continued, 'there is a certain wistfulness and momentary silence which betoken the many trials through which he has passed in the tragic history of his country...he has been schooled in suffering and in prayer'. Pope John Paul II listened attentively to Wheeler who came away wondering how, with all his cares, the Pope 'could give so inspiring a half-hour to one like me'. He had the impression that Pope John Paul II 'could cope with anything because he believes in the Cross and the Resurrection'.[62] Within a short time after his election in October 1978, the new and vigorous pope was definitely a star—a strong antidote to the popular image of the pope as an old man. To Wheeler, Pope John Paul II inherited the best qualities of his predecessors. He was 'a John XXIII man' with 'all the charisma of the Pope who flung open the windows and called the Second Vatican Council'. He saw him also as 'a Paul VI man, who so wisely and sensitively brought the Council's acts to fruition' and 'a John Paul I man with a smile on his face and a heart of boundless love and compassion coupled with a distaste for all the trappings of temporal power'.[63]

Of Pope John Paul II's three predecessors, Wheeler thought that Pope Paul VI had received a bad press. Pope Paul VI's pontificate was inevitably shaped by Pope John XXIII but he was a significantly different personality and the universal social and political circumstances of his reign were also contrasting. It was, Wheeler wrote, 'hard to succeed a success' and so it proved. Pope John XXIII may have opened the windows on the Church but Pope Paul VI had to deal with the chilly draughts which blew in from all directions. Nevertheless, he carried out the mandate of Pope John XXIII and during his pontificate the Church, so long European and Latin in geography and tradition, became more supra-national and less defined by a single culture. Under Pope Paul VI, all parts of the world came to share responsibility in the Church's life and mission and his pilgrimages brought national Churches together. Without mentioning the encyclical *Humanae Vitae*, which forbade all means of birth control, Wheeler wrote that Pope Paul VI had maintained the revealed Truth, the principles of morality and the unchanging Gospel message. History, he concluded, 'will be decidedly more sympathetic to this pious and deeply spiritual man than his contemporaries had been'.[64]

When Cardinal Hume and Archbishop Worlock delivered the *Easter People* to Pope John Paul II in August 1980, they invited him, in the name of the Bishops' Conference, to undertake a pastoral visit to the Catholic community of England and Wales. It was suggested that His Holiness visit in the summer of 1982 but no firm date or programme was offered. The Pope accepted the invitation in the context of a wider visit to Great Britain. Hume believed that great spiritual benefit would flow from the Pope's visit and that 'it will be a good ecumenical occasion'. The Holy Father, he wrote, 'was very insistent on that' in the light of visits made to Rome by previous Archbishops of Canterbury and other Christian leaders in Great Britain.[65] The political, diplomatic and logistical arrangements for such a visit were incredibly complex and at its meeting in November 1980 the Hierarchy set out guidelines and suggestions, one of which that the Pope would make short visits to each Province. It was subsequently agreed that as the National Pastoral Congress was centred on Christ, the Holy Spirit would be the guiding theme of the papal visit. The date of the visit was set for May 1982.[66] Cynics suggested that the Pope agreed to come in order to deflect interest from *The Easter People*.

The visit required much detailed planning and there were many aspects to consider, not the least of which was Pope John Paul II's understanding of and statements on ecumenism in England and Wales. Wheeler was asked by the Apostolic Delegate to prepare a memorandum on the subject 'in the light of my having been a convert from the Anglican ministry 45 years ago' and in it Wheeler stated his long-held position on the historical religious situation and his strong reservations about some aspects of the current ecumenical dialogue. He informed the Delegate that since the break with Rome, Anglicanism lacked any living magisterium, was a highly divided body theologically, dogmatically and morally, and 'embraced widely divergent views'. Consequently, it offered 'the vaguest of Christian teaching on almost every subject'. Continental Catholics who encountered a minority of High Anglicans had consistently failed to understand the historical significance of disunity in England and Wales and were unaware of the wide range of views across the Anglican Communion. Such uninformed European Catholics, he wrote, jumped the gun by wanting intercommunion and concelebration and placed Catholics in England and Wales and those working on the Anglican-Roman Catholic International Commission (ARCIC) at a huge disadvantage because they could not agree to such demands. The central issue, though, was the authority of the Catholic Church for 'until there is acceptance of the Papal Claims in their totality and the consequent acceptance of the magisterium in its fullness, there can be no guarantee of the validity of the Mass or of those Sacraments which postulate priesthood'. While dialogue should continue, the idea of a 'uniate' church, he averred 'would lead Catholics into a morass of indifferentism'. The background to Christian divisions in the country was highly significant and it was therefore critical that the Holy Father was briefed properly.[67] Wheeler thought it was also important to ensure that the Pope did not have to respond to Anglican or Free Church initiatives. The ARCIC dialogue, he wrote, should be welcomed but not approved although he would accept an Anglican move to explore what ecclesiastical structures might be needed for reconciliation and unity. He was of the opinion that there should be no Eucharistic services and that if the issue of married priests did arise then it should be recognized that such men would 'receive their mandate in a post-matrimonial context akin to the Orthodox'. In other words, men who had left the priesthood to marry would not be allowed back into the priestly ministry.[68]

The memorandum caused Wheeler some distress. Cardinal Hume seemed unaware of it being commissioned and Wheeler was shocked to hear that it had 'found itself on the Holy Father's desk'. Wheeler claimed that he had responded to a request made at the autumn meeting of the Hierarchy and had no inkling that it would entail a visit to the Pope to discuss it.[69] As it turned out, Bishop Alan Clark of East Anglia, who held the Ecumenism portfolio on the Bishops' Conference, was unperturbed and so Wheeler, with Hume's consent, accompanied the Cardinal and Clark on their visit to the Holy Father in February 1982. In audience, they discussed the Pope's forthcoming visit and Wheeler was amazed at his concentration and knowledge 'regarding the sensitivities to the difficulties of the English situation both civilly and ecumenically'. There was no discussion, however, on ecumenical issues. Wheeler noted that John Paul looked slimmer and much older than when he had last seen him but the Pope was recovering from gunshot wounds he had received when an attempt was made on his life on 13 May 1981.[70]

The future of the visit was thrown into doubt in April 1982 when in response to the Argentine invasion of the Falkland Islands, Britain sent a Task Force to expel the Argentine invaders and reclaim British territory. Like others, Wheeler was afraid that Pope John Paul II would cancel the visit due to the Falklands War and wrote a pleading letter to the Pontiff:

Dear Holy Father,

There is a deep sense of shock amongst all our people that your pastoral visit to us might be cancelled. It is felt that the reasons so far given for such a possibility just do not convince and there is a heartfelt longing for your presence more than ever in our present situation. I say this not only on behalf of our devoted Catholic people but also in the context of the ecumenical situation where there is great bewilderment.

Beloved Holy Father, you will know that your Catholic Bishops, Priests, Religious and Faithful will defend you to the utmost in whatever decision you make. But they will be put under terrible strain if they are called to do so. That is why we beg Our Lady of Fatima to whisper in your ear that for all of our sakes and for your sake too, you will come. The good that would thus result for Faith and ultimate unity would far outweigh any other considerations.[71]

In a press statement, Wheeler emphasised that people in Argentina and the United Kingdom were deeply concerned at the hostility between their nations and he urged politicians to enter into negotiations. He asked that 'all other means be exhausted before war is undertaken'. He made no mention of the Pope's visit.[72] A Statement from the Bishops' Conference called for peace as the Pope set out for Britain and a telegram from the Bishops of England and Wales to the Argentine Bishops assured them of heartfelt prayers for an end to the conflict, fraternal dialogue and future reconciliation.[73]It was important that there were no confusing or mixed messages.

Tensions and emotions were stoked up by the press and media. The *Catholic Herald* confidently proclaimed that the Pope would cancel his visit and *The Guardian* stated that 'The Pope will not be coming'.[74] The *Daily Mail*, meanwhile, hoped that 'the Pope can still come' while Norman St John Stevas wrote in the *Daily Express* that 'The Pope must still come to Britain'.[75] It was a close run thing and eleven days before the Pope's expected arrival at Gatwick, Archbishop Worlock of Liverpool and Archbishop Winning of Glasgow flew out to Rome 'to try to save the Pope's visit'.[76] In the Vatican, there were intense debates with the Secretary of State, Cardinal Casaroli opposing the visit. Archbishop Ubaldo Calabresi, papal nuncio in Argentina asked how the Pope could travel to Britain while British troops were spilling Argentine blood.[77] In Argentina Cardinal Primatesta of Cordoba called upon his countrymen to defend the Fatherland (which included the Falkland Islands or the

Malvinas) while in London Bishop Victor Guazzelli called for Britain to withdraw its forces and seek United Nations intervention.[78] Despite the Falklands War, the Pope decided to abide by his promise and it was, wrote Wheeler, 'a great relief to hear of that decision especially when one considers the great preparations which had been made for his visit'.[79]

The Pope landed at Gatwick on the morning of 28 May and then went to Westminster Cathedral to celebrate Mass. There, with other bishops, Wheeler met the Pope and in the afternoon travelled with him across the River Thames to Southwark Cathedral. Sadly, the need for Wheeler to prepare for the Pope's northern visit meant that he was unable to be with John Paul at Canterbury Cathedral and at the huge gathering at Wembley Stadium. With bishops of the Northern Province, Wheeler met the Pope at Speke Airport, Liverpool, on 30 May and took part in the great drive through the city to the Anglican Cathedral and then to the Metropolitan Cathedral of Christ the King. After having dinner with the Pope, the bishops and other guests, Wheeler crossed the Pennines so he could say an early Mass on the following day, 31 May, for the pilgrims awaiting the Holy Father's arrival at the Knavesmire in York. It was the Feast of the Visitation of the Blessed Virgin Mary.[80]

Wheeler, the other northern bishops and over 200,000 enthusiastic people gathered on the Knavesmire to welcome Pope John Paul II to Yorkshire. The Knavesmire had huge significance in the northern Catholic tradition as fifty-two martyrs for the faith had been executed there in penal times. Had the visit occurred two months earlier, the Pope would have touched down in the Diocese of Leeds but the two York parishes south of the River Ouse had recently been ceded to the Diocese of Middlesbrough as part of the restructuring that erected the Diocese of Hallam. There was, however, a strong Leeds connection with the papal visit for the initial preparations were co-ordinated by the Dominican Fr Francis Gresham, a Bradford priest and chaplain at York University. When Fr Gresham died suddenly in February 1982, he was replaced as co-ordinator of the papal visit to York by Wheeler's secretary, Fr Arthur Roche.

The York event was the only public gathering on the papal visit where the Pope did not celebrate Mass. However, the Feast of the Visitation of the Blessed Virgin Mary was most appropriate for the Holy Father's theme related to his recent exhortation *Familiaris Consortio* and he directed attention to the challenges presented to the Church and to the institution of marriage in the contemporary world. Marriage, the family and the renewal of vows took centre stage and thousands of couples renewed their marriage vows in front of the Pope while families rededicated themselves to each other and to the Church. The Pope stressed the home as a place of prayer and the importance of the role of women as equal partners in the Church. He likened those in mixed marriages to the difficulties faced by Christian Churches on the way to unity; he called for compassion for those in failed marriages; and he demanded opposition to abortion, contraception and scientific interference in the creation of human life. He urged authorities to defend the sanctity and institution of marriage in the modern world and as he had done on 22 May before he left for Britain, the Pope called for peace in the Falklands.[81] Wheeler wrote that John Paul II's visit to York was one of the outstanding events of the pontiff's itinerary. It was the only venue on the Pope's visit where the actual numbers exceeded those expected.[82]

From York, Pope John Paul II flew to Scotland and at the end of his Scottish visit returned south to Cardiff from where he left for Rome. Wheeler and other bishops concelebrated Mass with him in the Pontcanna Fields and were with him in Cardiff Castle when he received the Freedom of the City. For Wheeler, the Pope's visit was a significant event which had a huge impact. He wrote: 'It meant above all that the Catholic Church had really come to a certain maturity in this country'.[83] His use of 'maturity' in this context is unclear. If, by 'maturity' he meant that the domestic Church of 1982 was unlike the nineteenth and early-to-mid-twentieth century Church, characterised by a ghetto mentality, then he was correct. The crowds of 1982 were much more confident in the public expression of their faith. Yet the crowds of Catholics who met Pope John Paul II were significantly different from those who would have greeted him thirty years earlier. The pre-Vatican II Catholic community had fundamentally changed—bishops and priests were no longer the sole sources of authority, Catholic attitudes to sex, marriage and divorce had been transformed, the influence of the English recusant and Irish immigrant past was waning, Catholics were better educated, and Catholicism was no longer a ghetto culture. The National Pastoral Congress had already provided testimony that Catholic identity in the country was changing in terms of class and education and that Catholics were more challenging, sceptical and outward looking.[84] Although hundreds of thousands of Catholics turned out to welcome the Pope and participate in the religious events, many others did not.

In his Pastoral on the Papal Visit, Wheeler thanked all those who had prepared the events and those who had participated. The Pope's visit to York had especially moved him: 'I think particularly of our York event which will live especially in our memories and add for ever a new dimension to that Knavesmire, the field of the martyrs'. The Pope's addresses, he wrote, called people of all ages towards a deeper understanding of Christ and the value of the Sacraments. He asked parishes to establish groups to discuss the Pope's speeches on war and peace, on Christian Unity and on prayer, and to set up courses for Catholics and non-Catholics to study what the Pope had to say about the Sacraments.[85] Elsewhere, he wrote that John Paul's extraordinary visit challenged all to restore the spiritual dimension to their everyday lives.[86] To many, the Pope's visit blessed their country and enriched their faith.

Notes

1   B. Plumb, *Arundel to Zabi: A Biographical Dictionary of the Catholic Bishops of England and Wales (Deceased) 1623–1987* (Warrington, 1987).

2   *Daily Express*, 18 Feb 1975.

3   *The Sunday Times*, 28 Sept 1975.

4   A. Howard, *Basil Hume: The Monk Cardinal* (London: Headline, 2005), pp. 81–82.

5   *Catholic Herald*, 21 Nov 1975.

6   N. Schofield and G. Skinner, *The English Cardinals* (Oxford: Family Publications, 2007), p. 218.

7   A. Hastings, *A History of English Christianity 1920–1985* (London: Collins, 1986), p. 640.

8   *Catholic Herald*, 21 Nov 1975.

9   *The Sunday Times*, 28 Sept 1975.

10   C. Longley, *The Worlock Archive* (London: Geoffrey Chapman, 2000), p. 214.

11   G. Noel, *Miles: A Portrait of the 17th Duke of Norfolk* (Norwich: Michael Russell, 2004), pp. 118–119; P. Standford, *Cardinal Hume and the Changing Face of English Catholicism* (London: Geoffrey Chapman, 1993), pp. 13–14.

12   Longley, *The Worlock Archive*, p. 215.

13   *The Tablet*, 14 Oct 2006.

14   Personal testimony: Cardinal Cormac Murphy-O'Connor. The Duke of Norfolk's other house, Carlton Towers, was in Wheeler's diocese and Wheeler was a frequent visitor.

15   Howard, *Basil Hume: The Monk Cardinal*, p. 84.

16   Standford, *Cardinal Hume and the Changing Face of English Catholicism*, p. 16.

17   *The Tablet*, 21 Feb 1976.

18 Wheeler to Hume, 7 June 197. LDA, WDC, Cardinal Hume.
19 *Catholic Herald*, 28 May 1976.
20 W. G. Wheeler, *In Truth And Love* (Southport: Gowland and Co., 1990), pp. 116–117.
21 Standford, *Cardinal Hume and the Changing Face of English Catholicism*, p. 16.
22 *Catholic Herald*, 13 and 20 Feb 1976.
23 *Huddersfield Daily Examiner*, 18 Feb 1976.
24 *Yorkshire Post*, 18 Feb 1976.
25 Wheeler to Benelli, 24 March 1976. LDA, WDC, W39.
26 Standford, *Cardinal Hume and the Changing Face of English Catholicism*, pp. 19–20.
27 Longley, *The Worlock Archive*, pp 283–285.
28 *Liverpool 1980: Official Report of the National Pastoral Congress* (Slough: St Paul Publications, 1981), p. 3. Reports entitled *Pastoral Strategy* and *Time for Tomorrow* were presented to the Bishops' Conference in 1975 and 1976 by the Joint Working Party which had been set up in 1972.
29 *Responses: An account of the correspondence which followed 'The Church 2000' and 'A Time for Building'—the two reports of the Joint Working Party on Pastoral Strategy* (Catholic Information Services: Abbots Langley, 1980).
30 Longley, *The Worlock Archive*, pp 283–285.
31 *Liverpool 1980*, pp. 5–9, pp. 16–17.
32 K. Robbins, *Oxford History of the Christian Church: England, Ireland, Scotland, Wales: The Christian Church 1900–2000* (Oxford: Oxford University Press, 2008), p.432.
33 Hastings, *A History of English Christianity 1920–1985*, pp. 664–665.
34 *Catholic Gazette*, vol. 71, no. 5, May 1980.
35 Wheeler, *Ad Clerum*. National Pastoral Congress, Diocesan Report on Discussion Papers I—III. LDA, WDC, Wheeler Papers.
36 Wheeler, *Ad Clerum*. Congress News, Nov 1979. LDA, WDC, LDA, WDC, Wheeler Papers.
37 Wheeler, *Ad Clerum*. Joint Pastoral Letter of the Archbishops and Bishops of Wales on the National Pastoral Congress, 23 March 1980. LDA, WDC, Wheeler Papers.
38 *Liverpool 1980*, pp. 103–104.
39 *Ibid.*, pp. 258–259.
40 *Ibid.*, pp. 297–299.
41 *Ibid.1980*, pp. 111–295; *Catholic Herald*, 9 May 1980.The Leeds diocesan reports were submitted to thebishops on 30 May 1980. LDA, WDC, National Pastoral Congress.
42 *Liverpool 1980*, pp. 395–398.
43 *Catholic Herald*, 9 May 1980.
44 Minutes of Diocesan Pastoral Council, 20 Sept. 1980. LDA, WDC, National Pastoral Congress.
45 Wheeler, *Ad Clerum*, 25 Sep 1980. LDA, WDC, Wheeler Papers.
46 Wheeler, *Ad Clerum*, 30–31 Oct 1981. LDA, WDC, Wheeler Papers; *Catholic Voice*,

Nov 1980.

47   *Catholic Herald*, 8 Aug 1980; *Scepter Bulletin*, August-September 1980, pp. 3–8.

48   B. Quinn, 'Position Paper, Diocesan Pastoral Council', (n.d. 1980?). LDA, WDC, W12.

49   Wheeler, *Ad Clerum*, 23 Nov 1982, 'Leeds Diocesan Senate of Priests'. LDA, WDC, Wheeler Papers.

50   *Leeds Diocesan Directory* (1981), p. 5.

51   R. E. Finnigan, 'Bishop Wheeler, 1966–1985' in R. E. Finnigan and J. Hagerty, *The Bishops of Leeds—Essays in Honour of Bishop David Konstant* (Leeds: PBK Publications on behalf of the Diocese of Leeds, 2005),pp. 168–169.

52   *Catholic Voice*, Jan 1981.

53   *Catholic Voice*, Oct 1981.

54   Standford, *Cardinal Hume and the Changing Face of English Catholicism*, pp. 67–69; Longley, *The Worlock Archive*, p. 287.

55   *The Tablet*, 20 Nov 1999.

56   Longley, *The Worlock Archive*, pp 286–287.

57   E. Stourton, *John Paul II: Man of History*(London: Hodder and Stoughton, 2006), pp. 232–234.

58   *QR*, 1982, p. 6.

59   *Ibid.*, pp. 28–29.

60   J. Pereiro, 'Who Are The Laity ?' in V. A. McClelland and Michael Hodgetts (eds.), *From Without the Flaminian gate: 150 Years of Roman Catholicism in England and Wales 1850–2000* (London: Darton, Longman and Todd, 1999), pp. 184–185.

61   Longley, *The Worlock Archive*, p. 295.

62   *Huddersfield Daily Examiner*, 21 May 1979.

63   LDA, WPC, Papal Visit.

64   W. G. Wheeler, 'Pope Paul VI RIP'. LDA. WPC. The Popes.

65   Hume to Hierarchy, 29 Aug 1980. LDA, WPC, Wimbledon Letters.

66   Longley, *The Worlock Archive*, p. 288–289.

67   Wheeler to Apostolic Delegate, 3 Nov 1981. LDA, WPC, Papal Visit.

68   'Some Possible Suggestions Regarding the Ecumenical Aspects of the Papal Visit to Great Britain' (typescript, no date). LDA, WPC, Papal Visit.

69   Wheeler to Hume , 26 Jan 1982. LDA, WPC, Papal Visit.

70   Wheeler, Private Notes, 5 Feb 1982. LDA, WPC, Papal Visit.

71   Wheeler to H. H. Pope John Paul II, 15 May 1982. LDA, WPC, Wimbledon Letters. Wheeler had been advised by Mgr Michael Buckley on the impression that this statement might have on public opinion. Buckley to Wheeler, 15 May 1982. See LDA, WDC, W12a.

72   Statement by the Bishop of Leeds. LDA, WDC, W12a.

73   Draft Statement from the Bishops of England and Wales (no date); Draft Telegram to Argentine Bishops (no date). LDA, WDC, W12a.

[74] *Catholic Herald,* 14 May 1982; *The Guardian,* 18 May 1982.

[75] *Daily Mail,* 18 May 1982; *Daily Express,* 18 May 1982.

[76] *The Times,* 18 May 1982.

[77] *Time,* 7 June 1982.

[78] *Catholic Herald,* 14 May 1982.

[79] Wheeler, *In Truth And Love,* p. 121.

[80] *Ibid,* pp. 120–122.

[81] *The Tablet,* 5 June 1982.

[82] *Leeds Diocesan Catholic Voice,* Jan—July 1982.

[83] Wheeler, *In Truth And Love,* p. 122.

[84] T. Morris, 'The divisions that will welcome a Pope' in *The Guardian,* 25 May 1982.

[85] Pastoral Letter on the Papal Visit, 20 June 1982. LDA, WPC, Papal Visit.

[86] *Huddersfield Daily Examiner,* 18 June 1982.

14 ETHICS, SOCIETY AND POLITICS

Ethical and Moral Problems

ACH EPISCOPAL GENERATION can claim that it had to deal with a range of problems unknown to its predecessors but there can be no doubt that the bishops of Wheeler's generation were faced with a bewildering and challenging range of ethical and moral problems. Such problems were not traditional as in a just war, sporadic industrial disputes or intermittent social protest but were the result of seismic changes in morals and ethics which in some cases were enshrined in law. In response, the bishops affirmed the principles which underpinned the Church's doctrines and Christian life but their task was rendered more difficult by the changing social and cultural climate of the 1960s and subsequent decades which reversed traditional moral and ethical standards.

The biggest test for the bishops and Catholic community in the 1960s came with the legalisation of abortion. It was not, as *Humanae Vitae* was to become, an internal rejection of ecclesiastical authority, but an external assault by the state on the teaching of the Church. In 1965, Lord Silkin introduced a Bill into the House of Lords which sought extensions to legally acceptable conditions for the termination of pregnancy. Silkin sought to establish that an unwanted pregnancy could pose a potential mental threat to a mother and should be treated the same as a physical threat posed by an unwanted pregnancy. In addition, he proposed that unwanted pregnancies could be aborted if they were the result of a sexual offence or in cases of foetal deformity, impoverished social conditions, and maternal psychological frailty. Catholic opponents denied the need for further legal clarification and rejected Silkin's Bill arguing that it was inconsistent with Catholic teaching on the preservation and safeguarding of human life and that it would lead to abortion on demand.[1] Supporters of abortion saw the Hierarchy's intervention as attempt to impose Catholic morality on the law.[2]

In 1966, the Liberal MP David Steel introduced the Medical Termination of Pregnancy Bill in the House of Commons. This Bill not only included the proposals made by Silkin but endeavoured to enhance the respectability of termination and included a clause which legitimized abortion where the care of a child or an additional child might overstrain the mother. These aspects of the Bill introduced the possibility of external forces influencing the mother to undergo an abortion. In addition, the invocation of rape as justification for an abortion, the lax procedures concerning the official notification of abortions, the capacity for misinterpretation of the legislation and the spectre of abortion clinics alarmed the Hierarchy. In October 1966, the bishops issued a statement opposing the Bill and invoked the teaching of Vatican II which declared abortion unacceptable no matter what legal approbation there might be. At the same time, the Hierarchy was anxious to ensure that it was not seen to be imposing Catholic morality on the rest of society. They declared abortion wrong and asked for understanding where the faith and conscience of Catholic medical professionals might be compromised.[3]

Some Catholics described the Bishops' statement as the product of 'loose thinking' and Catholic parliamentarians complained that the bishops were not forceful enough in marshalling and leading opposition in Parliament to Steel's Bill.[4] Others felt that the bishops had held back and waited while the laity opposed the Bill and actively lobbied for its withdrawal. Lee and Stanford concluded that the bishops were inept in their opposition: 'They organized too late, in too amateurish a fashion, and they failed to block Steel's Bill from becoming law'.[5] Cardinal Heenan later admitted to Lord Longford that 'he regretted the failure of the Catholic Church in England to come out fighting more fiercely when the Abortion Law Reform Bill was being passed'. Waiting for the Anglicans to take the lead, he said, was a miscalculation.[6] So too was any expectation that Catholic politicians would have either the power or determination to oppose the Bill. The anti-abortion lobby in parishes and dioceses, however, was well organised and vocal in its opposition.

It was a difficult situation for the bishops. According to Wilson, 'the manifestation of varying degrees of dissatisfaction regarding Catholic inertia and ineffectiveness in engaging with the abortion debate testifies to the complex interaction of religious morality with public policy and the hesitant role of ecclesiastical authority in brokering the two'. He adds that in the post-Conciliar Church, with its own intensifying debate about contraception, perceptions surrounding the immutability of the Catholic stance on abortion were rendered less than certain.[7] A national petition was presented to Prime Minister Harold Wilson asking for a Royal Commission on the problem of abortion and calling for 'a moderate measure of reform' of the abortion law. Wilson listened with interest and concern to the Hierarchy's anxieties but did nothing to prevent the Bill going forward.[8] Meanwhile, a Gallop Poll for the *Sunday Telegraph* in March 1967 showed that the majority of Catholics who were canvassed favoured abortion if the life of the mother was at risk but disapproved where a child might be born deformed and strongly disapproved 'where a mother wants it'.[9]

The Abortion Bill became law in April 1968. A conscience clause placed the burden of proof on the doctor or nurse objecting to involvement in abortions and Catholics who declined to co-operate with the unethical conduct of the patient, were not seen as forcing their views on the patient but asserting their right not to have their own personal actions compelled by the ethical views of the patient. There remained, however, circumstances where Catholic medical staff were inevitably compromised. The bishops acknowledged the problems confronting Catholic medical staff and con-cluded that Catholic healthcare professionals should not participate in abortions unless there were sufficiently grave reasons for them to do so. It was decided that this should be done in accordance with personal conscience.[10]

The bishops initially provided no practical alternative to abortion. At their Low Week meeting in April 1969, they discussed abortion, euthanasia and other 'important moral and ethical questions' and in 1970 dedicated the Feast of the Holy Innocents as a day of prayer for the unborn victims of abortion. In 1970 Bishop Casey of Brentwood issued further guidelines for medical staff and in the same year the Hierarchy published a *Statement Concerning Moral Questions* in which it emphasized that 'whatever civil law might permit, Christians, together with other consci-entious objectors, should not, and could not, actively be expected to assist in abortion'.[11] In another letter Casey expressed further disquiet at the discrimination against Catholics in the medical professions: 'in most walks of life today Christian witness is a painful and materially unrewarding activity, and in few more so that in medicine and nursing...'[12] Conscien-tious objectors were increasingly victimized by exclusion from areas of specialization and the Hierarchy again expressed its concerns to Prime Minister Wilson. There was, however, no real Catholic strategy to offset the legislation or its social effects. In October 1972, the Hierarchy could only encourage alternatives to abortion and placed the issue before its

Social Welfare Commission.[13] In 1973, Cardinal Heenan admitted there had been a lack of direction when he said that the Catholic Church deliberately made no pronouncement against the Abortion Bill because if it did it would confirm the humanist argument that only Catholics objected to abortion. There was a need, he said, 'for a Catholic strategy on abortion which must be firm where firmness is required and compassionate where compassion is possible'.[14] Such a national strategy, however, failed to materialise. It was only later that bishops such as Grasar and Brewer of Shrewsbury provided practical help for mothers and babies along the lines of traditional 'Catholic rescue societies'.[15]

The Lane Report of 1974 recommended that Catholics in the medical profession be allowed to address the practical ramifications of the Act such as the tightening up of regulations on abortion in private clinics but according to Heenan it did not address the impact of abortion on ethical standards in public life and that abortion 'engendered a moral mentality devoid of unequivocal acceptance of the right to life...' The Act was operating in a way unintended by its promoters and the approach to unborn life was discriminatory, illogical and eugenic. The nation was, Cardinal Heenan argued, only a step away from euthanasia. In this and in his comments on some other aspects of abortion, the Cardinal was supported by the Church of England's Board of Social responsibility. In 1975 a House of Commons Select Committee on Abortion was convened to consider amendments in order to improve the regulation of the Act. The Hierarchy's submission, based on the immoral and unwarranted destruction of human life, called for social alternatives to abortion. The Commission replied that if the Catholic Church allowed contraception then abortion might not be required.[16]

Wheeler was appalled by the legislation and its effects and referred to abortion 'as one of the most terrifying things that has happened in the twentieth century'. It was, he wrote, a move towards paganism and for allowing it 'the country deserved to be punished' by 'the vengeance of Heaven'. However, the country alone was not to blame for like Cardinal Heenan, he recognised that the bishops and Catholic community 'haven't played the part we should have done in seeing that this sort of anti-Christian teaching is never made legal'. One of his solutions was the increased involvement of Catholics and Christians in political and public life.[17]

Wheeler's approach reflected that of the Hierarchy whereby his general opposition to abortion ran alongside specific diocesan endeavours to alleviate the problem while acknowledging that the law would not be rescinded but might be amended. In the diocese, he actively promoted opposition to the legislation and encouraged practical steps to help those immediately affected by it. He had not been confident of success in the campaign against the Bill but this did not prevent him from mobilizing opposition or lobbying the forty-four MPs representing constituencies in the diocese. In his *Ad Clerum* of August 1966, he said that 'the bill now before Parliament is the most serious de-Christianization of our legal system...and everything possible should be done... to oppose a measure which attacks the whole moral law and the sanctity of human life'. He called for his priests to rally non-Catholic and non-Christian support 'for us in our lone defence of a principle which, if abrogated, could have far reaching effects on the whole of community'.[18] In his next *Ad Clerum*, he admitted pessimistically that 'we must be quite realistic and recognize that there is little hope of repealing the Bill...' It remained, however, a Christian's duty to fight against it and bear witness to the belief that abortion was both opposed to God's law and the good of society. He suggested ways in which individuals and local groups could voice their opposition to the Bill but in a way that 'would merit the respect of those who cannot agree with us' and not 'call into question the integrity and honesty of purpose of those who support it'.[19]

Subsequent Pastorals and *Ad Clerum* maintained the impetus with Wheeler encouraging attendance at anti-abortion rallies, petitions to Parliament and pertinent questions placed before prospective parliamentary candidates. He called for prayers for Catholic medical professionals whose faith and conscience were being compromised and ensured that the Diocesan Pastoral Council took a diocesan lead in concerted opposition to the Abortion Bill and the Abortion Act.[20] The Leeds Diocesan Rescue, Protection and Child Welfare Society, led by Mgr J. J. Kelly and Fr John Murphy, continued to provide practical support as an alternative to abortion and Wheeler ensured that it liaised closely with other Catholic anti-abortion groups such as the Society for the Protection of Unborn Children (SPUC), Right to Life Groups and the Bishops' Conference Catholic Child Welfare Council.[21] He was also anxious to enlist Anglican backing and expressed his gratitude to the Archbishop of York and the Bishop of Ripon for their support.[22]

Over 163,000 abortions per year were being carried out in England and Wales by 1975 and Wheeler called upon priests and people 'to make it clear in no uncertain terms that they are not prepared to sit back and allow the appalling toll of deaths perpetrated under the 1967 Abortion Act to continue in their name'. An Abortion Amendment Bill prepared by James White MP was placed before Parliament in 1975 and, although its objective was not to rescind the Abortion Act, it did seek to limit the worst abuses of the legislation, reduce the number of abortions and protect medical professionals who had conscientious objections to being involved with abortions. Wheeler called upon his priests to be fully informed of the issue and to encourage parishioners to support public campaigns against abortion. In October 1975, there were silent rallies within the diocese and Bishop Moverley led the diocesan contingent to a mass protest rally held in London.[23] Wheeler recognised that such demonstrations gave vital public support to Catholic and other anti-abortion MPs in their attempts to mitigate a difficult situation. A House of Commons Select Committee on Abortion was established and considered White's amendment among other proposals but the political atmosphere was charged and the Catholic MPs on the Committee endured a gruelling time.[24] The publication of the Committee's report in July 1976 did little to placate the pro-life lobby and with Archbishop Worlock and other northern bishops, Wheeler attended a huge anti-abortion rally in Bradford.[25]

As with contraception and abortion, the Church continued to prohibit euthanasia and mercy killing. Vatican II specifically rejected euthanasia 'and post-conciliar Catholic ethics maintained principled intransigence in the face of rapidly developing medical technology' and an increasingly secular social climate. Cardinal Heenan had correctly warned that if successful the abortion campaign would lead to calls for euthanasia and in 1969, Lord Raglan introduced the Voluntary Euthanasia Bill. It brought the issue to the surface with the prospect of legislative authority.[26]

The bishops were determined not be left behind in the euthanasia debate as they had been with abortion and the Hierarchy's *Statement Concerning Moral Questions* addressed the issue forcefully in the context of the Christian concept of 'a happy death'. The bishops stressed the Christian acceptance of death as 'glorious fulfilment' and not as something to be either postponed or induced by medicine and technology. The availability of palliative care offered an alternative of letting nature take its course within an environment of relative comfort and expert medical attention and the bishops concluded by clarifying the Christian mandate of facing death confidently and hopefully.[27] Wheeler lamented that the permissive society had 'seeped into the very foundations of morality' and warned that terrible personal tensions would arise out of so-called 'voluntary euthanasia'.[28] Like others, he was fearful that there was a distinct possibility that just as legalised abortion had created an abortion-minded society so too could legalised euthanasia lead to a euthanasia-minded society with terrible consequences for families and communities.[29]

The Guild of Catholic Doctors, including members in the Leeds Diocese, marshalled their forces to oppose the proposed legislation and publicize the Catholic position. The Hierarchy supported them but despite its best efforts, it appeared once again to lag behind the Catholic laity. In 1974, it issued a statement to be read in all dioceses which confirmed its rejection of euthanasia and stressed that authentic and compassionate palliative care for the terminally ill was the alternative to illegal methods which deliberately ended life. Euthanasia was likened to 'murderous killing prohibited by divine and civil law'. Acceptance of euthanasia would detrimentally affect social attitudes, the statement continued, and the bishops 'invited universal testimony to the worth of human life through loving support and care for the dying'.[30] The Anglican publication, *On Dying Well*, published in 1975, also rejected the practice of voluntary euthanasia and supported the provision of specialist palliative care.[31]

In his own Diocese, Wheeler endeavoured to provide caring facilities and was instrumental in the opening and development of St Gemma's Hospice in 1978. Negotiations with the Sisters of the Cross and Passion, Canon Joseph McShane and Dr Kevin Rooney led to the former St Gemma's private school being converted into a hospice for the terminally ill. Wheeler blessed the foundation stone of the new building complex in September 1981 and, in March 1982, was present for the visit of Prince Charles and Princess Diana.[32]

Medical and ethical issues continued to confront the bishops. In 1973, the Hierarchy gave consent for the opening of a Catholic research centre to engage with the moral questions arising in clinical practice and biomedical research and study how these related to the principles of natural law, ethics, and the teaching of the Church. It was to advise Catholics in the medical professions and the Hierarchy's Social Welfare Commission. In 1974, the Linacre Centre for Ethics and Health Care was opened in London.[33]

Yet another ethical and moral problem to confront the Hierarchy came with the Committee of Inquiry into Human Fertilization and Embryology which met from 1982 to 1984 and was chaired by Mary Warnock, a Cambridge academic, a former headteacher and a member of the Independent Broadcasting Authority. Warnock's report gave rise to the Human Fertilization and Embryology Act of 1990 which, through the Human Fertilization and Embryology Authority, now governs human fertility treatment and experimentation using human embryos. Its effect has been to require licensing for procedures such as in vitro fertilization (IVF) and to ban research using human embryos more than fourteen days old.

The Hierarchy established a Joint Committee on Bio-ethical Issues to marshal its own evidence to Warnock's Committee of Inquiry but also called upon the specific support of the Catholic Union of Great Britain, the Guild of Catholic Doctors, the national Board of Catholic Women, the Society for the Protection of Unborn Children and the more general but nonetheless important support of the Catholic community. In summary, the bishops and their supporters rested their case on two main principles: the right to life of any human being and the fundamental importance in society of marriage and the family. The former had a bearing on the laboratory techniques involved in *in vitro fertilization* and related procedures while the latter had a significant bearing on the applicability of the method itself. One was related to the scientific interference in the transmission of life while the other related to the moral, ethical and legal issues attendant on IVF. In the opinion of the bishops 'there is no other clearly recognizable point at which human life and therefore rights can be deemed to begin than at the moment of fertilization'. 'No human being, nor any society', their Lordships proclaimed, 'can claim for itself or give to others absolute powers over life and death'.[34]

While supporting the Hierarchy's position, Wheeler mobilized opposition to IVF within his own diocese. He himself took advice from moral theologians and engaged in correspondence with politicians of all denominations while the diocesan newspaper—*The Catholic Voice*—ran features comparing the work of the Diocesan Child Welfare Society with the frightening prospects of scientific experimentation in the formation of life.[35] With Wheeler's approval, a conference for hospital chaplains on 'Moral Choices in Medicine' was convened by the Linacre Centre at Wood Hall in November 1984. By December, Warnock's Committee ceased to receive evidence but Catholic opposition continued. A study day on 'Early days of Life' was held at Trinity and All Saints College, Leeds, in February 1985 and the Hierarchy continued its lobbying of parliament. Meanwhile, Enoch Powell MP introduced a Private Members Bill to prevent IVF. By the time of Wheeler's retirement in 1985, the issue was still under parliamentary scrutiny.

Northern Ireland

Throughout Wheeler's episcopate, the Province of Ulster—the six northern counties of Ireland—was the site of a violent and bitter inter-communal conflict often referred to as 'The Troubles'. Many Catholics in England and Wales were dismayed by the Hierarchy's silence and by implication its lack of moral leadership on the problem. Nearer home, Bishop Wheeler and Bishop Moverley became involved in a serious controversy surrounding the pastoral care of an IRA hunger striker in Wakefield Top Security Prison.

The savage internecine conflict in Ulster was caused by sectarian and political divisions between Nationalists, who saw themselves as Irish and were predominantly Roman Catholic, and Unionists, who regarded themselves as British and who were predominantly Protestant. The Unionists wanted Northern Ireland to remain part of the United Kingdom while the Nationalists wanted reunification with the rest of Ireland and independence from British rule. The roots of the conflict were deep and tortuous and twentieth-century Ireland had rarely been free from violence. Religious discrimination against Catholics in Ulster was endemic and Stormont Castle, the Royal Ulster Constabulary, the Harland and Wolff Shipyard in Belfast and the allocation of council houses were the most obvious symbols of political, legal, economic and social divisions.

'The Troubles' began in 1968 when the Royal Ulster Constabulary (RUC) baton-charged a civil rights group marching from Belfast to Derry. In 1969, as the Province slid into violence, the Labour government sent in troops and there followed a series of bloody and murderous incidents which marked the beginning of a prolonged communal conflict.[36] The major but not the only issues were the constitutional status of Northern Ireland as part of the United Kingdom and the relationship between the Protestant Unionist and the Catholic Nationalist communities. On the streets, 'The Troubles' involved the Irish Republican Army (IRA), the Ulster Volunteer Force (UVF) and Ulster Defence Association (UDA), other splinter paramilitaries such as the Provisional Irish Republican Army ('the Provos'), the British Army, and the security forces of Ulster and the Irish Republic. At the political level they involved the governments at Westminster, Stormont and Dublin. Catholics demanded civil rights, social justice and an end to political gerrymandering while Protestants insisted on their right to hold Orange Parades and continued control of the Province. There were large scale civil disturbances with street battles and rioting enjoining police, troops and paramilitaries in bloody battles. Between 1969 and 2001, over 3,500 people—soldiers, police officers and civilians on both sides of the sectarian divide—were killed in the conflict; many were maimed; houses and businesses were destroyed and no-go areas were established.

Bombings and assassinations on mainland Britain heightened tensions and gave rise to friction and suspicion between the Irish community in England and the rest of the population. The Diocese of Leeds had many Catholics of Irish descent and many of these sympathized with the condition of Ulster Catholics and favoured Irish reunification if not the violent methods of the IRA. There were voluntary collections in the diocese for the relief of Ulster Catholics evicted from their homes or who were suffering in some other way as a result of 'The Troubles'. Wheeler was personally happy to support these and more formal organizations such as the Leeds Branch of the Campaign for Social Justice in Northern Ireland[37] but the whole thing took on an overtly political tone in 1971 when the British government introduced internment without trial. Some diocesan Irish priests, already disturbed by the ugly events in Ulster, saw internment as the mark of a totalitarian government determined to silence constitutional rather than military opposition. From St. Patrick's Huddersfield, Fr Leo Walsh told Wheeler that he could not continue to exercise his priestly office in the United Kingdom as long as internment was maintained.[38] Wheeler subsequently issued a Pastoral on the Northern Ireland situation but refrained from criticizing government policy on internment. It was a silence which worried many of his correspondents. One wrote: 'My Lord, I ask you now to speak out against this evil act. I know young Irishmen and girls who are turning to other organizations in an effort to expose the corrupt government in Northern Ireland and feel badly let down by their own Church leaders'.[39] Wheeler replied that the Hierarchy was 'doing far more than you can imagine...about the Northern Ireland situation...but...it could spoil things if there were any publicity about this just now'.[40]

Many deplored the silence of the Hierarchies both in England and Wales and in Ireland but the bishops were cautious in their utterances. To a request from the Vatican via Archbishop Domenico Enrici, the Apostolic Delegate, that the English and Welsh Hierarchy should join the Irish bishops in a public call for peace, Cardinal Heenan rejected the suggestion saying that 'no country is so sensitive as Ireland' and that close contact was maintained with the Irish Hierarchy and the British government.[41] The Combined Irish Organizations and the National Council of Priests called upon 'the Bishops of England and Wales to give positive guidance to the troubled consciences of so many people confronted with the anguish, fear and terror experienced by Catholics in Northern Ireland'. They concluded that 'the continued silence of the British Church can only mean that diplomacy has priority over the spirit of the Gospel'.[42] Wheeler explained that the Hierarchy was fully in accord with the Irish Hierarchy with whom it had 'the closest possible relationship'.[43] This relationship, of course, was the reason why on so many Irish matters the English and Welsh bishops had to remain silent: Ireland was not within their canonical jurisdiction and the Irish bishops would not welcome unwarranted or unhelpful intrusion. Organizations such as Pax Christi regarded this stance as something of an excuse and argued for direct political action by the English and Welsh Catholic community, not to inflame the situation but to allay the fears of Protestants and obtain justice for all.[44]

On 23 November 1971, Archbishop Dwyer of Birmingham and Cardinal Conway of Armagh, the Primate of All Ireland, unequivocally condemned the inhuman treatment of detainees, the violence and the murder of innocent people in Ulster. Too often, Dwyer said, 'for the sake of a quiet life, we are inclined to turn a blind eye to injustice—when it is done to others'. He called for public opinion 'to force injustice to be righted' and for Catholics to approach politicians in order to effect change in Northern Ireland.[45] As might be expected, Cardinal Conway, himself the product of divided Belfast, issued many more statements in reaction to sickening events and in a search for a just and peaceful conclusion to the problem. To Wheeler, Conway wrote that the collection of his Statements would 'help to refute the canard that the Catholic Church in Ireland has remained silent during most of the crisis or has not condemned in sufficiently forthright terms the campaign of violence or individual bombings and assassinations'.[46] Meanwhile to most of the British press and the country at large, those fighting the army were terrorists and propaganda became a powerful weapon. *The Sun* contained illustrated stories of Catholic women and girls in Londonderry making petrol bombs as part of the 'civil war effort against the British Army in Ulster'. The IRA, it claimed, recruits 'the terrorists' at a young age.[47]

In truth, there was little Wheeler or the Hierarchy could do in the face of repeated atrocities and implacable sectarian and political bigotry. When asked for guidance on the morality of resorting civil violence to achieve reforms, the Hierarchy had expressed the view that it in some cases it was not possible to issue a blanket condemnation of those who engaged in protests and civil violence if there was no prospect of injustice being ended or if governments resorted to violence to maintain an unlawful position. The IRA, of course, perceived both the British government's position and its actions as unlawful.[48]

The bishops had also pointed out the tragic consequences of civil violence and in February 1972, Bishop Moverley drafted a Pastoral expressing his and Wheeler's revulsion at the repression, violence and death in the Province. He called for prayers, trust and love to counteract 'the spread and intensity of hatred' and for justice for the Catholic minority and for all people of Northern Ireland.[49] In May 1972 Wheeler informed the Leeds Council of Priests that the Hierarchy had expressed its solidarity with Cardinal Conway who had called for the government to take notice of Catholic accounts of events in Northern Ireland 'instead of giving unqualified credence to the security forces' point of view'.[50] At a more practical level, Cardinal Heenan called for episcopal support for self-help initiatives like Catholics and Protestants joining forces to rebuild homes destroyed in The Troubles.[51] Wheeler supported Coventry Cathedral's Corrymeela Venture which planned for a House of Reconciliation between Protestants and Catholics[52] and the Northern Ireland Children's Holiday Scheme.[53] Events, however, made the situation worse. In January 1972, following the alleged shooting of civilians in Derry by British troops, Heenan wrote to Prime Minister Heath calling for an independent enquiry into the tragedy. In the shadow of the shootings, he continued, he thought it wise 'if you were to cancel the dinner you kindly proposed to give our Bishops on the 14th February. Yesterday's tragic events have made the whole situation immensely delicate'. He concluded: 'I assure you there are no personal feelings involved' but 'a social visit by the Hierarchy to Downing Street at the moment might easily give rise to misunderstandings'.[54] This action did not end meetings between Heenan and the government, however, and he maintained contact with the Secretary of State for Northern Ireland.

There was frustration among the priests at the Hierarchy's lack of action, although all must have recognized the political and ecclesiastical difficulties confronting the bishops. Archbishop Beck of Liverpool coordinated the Bishops' Conference initiatives on Northern Ireland but these were confined to calls for prayers, practical relief and communication with the Irish Hierarchy and the government. Priests of the Archdiocese of Westminster and other dioceses openly associated themselves with all groups working for peace and justice in Northern Ireland and called for an end to internment and for financial investment and a political solution.[55] There was no point, they claimed, Vatican II proclaiming that the Church stood for Justice and Peace if it took no action in Northern Ireland. Priests in Cardiff tried to organize a rally for peace but Archbishop Murphy was anxious lest it became politicized.[56] To Irish priests The Troubles could not be anything less than political and to Northern Irish priests the violence was close to their homes and families. To one, Wheeler wrote: 'We are all deeply concerned in this problem, and of course, it is a matter that affects those priests whose homes are in Northern Ireland more than any others. One very much hopes that the various groupings will get together to see that justice is done for Northern Ireland'.[57] Wheeler was aware of the injustices but thought that others— 'communists and anarchical groups'—'are using the situation to bring about their own ends'.[58]

Although there may have been fringe elements trying to exploit the situation, the problem was essentially an Anglo-Irish one and was seen by Catholics in Northern Ireland as them versus the largely Protestant security forces. In 1972 Wheeler, and presumably other bishops, was given numerous examples of the inhumane and unjust treatment meted out to some Catholics in Ulster by the police and British army. The Belfast-based Association for Legal Justice sent Wheeler a dossier of files compiled by those Catholics who had suffered arrest, imprisonment, interrogation and torture at the hands of the security forces and those whose homes had been forcibly entered under the Special Powers Act.[59] With evidence such as this and the daily violence and urban mayhem over which it had no influence, the Hierarchy asked for prayers and 'genuine reconciliation and true comradeship among men and women of every creed and party'.[60]

In 1975 'The Troubles' came to Wheeler's doorstep when Frank Stagg, a convicted IRA man from County Mayo was transferred from Long Lartin High Security Prison in Worcestershire to Wakefield Prison. At Wakefield, the prison authorities demanded that Stagg do prison work which he had refused at Long Lartin. Stagg refused again and was placed in solitary confinement. His subsequent demands for repatriation to Ireland, an end to solitary confinement and no prison work were refused by the British government and on 14 December 1975 he embarked on a hunger strike along with a number of other Republican prisoners. Stagg died on 12 February 1976 after sixty-two days without food. He was buried in Ballina, a town familiar to many of the Yorkshire Irish from County Mayo.

Stagg's death brought Wheeler and Moverley condemnation and opprobrium. In Wheeler's absence on vacation, Bishop Moverley had ensured that Stagg received the ministrations of the prison chaplain, Fr Michael Byrne, but refused to allow Mass to be celebrated in Stagg's cell. Stagg then declined Holy Communion from the chaplain but insisted on Mass being celebrated in his cell. News of Moverley's firm stance inevitably got out. Frs Brian Brady and Denis Faul telegrammed Wheeler from Northern Ireland 'respectfully requesting' that 'the opportunity to assist at Holy Mass be given to Frank Stagg in his hour of extreme spiritual need'.[61] A New Yorker of Irish descent said he was 'ashamed' of Wheeler for denying Stagg Mass in his cell.[62] From Dundalk, he received a letter which accused him of heresy[63] while a Dublin family was 'disgusted' with his actions.[64] From Boston, Massachusetts, a correspondent told Wheeler that 'if the Irish people should ever lose the Faith, the blame can be placed squarely on the Church hierarchy and men of your caliber'.[65]Another from Brooklyn told Wheeler 'you have failed in your duty to God'.[66] Wheeler answered them all sympathetically but firmly. The prisoner, he wrote, had received compassion, had been offered the ministrations of the chaplain, and had not been denied the Sacraments. When Bishop Moverley refused to allow Mass to be celebrated in Stagg's cell, the prisoner had refused to receive Holy Communion; the Bishop had not denied him the Sacrament. Nor was Stagg being treated differently from any other hospital patient who would not expect Mass to be celebrated at the bedside.

Bishop Moverley's decision was dictated in part by the fear of exploitation of the Church's offices for political ends. There had been numerous cases where the Church's concern for the spiritual welfare of an individual had been interpreted as support for Irish Republicanism. Wheeler too saw a political dimension to Stagg's request and aware that the situation was receiving national attention, he informed the Apostolic

Delegate of the reasons for Moverley's actions which he supported. Stagg, he wrote was being 'well looked after materially and is most comfortably placed'. In addition, 'we have given him the benefit of the doubt re conscience in allowing him the Sacrament of the Sick and daily Holy Communion: which he received up to yesterday'. He concluded: 'we feel that this is an attempt to pressurize the Church to put itself on the side of the hunger striker and do not think we should concur without causing misunderstanding'.[67] To the prison chaplain and prison officers he wrote that they had all behaved in an exemplary fashion and hoped there would be no violent recriminations. He concluded: 'It is all a sad story and as you will realize entirely bedevilled by politics of a sinister kind and calculated all too often to bring religion into disrepute.[68] Meanwhile, Wheeler continued to lead his diocese in prayers for peace and on Sunday 10 October 1976 led a procession of 5,000 through the streets of Leeds with the Anglican vicar of St Michael-le-Belfrey, York, the Reverend David Watson together with Mairead Corrigan, co-founder with Betty Williams, of the Northern Ireland Women's Peace Movement.[69] In the same year, Corrigan and Williams were awarded the Nobel Peace Prize.[70]

Further episcopal pleas to end the violence went unheard. Bishop Cahal Daly of Ardagh, speaking in 1979 after the killing of a party of soldiers and Lord Mountbatten and some of his family, said that the resentment in the Catholic minority community stemmed from its permanent and apparently unchangeable exclusion from the decision making processes of government. Until this changed the violence would continue. The only answer, he maintained, was to see the conflict not simply in religious terms but in the need to create political institutions providing possibilities for non-violent social change and for peaceful movement towards a more just society.[71] It was a view that Daly's episcopal brethren in England and Wales could only accept. Wheeler and other Church leaders in West Yorkshire continued to hold joint prayers for peace and encouraged others to do likewise.[72]

The situation further deteriorated when in 1981 Republican internees in the Maze Prison began hunger strikes to draw attention to both their treatment by prison authorities and to their call for political prisoner status. In May 1981, one of the hunger strikers, Bobby Sands, died and his funeral in Belfast was attended by over 100,000 people. The Irish Justice and Peace Commission called for government intervention to address the complaints of the republican prisoners and for the nationalist community not to express demands in terms that the British government could not accept. The Leeds Diocesan Justice and Peace Commission supported the stance of the Irish Commission and expressed concern that the effect of the hunger strikes would be to further alienate the opposing communities in Ulster. The Leeds Commission, of which Wheeler was President, sent messages to the Prime Minister and to Members of Parliament calling for an amelioration of the prison regime, a less violent approach to the imposition of law and order, and an acceptable wider solution to the Ulster problem. The Commission's Coordinator, Anne Forbes, visited Northern Ireland in the summer of 1981 and on her return briefed Wheeler on the situation.[73] He supported the Commission's actions. The British government took no action, however, and by October 1981 another nine hunger strikers had died.[74] The Hierarchy welcomed the Holy See's intervention, liaised with Cardinal Ó Fiaich, collaborated with the Irish justice and Peace Commission, and called for prayers but none of these initiatives lessened the determination of the hunger strikers to die for their cause. Nevertheless, the Hierarchy continued to work behind the scenes and Cardinal Hume in particular fought to have alleged miscarriages of justice over Irish prisoners reviewed. Between 1978 and 1989 he campaigned successfully on behalf of the Guildford Four and the Birmingham Six to have their convictions overturned.[75]

Justice and Peace and Social Responsibility

Vatican II emphasized the Church's responsibility to become involved in the struggle for universal justice and peace and in 1970 the Bishops' Conference of England and Wales published a *Statement Concerning Moral Questions* which defined the Catholic position on a range of issues including civil unrest and violence, race relations, and social justice at home and abroad. In the post-conciliar world, wars, international political instability and widening trade gaps together with urban disturbances and civil strife continued to impinge on the debates and actions of the Hierarchy as they did on those of national governments and international organizations. As the bishops called for prayers for peace in war zones such as Vietnam, Biafra, the Middle East and the Falklands, so too did they call for direct personal, communal and governmental action on world poverty and health and unfair trade arrangements which penalized poorer countries. Nearer home they called for and a more tolerant and equitable society to avoid racial and social unrest.[76]

Wheeler's interest in justice and peace and social responsibility was rooted in his own social conscience and also in the belief that the Church and particularly the laity should be engaged in society and politics at all levels for the benefit of the whole community. He had contributed to the conciliar debate on world poverty and disarmament and took up the challenge as soon as he arrived in Leeds adding a range of initiatives to existing diocesan charitable agencies which were concerned, for example, with housing, disabled children, family and social action, and world poverty.[77]

His own involvement was occasionally direct. After the Second World War, the Diocese of Leeds had become home to many immigrant Catholics and, irrespective of their national origins, they often bore the brunt of racial discrimination, injustice and multiple deprivation. The Holy Rosary parish was located in the multi-racial Chapletown area of Leeds and Wheeler knew of the challenges that ethnic minority groups faced. In autumn 1976, he convened a meeting at the Holy Rosary Parish Hall to meet parishioners and others concerned about the discrimination in employment and housing which they faced. In November 1976 he issued a Pastoral on Racial Justice. In May of the following year, Cardinal Hume visited Chapeltown to see first-hand the neighbourhood and meet the community. However small these initiatives were on the scale of problems facing the community they were symbolic of the Church's support and led to a closer involvement between the diocese and the local community.[78]

At the diocesan level, structures had already begun to emerge under Wheeler's intervention and guidance to address these and wider social problems. The Pontifical Justice and Peace Commission was established in 1967 in response to Vatican II's call for attention to be focused on the gap between rich and poor nations and the many political injustices existing throughout the world. Unless the Christian message of love and justice was manifested through action, there was little chance that the message would be heard and hierarchies were encouraged to form similar commissions.[79] In England and Wales, there was an impressive range of long-established Catholic social and charitable organizations but there was no Catholic equivalent, for example, to the Social Responsibility Department of the British Council of Churches. The Hierarchy rectified this situation and established a Social Welfare Commission to oversee Catholic social action in England and Wales and a Justice and Peace Commission 'for education and political action'.[80] In April 1968, Bishop Moverley was appointed to the National Justice and Peace Commission which in the following year brought together the CIIR (Catholic Institute for International Relations) and CAFOD (Catholic Fund for Overseas Development) in an effort to coordinate international Catholic activities. The Commission, which included some high powered and high profile Catholics, was given competence for the work of development and international social justice as recommended in *Populorum Progressio*, and for education in the cause of peace and human rights as expressed in *Gaudiam et Spes*.[81]

In 1967 Wheeler followed up his earlier questionnaire on *The Apostolate of the Laity* with a more wide-ranging one on *The Church in the World of Our Time*. Among the topics addressed were Man in Society, Social Problems, Politics, and The Search for Peace. Drawing inspiration from Council documents, Wheeler sought to focus his diocese on those issues which divided mankind and more importantly asked it what it could do to eradicate divisions and promote the common good.[82] His Advent Pastoral of 1967—*The Christian Community*—drew the two question-naires together and placed the onus of developing the diocese as a Christian community firmly on the parish which, he hoped, would address issues beyond its geographical confines and be associated with but not necessarily directed by the diocese.[83] In 1968 another Pastoral placed before the diocese the teachings of *Populorum Progressio*, outlined the problems of world poverty and called for a more charitable and under-standing approach to the plight of the less fortunate.[84]

In his *Ad Limina* of 1972 Wheeler reported that a diocesan 'Commis-sion of Justice and Peace and Social Responsibility' was in the process of formation[85] and during 1973 meetings were held to prepare for the launch of a Justice and Peace Commission.[86] In July 1973, two meetings took place at St Augustine's, Leeds, when Fr Michael Kelly, Chris Seneviratne, Paul Rogers, Walter Steyn and Anne Forbes were invited by Wheeler to consider forming, staffing and directing a Diocesan Justice and Peace Commission. The Commission was duly established and Wheeler asked parish priests to form Justice and Peace groups which would liaise with the Diocesan Commission.[87] In November 1973 Wheeler issued a Pastoral on *The Third World*. It was unlike previous pastorals inasmuch as it was designed to raise awareness about global economic injustices in which Catholics were unwitting partners. While parishioners were generous in charitable giving, he wrote, they may be unaware of the impact of their plentiful diet and relatively comfortable lifestyles for cheap prices in the developed world came at a cost to those in the Third World. 'In today's world', Wheeler wrote, 'the share out is less than fair, and there is grave injustice in the treatment of our brothers in the poorer countries'. 'Rich countries', he continued, 'use their strength and wealth for selfish and therefore un-Christian purposes'. He encouraged the formation of parish Justice and Peace groups to 'be informed of the situation and decide what local action may be taken to remedy problems which come to light'.[88]

The Diocesan Justice and Peace Commission, wrote Wheeler, emerged 'specifically from Vatican II' and attracted a considerable amount of interest.[89] In 1976, Fr Eamonn O'Brien, a Columban Father, was appointed full-time salaried Co-ordinator, the first in the country, and the Commission became one of the most dynamic organizations in the diocese, assuming a national and international stature. Justice and Peace groups were set up in schools and parishes across the diocese and courses and conferences were convened to increase awareness and galvanize efforts relating to national and international problems. In his 1977 *Ad Limina* Wheeler reported that since 1972 there had been considerable development and 'an increasing awareness and concern for the hungry, the deprived and the oppressed has led to the foundation of a number of active and zealous Justice and Peace groups in the diocese'.[90] These developments were the result of his direct involvement and his intention to integrate the work of the Justice and Peace Commission with the Area Pastoral Councils and the Diocesan Pastoral Council thus widening the impact of the Commission's work and influence.[91]

An elected Diocesan Coordinating Council assumed responsibility for overall direction and by the end of 1979 a vibrant programme of courses had been mounted and initiatives undertaken relating to the arms trade, racial justice, fair trade, and world poverty. Solidarity was expressed with movements for human rights in South Africa, Rhodesia, Northern Ireland and Latin America. The Commission was also successful in inviting eminent speakers and notable figures to the diocese including Bishop Cahal Daly and Bishop Edward Daly from Northern Ireland, Fr Bryan Hehir from the USA, and Fr Michael Hollings from London.[92] Perhaps the most prominent visitor was Archbishop Hélder Câmara of Olinda and Recife, Brazil, whose outspoken comments about poverty won him admirers and enemies. Censored in Brazil, Câmara visited London and spoke to a packed Leeds Town Hall on 21 October 1975. The clergy were urged to encourage attendance and Wheeler 'hoped that many will come to listen to this great man'.[93] The Bishop was not present at the meeting, which had been arranged with CIIR, although he gave his blessing and support to Câmara as he did to refugees in his diocese from President Allende's regime in Chile.[94] However, his thoughts on Liberation Theology, the direct political intervention of the Church in Latin American politics, were kept very much to himself.

Anxious that any public expression by laypeople on behalf of the diocese should be in balanced terms, Wheeler placed confidence in a number of key individuals as the need arose. He was fortunate in that he could call on the services and advice of Catholics who were deeply involved in local and national politics as MPs, mayors, aldermen, councillors, magistrates and members of public bodies. Stanley Cohen was Labour MP for Leeds South East; Paddy Crotty was a Councillor and Lord Mayor of Leeds as was Bill Kilgallon; John Battle was a member of Leeds City Council and national coordinator of Church Action on Poverty; Danny Coughlin served as Lord Mayor of Bradford, while John Power served as a leading magistrate in Leeds and was a Deputy Lord Lieutenant of West Yorkshire. Dr Brian Quinn was prominent in the medical profession and Chairman of the Diocesan Pastoral Council. In Sheffield, D. J. O'Neill was a City Alderman, Mrs L. Fitzpatrick was a County Alderman of the West Riding and in Wakefield, J. Marsh and M. Fitzpatrick were Aldermen.[95] 'The Christian Voice', said Wheeler, was needed and 'Our people should be urged to proclaim their faith in all spheres of government and society'. If it could not be articulated by many then a few should undertake that responsibility but he was of the opinion that Catholic bishops should not sit in the House of Lords and thus become directly involved in politics and the legislative process.[96]

In the Diocese of Leeds there were large industrial conurbations and within these there were opportunities for the Church to be involved in social problems. In his first *Ad Limina* he reported on the changes in industrial patterns across his diocese; in his last, he identified specific problems of ethnic integration, racial disharmony and unemployment.[97] Shortly after his translation to Leeds, he became involved in the Yorkshire Council of Social Service founded in 1963 to bring together representatives of local community, political, industrial, commercial and religious groups. Its field of interest was wide ranging encompassing industrial relations, race relations, community arts and social problems. It recognized that Yorkshire was changing rapidly in economic, ethnic and social terms and it was concerned that the value of life in the county should be enhanced.[98] Religious leadership was provided by the Anglicans but Wheeler felt the need for Catholics to be engaged and appointed Fr Michael Keegan and John Power to be his clerical and lay deputies.[99] When the YCSS discussed 'The Churches and Regionalism' at York in January 1968, it was evident that the Anglican presence was not only large but its representatives had effectively investigated and assessed the current situation and problems regarding regional development, housing, welfare, transport, education and immigration and emigration, issues which directly affected Wheeler and his diocese. The Archbishop of York called for churches to co-operate with each other to promote social action and exercise social responsibility[100] and an outcome of the York meeting was the formation in March 1968 of a Yorkshire Churches Group which had Wheeler's support. The task given to the Yorkshire Churches Group, however—to explain the social needs of the region, to suggest means and ways of ecumenical cooperation, to engage in discussion and planning with public bodies, and to mobilize interest in the region's prosperity and progress—was enormous and impossible to achieve. Priests, ministers and religious groups could do little other than engage in lobbying and in local, practical self-help initiatives.[101] The YCSS, meanwhile, managed to draw in financial support, hosted a number of conferences and spawned a range of committees including a Ladies Social Committee and a Ladies Luncheon Club.[102]

The Catholic Church was not unaware of social problems and had a good record, in the Diocese of Leeds and elsewhere, of active charitable involvement in urban areas. On Wheeler's elevation to the episcopate, the Hierarchy, through its Social Welfare and Justice and Peace Commissions, was dealing with race relations, migration, prisoners' aid and child welfare. In 1979, the Hierarchy considered 'Good News to the Poor', the Social Welfare Commission's report on the Church and urban problems. It highlighted the problems of city life and the inevitable tensions arising from them. The Church, it emphasized, had to reach out to people who were trapped in despair and hopelessness for social, economic and racial reasons. It was, the report, suggested, a huge problem but one which had to be addressed.[103]

The Leeds Industrial Mission was one way among many in which the diocese expressed its care and interest and became actively involved in economic and social matters. Considerable progress had been made by the Churches in Britain towards establishing good practice for industrial mission and Wheeler saw it as a means of Catholic involvement in the modern world. Once again, the lead had been taken by the Anglican Diocese of Ripon but Wheeler encouraged Catholic clerical and lay involvement in the mission. It was difficult to spare priests engaged in parish work to undertake such heavy commitments to industry and even more difficult to persuade parish priests to contribute to the funding of the mission[104] but Fr Paul Moxon successfully undertook an industrial chaplaincy and other priests became involved in chaplaincy work in the Selby Coalfield and the neighbouring power stations.[105]

Wheeler's involvement in community relations was not simply confined to encouraging others; there were occasions when his presence and intervention was necessary for the sake of defusing volatile situations and improving community relations. In the 1970s and 1980s, his diocese like many others with large urban concentrations, suffered civil unrest linked to unemployment, poor housing, poverty, racism and police and community relations. In 1975 and 1981 the Chapeltown district of Leeds witnessed particularly serious rioting[106] and Wheeler saw the value of a joint approach to addressing the root causes of such outbursts of community frustration. In 1983 he signed a joint ecumenical statement on the high level of unemployment, calling for the better use of human resources and an end to the bitterness and division caused by uneven unemployment.[107] Meanwhile, the Diocesan Justice and Peace Commission had produced *Towards a Better Life—The World of Work*, which encouraged Catholics and others to address unemployment and other social problems in practical terms and in the context of recent Church teaching and declarations.[108] At Wood Hall Mgr Basil Loftus introduced a job-creation scheme and parishes undertook similar initiatives on a smaller scale.[109]

Another diocesan community initiative supported by Wheeler was St Anne's Shelter and Housing Action which was founded in December 1971. It was one of the first day shelters to be opened in the country and its first Director was Fr Paulinus Healy CP.[110] Its function was to work with single homeless people and its first venture was the St Anne's Day Shelter located in a basement behind Leeds Cathedral. There it provided medical care, food and shelter, and other services. Aware of the high incidence of drinking problems among the homeless, in 1973 St Anne's opened a house for recovering homeless alcoholics. Another house was opened in 1974 and by 1978 there were six houses providing shelter, care and assistance. In due course a detoxification centre was opened designed to provide an alternative to the penal system for those habitually arrested for public drunkenness and to provide to the homeless alcoholic an opportunity to escape his present destructive lifestyle. With national and local government support, both initiatives were well managed by Bill Kilgallon and were extremely successful. Wheeler gave his support to the centres by visiting them and by providing cash grants. He was also anxious to enlist the support of Parliament and MPs but always preferred to do this in conjunction with other denominations.[111] Shortly before he retired he was anxious that the Faith in the City Project, with its emphasis on caring for the urban poor, should be an ecumenical venture and by January 1985 all the major denominations were involved in the Leeds Churches Community Involvement project.[112]

The Miners' Strike 1984–1985

Whatever his views on social justice and care for the poor and marginalized, Wheeler, like other church leaders, was unable to influence the course or alter the outcome of the coal miners' strike of 1984–85. This major industrial dispute affected the Diocese of Leeds and that of Hallam inasmuch as both had a large number of coalmines within their boundaries.

The strike was a defining moment in the history of British industrial relations. Its failure significantly weakened the British trade union movement and was seen as a major political victory for Prime Minister Margaret Thatcher whose aim was to modernize British industry even if this meant dismantling forty years of state ownership. The strike became a symbolic struggle, as the National Union of Mineworkers (NUM), one of the strongest unions in the country, was viewed by many as having brought down Edward Heath's Conservative government as a result of the union's strike in 1974. To Thatcher's Conservative administration it could not be allowed to happen again and the strike of 1984–1985 ended with the miners' defeat and the political power of the NUM permanently broken.

In March 1984, the National Coal Board announced its intention to close twenty coal mines, with a loss of 20,000 jobs, and many communities in the North of England, Scotland and Wales would lose their primary source of employment. Fearing secondary strikes, the government had prepared for industrial action by stockpiling coal, converting some power stations to burn heavy fuel oil, and arranging for coal to be transported by road in case sympathetic railway men went on strike to support the miners. Arthur Scargill, president of the NUM, responded by declaring, without the support of a ballot, that there was to be a national strike in protest against the NCB's plans. The strike lasted for a year and was marked by violent clashes between police and strikers and by bitter social divisions across the country and within mining communities. In Yorkshire, over 97% of the 56,000 miners went on strike and 83% were still on strike at the end of the action. In North Derbyshire, in Hallam Diocese, 67% of 10,500 miners went on strike but only 40% were on strike at the end.

Wheeler called upon his diocese for prayers that the dispute might end and for practical assistance to be given to the mining families who were suffering severe hardship. To the priests he wrote:

> Please fulfil the request made to you regarding Exposition and prayers for a just and peaceful settlement to the present industrial strike… In addition—since there is considerable suffering in the mining area—I should be glad to hear of special collections which could be channelled to the Society of St Vincent de Paul in the Pontefract area.

He concluded: 'This is a matter of compassion and not of any political alignment in the matter'.[113] Mgr Michael Buckley, now at Tadcaster, agreed that the Church should not take sides but Wheeler and other church leaders, he claimed, were 'ominously silent' for fear of alienating either one or both sides of their mining communities. Politics and religion, he wrote, cannot always be separated especially when basic freedoms are denied.[114] Wheeler's reaction to Buckley's statement is not recorded.

The Hierarchy was naturally deeply concerned by the protracted dispute and its ramifications and was particularly alarmed by the inflexibility of both sides. In an ecumenical attempt to bring the dispute to an end Archbishop Habgood of York, Archbishop Worlock of Liverpool and other church leaders met with miners' leaders at Bishopthorpe Palace in York but the meeting was fruitless. Archbishop Worlock stated publicly that such violent disputes arising from radical government policies were leading to the alienation of large urban communities and that no one had really planned for the consequences of a defeat for the miners.[115] As Robbins suggests, the meeting was a symbolic intervention rather than one to determine the end or outcome of the strike.[116]

Notes

1 ALA, GHC/S1/2/A; J. Wilson, 'Abortion, Reproductive Technology and Euthanasia: Post-Conciliar Responses from within the Roman Catholic Church in England and Wales 1965–2000' (University of Durham: unpublished Ph.D. thesis, 2004), p. 62.

2 S. Lee and P. Stanford, *Believing Bishops* (London: Faber and Faber, 1990), pp. 71, 73.

3 *The Tablet*, 29 Oct 1966; ALA, BEC/S2/9/A; Wilson, 'Abortion, Reproductive Technology and Euthanasia: Post-Conciliar Responses', p. 63.

4 Personal reminiscences of Kevin McNamara, MP for Hull North (1966–1974), Hull Central (1974–1983) and Hull North (1983–2005).

5 Lee and Stanford, *Believing Bishops*, p.73.

6 F. Longford, *The Bishops: A Study of Leaders in the Church Today* (London: Sidgwick and Jackson, 1986), p. 124.

7 Wilson, 'Abortion, Reproductive Technology and Euthanasia: Post-Conciliar Responses', p. 64.

8 *Ad Clerum*, 16 March 1967. LDA, Wheeler Papers; P. Stanford, *Cardinal Hume and the Changing Face of English Catholicism* (London: Geoffrey Chapman, 1993), p. 51; *Catholic Herald*, 14 Nov 1975.

9 *Sunday Telegraph*, 26 March 1967.

10 ALA, BEC/S2/9/A; Wilson, 'Abortion, Reproductive Technology and Euthanasia: Post-Conciliar Responses', pp. 66–67.

11 Bishops' Conference of England and Wales, *Statement Concerning Moral Questions* (London: Catholic Truth Society, 1970), pp. 15–16.

12 Bishop Patrick Casey, Letter to the Catholic Nurses Guilds of England and Wales and to the Guild of St Luke and SS Cosmas and Damian, January 1971. LDA, WDC, Wheeler Papers.

13 ALA, BEC/S2/9/A; *Obituaries From The Times 1971–1975*, pp. 234–237.

14 Wilson, 'Abortion, Reproductive Technology and Euthanasia: Post-Conciliar Responses', p. 73.

15 *Ibid.*, pp. 69–72.

16 *Ibid.*, pp. 73–80.

17 W. G. Wheeler, *In Truth And Love* (Southport: Gowland and Co., 1990), p. 107.

18 Wheeler, *Ad Clerum*, 30 Aug 1966. LDA, WDC, Wheeler Papers.

19 Wheeler, *Ad Clerum*, 10 Oct 1966. LDA, WDC, Wheeler Papers.

20 See Wheeler, *Ad Clerum*, 24 March 1971, 21 Jan 1972 and 29 Feb 1972; Wheeler, Pastoral Letters of Dec 1971 and 30 April 1972; Council of Laity Minutes, 29 April 1972. LDA, WDC, Wheeler Papers.

21 LDA, WDC, W64. Abortion. I am indebted to Mgr John Murphy for his help and advice on this section.

22 Wheeler to Fr A Byron, 7 Dec 1973. LDA, WDC, W64, Abortion.

23   Wheeler to Clergy, 12 Aug 1975; K Heslop to Wheeler, 16 Sept 1975. LDA, WDC, W64, Abortion.

24   Kevin Mcnamara MP to Wheeler, 3 Aug 1976. LDA, WDC, W64, Abortion. McNamara was a member of the Commons Select Committee on Abortion and was anxious that support for Catholic MPs was maintained. He expressed concern to Wheeler that if Catholic anti-abortionists misinterpreted the Committee's report it would give the impression of Catholic disunity.

25   Wheeler to Priests, 5 Oct 1976. LDA, WDC, W64, Abortion.

26   Heenan to St John Stevas, 14 March 1969. LPL, Ramsey, vol. 158, 15.

27   *Statement Concerning Moral Questions*, pp. 16–17; Wilson, 'Abortion, Reproductive Technology and Euthanasia: Post-Conciliar Responses', p. 197.

28   Wheeler, 'Euthanasia', May 1969. LDA, WDC, Wheeler Papers.

29   Wilson, 'Abortion, Reproductive Technology and Euthanasia: Post-Conciliar Responses', p. 185.

30   ALA, WOR/S6/9/E3; Wilson, 'Abortion, Reproductive Technology and Euthanasia: Post-Conciliar Responses', pp. 191–192.

31   Wilson, 'Abortion, Reproductive Technology and Euthanasia: Post-Conciliar Responses', pp. 192–193.

32   *Catholic Voice*, April 1982; *Leeds Diocesan Directory* (1983), p. 9.

33   ALA, BEC/S2/9/A and ALA, WOR/S6/9/E3.

34   *Briefing 83*, 5 Aug 1983.

35   *Catholic Voice*, Aug 1984; Wheeler to McReavy, 30 Nov 1984. LDA, WPC, Warnock Report 1984.

36   K. Robbins, *Oxford History of the Christian Church: England, Ireland, Scotland, Wales: The Christian Church 1900–2000* (Oxford: Oxford University Press, 2008), pp. 341–345.

37   Wheeler to J. McGinley, Secretary, Convening Committee, Northern Ireland Relief Fund, 1 Sep 1969. LDA, WDC, W10.

38   L. Walsh to Wheeler, 24 Aug 1971. LDA, WDC, W10.

39   L. B. Kearns to Wheeler, 25 Oct 1971. LDA, WDC, W10.

40   Wheeler to Kearns, 27 Oct 1971. LDA, WDC, W10.

41   Heenan to Enrici, 29 July 1970. AAW, He1/A5 (b).

42   J. Bourke to Wheeler, 25 Oct 1971. LDA, WDC, W10.

43   Wheeler to Bourke, 27 Oct 1971. LDA, WDC, W10.

44   'English Pax Christi Statement on Northern Ireland', 27 Nov 1971. LDA, WDC, W10.

45   B. O'Hagan, 'A Letter to the Roman Catholic Bishops of Ireland, North and South, England, Scotland and Wales', 30 Nov 1971. LDA, WDC, W10.

46   Conway to Wheeler, 17 Oct 1972. Between October 1968 and July 1972, Conway issued fifty statements, either alone or with the Irish Hierarchy or leaders of other denominations. 'Statements by Cardinal Conway and Joint Statements on Northern Ireland Situation 1968/72'. LDA, WDC, W10.

47   *The Sun*, 18 Dec 1971.

48   *Statement Concerning Moral Questions*, pp. 12–13.

49   Wheeler, *Ad Clerum*, Feb 1972 and Pastoral on Northern Ireland. LDA, WDC, Wheeler Papers.

50   LDA, WDC, Leeds Council of Priests. May 1972.

51   Heenan, 'A Bridge in Belfast', 13 Dec 1971. LDA, WDC, W10.

52   G. H. Dammers to Wheeler, Sept 1972. LDA, WDC, W10.

53   Wheeler to Reverend John Wright, 19 March 1973. LDA, WDC, W10.

54   Heenan to the Prime Minister, 31 Jan 1972. LDA, WDC, W10.

55   'Statement on Northern Ireland by Priests of the Archdiocese of Westminster', 31 Dec 1971. LDA, WDC, W10.

56   Archbishop Murphy to the Priests of the Archdiocese of Cardiff, 11 Feb 1972. LDA, WDC, W10.

57   Wheeler to Fr John Sullivan, 18 Feb 1972. LDA, WDC, W10.

58   Wheeler to J. E. McInerney, 18 Aug 1972. LDA, WDC, W10.

59   Association for Legal Justice. LDA, WDC, W10.

60   Wheeler to Priests, Oct 1973. LDA, WDC, W10.

61   Brady and Faul to Wheeler, 2 Feb 1976. LDA, WDC, W24, Frank Stagg.

62   McPolin to Wheeler, 6 Feb 1976. LDA, WDC, W24, Frank Stagg.

63   Toal to Wheeler, 11 Feb 1976. LDA, WDC, W24, Frank Stagg.

64   Stoker to Wheeler, 3 Feb 1976. LDA, WDC, W24, Frank Stagg.

65   Sheehan to Wheeler, 22 Feb 1976. LDA, WDC, W24, Frank Stagg.

66   Gill to Wheeler, 7 March 1976. LDA, WDC, W24, Frank Stagg.

67   Wheeler to Apostolic Delegate, 3 Feb 1976. LDA, WDC, W24, Frank Stagg.

68   Wheeler to Fr M. Byrne, B. Davis and D. Peterson, 13 Feb 1976. LDA, WDC, W24, Frank Stagg.

69   *The Tablet*, 16 Oct 1976.

70   *Catholic Herald*, 14 Oct 1977.

71   C. B. Daly, *Northern Ireland: From Impasse to Initiative*, Oct 1979. LDA, WDC, W10.

72   Wheeler to the Anglican Bishops of Ripon, Bradford, Wakefield and the Vicar of Leeds, 29 Nov 1978. LDA, WDC, Northern Ireland 1978.

73   Forbes to Wheeler, 14 Aug 1981. LDA, WDC, W14; A. Forbes, 'Deadlock at the Maze', *The Times*, 11 Aug 1981.

74   See cain.ulster.ac.uk

75   *Briefing*, vol. 29, July 1999, p. 15.

76   *Statement Concerning Moral Questions*. This publication was the subject of Wheeler's Lenten Pastoral of 1971. Between 1979 and 1986, the Hierarchy also published statements on the revision of the British Nationality Law and on Racial Justice. See *Race Relations and Racial Justice: Statements by the Catholic Bishops' Conference of England and Wales 1979–1995* (London: Committee for Community Relations, 1995).

77 *Leeds Diocesan Directory* (1967), pp. 159–190.
78 *Holy Rosary, Parish Stories*, Sept 2012. I am grateful to Anne Forbes for this information.
79 Diocese of Leeds, *Justice and Peace Commission, 1979 Report*. LDA, WDC, Justice and Peace. I am grateful to Anne Forbes for her advice on this section.
80 *The Tablet* 14 Jan and 23 Dec 1967.
81 *Ibid,* 22 April 1972.
82 Wheeler, *Ad Clerum*, 1973, *The Church in the World of Our Time*. LDA, WDC, Wheeler Papers.
83 Wheeler, Advent Pastoral, 1967 and *Ad Clerum*, 1967. LDA, WDC, Wheeler Papers.
84 Wheeler, Pastoral, Sept 1968. LDA, WDC, Wheeler Papers.
85 *QR*, 1967–1972.
86 Wheeler, *Ad Clerum*, Feb and June 1973. LDA, WDC, Wheeler Papers.
87 Wheeler, *Ad Clerum*, Nov 1973. LDA, WDC, Wheeler Papers.
88 Pastoral Letter, Nov 1973 and, *Ad Clerum*, 1967. LDA, WDC, Wheeler Papers.
89 Wheeler, *In Truth And Love*, p. 108.
90 *QR*, 1972–1977.
91 Wheeler to Forbes, 10 March 1973. Courtesy of Anne Forbes.
92 Diocese of Leeds, *Justice and Peace Commission, 1979 Report*. LDA, WDC, Justice and Peace.
93 Wheeler, *Ad Clerum*, Oct 1975. LDA, WDC, Wheeler Papers.
94 *QR*, 1977–182. When Câmara was leaving Eltofts, the Sisters knelt before him and asked for a blessing. Câmara looked at them and said: 'After you bless me!' I owe this reference to Archbishop Arthur Roche.
95 *Leeds Diocesan Directory*, various dates.
96 Wheeler, *In Truth And Love*, pp. 107–109.
97 *QR*, 1967–72; 1977–1982.
98 Yorkshire Council of Social Service, *Fourth Annual Report 1966–67*.
99 Wheeler to R. T. Clarke, 10 May 1967. R. T. Clarke to Wheeler, 16 May 1968. LDA, WDC, W63.
100 'Churches and Regionalism'. Notes of a meeting held by the Yorkshire Council of Social Service, York 22 Jan 1968. LDA, WDC, W63.
101 *Freelance*, Notes and Comments compiled by the Yorkshire Council of Social Service, March 1968;'The Task of the Yorkshire Churches Group', March 1968. LDA, WDC, W63.
102 Yorkshire Council of Social Service, *Fifth Annual Report 1967–68*.
103 'Good News to the Poor—The Church and City Problems', Bishops' Conference, Oct 1979.
104 See correspondence on the Leeds Industrial Mission, 1980. LDA, WDC, W63, Leeds Industrial Mission.

[105] J. Y. W. Ritchie to Wheeler, 26 Nov 1982 and Wheeler to Ritchie, 29 Nov 1982. LDA, WDC. Leeds Industrial Mission, W63.

[106] See *The Guardian*, 8 August 2011, 'Urban Riots: Thirty Years after Brixton'. At the time of the Chapeltown Riots in Leeds in 1981, there were serious outburst of urban rioting in Brixton in London and Toxteth in Liverpool.

[107] Joint Statement by the Leaders of the West Yorkshire Churches, 26 March 103. LDA, WDC, Leeds Industrial Mission, W63.

[108] *Towards a Better Life—The World of Work*, Diocese of Leeds, Justice and Peace Commission, 1980.

[109] *QR*, 1977–1982; *Catholic Herald*, 23 Sept 1983.

[110] *Catholic Herald*, 11 Feb 1972.

[111] LDA, WDC. St Anne's. W16.

[112] I am grateful to Anne Forbes for this reference.

[113] *Ad Clerum*, 3 Oct 1984. LDA, WDC, Wheeler Papers. There were no comments and only one letter in the diocesan newspaper relating to the strike. The letter supported the miners. On the conclusion of the strike, Fr Donal Bambury of Denaby Main in the Hallam Diocese was presented with a miner's lamp for providing financial and material support to the striking miners and their families. *Catholic Herald*, 26 April 1985.

[114] *Catholic Herald*, 5 Oct 1984.

[115] *Ibid.*, 10 Nov 1984

[116] Robbins, *Oxford History of the Christian Church: England, Ireland, Scotland, Wales: The Christian Church 1900–2000*, pp. 426–427.

15 TOWARDS RETIREMENT

Diocesan Centenary and Ad Limina 1977–1982

I N 1978–1979, THE Diocese celebrated the centenary of its foundation.[1] On 20 December 1978, Wheeler presided over a concelebrated Mass of Thanksgiving at St Anne's Cathedral, Leeds, in the presence of Cardinal Basil Hume, Archbishop Bruno Heim, Archbishop Derek Worlock of Liverpool and Bishops of the Northern Province including the newly appointed Bishop Augustine Harris of Middlesbrough and his Cathedral Chapter. The sermon was preached by Archbishop Dwyer of Birmingham, Wheeler's predecessor in Leeds. From Pope John Paul II there came a letter of congratulation and thanks to Wheeler and the diocese.

> We rejoice wholeheartedly first of all with you, esteemed Brother, and then with the whole of your flock over which you have been placed, on the occasion of your approaching centenary of the diocese and on the outstanding service and activity of Catholic life which has in a praiseworthy fashion continued uninterruptedly among you for one hundred years. Likewise, we warmly congratulate you on the signs given throughout these hundred years of a desirable renewal and of the truly flourishing condition of Christian devotion and the practice of religion within the confines of the Diocese of Leeds. This we have learnt to our great comfort from several documents.

The Pope offered his heartfelt thanks and loving praise to the Lord 'who, by His heavenly help brought about that not only should the institution of the Catholic church be so happily revived there, but also that it should meanwhile continuously go from strength to strength with a threefold increase in the numbers of priests, faithful and places for divine worship'.[2]

During the next six months, Wheeler and Bishop Moverley presided at twelve other concelebrated Masses across the diocese—in Bradford, Dewsbury, Rotherham, Barnsley, Doncaster, Sheffield, Halifax, Wakefield, Skipton, Harrogate, Leeds and York. In June 1979, Cardinal Hume preached at a special event at Ampleforth for the Dioceses of Leeds and Middlesbrough and in July, the Apostolic Delegate presided over another joint event at Hazlewood Castle. The Duke of Norfolk opened a Centenary Exhibition in the Leeds Art Gallery of Catholic treasures from the history of the area and other notable events included pilgrimages to Walsingham and Rome. For Wheeler the themes running throughout the celebrations were thanksgiving and renewed commitment for the future.[3]

One of the documents the Pope referred to in his letter of congratulation and thanks was the *Ad Limina* reports sent to Rome and in 1982 the time came for Wheeler to present his final *Ad Limina*. It was a much more comprehensive document than its predecessors but curiously included no demographic statistics. Wheeler reported that the major change had been the loss in 1981 of fifty parishes to the new Diocese of Hallam and two parishes in the City of York to the Diocese of Middlesbrough. The diocese now had 131 parishes with 131 parish churches, forty-two chapels of ease and twenty-three Mass centres. Seven of the parishes were entrusted to religious orders which had forty-eight priests working in the diocese. At the close of 1981, 209 diocesan priests were on active work in the diocese and twenty-one were working outside the diocese as Chaplains to the Forces, on seminary and higher education faculties, and in Peru. 'There was', he wrote, 'a wholesome and easy relationship between Ordinary and clergy of the diocese' and reported that there was frequent consultation and in-service training for the priests.

Although a Diocesan Synod had not been convened 'for some years' Wheeler felt a meeting of 'the entire Presbyterium' after the National Pastoral Congress served the same function. Celibacy was 'held in the highest esteem' and although there had been defections, it was by no means easy to analyse the real reason for them. Fortunately, none of the priests were 'engaged in the political scene' and 'there is no problem of priests aligning themselves to extreme politics of either wing'. Eighteen men were training for the priesthood (although he lamented the fact that the general level of their education did not seem high) and while this figure appeared healthy, the age profile of the clergy presented a future problem. Only six men were ordained in 1981 and solutions to the projected shortage included married deacons and women priests. He accepted the former but not the latter. 'With the increasing development of the feminist movement', he wrote, 'it was inevitable that some people should hold the view, even in the Catholic community, that women ought to be ordained'. To this, 'the only answer is to listen and to present the teaching of the Church with balance, sensitivity and charity'. He concluded: 'It is an aspiration that would be rejected by the vast majority in this diocese'.

There was a sound diocesan infrastructure and administrative, consultative and pastoral responsibilities were fulfilled successfully by the Diocesan Curia, the Cathedral Chapter, the Diocesan Tribunal, the Diocesan Pastoral Council, Area Pastoral Councils, Deanery Parish Councils, Parish Councils, the Diocesan Council of Priests and the Senate of Priests. Commissions existed for Liturgy, Justice and Peace, Finance, Christian Unity, and Diocesan Schools.[4]

Diocese, Priests and People

Three years after the submission of his final *Ad Limina*, the time came for Wheeler to leave the diocese and take stock of his episcopate. It had been a time of enormous ecclesiastical change and turbulent social upheaval. Wheeler had good cause to be proud of many of his achievements but there could be no masking the rise of secularism or the decline in religious belief and practice.

Two inter-related developments which particularly distressed Wheeler during his episcopate were the loss of priests and the decline in vocations. Between 1966 and 1985, Wheeler ordained 135 men for the Diocese of Leeds. Of these, ninety-two were ordained during the period 1966–1976 and forty-three between 1976 and 1985. Of the 135 priests ordained by Wheeler, thirty-three (24%) left the priesthood either during Wheeler's episcopate or after his retirement in 1985. Another twenty priests who had been ordained before Wheeler arrived in Leeds left their ministry between 1966 and 1985. Few things, if any, wrote Finnigan, ... caused Bishop Wheeler more distress during his time in office than when a priest abandoned his ministry. To him it was the breaking of a sacred vow, and in many cases, he witnessed the departure of men who had ability and potential. Looking back on this period in 1990, he said he could not understand why it had happened on such a scale, although he acknowledged that in the majority of cases it stemmed from a desire to marry. If there was an explanation, it was not any fault of Vatican II but a reflection of contemporary secular society. 'It was something', he said, 'which was part of a sociological phenomenon'.

The resignation of priests from the active ministry was exacerbated by the fact that fewer men were presenting themselves for the priesthood. In his last five years as bishop, Wheeler ordained fourteen priests—the same number he had ordained during his first year in Leeds.[5] By 1985, there were six diocesan candidates for the priesthood in the junior seminaries and forty-three in the senior seminaries.[6]

Sociological reasons and Vatican II were not alone responsible for the reduction of priests and parishes within the Diocese of Leeds; the erection of Hallam had a significant impact on diocesan statistics. In 1966, Wheeler inherited a diocese consisting of 173 parishes in twenty-six Rural Deaneries, 288 secular priests and seventy-five priests representing eleven religious orders.[7] The creation of Hallam reduced the number of parishes and on Wheeler's retirement there were 131 parishes with forty-one chapels-of-ease and twenty-one Mass Centres. In 1985, notwithstanding the loss of some priests to the Diocese of Hallam, there were 277 priests, of whom 237 were priests of the diocese, including retired priests and those working outside the diocese. Only 200 of these were on active duty in the diocese. There were twelve foreign chaplains and thirty-eight priests from religious orders.[8]

In addition to these worrying trends, other developments meant that the diocese was significantly different at the end of Wheeler's episcopate than it had been at the beginning with statistics indicating a shrinking of the Catholic population and a decline in religious practice. Mass attendance, for example, was 135,725 in 1966; by 1970, it was 121,677.[9] In those parishes remaining in the Diocese of Leeds following the creation of the Hallam Diocese, Mass attendance fell from 90,645 in 1966 to 68,224 in 1985.[10] Marriages dropped from 2,810 in 1966 to 1,580 in 1980 and 1,248 in 1985. Infant baptisms dropped from 8,431 in 1966 to 3,422 in 1980 and 3,328 in 1985.[11] Conversions to the faith also declined.

Whereas his two immediate predecessors were required to provide more churches and schools, Wheeler found himself in a very different situation. Temporary churches which had been built to meet the needs of Catholics on inter- and post-war suburban housing estates now had to be replaced and nearly all churches had to be reordered following Vatican II. Between 1966 and 1985, Wheeler opened the new churches of St Francis, St Gregory and St Joseph in Leeds, St Theresa and St Winefride in Bradford, English Martyrs in Huddersfield, St Patrick in Birstall, St Joseph in Sherburn-in Elmet, St Margaret Clitherow in Threshfield, St Anthony in Windhill and Holy Innocents in Wyke. Some churches, for example St Francis in Bradford, were extended while St Andrew in Huddersfield was one of a number of redundant churches were purchased from other Christian denominations.

Educational priories in the diocese were affected by the differing responses of Local Education Authorities to government policies, the most radical of which was the introduction of secondary comprehensive schools in the late-1960s. Local Education Authorities each drew up different plans for educational organization and each individual scheme was another financial burden on the diocese. Like many other priests, Wheeler was a firm advocate of the primary school being essential to the vitality of parish life and future development. Six new primary schools (St Andrew, St Dominic, St Francis, Holy Name, Holy Rosary, and SS Peter and Paul) were opened in Leeds and three in Bradford (St Cuthbert, St Matthew and St Patrick), while elsewhere new or replacement primaries were opened in Batley, Boston Spa, Bingley, Chequerfield, Garforth, Goole, Halifax, Harrogate, Horsforth, Huddersfield, Otley, Selby, Wetherby and Windhill.

Wheeler was less convinced about the value of secondary comprehensive provision but maintained that every Catholic child should at least have access to Catholic education at all levels. The abolition of grammar schools caused anguish among some clergy and parents but joy among others. Wheeler was somewhat ambivalent: 'In their day the Catholic grammar schools did a great work. Many of the Catholic public schools likewise have performed in a highly dedicated manner both academically and from the religious point of view'. He felt that there were some advantages to Catholic children being in non-Catholic schools but concluded that most children 'often need the support of a school which has an avowedly Catholic ethos'.[12] New secondary schools were opened in Leeds, Bradford and Carlton but although planned as secondary modern schools their ultimate nature depended on the plans of the Local Authorities. Thus in Bradford, St George, planned as a secondary modern school, became a middle school. In Authorities such as Leeds, some schools which had been planned as primary schools became middle schools. The time lag between planning, agreement, funding and building was usually considerable and some developments took over a decade to reach fruition. In Huddersfield, St Augustine's Secondary Modern School and St Gregory's Grammar School, both occupying one site, were amalgamated to form All Saints' High School.[13]

Wheeler was of the opinion that the post-Conciliar Catholic educational system in England and Wales was partly to blame for the decline in vocations. The cause was not due to structural or organizational problems but could be ascribed to new pedagogical methods. In particular, he considered that the demise of rote learning and the speedy introduction of radical new teaching methods, especially in religious instruction, had left teachers bewildered and children with no real knowledge of their faith. The old system of the structured catechism, he felt, was a much better way of imparting knowledge of the truth although he personally never experienced the Catholic *Penny Catechism* as a child. 'Despising the faculty of memory' he wrote, 'is highly regrettable; after all it is one of the three faculties of the soul'.[14]

A Fond Farewell

In October 1984, as Wheeler approached his seventy-fifth birthday and in accordance with Canon Law, he submitted his resignation from office.[15] He hoped for a smooth transition and told the Apostolic Nuncio that he was ready to hand over his accommodation and that 'it will be possible for my successor to enter into his inheritance the moment he is free to do so and in totality'. He added: 'I have no desire to plug any particular candidate...'[16] In January 1985, he was informed by the Apostolic Nuncio that the Holy Father had accepted his resignation and the process of choosing his successor would begin. Archbishop Heim also took the opportunity to congratulate Wheeler on being awarded an honorary doctorate by the University of Leeds: 'it reflects the esteem and the affection you have earned through the years', he wrote. [17]

After nineteen years, Wheeler had to relinquish the See of Leeds. 'As you can imagine', he wrote, 'I do so with mixed feelings because whilst I sometimes get somewhat exhausted physically with all the demands to be fulfilled, yet I have a great love for you all and great joy from your response and your wonderful help and co-operation in so many ways'. He thanked God for the opportunity to serve the diocese and felt confident that its people would support his successor in the same way.

He advised that suggestions as to who the next bishop might be should be sent to the Apostolic Nuncio and that his resignation would not become effective until the name of his successor was announced by the Holy See. Meanwhile, he asked that prayers be said that the Holy Father would appoint 'a wise and holy man' to be the next Bishop of Leeds'.[18] In July 1985, it was announced that Bishop David Konstant, an Auxiliary Bishop in Westminster was to be Wheeler's successor. The diocesan clergy were informed, a press conference was arranged at which Wheeler and

Konstant appeared together, and a Pastoral informing the laity was sent to the parishes.[19]

On 18 September 1985, Wheeler was guest of honour at a civic dinner to mark his retirement and on the following night he bade an emotional farewell to his flock at Leeds Town Hall. With his successor, Bishop Konstant, and his former Auxiliary, Bishop Moverley, he concelebrated Mass before a huge congregation and was clearly moved by presence of so many priests and people, the warm reception and the glowing tributes. On behalf of the priests, Provost Mgr Harry Thompson, a former Vicar General of the diocese, presented him with the keys of a new car and said that Bishop Wheeler was a man of great compassion who was generous not only in helping others and but also in acknowledging the debt he owed to others. Dr Brian Quinn, Chair of the Diocesan Pastoral Council, thanked him for his work with the laity and youth and presented him with a cheque for £15,000, the sum collected across the diocese. Mgr George Bradley, the Diocesan Archivist, presented him with a bound copy of specially commissioned essays on Yorkshire Catholics, while the Union of Catholic Mothers gave him a 'Mouseman' oak bookrest and St John's School for the Deaf at Boston Spa gave him a table. Wheeler was overwhelmed by the kind wishes, prayers and generosity of his diocese. He thanked all those who had helped him and said: 'It is a very lovely and a wonderful thing that you have come together like this. It means far more to me than I can possibly say'.[20]

Wheeler was now confronted with the reality of having to leave his beloved Eltofts and finding somewhere to live. He considered retiring to Downside but realised that although this would provide security, comfort and access to the spiritual life, it would be far removed from his family and many friends. Eventually, having secured gracious permission from Bishop Konstant, he decided to stay in the diocese and took up residence at Marydene, an apartment within the College of the Blessed Virgin Mary at Headingley. There, surrounded by some of his most beautiful and valuable pieces of antique furniture, he settled down to an active retirement.

An early assessment of Wheeler's tenure as Bishop of Leeds came from Michael Brown, the Churches Correspondent of *The Yorkshire Post*. Headed 'Lesson on the Trail of Unity' it was an honest if brief evaluation of Wheeler's contribution to his diocese and especially the wider ecumenical movement. Brown claimed that Wheeler had acquired the image of a reactionary and although 'a pastor of warm and kindly leadership' and even 'a churchman of prophetic vision', he was to some 'a man who by temperament was programmed for a more autocratic age'. Some went so far as to dismiss Wheeler as 'one of the most reactionary bishops now on the Roman Catholic Bench of England and Wales'—'a Bishop of London in Roman clothes'. Yet to Brown this was not a balanced judgement of Wheeler for he was no Lefebvrist and would have nothing to do with the right wing radicals in the Church. For Wheeler, fidelity to Vatican II was supreme and 'that meant fidelity to all the conciliar reforms, including the liturgical and ecumenical ones'. Wood Hall was the manifestation of Wheeler's most cherished ambition to make the message of Vatican II come alive in his diocese and as Mgr Michael Buckley had said, 'To do this was 'prophetic and courageous'. This visionary and imaginative pastoral and ecumenical development was a trailblazer and subsequently attracted leading religious figures. Yet, opined Buckley, Wheeler was not instinctively prepared for Vatican II and it was to his credit that he opened Wood Hall, a venture which, aesthetically, held little attraction for him. In the 1930s, he had entered a Church whose monolithic and unchanging doctrine and authority he found appealing. Not all the changes emanating from the traumatic Vatican II, therefore, were welcomed by Wheeler but Bishop Moverley, echoing Mgr Buckley's observations, wrote that he 'had the vision of the pastures opened up by the Council, and he strove to lead people into them'. Cardinal Hume recalled Wheeler's surprise appointment to Middlesbrough where he quickly endeared himself to a diocese which was subsequently sad to see him leave for Leeds. He had, said Hume, 'made a great contribution not only to the Leeds diocese but to the Church in this country in general'. Brown concluded: 'Gordon Wheeler will be a difficult man to follow'.[21]

Notes

1   On 20 December 1878, the Diocese of Beverley was sub-divided into the Dioceses of Leeds and Middlesbrough.

2   www.vatican.va/holy_father/john_paul_ii/letters/1978/documents.

3   *Leeds Diocesan Directory* (1980), pp. 4–5.

4   *QR*, 1977–1982.

5   R. E. Finnigan, 'Bishop Wheeler 1966–1985' in R. E. Finnigan and J. Hagerty, *The Bishops of Leeds—Essays in Honour of Bishop David Konstant* (Leeds: PBK Publications on behalf of the Diocese of Leeds, 2005), p. 172.

6   *Catholic Directory* (1986), p. 250.

7   LDA, WDC, Council of Clergy, 8 Jan. 1967.

8   *Leeds Diocesan Directory* (1986), p. 69.

9   *Ibid*, (1967), p. 87; (1971), p. 78.

10 Finnigan, 'Bishop Wheeler 1966–1985', p. 173.

11 *Leeds Diocesan Directory* (1967), p. 87; (1982), p. 82; *Catholic Directory* (1986), p. 250.

12 W. G. Wheeler, *In Truth And Love* (Southport: Gowland and Co., 1990), pp. 99.

13 Finnigan, 'Bishop Wheeler 1966–1985', pp. 173–175.

14 Wheeler, *In Truth And Love*, pp. 97–98.

15 Wheeler to Heim, 1 Oct 1984. LDA, WPC, Letters 1984.

16 Wheeler to Heim, 5 Oct 1984. LDA, WPC, Letters 1984.

17 Heim to Wheeler, 23 Jan 1985. LDA, WPC, Appointment of Bishop David Konstant.

18 *Catholic Voice*, Jan 1985.

19 LDA, WPC, Appointment of Bishop David Konstant.

20 *Yorkshire Post*, 20 Sept 1985. In his will, Wheeler left the £15,000 to the Little Sisters of the Poor.

21 *Yorkshire Post*, 6 May 1985.

16 AD MULTOS ANNOS

An Active Retirement

WHEELER APPROACHED RETIREMENT with trepidation. He had been actively involved in religious affairs since his Anglican ordination in 1933 and he did not look forward with enthusiasm to what E. M. Forster called 'that seductive combination of increased wisdom and decaying powers'.[1] Yet his retirement proved active and fulfilling because he remained mentally active, quite fit physically, and involved with a number of causes near to his heart. He was also well cared for and surrounded by people who knew and loved him. He drew much comfort from the Scriptures, the Classics and Church history with their examples of the elderly not necessarily being inactive, unhappy or isolated but being remarkably inspirational.

Retirement allowed him the time and opportunity to read and write, visit old friends and places of interest, and listen to music. He continued to receive documents from the Bishops' Conference, the Apostolic Nunciature and the Holy See and this helped him to remain in touch and, as he said, 'very much part of our Mother the Church'. He also received regular invitations to speak at commemorative events and ceremonies, all of which gave him scope to draw on his huge experience and use his historical, literary and oratorical gifts. In 1986, he wrote to Archbishop Couve de Murville that he 'had got over the trauma of retirement' and that he was 'now enjoying it'.[2]

With the assistance of Robert Finnigan, he also produced two books— *In Truth and Love* and *More Truth and Love*—the former a memoir of his life and ministry, the latter a collection of articles, sermons and eulogies. The subjects of the sections which follow are largely based on his second volume and illustrate dimensions of Wheeler's life and interests which he did not or was unable to give prominence to in his episcopate or which referred to events which occurred after his retirement. It concludes with Wheeler's reflection on priesthood, especially in retirement.

The Knights of Malta

The Sovereign Military Hospitaller Order of Saint John of Jerusalem of Rhodes and of Malta, also known as the Sovereign Military Order of

Malta, the Order of Malta, and the Knights of Malta, is a Catholic lay religious order with humanitarian, military, chivalrous and noble origins. It was into this exclusive Order that Wheeler was admitted in 1958 and it was an honour in which he took great delight. Steeped in history yet relevant in the contemporary world, the Order enabled Wheeler to meet with Catholic men, usually of financial substance and descendants of European and British nobility, who like their predecessors continued to care for those in need of medical and charitable assistance.

The Order dates from the mid-eleventh century when merchants from the Republic of Amalfi obtained authorization from the Caliph of Egypt to build a church, convent and hospital in Jerusalem to care for pilgrims of any religious faith or race. The Order of St. John of Jerusalem—the monastic community which ran the hospital for pilgrims in the Holy Land—became independent under the guidance of its founder, Blessed Gérard Thom. After the conquest of Jerusalem in 1099 during the First Crusade, the Hospitallers became a military order. By the Bull of 15 February 1113, Pope Paschal II approved the foundation of the Hospital in Jerusalem placing it under the authority and protection of the Holy See and granting it the right to elect its superiors without interference from other secular or religious authorities. The Hospitallers, religious bound by the monastic vows of poverty, chastity and obedience, were obliged by the constitution of the Christian Kingdom of Jerusalem to defend the sick, the pilgrims and the territories that the crusaders had captured from the Muslims. As the military situation worsened for the Crusaders, the Order thus added the military task of defending the faith to its original mission. The Order subsequently adopted the white eight-pointed Cross representing the eight beatitudes. Following the loss of Christian held territories in the Holy Land to Muslims, the Order operated from Rhodes (1310–1523), and later from Malta (1530–1798), over which it was sovereign. After Napoleon's capture of Malta in 1798, the Order became dispersed throughout Europe and in the nineteenth century redirected itself toward international humanitarian and religious causes.

In 1834, the Order, now known as the Sovereign Military Order of Malta, acquired new headquarters in Rome where it has remained ever since. Its modern work is international in scope, essentially humanitarian and reflects its original purpose. The Order has established hospitals, schools and other facilities throughout the world to care for the sick, those suffering from hunger and the homeless and deprived. The Sovereign

Military Order of Malta is considered a sovereign subject of international law and has permanent observer status at the United Nations.[3]

According to its Constitution, members of the Order are divided into three Classes. They are expected to conduct their lives in an exemplary manner in conformity with the teachings and precepts of the Catholic Church and devote themselves to the humanitarian activities of the Order. Within the Third Class are Chaplains of Magistral Obedience whose duties are to dedicate themselves to the pastoral care of the members and provide religious assistance to the Order's charitable and missionary works and to the service of its churches.[4] It was into this division of the British Association of the Order that Wheeler was enrolled on 9 November 1958. At this time, he was a priest in Westminster and Archbishop David Mathew proposed his application.[5] The Order had within its ranks many of Wheeler's wealthy friends and acquaintances, including Viscount Furness who had been in the Order since 1946. Duties at Westminster Cathedral and subsequently in Middlesbrough and Leeds left Wheeler little time for involvement but on his frequent trips to Rome, he would visit the Order's Magistral Palace on the Via Condotti and its villa on the Aventine Hill. In October 1965, Wheeler was promoted to Conventual Chaplain *ad honorem*. Four of his confrères carried the canopy at his enthronement in Leeds on 27 June 1966 and exactly a year later, he celebrated High Mass at the Order's Annual Assembly.[6]

Despite the fact that Wheeler's attendance at the Order's events and his involvement in its affairs was necessarily spasmodic, he was nevertheless awarded the Order's Grand Cross Pro Piis Meritis 'Pro Merito Melitensi' on his retirement in 1985 in recognition of his activities that had brought honour and prestige to the Order. His surprise was considerable and he wrote to Sir Peter Drummond-Murray that 'As I have been so rarely able to attend the various Assemblies for the twenty-one years that I have been a Bishop in Yorkshire, I feel entirely unworthy of such a decoration'. Diocesan commitments however, prevented him from receiving the award until 1986.[7] Once he was free from his busy episcopal timetable, Wheeler was able attend the Order's functions and preach retreats for them as he did at Hazlewood in March 1987.[8] He was also able to participate in the Chaplains meetings under the direction of Archbishop Maurice Couve de Murville, Archbishop of Birmingham and Principal Chaplain of the British Association. By the end of 1988, he had preached at Arundel, celebrated Mass for the Order at Westminster Cathedral, was novice master to an aspirant member, and was helping the Association's Vice Chancellor with the translation of the *Supplement of Propers* for the Association's Prayer Book.[9] Three years later, the President, Lord Craigmyle, wrote to Wheeler inviting him to become Principal Chaplain following the termination of Archbishop Couve de Murville's term of office. It was not a particularly onerous responsibility and despite his age, Wheeler felt able to accept.[10] From then on, he chaired the meetings of the chaplains, accompanied the Association on pilgrimages to Lourdes, celebrated Mass, wrote Lenten reflections for the members, preached retreats and continued to attended social functions. His messages and sermons were always simple and direct: the Order may be ancient but its function, based on the Scriptures, the life of Christ and personal piety, remained relevant and necessary in the contemporary world.[11]

Wheeler enjoyed his time as Principal Chaplain but his tenure was marred by the sudden death of his great friend Tony Furness in May 1995. His other great regret was that he was unable to see Hazelwood Castle become a northern centre for the Order following the withdrawal of the Carmelite Friars in 1995.[12] Wheeler and Bishop David Konstant felt that if possible, the Castle with its chapel and shrine had to be kept in Catholic hands but the cost of maintaining a Grade 1 listed building would have been a considerable financial burden on the diocese.[13] Wheeler therefore approached the Order suggesting that it might invest in the Castle as a retreat house. Lord Gainsborough agreed with Wheeler that it would be a tragedy if the Castle was to be lost to the Catholic Church 'after so many years and after all the efforts you made to save it' but the Order felt unable to embark on such a huge and expensive project.[14]

Wheeler was succeeded as Principal Chaplain in 1995 by Bishop Mario Conti of Aberdeen.[15] Sir Peter Drummond-Murray wrote to Wheeler: 'You have been an inspiration and example to all of us during a very difficult period in the Church's history—particularly difficult for those of us who are attached to the traditional Mass'.[16] In May 1995, he learned that the Order had promoted him to Grand Cross Conventual Chaplain *ad honorem*.[17]

Opus Dei

Opus Dei is a Catholic institution founded by Saint Josemaría Escrivá (1902–1975). Its mission is to spread the message that work and the circumstances of everyday life are occasions for growing closer to God, for serving others and for improving society. Opus Dei received Church approval in 1941 and although Escrivá originally saw it as a lay organization, he widened the movement to include priests when, in 1943, he founded the Priestly Society of the Holy Cross.[18] In 1947, Opus Dei became a worldwide institution of the Church and received pontifical approval from Pope Pius XII in 1950. In 1983, Pope John Paul II erected Opus Dei as a Personal Prelature; on 17 May 1992, he beatified Escrivá and on 6 October 2002, proclaimed him a saint.[19]

Opus Dei began in England in December 1946 with the arrival in London of a Spaniard called Juan Antonio Galarraga who had joined Opus Dei as a Numerary in 1940. In 1946, Galarraga obtained a research scholarship at London University and he met Wheeler in the early 1950s at the Newman Centre in Portland Square. When Wheeler became chaplain to London University, he saw much more of Galarraga who later became a priest of the Society of the Holy Cross. From Galarraga and a growing number of Numeraries at the University, Wheeler learnt a great deal about Escrivá and when Opus Dei opened a residence at Netherhall House, Wheeler recommended it to students.[20] It was not until 1959, however, when he was Administrator of Westminster Cathedral that Wheeler met Escrivá and on that occasion, the Founder gave him a leather-bound copy of *The Way*.[21]

The Founder had good reason to be pleased with Wheeler's assistance. During his first visit to England in 1958, Escrivá let it be known that he was anxious for an Opus Dei house to be opened as soon as possible in Oxford. His intention was to set up the equivalent of the *colegios mayores* which were a feature of university life in Spain. A combination of hall of residence and tutorial college, they offered educational and cultural programmes in combination with the university degree courses. However, there was no room in the British university system for such a venture. Eventually, through Wheeler's intervention, a suitable property for a centre was found. It was Grandpont House, located to the south of Oxford in the Diocese of Portsmouth. The Hierarchy of England and Wales had an earlier option to buy the house but had decided against its purchase. In 1959, with the encouragement of Cardinal Godfrey of Westminster and Archbishop King of Portsmouth, Opus Dei went ahead and established a centre there for a male apostolate.[22]

That Wheeler maintained contact with the priests of Opus Dei is evidenced by the letters of congratulation he received from them and from

Escrivá on his appointment to Middlesbrough in 1964 but there is no evidence to suggest that he made an effort to introduce Opus Dei into either Middlesbrough or Leeds, possibly because of the adverse media coverage the movement attracted. However, he welcomed their visits to the Diocese of Leeds to hold Days of Recollection, retreats and to meet with sixth-formers and university students. Throughout the 1970s, he maintained correspondence with Opus Dei in London and suggested speakers for their weekly talks at Netherhall House.[23] In 1980, he accepted an invitation to speak on 'The Kind of Priests the Church Needs' at a conference organised by the Centro Romano di Incontri Sacerdotali which had been founded by priests of Opus Dei. He found a parallel to the teaching of *Lumen Gentium* in the writings of Escrivá.[24]

Wheeler's admiration of Opus Dei and respect for its aims and values remained strong. In 1982, he wrote a very complimentary article about Opus Dei in *the Scottish Catholic Observer* and praised it for 'Christianising the civilization of our times'. He considered that he was in a unique position to talk about what could be called the universality of the spirit of Opus Dei, 'having seen its activities all over the world'. While in Peru, he had visited the house of the Work in Lima and was interested to see how Opus Dei had penetrated to such remote parts of the world and had taken root among peoples of such different backgrounds. The thing that enchanted him about Opus Dei houses, he wrote, was 'the spirit of civilisation—the right kind of civilisation. There was no excessive grandeur; there was always a tasteful understatement, and yet a real Christianising of the civilisation of our time'. In such a way and through it deeds Opus Dei stood out for Christianity and Catholicism. There were, he recalled, a family spirit and a sense of great personal discipline and integrity. The Founder had achieved the balance of life, work and prayer that to Wheeler was the pattern that should be followed by all sorts of people. He treasured the copy of Escrivá's book, *The Way*, which the Founder had given to him and in which he had written an inscription. Wheeler wrote of *The Way*: 'I've always loved its simplicity'.

According to Wheeler, Escrivá radiated an enormous appreciation of the spiritual life. He had a great desire to lead people on in the most simple and straightforward way—a Biblical way. Here he was ahead of his time. He was also ahead of his time regarding Vatican II, with the concept of the laity playing a fuller part in the life of the Church and being contemplatives in their ordinary lives. He had the mind of Vatican II and in the very difficult post-Conciliar period, 'when many in the Church went through something of a silly season', Opus Dei weathered things in a way that could be a great example to the rest. He wrote: 'I think this is because it has struck the right balance between *aggiornamento* and tradition, with all the time an eye cocked on the situation in the world today'.

Wheeler remembered Escrivá as a light-hearted companion and recalled an occasion when some bishops were tackling the Founder on a number of points over lunch one day. He broke down any resistance by the great love he radiated, wrote Wheeler: 'You felt that he loved everybody that came his way and you couldn't help responding'. He continued, 'I felt I had met a very holy person who was a very human person. After all, true holiness builds upon the nature we have already been given by God. God enriched him very much in every way'. Escrivá gave Wheeler a little laughing donkey one day in Rome and said: "Put that on the mantelpiece in your study, and every time you look at it, it will remind you to pray for me." 'I still have it', wrote Wheeler, 'It stands permanently on my mantelpiece and sometimes inspires me when I'm taking things too seriously'. Escrivá gave a special significance to the donkey; he used to call himself "a beast of burden for Our Lord".

One aspect of Opus Dei's apostolate which Wheeler claimed to know especially well was its work with university students, with the laity and with families. It was remarkable, he said, that at a time when families as a whole were suffering from the impact of the permissive society in Europe generally, they seem to gain enormous strength and stimulus from the work of Opus Dei. It was his experience that there was a close parallel between the members of the Work and the early Christians—people of different walks of life with something of the same spirit, in the middle of the world, trying to sanctify their ordinary activities. Escrivá stressed this and the notion of the apostolate of the laity was enshrined, according to this model, in one of the Decrees of the Vatican Council. He concluded that through his writings and memories of him, Escrivá 'will emerge a figure of a man who had a very great impact on the life of the whole Christian people' for he had roused people from spiritual apathy.[25]

Following his resignation from Leeds, Wheeler's open contact with the Prelature increased both in England and in Rome. On 26 June 1993, the eighteenth anniversary of Escrivá's death, he preached a moving and complimentary homily at a Memorial Mass celebrated in Westminster Cathedral. Escrivá, said Wheeler, had played a great part in the lives of vast numbers of people who like the Founder persevere in striving to Christian-ise contemporary civilization. He recalled how, in 1992, he had attended Escrivá's beatification ceremony in St Peter's where he remembered his 'little memories' of him, and the Founder's great love for the Church and for the priesthood. The Beatification Mass, he said, 'was one of joyful tranquillity and a deepening of Faith despite the presence of the great evils in our times'. Pope John Paul II had said that like members of Opus Dei 'the whole people of God can find new models of holiness and a new witness of heroic virtue lived in the ordinary everyday circumstances of human existence'. Wheeler took from this the reference from the Pope's Apostolic Exhortation *Christifidelis Laici* in which he intended to promote a deeper awareness among all the faithful of the gift and responsibility they share, both as a group and as individuals, in the communion and mission of the Church. For Wheeler, Opus Dei responded directly to that and inspired by Escrivá its outstanding influence was a total acceptance and reliance on the unchanging fundamentals of the Faith combined with the call of Vatican II to place an increased emphasis on the role of the laity in the Church. From these two sources, there emerged a new vision of work—of the lay vocation—enriched by holiness, spirituality and contemplation. A dedicated life of prayer, work and apostolate resulted in a harmonious unity which sanctified ordinary work and all human activities and situations.[26] In recognition of his support for Opus Dei in Great Britain, Wheeler was appointed a Co-operator of the Prelature.[27]

Wheeler's respect for Escrivá and Opus Dei was not shared by all. One priest of the Society of the Holy Cross wrote to Wheeler that they were treated in the English press with a hatred akin to that reserved for the Ku Klux Klan and complained that no one was brave enough to support publicly Opus Dei. Although Wheeler inadvertently omitted from his first memoir any mention of his encounters with Escrivá he rectified this in *More Truth and Love* when he admitted that he was deeply saddened that Opus Dei 'had not found everywhere in this country the understand-ing and appreciation which it has richly deserved'.[28]

Saints and Martyrs

As an intelligent and perceptive student of history, Wheeler had a firm understanding of the Church's past and how it influenced its present at both an institutional and a personal level. He was particularly impressed and moved by the lives of the saints and their powers of intercession, and as he had written in 1967, he felt that there was a danger that modern trends within the Church would eventually consign the pious adoration of the saints to the past. Such a development, he argued, was mistaken and contrary to the Conciliar Decree *Lumen Gentium* which stated that saints should continue to be recognised as mediators between God and man and a link between the Pilgrim Church and the Church Triumphant. Some of Wheeler's earliest sermons and articles had been concerned with the saints and martyrs and he never tired of speaking and writing on the lives of the many remarkable men and women who had given outstanding witness or who performed some special service in the history of the Church. In his conversion to Catholicism, he too had suffered and he felt some affinity with those who had steadfastly borne witness to the faith.[29]

Three saints who appealed to Wheeler for different reasons and about whom he wrote and recalled in retirement were St William of York and the Carthusians St Hugh of Lincoln and St Augustine Webster. For Wheeler, St William Fitzherbert, Archbishop of York, was not only a man with whom he shared a name. Wheeler's diocese and many of its shrines and places of worship lay within the Province of York. The narrative of William's life and witness also appealed to Wheeler. Elected in 1143, William served until 1147 when dissenting electors had him removed and he 'fled from the pomp of the world'. Subsequent acrimonious disputes involved Pope Eugenius III, St Bernard of Clairvaux and the Cistercians at Fountains Abbey. William was then re-elected in 1154 and returned in triumph to York. In the midst of the celebrations, a bridge over the River Ouse collapsed but no one was drowned or injured. His miraculous powers were ascribed to this incident and his tomb in York Minster became a place of pilgrimage. 'Deep in the ground', wrote Wheeler, William was 'worthy of exaltation'. To Wheeler, William was a model of discretion and humility and 'knew the dissensions of Christendom even in the days of greater unity'.[30]

The Carthusians Hugh of Lincoln and Augustine Webster provided other examples of Christian virtue through their solitary, penitential, prayerful regimen and, in the case of Webster, martyrdom. In his Apostolic Constitution *Umbrilatem*, Pope Pius XI wrote: 'Those who assiduously fulfil the duty of prayer and penance contribute much more to the increase of the Church and the welfare of mankind than those who labour in tilling the Master's field'. Concerned as he was with working 'in the field', Wheeler, wrote that 'such a background can be a great bonus in the exercise of any episcopate'. In Hugh of Lincoln, he saw a man taken from his monastic calling and placed in the secular world. There, faced with the awesome responsibilities attached to that office, he became the paradigm of a bishop. To Wheeler the saint's spiritual reserves accumulated through his dedicated life of prayer were not only of vast inspiration but also brought 'to the office of Bishop a man of full stature, possessed of inner tranquillity and habitual serenity'. Moreover, Hugh was a true European, sympathetic to every dimension of society from the highest to the lowest. He was a patron of the arts, a man of learning, and he dispensed great hospitality. Hugh's personal austerity, wrote Wheeler, 'was gentle and his intransigence tender. He administered his diocese wisely and well choosing men of integrity to assist him and share his labours'. Not that Hugh was without human failings and foibles, however, as Wheeler pointed out.[31] Perhaps Wheeler saw something resembling his own experiences in Hugh's life. In 1936, he had wished for the spirituality of the monastic rule.

St Augustine Webster was a Carthusian who was executed at Tyburn in 1535, a victim of Henry VIII's Reformation. His life of prayer and solitude had been rudely shattered by the demand of royal supremacy in ecclesiastical affairs. His monastery and many others were dissolved. To Wheeler, Webster was a supreme example of loyalty to the true Faith, a priest of outstanding courage and deep spirituality. The contemporary world, wrote Wheeler, not only needed the intercession of martyrs like Webster but also the continuing prayers of modern Carthusians who carried on their timeless vocation and dedication to prayer. The ecumenical dimension of the lives and veneration of Sts Hugh and Augustine should not be overlooked, he claimed, for the spiritual example of the lives provides 'a special enrichment' which stresses 'ecumenically shared values' and 'transcends all denominations of Christianity'.[32]

The Beatification of the Eighty-Five Martyrs of England, Scotland and Wales in 1987 was an event in which Wheeler was closely involved. The canonization of the Forty Martyrs of England and Wales in 1970 was followed almost immediately by a proposal to beatify other English, Welsh and Scottish martyrs executed between 1584 and 1679. In 1971, the Hierarchy received a memorandum from the Cause of the English Martyrs to initiate the beatification process of the Venerable Martyrs unsuccessfully proposed for beatification in 1929. There were strong links with Yorkshire for thirty of the eighty-five eventually beatified were from

Yorkshire while many others had been executed at York. Thirty-four were also associated either through birth, residency or ministry with the area covered by the Diocese of Leeds and the area co-terminus with the Diocese of Middlesbrough.[33] Despite initial optimism,[34] the process was lengthy and difficult as so many criteria had to be met. It was not until 22 November 1987 that the beatification of eighty-five martyrs was complete and by which time Wheeler had retired. Nevertheless, he was closely involved in the beatification ceremonies in Rome which were marked by the usual celebrations.

On the eve of the ceremony, Cardinal Hume and Dr Robert Runcie, the Archbishop of Canterbury, issued a joint statement of unity and thanksgiving in order to defuse the inevitable controversy which accompanied such ceremonies. The reconciliation of painful memories and a common commitment to unity involved no disloyalty to churches and history, they said, and modern Christians had grown to recognize that those who were put to death on both sides of the Reformation divide were martyred by their brothers and sisters in Christ. To the Cardinal, 'men and women strong in faith, like the martyrs, make the best ecumenists'. Dr Runcie said that in the past, 'this announcement would have fuelled controversy and communal rivalry. Today we can all celebrate their heroic Christian witness and together deplore the intolerance of the age which flawed Christian conviction'.[35] These were sentiments with which Wheeler heartily agreed and to which Pope John Paul II referred at the Mass on the following day, the Feast of Christ the King. Accompanying the Pilgrimage was the Westminster Cathedral Choir singing Gregorian chant, Palestrina motets and a hymn composed by Nicholas Postgate, one of the eighty-five martyrs, while awaiting his execution at York in 1679. Cardinal Hume, accompanied by Fr Paolo Molinari SJ, Promoter of the Cause of the Martyrs, presented the petition to the Pope. The Cardinal was also joined in St Peter's by Bishop Mark Santer of Birmingham representing Dr Runcie.

In the evening Vespers were sung at the sixteenth-century church of Chiesa Nuova which was, Wheeler noted, linked through its builder St Philip Neri with Cardinal Newman and the Oratorians. No service books were provided at the end, without prompting, the congregation rose and sang a lusty rendition of *Faith of Our Fathers*. Hume and Wheeler were highly delighted! On Monday Wheeler preached at a Mass celebrated at St Paul's Outside-the-walls, a church with special links with England for

Medieval Kings of England were Canons of St Paul while its abbot automatically received the Order of the Garter. It was an occasion and setting which Wheeler relished. He spoke with great emotion about the example of the martyrs and their modern relevance and his sermon contained many of the points he had adumbrated in *The Tablet* in 1967 about the importance of the canonization of the Forty Martyrs. The martyrs, he said, were the symbols of resistance and constancy in the bloody struggle to retain Faith in England during and after the Reformation, while the continental seminaries, supported by the papacy and the French and Spanish monarchies, had ensured the supply of priests. Such colleges, he said, continued to provide 'enrichment in culture and in faith important for countries like ours which sometimes suffer from their insularity.' The deaths of so many young men and women in Penal Times was akin to the sacrifices made by his generation and his father's generation in the two World Wars of the twentieth century. Yet the shedding of the martyrs' blood 'brought about a resurrection of the Faith beyond all human inspiration'. Like Cardinal Hume and Archbishop Runcie, Wheeler saw the Beatification not as a divisive issue but as 'a greater incentive to the unity for which Christ prayed'. This was, he said, the approach taken by Pope Paul at the Canonization of the Forty Martyrs in 1970 when he asked for the witness of the martyrs' deaths to be an example to all in the move towards unity and in the struggle against the material paganism of the modern world. Wheeler concluded: 'one of the most beautiful things about these martyrs of ours lies not only in their loyalty to the Faith but also to their country'. At their deaths they bore no trace of malice and demonstrated the full maturity of their love by forgiving others as Christ had done.[36]

Catholic History and a Catholic Historian

In March 1989, Christina Scott, daughter of the Catholic historian Christopher Dawson, invited Wheeler to commemorate the centenary of her father's birth.[37] Wheeler saw many parallels in the lives of John Henry Newman and Dawson. Both were converts, both approached Catholicism through a study of history and both strove to revitalise Christian society. To Wheeler, Dawson was 'without question' one of the greatest influences of the twentieth century as Newman had been of the nineteenth. Dawson's journey of faith (and Newman's) bore similarities to that of

Wheeler and his historical theories and writings very much appealed to the Bishop; for these reasons he was delighted to accept the invitation.

Dawson, an Anglican who converted to Catholicism in 1914, was born at Hay Castle in the Wye Valley but his family home was Hartlington Hall between Burnsall and Bolton Abbey in Yorkshire and located in the Diocese of Leeds. The Dawson family arranged for the centenary service to be held in October 1989 at the Anglican Church of St Wilfred in Burnsall where Dawson and his wife were buried and there Wheeler celebrated the first Mass in the church since the Reformation. It was an occasion hugely enjoyed by Wheeler—celebrating Mass in a pre-Reformation church and preaching on an academic luminary who had been driven on by the courage of his faith.

In his address, Wheeler recalled that Dawson was educated at Winchester and Trinity College, Oxford, where he read History and where he encountered Anglo-Catholics such as Ronald Knox, E. I. Watkin, Vernon Johnson and Dr Darwell Stone, all of whom subsequently influenced Wheeler. A visit to Rome in 1909 opened Dawson's eyes to a new world of religion and culture and in 1914, following a meeting with his future wife, the Catholic Valery Mills, he joined the Catholic Church. Dawson carved out a formidable university reputation at Exeter, Liverpool and Edinburgh Universities as a historian and man of letters. Three of his major volumes—*The Age of the Gods, Progress and Religion,* and *The Making of Europe*—were published to great acclaim but he was unable to obtain a professorial post because of his religion. He was successively a director of *The Tablet* and, for a brief period, editor of *The Dublin Review.* A substantial family fortune enabled Dawson to leave university teaching and operate as an independent scholar and from their home in Yorkshire, Dawson and his wife entertained the Catholic *literati* of the time including Douglas Woodruff, Evelyn Waugh, Eric Gill, Fr J. H. Pollen and G. K. Chesterton. In the 1950s, Dawson received many invitations to lecture in the United States and in 1958 was appointed Professor of Roman Catholic Studies at Harvard University. At Harvard, his output was prolific and there followed, among other works, *The Historic Reality of Christian Culture* (1960), *The Dividing of Christendom* (1965), *The Formation of Christendom* (1967) and *Religion and World History* (1975).

Dawson studied the influence of religion of culture and his sweeping narratives of European history demonstrated how Western society, once based on the teachings, power and influence of the medieval Catholic

Church, had declined because its bedrock of Christian spirituality had disintegrated. To Dawson, the Catholic tradition of 'divine energy'— expressed through art, literature, music and architecture—was the inspiration which created Christian civilization. The Christian vision of history, therefore, 'is essentially theological in character, reflecting divine revelation rather than a philosophical effort elaborated by Christian scholars'. It was a familiar theme to Wheeler; one which he welcomed and one on which he had preached. To Dawson, and to Wheeler, Western society 'was withering' because it had lost touch with its Classical, religious and spiritual roots. Religion is 'the spirit that informs every culture' and if this is lost then the moral foundations of civilization will be weakened and the soul of man 'which is the beginning and end of all culture' will be destroyed. With the contemporary growth of the European ideal and the prospect of greater political and economic unity, said Wheeler, the moment had come for a major re-evaluation of Dawson's works.[38]

The Retired Priest

In 1980, after the National Pastoral Congress at Liverpool, Wheeler addressed the diocesan priests at Hazelwood Castle on 'Our Priesthood'. He addressed them on what had emerged, or was likely to emerge from the Congress, and in the context of a contemporary crisis of clerical identity and authority. He took care to re-affirm their apostolate and expressed his optimism that doubts and crises would diminish as priests realised what was expected of them by the Church and by those whom they served. Five years later, Wheeler's own active apostolate ended and he was confronted with the prospect of a different facet of priesthood—retirement.

The priesthood, wrote Wheeler, is something which is ever progressing and ever developing and therefore the retirement of a priest should be considered an opportunity and not a disaster. He wrote:

> Our daily Mass, our recitation of the Divine Office—that prayer
> of the Church which is the prayer of Christ—our Rosary and our
> offering of ourselves anew to God, can do more for God and His
> Church, and all his people than all the activity of former years.

Retirement, he reflected, brought the opportunity for a spiritual growth 'which can prepare us for the eternal destination'. It was in retirement that the priest could take on a contemplative role by replacing the active apostolate with a prayerful apostolate. Many previous priests and bishops, monks and abbots, especially in Medieval Yorkshire, he wrote, had developed lives of prayer and as they grew older went away 'to make their souls'. A retired priest or bishop, he continued, should choose a situation in which he can best realise God's will in the continuation of his vocation. The priest still had a two-fold apostolate in the sense of a subdued activity and a prayerful tranquillity while the revival or development of friendships was a way of avoiding one person's loneliness. Seminaries may wish to enlist the wisdom and experience of a retired priest without burdening him with the administrative or liturgical demands of those still actively involved. The absence of specific duties, he wrote, permitted the retired priest to be active and committed in proportion to his physical and mental capabilities.

The 'Ascent' movement in France, wrote Wheeler, demonstrated how through prayer and spirituality, the thoughts of old people, including retired priests, could turn in a positive way to the meaning of life and death. It was not a new concept or a new approach for prayer and spirituality had forever been at the heart of the Church. It was, though, a sign of a return to spiritual insights and an increased appreciation of contemplation as one of the primary functions in everyday life. He concluded: 'Our latter days are the most important for our lives and so we can love even in old age and retirement. For we never need be redundant as we follow God's call'.[39]

Notes

1   W. G. Wheeler, *More Truth And Love* (Southport: Gowland and Co., 1994), p. 19.

2   Wheeler to Archbishop Couve de Murville, 15 March 1986. ABA, Archbishop Couve de Murville, MCM/B/W/65.

3   For general histories of the Knights of Malta See G. Ollivier, *A Short History of the Sovereign Order of Malta* (Paris: Nagel, 1966) and J. Galvin, *The Order of Malta* (Dublin: nd).

4   *Code of The Sovereign Military Hospitaller Order of Malta of St John of Jerusalem of Rhodes and Malta* (Rome, 1966), pp.16–18.

5   LDA, WPC, Knights of Malta.

6   British Association of the Sovereign Military Order of Malta, *Report of the Chancellor for Year 1966–7*, pp. 9–10.

7   Wheeler to Drummond-Murray, 5 June 1985. LDA, WPC, Knights of Malta.

8   Lord Craigmyle to Wheeler, 6 March 1987. LDA, WPC, Knights of Malta.

9   Minutes of the Annual Meeting of the Chaplains of the British Association of the Sovereign Military Order of Malta, 16 Nov 1988. LDA, WPC, Knights of Malta.

10   Lord Craigmyle to Wheeler, 6 June 1991. LDA, WPC, Knights of Malta.

11   See for example, Wheeler's Lenten Messages of 1993, 1994 and 1995, and his sermon of 24 June 1994. LDA, WPC, Knights of Malta.

12   Wheeler to the Grand Master, 15 May 1995. LDA, WPC, Knights of Malta.

13   Konstant to Fr J. Chalmers, O. Carm., 20 April 1995. LDA, WPC, Hazlewood Castle.

14   Fra' M. Festing to Wheeler, 18 April 1995; Gainsborough to Wheeler, 24 July 1995. LDA, WPC, Hazlewood Castle.

15   Conti to Wheeler, 8 Feb 1995. LDA, WPC, Knights of Malta.

16   Drummond-Murray to Wheeler, 3 March 1995. LDA, WPC, Knights of Malta.

17   Prince Rupert zu Loewenstein to Wheeler, 10 May 1995. LDA, WPC, Knights of Malta.

18   P. Bristow, *Opus Dei: Christians in the Midst of the World* (London: CTS, 2001), pp. 3–15.

19   See www.opusdei.org.au

20   *Scottish Catholic Observer*, 23 April 1982

21   W. G. Wheeler, 'Josemaría Escrivá—a special charisma'. Homily preached at Westminster Cathedral, 26 June 1993. LDA, WPC, W69, Opus Dei. *The Way* was an account of Escrivá's life as a priest to which were added spiritual considerations on aspects of the human condition and the Christian life.

22   www.opusdei.org.uk

23   See for example, S. Reynolds to Wheeler, 5 March 1970 and R. Stork to Wheeler, 4 May 1973. LDA, WDC, W69, Opus Dei.

24   *The Universe*, 8 Aug 1980.

25   *Scottish Catholic Observer*, 23 April 1982.

26   Wheeler, 'Josemaría Escrivá—a special charisma'.

27   LDA, WPC, W69, Opus Dei.

28   Wheeler, *More Truth And Love*, p. 60.

29   *Ibid.*, p. 72.

30   W. G. Wheeler, *St William of York* (London: Catholic Truth Society, 1974).

31   Wheeler, *More Truth And Love*, pp. 74–80. In 1986 Wheeler preached at Westminster Abbey on the eighth centenary of St Hugh's consecration.

32   *Ibid.*, pp. 81–85. In 1987, Wheeler preached on the life of St Augustine near the site of Axeholme Priory.

33   Fr James Walsh to Wheeler, Nov 1971. LDA, WDC, W68, Cause of the Martyrs.

34   It was estimated that the beatification process would take about three years. *ACTA*, April 1971.

35   *Catholic Herald*, 27 Nov 1987; *The Times*, 23 Nov 1987.

36   Wheeler, *More Truth And Love*, pp. 101–102. Wheeler repeated his views on the contemporary relevance of the saints and martyrs when he preached at the fiftieth anniversary of the canonization of SS John Fisher and Thomas More in June 1985

at Westminster Cathedral. LDA, WPC, SS John Fisher and Thomas More.

37 Scott to Wheeler, 28 March 1989. LDA, WPC, Letters 1989.

38 Wheeler, *More Truth And Love*, pp. 42–47; *Craven Herald and Pioneer*, 3 Nov 1989.

39 Wheeler, *More Truth And Love*, pp. 20–23.

17 EPILOGUE

ISHOP WHEELER'S LAST public appearance was at St Marie's Cathedral, Sheffield, on 3 July 1997 at the installation of Bishop John Rawsthorne as the Second Bishop of Hallam. He became ill during that same summer and his health gradually deteriorated. The Little Sisters of the Poor cared for him with love and great tenderness in his home at Mount St Joseph's, Headingley, where he died on 20 February 1998.[1] His body lay in the Little Sisters' Chapel for one day before being received at St Anne's Cathedral where Provost Mgr John Murphy led the Cathedral Chapter in singing Solemn Vespers. In the evening, Mgr Peter McGuire, the Cathedral Administrator and like Mgr Murphy one of Wheeler's Vicars General, celebrated a Requiem Mass attended by priests and people from across the diocese. He paid tribute to 'the beauty of holiness' which had been 'so evident in Bishop Wheeler's life' and said that 'there cannot be but sadness, the sadness of a parting, as we give back to God the good and gentle man who was our bishop, our gracious shepherd, for almost twenty years'.[2]

Wheeler's funeral Mass was celebrated in the Cathedral on 3 March. As might be expected for a man who had served God and His Church for so long and who was known to so many, Wheeler's requiem was a very public occasion attended by prelates and priests, public figures and civic dignitaries, representatives of other religious denominations and people from all walks-of-life. It was how he would have wished it and he would have taken great pleasure in the colour and spectacle, the choreographed ceremony, the carefully selected organ music, the beautifully sung hymns (including Newman's *Praise to the Holiest in the Height*), the well-chosen words of tribute and, perhaps above all, the genuine sense of love and affection felt for this familiar and popular figure of a bye-gone age.

In his homily, Bishop David Konstant said that Wheeler had never wavered from his total fidelity to the Church:

> He was never even remotely apologetic for his faith or for the Church. His home was there. He was proud to belong. Moreover, he wanted all members of the Church equally to be proud and happy of their belonging, even if for one reason or another they

might find the institutional Church lacking in understanding or compassion.

In a simple expression of his faith, continued Bishop Konstant, Bishop Wheeler had prefaced his last will and testament with the words: 'I thank almighty God above all things for the gift of the Holy Roman Catholic and Apostolic Church, in which by His grace I live and die'. He had concluded by asking forgiveness of all he may have offended and begged for the prayers of 'my beloved priests, deacons, religious and people'. Like the psalmist, said Bishop Konstant, Bishop Wheeler placed all his trust in God's saving help for 'he knew that with the Lord there is mercy and fullness of redemption'. Reminding the congregation of Wheeler's irrepressible sense of humour, his acute sense of place and status, and forthcoming burial at St Edward's, Clifford, Bishop Konstant quoted one of his predecessor's limericks:

Perhaps to be seen at St Edward's Clifford

The graves of Leeds' Bishops are found
In a number of places around
But as Heenan and Dwyer
Most kindly moved higher
The next lot's achieved the *best* ground.[3]

In his tribute, Cardinal Hume recalled happy memories of Wheeler in Middlesbrough but recognised the correctness in translating him to Leeds. 'He had so much to contribute', said the Cardinal, and 'so it fell to him to implement in his new diocese the requirements of the Second Vatican Council'. He did so loyally, but it was not easy and he had to struggle to counter his conservative instincts: 'Like the rest of us he had to leave the temple of Solomon with its certainties and securities and set out, like Abraham, on the pilgrim way to an unknown future'. He set about the task with resolution and was successful in so many initiatives. In Leeds as in Middlesbrough, he quickly identified with diocesan priests and demonstrated his special gift for friendship, great charm of manner, a genuine interest in everyone he met, a sense of humour and a capacity to poke fun at human foibles and eccentricities, always charitably, but amusingly. He was, said the Cardinal, a marvellous after-dinner speaker and an 'an excellent raconteur'. He was also a man of style, of warm hospitality, gracious manners and the highest standards. Wheeler had to do things properly and the Cardinal recalled that when summoned to

Wimbledon to be informed by the Apostolic Nuncio of his appointment to Leeds he did so in full episcopal regalia. 'Not for Gordon', continued the Cardinal, 'the shedding of the Cappa Magna or any playing down of what was traditionally appropriate for a bishop'. However, behind this sartorial rectitude and fine hospitality there was a man of strong faith and deep prayer. Wheeler was a man of great charity and according to Hume this was his most characteristic quality.[4]

After the final commendation, Bishop Wheeler was carried in a hearse preceded by a police outrider and laid to rest in the crypt of the Church of St Edward at Clifford. His wish was to have been buried in the cemetery at Hazlewood Castle near one of his predecessors, Bishop Briggs, and the Shrine of the Forty Martyrs but the property had been sold by the Carmelites and the prospects of it remaining in Catholic hands receded.[5]

Wheeler was remembered elsewhere. On the day of the funeral, staff and students at the Beda placed his portrait in front of the altar and prayed for the repose of the soul of one of their *alumni* and most devoted supporters. In the evening, candles were placed on either side of the portrait as the college sang Vespers.[6] On 11 May, a Memorial Mass for Wheeler, attended by Bishop Konstant, Wheeler's sister Betty, and a small contingent of Leeds priests, was celebrated at Westminster Cathedral by Cardinal Hume.

The obituaries shared the narrative of Wheeler's life and ministry but each emphasized different aspects of his personality and achievements. To *The Universe* the 'Loved Pastor was a true man of vision'[7] while *Oremus*, the bulletin of Westminster Cathedral, described him as a man of ability, courtesy and imagination.[8] Most obituaries referred to his reaction to Vatican II and to his 'vision' and pragmatism in implementing its decrees. Bishop Konstant wrote that 'it could not have been easy being a bishop in those heady post-Vatican II years' and 'in this climate the place of the progressive traditionalist which Gordon Wheeler was by temperament and experience, was difficult to maintain with equilibrium'. He was unfailing, however, in supporting the introduction of liturgical and other reforms.[9] *The Daily Telegraph* described him as the urbane, cultured and witty bishop 'whose sympathetic orthodoxy endeared him to those troubled by the innovations of the Second Vatican Council'. It continued: '... his two decades in Leeds were remarkable for the gentleness with which those drastic changes were introduced'.[10] *The Times* obituary also described him as urbane and as an effective diocesan bishop and capable administrator but a man of deep culture with a wide intellectual grasp. He was, it continued, a liturgical and theological conservative 'who nevertheless could see the need for intelligent innovation in the Church'. By nature he was a traditionalist but 'with a mixture of tact and charm' he saw to it that the changes wrought by Vatican II were made without too much disruption.[11]

The *Yorkshire Post* claimed that Wheeler was a traditionalist, an autocrat, a man of a former age, something of an anachronism who allowed things to happen after Vatican II 'for which aesthetically he had little attraction or sympathy'. That he did 'was a measure of his fidelity to the reforms of the Council', including the liturgical and ecumenical ones.[12] *The Independent* recalled that in line with Vatican II Wheeler established the Wood Hall Pastoral and Ecumenical Centre and the first Catholic Diocesan Council. In later years, it continued, he was apt to regret that the latter initiative did not achieve more by way of disseminating the authentic fruits of Vatican II and speculated that it would have been better to concentrate on promoting this aim in the parishes, among priests and people at the grass roots. Nevertheless, Wood Hall epitomized Wheeler's vision of a church enriched by careful reflection on the work of the Vatican Council, in contrast to what he saw as the frequent, and sometimes deliberate, misinterpretations and distortions of conciliar teachings. His loyalty to the Second Vatican Council was also apparent in 1980 when he was largely responsible for creating the Diocese of Hallam. This move conformed to the principle that dioceses should be of a size which permits effective pastoral care and administration by a single bishop; but, for a man with a keen sense of history, the division of a diocese which had existed since 1878 caused not a little sorrow.[13]

Many paid tribute to Wheeler's grace and style. The *Catholic Herald* recorded that at Leeds Cathedral Wheeler insisted that Mass should be celebrated beautifully. On Easter Sunday morning, he would be dressed up in the long purple train of his Cappa Magna with two small altar servers in tow, and would sweep up the nave towards the High Altar, turning right at the last moment to visit the Blessed Sacrament Chapel and kneel on a *prie dieu*. There, in front of the beautiful Pugin reredos, he would pass a few moments in silent prayer. When asked why he was the last bishop in Britain to wear the Cappa Magna, he would reply that there was surely no better lesson in the reality of the Real Presence than for his flock to see their bishop in his finery kneeling before the Blessed

Sacrament.[14] *The Daily Telegraph* claimed that Wheeler made St Anne's 'a sort of liturgical showpiece' in which he, 'a man of unassuming piety, demonstrated that the new order was not incompatible with beauty and solemnity'.[15] So too did Wheeler recognize that preaching the Word of God was something of an art form and his sermons were famous for their elegance and force. He would preach with particular passion on the Resurrection standing not at a lectern, but directly in front of his congregation. 'Propping his frail frame on his heavy brass crozier, the two halves of which were wedged firmly together by a bus-ticket traditionally supplied by the Master of Ceremonies and swaying slightly between two altar servers who were ready to catch him if ill-health should overcome him, he electrified his audience with the vigour of the simple statement that they were celebrating the Resurrection because it was true'.[16]

The Guardian called Wheeler 'God's Witty Apostle' and opined that he was 'perhaps the finest intellect among the Roman Catholic bishops of England and Wales'. Only frail health, it claimed, prevented him from succeeding Cardinal Heenan at Westminster. Bishop Wheeler had a rapier-like, but always kindly, tongue with which he would fondly tease his brother bishops. When Pope John Paul II was due to visit Britain and to emphasize each of the seven Sacraments in a different diocese, he suggested that one particular diocese should have confession as its theme because then, perhaps, its bishop might take the opportunity to avail himself of the Sacrament of Reconciliation.[17] On a more serious point, however, it was noted in *The Daily Telegraph* that Wheeler's social style and conservative theology, typical of many former Anglicans, were so obviously very different from those of his brother bishops. To the traditionalists and Catholic aristocrats, Wheeler was seen 'as their man in the hierarchy' and he remained 'theologically and culturally opposed to the bland liberalism of many of his episcopal colleagues'.[18]

Writing seven years after the Bishop's death, Robert Finnigan provided a more analytical and balanced assessment of Wheeler's life. Finnigan rightly judged that Wheeler 'would certainly have found being a diocesan bishop more congenial in in the certainties of an earlier age but that is not to say he lived in the past'. He viewed some of the changes ushered in by Vatican II with mixed feelings but acknowledged that many were welcomed by others. Conservative by temperament and background he was nonetheless progressive in certain respects. Without ceding the bishop's traditional teaching and organizational responsibilities, he introduced structural change and advisory and consultative processes. To renew and reform liturgical life he laid much emphasis on the Diocesan Liturgy Commission whose remit was a balanced implementation of the Council's decrees. He never disguised his love for the Latin Rite but accepted that the vernacular had its advantages in encouraging active participation in the Mass and the liturgy. He contended that Latin was a way of ensuring that the modern Catholic community maintained its liturgical inheritance and was conscious of the Church's long history and heritage. Aware of the historical primacy of Rome, he argued that every priest should be able to say the Latin Mass 'which associates him and his people in a special way with the Petrine See and Office'. As Chair of the National Liturgical Commission, he represented the Hierarchy on the International Commission for English in the Liturgy but his interventions were infrequent and therefore his influence was never very strong. He did not care for some of the translations and disliked especially the fact that the translation of the Roman Missal was unduly influenced by the USA. He did, however, ensure the appointment of an on-going committee to 'to evaluate the English liturgical texts with a view to revision in the light of experience'.[19]

Wheeler had recorded his own examples of his self-deprecating humour. After he had deputized for a sick organist at Westminster one visiting priest asked another: "Was that Gordon playing the organ?" "Yes" came the reply. To which the first priest said: "It sounded like a seaside landlady entertaining her lodgers on a wet Sunday afternoon."[20] The Bishop relished the liturgical richness of his adoptive Church and to his death he remained fond of the Tridentine liturgy. He would celebrate the Pope Pius V Mass infrequently but only on special requests. After Douglas Woodruff's Requiem Mass, Lady Acton said to Wheeler: "If the Mass had been as old fashioned as that four years ago, I wouldn't have become a Catholic." Wheeler replied: "Well, if the Mass hadn't been as old-fashioned as that 40 years ago, I wouldn't have become a Catholic."[21]

His skill as a raconteur was recorded elsewhere. To the *Catholic Herald*, he was by far the best public speaker among the bishops and was much in demand, not only for sermons and retreats but also for after-dinner speeches. In one address, to the Converts' Aid Society, he said:

> And Jesus said unto the liberal theologians, 'Whom do you say I am?' And they answered and said, 'Thou art the eschatological manifestation of the ground of our being, the kerygma of which

we discern the ultimate meaning in our interpersonal relationships.'
And Jesus said: 'What?'[22]

Under the title 'Prince Bishop', *The Tablet* included the following wonderful cameo:

> As the song goes, you've either got, or you haven't got, style. One man who had it in spades was Bishop Gordon Wheeler, who died last weekend. In retirement at Eltofts, near Leeds, which was then the bishop's residence, he would have coffee at 11, sherry before lunch and tea at 4. In summer, refreshment would be taken under umbrellas bearing the papal colours, set out on the lawn.
>
> The residence at Eltofts was the centre of a small community. The neighbouring stables were converted into cottages, where Bishop Wheeler, a former Anglican, housed a number of vicars' widows. It was a congenial arrangement, with the widows appearing every evening at 8 p.m. for Scrabble and a little glass of something.
>
> Another well-bred resident of Eltofts was the bishop's beloved dog Finn, who would appear for Benediction in the beautiful chapel and sang along with the *Tantum Ergo* and the *O Salutaris*. Later, Finn lived at Eltofts with Bishop Konstant, the current Bishop of Leeds, who opted for a reordered chapel and modern hymns. It is said that the dog, who like his former master was something of a conservative in his liturgical preferences, ceased his public practice of the faith.[23]

A more tangible reminder of Bishop Wheeler, and one in which he would have taken much pleasure, appeared in 2001 when a blue commemorative plaque was placed on the wall of Sacred Heart and St William Church in Uppermill near Wheeler's birthplace at Dobcross. Uppermill parish had been erected by Bishop Heenan in 1952 and was staffed by Missionaries of the Scared Heart. The first priests resided at Ladcastle Hall, which also served as the Mass centre, but later bought the chapel of the Ebenezer-Congregationalist chapel in Uppermill. Wheeler opened and blessed the new church on his birthday, 5 May 1967.[24] Another link came with the naming of the Pastoral and Conference Centre at St Anne's Cathedral, Leeds, in his memory and in March 2013, Catholic primary and secondary schools in north-west Leeds joined together to gain Academy status from the government, as a Catholic Multi-Academy Trust. The Trust, the second in Diocese of Leeds, took the name 'The Bishop Wheeler Catholic Multi-Academy Trust'.

Wheeler's lasting legacy, however, is not to be discovered only on plaques or in buildings bearing his name. His life was so long and his ministry so varied that he deserves to be remembered in many ways. Some will recall him primarily as conservative in theology, in liturgical inclination, and in episcopal outlook, dress and behaviour. Others may recall him as an enthusiastic yet pragmatic modernizer of the local Church in accord with the decrees and constitutions of Vatican II and the dictates of Rome. In Anglican circles, he will be remembered as one with a promising clerical future who went over to Rome but kept contact with his Anglican friends while simultaneously retaining his deep admiration for Anglican prose and prayer. In Westminster, his substantial legacy lies in the work he did as a curate in wartime Edmonton, as a chaplain at London University and as a successful Administrator of Westminster Cathedral. To many in the north he remained a Westminster priest despite living outside the diocese for thirty-four years. To the Middlesbrough Diocese he will probably be seen as the 'one who got away'. In the Diocese of Leeds he will be fondly remembered as the bishop with abundant style and charm and for the firm yet gentle way in which he guided the diocese through a tumultuous and troubled period in its history. Above all, his memory evokes a devout and sincere man dedicated to God's work on earth.

Notes

1.   *Leeds Diocesan Directory* (1999), pp. 117–120.
2.   *Catholic Post*, April 1988.
3.   Bishop David Konstant, Homily at the funeral of Bishop William Gordon Wheeler, 3 March 1998. LDA, WPC, Funeral.
4.   'A Tribute Given by Cardinal Hume at the Conclusion of the Funeral mass for Bishop Gordon Wheeler', 3 March 1998. LDA, WPC, Funeral.
5.   *Catholic Post*, April 1988. The Carmelites had agreed to Wheeler's request.
6.   *The Beda Review*, May 1998.
7.   *The Universe*, 1March 1998.
8.   *Oremus*, no. 15, April 1998.
9.   *The Tablet*, 28 Feb 1998.
10.   *The Daily Telegraph*, 28 Feb 1998.
11.   *The Times*, 25 Feb 1998.
12.   *Yorkshire Post*, 23 Feb 1998.
13.   *The Independent* 7 March 1998.

[14]   *Catholic Herald*, 27 Feb1998.

[15]   *The Daily Telegraph*, 28 Feb 1998.

[16]   *Catholic Herald*, 27 Feb1998.

[17]   *The Guardian*, 27 Feb 1998.

[18]   *The Daily Telegraph*, 28 Feb 1998.

[19]   Robert Finnigan, 'Bishop Wheeler 1966–1985' in R. E. Finnigan and J. Hagerty, *The Bishops of Leeds 1878 -1985* (Keighley: PBK Publishing, 2005), pp. 175–178.

[20]   W. G. Wheeler, *In Truth And Love* (Southport: Gowland and Co., 1990), pp. 59–60.

[21]   *Catholic Herald*, 27 Feb 1998.

[22]   *Ibid.*

[23]   *The Tablet*, 28 Feb 1998.

[24]   *Oldham Chronicle*, 15 March 2001 and 17 Dec 2001; *Catholic Post*, Feb 2002.

SOURCES AND BIBLIOGRAPHY

PRIMARY SOURCES

Archives of the Archbishop of Westminster:
Cardinal Griffin Papers
Cardinal Godfrey Papers
Cardinal Heenan Papers

Archdiocese of Birmingham Archives:
Archbishop Dwyer Papers
Archbishop Couve de Murville Papers

Archdiocese of Liverpool Archives:
Godfrey-Heenan Collection
Archbishop Beck Papers
Archbishop Worlock Papers

Brentwood Diocesan Archives:
Bishop Patrick Casey Papers

Downside Abbey Archives:
Bishop Christopher Butler Papers

Leeds Diocesan Archives:
Bishop George Patrick Dwyer Papers
Bishop William Gordon Wheeler Diocesan Collection
Bishop William Gordon Wheeler Personal Collection
Diocesan Returns to Rome
Diocesan Photographic Collection
John F. Power Collection

Nottingham Diocesan Archives:
Bishop Edward Ellis Papers

Salford Diocesan Archives:
Bishop Thomas Holland Papers

Pontifical Beda College:
Log Books

Manchester Grammar School Archives:
Student records and photographs

PRINTED PRIMARY SOURCES

Directories and Annual Reviews:
Catholic Directory
Dictionary of National Biography
Hallam Diocesan Year Book
Kelly's Directory of the West Riding 1912
Leeds Diocesan Directory
Middlesbrough Diocesan Yearbook
The Catholic Building Review
The Catholic Who's Who
The Nottingham Diocesan Year Book

Newspapers and Journals:
Briefing (Catholic Information Services of the Bishops' Conference of England
    and Wales)
Catholic Gazette
Communio
Daily American
Diorama
Huddersfield Daily Examiner
Leeds Diocesan Catholic Post
Leeds Diocesan Catholic Voice
Leeds Diocesan Gazette

Liturgy

L'Osservatore Romano

Music and Liturgy

New Blackfriars

Northern Echo

Novena

Oldham Chronicle

Priests & People

Scepter Bulletin

The Beda Review

The Catholic Herald

The Catholic Worker

The Church Times

The Clergy Review

The Community

The Daily Telegraph

The Guardian

The Messenger of the Catholic League

The Sunday Telegraph

The Sunday Times

The Tablet

The Times

The Universe

Westminster Cathedral Chronicle

Yorkshire Post

Other Sources:

A Biographical Register of Old Mancunians 1888–1951 (Manchester: Manchester Grammar School, 1965).

Census, 1901, 1911.

Liverpool 1980: Official Report of the National Pastoral Congress (Slough: St Paul Publications, 1981).

SECONDARY SOURCES

Books:

G. Alberigo, A Brief History of Vatican II (Maryknoll, New York: Orbis, 2008).

G. A. Beck, *The English Catholics 1850–1950* (London: Burns Oates, 1950).

D. M. Board, *Responses: An account of the correspondence which followed 'The Church 2000' and 'A Time for Building'—the two reports of the Joint Working Party on Pastoral Strategy* (Abbots Langley: Catholic Information Services, 1980).

P. Bristow, *Opus Dei: Christians in the Midst of the World* (London: CTS, 2001).

B. C. Butler, *The Church and Unity* (London: Geoffrey Chapman, 1979).

R. Carson, *The First Hundred Years: A History of the Diocese of Middlesbrough 1878–1978* (Middlesbrough: Middlesbrough Diocesan Trustees, 1978).

A. Chandler and C. Hansen (eds.), *Observing Vatican II: The Confidential Reports of the Archbishop of Canterbury's Representative, Bernard Pawley, 1961–1964* (Camden Fifth Series, volume 43). (Cambridge: Cambridge University Press for the Royal Historical Society, 2013).

J. Coulson and A. M. Allchin, *The Rediscovery of Newman* (London: Sheed and Ward, 1967).

R. Currie, A. Gilbert, L. Horsley, *Churches and Churchgoers: Patterns of Church Growth in the British Isles since 1700* (Oxford: Clarendon Press, 1977).

M. de la Bedoyere, *Cardinal Bernard Griffin* (London: Rockliff, 1955).

M. de la Bedoyere (ed.), *Objections to Roman Catholicism* (London: Constable and Co., 1964).

P. Doyle, *Westminster Cathedral 1895–1995* (London: Geoffrey Chapman, 1995).

R. E. Finnigan, The Cathedral Church of St. Anne, Leeds: A History and Guide (London: Universe Publications Company Ltd., 1988).

R. E. Finnigan, *St Anne's Centenary: Leeds Cathedral 1904–2004* (Keighley, PBK Publishing Ltd., 2004).

R. E. Finnigan and J. Hagerty, *The Bishops of Leeds—Essays in Honour of Bishop David Konstant* (Leeds: PBK Publications on behalf of the Diocese of Leeds, 2005).

C. Fisher, *Walsingham Lives On* (London: CTS, 1979).

A. Flannery (ed.), *Vatican II: The Liturgy Constitution* (Dublin: Scepter Books, 1965).

M. Fox and P. Fox, *Saddleworth Album* (Oldham: Taylor and Clifton, 1995).

M. Fox and P. Fox, *Victorian Saddleworth* (Uppermill: Saddleworth Museum & Art Gallery, 1995).

H. M. Gillett, *The Pilgrim's Walsingham* (London: Samuel Walker, 1948).

J. Hagerty, *Cardinal Hinsley: Priest and Patriot* (Oxford: Family Publications, 2008).

J. Hagerty, *Cardinal John Carmel Heenan: Priest of the People, Prince of the Church* (Leominster: Gracewing, 2012).

B. Handford, *Lancing College: History and Memoir* (Chichester: Phillimore, 1986).

G. Hanlon, *In A Far Country—Leeds Diocesan Mission to Peru* (privately printed, 2011).

A. Hastings, *A History of English Christianity 1920–1985* (London: Collins, 1986).

A. Hastings (ed.), *Bishops and Writers* (Wheathampstead: Anthony Clarke, 1977).

P. Hebblethwaite, *The Runaway Church* (London: Collins, 1975).

J. C. Heenan, *A Crown of Thorns* (London: Hodder and Stoughton, 1974).

J. C. Heenan, *Council and Clergy* (London: Geoffrey Chapman, 1966).

T. Holland, *For Better and For Worse* (Salford: Salford Diocesan Catholic Children's Society, 1989).

M. P. Hornsby-Smith, *Roman Catholics in England* (Cambridge: Cambridge University Press, 1987).

A. Howard, *Basil Hume: The Monk Cardinal* (London: Headline, 2005).

H. Johnson, *Roy de Maistre: The English Years 1930–1968* (New South Wales: Craftsman House, 1995).

G. P. Joyce, *St Edmund's Edmonton: A Short History* (London: Fr G. P. Joyce, 1991).

P. Kennedy, *The Catholic Church in England and Wales, 1500–2000* (Keighley: PBK Publishing Ltd., 2000).

S. Lee and P. Stanford, *Believing Bishops* (London: Faber and Faber, 1990).

B. Levin, *The Pendulum Years: Britain and the Sixties* (London: Jonathan Cape, 1970).

H. W. R. Lillie, *England The Dowry of Mary* (London: CTS, 1953).

B. Little, *Catholic Churches Since 1623* (London: Robert Hale, 1966).

R. Lloyd, *The Church of England 1900–1965* (London: SCM Press, 1966).

C. Longley, *The Worlock Archive* (London: Geoffrey Chapman, 2000).

M. Manktelow, *John Moorman: Anglican, Franciscan, Independent* (Norwich, Canterbury Press, 1999).

A. Mason (ed.), *Religion in Leeds* (Stroud: Alan Sutton, 1994).

H. T. Milliken, *Changing Scene: Two Hundred Years of Church and Parish Life in Worsley* (Worsley: H. Duffy, 1985).

J. Minnis with T. Mitchell, *Religion and Place in Leeds* (Swindon: English Heritage, 2007).

G. Noel, *Miles: A Portrait of the 17th Duke of Norfolk* (Norwich: Michael Russell, 2004).

E. Norman, *Roman Catholicism in England* (Oxford: Oxford University Press, 1986).

C. P. O'Connor, *Classic Catholic Converts* (San Francisco: Ignatius Press, 2001).

G. Ollivier, *A Short History of the Sovereign Order of Malta* (Nagel: Paris, 1966).

B. Parry, *From Erin's Green Valleys: A Celebration of 150 years of St Patrick's Bradford 1853–2003* (Bradford: 2003).

N. Pevsner, *Yorkshire: The West Riding* (Harmondsworth: Penguin Books, 1959).

J. Porter, *The Making of the Central Pennines* (Broughton Gifford: Ash Grove Books, 1980).

B. Plumb, *Arundel to Zabi: A Biographical Dictionary of the Catholic Bishops of England and Wales (Deceased) 1623–1987* (Warrington: 1987).

K. Robbins, *Oxford History of the Christian Church: England, Ireland, Scotland, Wales. The Christian Church 1900–2000* (Oxford: Oxford University Press, 2008).

P. Rollings, *Walsingham: England's Nazareth* (Walsingham: Roman Catholic National Shrine, 1998).

N. Schofield and G. Skinner, *The English Cardinals* (Oxford: Family Publications, 2007).

G. Scott, The RCs: a report on Roman Catholics in Britain today (London: Hutchinson, 1967).

A. Stacpoole, *Vatican II by those who were there* (London: Continuum, 1986).

P. Stanford, *Cardinal Hume and the Changing face of English Catholicism* (London: Geoffrey Chapman, 1993).

W. Steele, *Ecumenism for Catholics* (Oxford: Blackfriars Publications, 2003).

E. Stourton, *John Paul II: Man of History* (London: Hodder and Stoughton, 2006).

R. Strange, *John Henry Newman: A Mind Alive* (London: Darton, Longman & Todd, 2008).

T. Tastard, *Ronald Knox and English Catholicism* (Leominster: Gracewing, 2009).

P. Vickery, *Justice and Truth: The Guildford Four and Maguire Seven* (London: Sinclair-Stevenson, 2010).

E. Waugh, *Monsignor Ronald Knox* (Boston: Little Brown, 1959).

L. E. Whatmore, *The Story of Our Lady of Ransom, Eastbourne* (Sussex: privately printed, 1977).

W. G. Wheeler, *The Council at a Glance* (London: Burns and Oates, 1966).

W. G. Wheeler, *Let's Get This Straight: The Church after Vatican II* (London: Catholic Truth Society, 1969).

W. G. Wheeler, *In Truth And Love* (Southport: Gowland & Co., 1990).

W. G. Wheeler, *More Truth And Love* (Southport: Gowland & Co., 1994).

C. Williams, *Harold Macmillan* (London: Phoenix Books, 2010).

D. Worlock, *English Bishops at the Council: Third Session* (London: Burns and Oates, 1965).

X. Wrynne, *The Third Session* (London: Faber and Faber, 1965).

X. Wrynne, *The Fourth Session* (London: Faber and Faber, 1965).

M. Yelton, *The South India Controversy and the Converts of 1955–1956: An Episode in Recent Anglo-Catholic History* (London: Anglo-Catholic History Society, 2010).

The Pictorial Story of Westminster Cathedral (London: Pitkin Pictorial Ltd., no date).

Articles:

B. Bergonzi, 'The English Catholics' in *Encounter*, Jan 1965, pp. 19–30.

O.B. de Berranger, 'Becoming Catholic: John Henry Newman' in *Communio*, vol. XL, no. 1, Spring 1913.

C. L. H. Duchemin, 'The Beda' in *The Catholic Herald*, 19 Sept 1941.

C. L. H. Duchemin, 'The Evolution of the Beda' in *The Beda Review*, Sept 1942, vol. 4, no. 8.

B. Harbert, 'Flaminian Gate to Eccleston Square' in *Priests & People*, Oct 2000, vol. 14, no. 10.

A. Harris, 'A Fresh Stripping of the Altars? Liturgical Language and the Legacy of the Reformation, 1964–1984'. Paper read at the Annual Conference of the Catholic Record Society, Cambridge, 2013.

A. A. King, 'The Consecration of Bishop Wheeler' in *Westminster Cathedral Chronicle*, April 1964.

M. J. McConnon, 'The Pontifical Beda College: A History' in *The Beda Review*, June 1985, vol. 12, no. 1.

W. G. Wheeler, 'Salvete Flores Martyrum' in *The Beda Review*, March 1941, vol. 4, no 5.

W. G. Wheeler, 'Arundel's Glory' in *The Beda Review*, Sept 1942, vol. 4, no 8.

W. G. Wheeler, 'The Song of David' in *The Beda Review*, Sept 1943, vol. 5, no 2.

W. G. Wheeler, *The Beda Review*, Sept 1947, vol. 5, no 10.

W. G. Wheeler, 'Catholics and the Universities' in *New Blackfriars*, vol. 46, no. 533, Nov 1964.

W. G. Wheeler, 'The Bishop and the Liturgy' in *Liturgy*, vol. xxxv, no. 1, Jan 1966.

Theses:

E. Palloc, *Une Eglise En Marche: Vatican II dans Le diocese de Leeds (Angleterre) 1959–1980* (unpublished memoire de maîtrise, Université Lyon II Lumière, 1992).

J. Wilson, *Abortion, Reproductive Technology and Euthanasia: Post-Conciliar Responses from within the Roman Catholic Church in England and Wales 1965–2000* (unpublished Ph.D. thesis, University of Durham, 2004).

INDEX

Lightning Source UK Ltd.
Milton Keynes UK
UKOW02f0008011016

284226UK00001B/9/P